THE DYNAMICS OF PERSUASION

COMMUNICATION
TEXTBOOK SERIES

Jennings Bryant — Editor

General Communication Theory and Methodology

Jennings Bryant — Advisor

THE DYNAMICS OF PERSUASION

Richard M. Perloff
Cleveland State University

LAWRENCE ERLBAUM ASSOCIATES, PUBLISHERS
1993   Hillsdale, New Jersey   Hove and London

Lawrence Erlbaum Associates, Inc., Publishers
365 Broadway
Hillsdale, New Jersey 07642

Library of Congress Cataloging in Publication Data

Perloff, Richard M.
    The dynamics of persuasion / Richard M. Perloff.
        p. cm. − (Communication textbook series. General communication theory and methodology)
    Includes bibliographical references and indexes.
    ISBN 0-8058-0490-0 (c)   ISBN 0-8058-1377-2 (p)
    1. Persuasion (Psychology) 2. Mass media−Psychological aspects.
    3. Attitude change. I. Title. II. Series.
    BF637.P4P39 1993
        153.8′52−dc20   92-35942
                                                                          CIP

Books published by Lawrence Erlbaum Associates are printed on acid-free paper, and their bindings are chosen for strength and durability.

Printed in the United States of America
10 9 8 7 6 5 4 3 2

Contents

PART III: COMMUNICATION APPROACHES

Preface

Persuasion is one of the oldest fields of academic study—it dates back thousands of years; indeed Aristotle was arguably the Western world's first great persuasion theorist. In our own era, persuasion has been studied primarily by means of the theories and methods of social science research. Numerous scholars have made contributions to our knowledge of persuasion, and the field has generated a host of intriguing concepts and an impressive body of knowledge on persuasion processes and effects.

Persuasion is not simply a science, however. It is also an art. In the 16th century, the Italian writer Machiavelli wrote a book entitled *The Prince*, in which he counseled politicians on how to use power and social influence techniques to manipulate the masses and to achieve personal and political goals. Since then, politicians and rulers have made considerable use of persuasion techniques. Unfortunately, these techniques have been employed successfully by the likes of Hitler and Stalin; fortunately, they have been used to accomplish positive end-states by individuals ranging from Thomas Jefferson to Susan B. Anthony. Today, there is a burgeoning persuasion industry that includes advertising, sales, public relations, political consulting firms, and a host of private and public companies that seek to change attitudes and influence social behaviors.

This book is designed to enhance students' understanding of persuasion theory and its applications to everyday situations. The volume presents an up-to-date review of persuasion theory and research; it also attempts to show students how these theories can deepen our understanding of how persuasion is practiced in a variety of real-life situations. The book is designed as a text for undergraduate students who have heard the terms *attitude* and *persuasion* bandied about, and who wish to know more about these fascinating concepts. The book is also designed to introduce graduate students to theory and research in the field of persuasion. Finally, the book

vii

provides faculty members and other professionals with an up-to-date review of research in the field of persuasion.

This book takes a broad look at persuasion research. It examines psychological approaches to persuasion, interpersonal communication theories, and the interface between persuasion and mass communications, in particular mass media information campaigns. Thus, the book examines research on cognitive processing of persuasive messages, compliance-gaining in interpersonal contexts, and the effects of large-scale health communication campaigns. By necessity, some contexts have been excluded. For example, political persuasion and public opinion—which happen to be research interests of mine—have been discussed only in passing and by example, for a full-scale discussion of these issues would have required another volume, or hundreds more pages at the very least.

The book is organized into three sections. The first section, *Foundations of Persuasion*, provides an introduction to basic terms and concepts (notably, persuasion and attitude). The next chapters in this section focus on the formation of attitudes and on the issue of consistency between attitudes and behavior. The second section, *Changing Attitudes and Behaviors*, examines theory and research on attitude change. The focus of this section is predominately psychological, as I examine theories and empirical investigations that are directed at individual-level variables, such as cognitions and affects. The third section of the book, *Communication Approaches*, focuses on the contributions that interpersonal and mass communication scholars have made to our understanding of persuasion. It examines persuasion in interpersonal contexts, and it explores the complex effects of mass media information campaigns. The final chapter tries to integrate persuasion theories with mass communication issues by providing a discussion of the implications of persuasion concepts for media information campaigns.

ACKNOWLEDGMENTS

This book has benefited from the comments and assistance of a number of individuals. The following persons read over various chapters from the book and provided thoughtful comments: Charles Atkin, Robert Bornstein, Franklin Boster, Timothy Brock, Kenneth DeBono, James Dillard, Alice Eagly, Leo Jeffres, Robert Kraftowitz, Kimberly Neuendorf, Linda Perloff, Gary Pettey, Richard Petty, Michael Pfau, Anthony Pratkanis, George Ray, Ronald Rogers, Jill Rudd, Charles Salmon, Sharon Shavitt, Mark Snyder, and Claude Steele. I also wish to thank one of the LEA reviewers, who offered an insightful and thoughtful review of an earlier version of the book.

I also appreciate the assistance that I received from a number of local libraries, including the Cleveland State University Library, Case Western Reserve University's Freiberger Library, and the John Carroll University Library.

I am also grateful for the help that Denise Schur provided in word processing the book. Her patience and dependable assistance were invaluable.

Finally, I am grateful to my wife, Julie, for the support and encouragement she provided throughout this project.

—*Richard M. Perloff*

Credits

FIG. 5.2: From McGuire, W. J. (1970). A vaccine for brainwash. *Psychology Today, 3,* 39. Adapted with permission from Psychology Today Magazine. Copyright © 1970 (Sussex Publishers, Inc.)

FIG. 5.3: From Petty, R. E., & Cacioppo, J. T. (1986). The elaboration likelihood model of persuasion. In L. Berkowitz (Ed.), *Advances in experimental social psychology* (Vol. 19, p. 126). Copyright © 1986 by Academic Press. Reprinted by permission.

FIG. 5.4: From Petty, R. E., Cacioppo, J. T., & Goldman, R. (1981). Personal involvement as a determinant of argument-based persuasion. *Journal of Personality and Social Psychology, 41,* 852. Copyright © 1981 by the American Psychological Association. Reprinted by permission.

FIG. 7.1: From *Journal of Psychology, 91,* 99, 1975. Reprinted and adapted with permission of the Helen Dwight Reid Educational Foundation. Published by Heldref Publications, 1319 Eighteenth St., N.W., Washington, DC 20036-1802. Copyright © 1975.

"Lady Killer": Used by permission of American Cancer Society, Inc.

FIG. 7.2: From Gruder, C. L., Cook, T. D., Hennigan, K. M., Flay, B. R., Alessis, C., & Halamaj, J. (1978). Empirical tests of the absolute sleeper effect predicted from the discounting cue hypothesis., *Journal of Personality and Social Psychology, 36,* 1066. Copyright © 1978 by the American Psychological Association. Reprinted by permission.

FIG. 9.1: From Kiesler, C. A., Collins, B. E., & Miller, N. (1969). *Attitude change: A critical analysis of theoretical approaches.* Copyright © 1969 by John Wiley & Sons, Inc. Reprinted by permission of John Wiley & Sons, Inc.

FIG. 9.3: From Bochner, S., & Insko, C. A. (1966). Communicator discrepancy, source credibility, and opinion change. *Journal of Personality and Social Psychology, 4,* 618. Copyright © 1966 by the American Psychological Association. Reprinted by permission.

Table 10.1: From Festinger, L., & Carlsmith, J. M. (1959). Cognitive consequences of forced compliance. *Journal of Abnormal and Social Psychology, 58,* 207. Copyright © by the American Psychological Association.

FIG. 10.1: Data from Zanna, M. P., & Cooper, J. (1974). Dissonance and the pill: An attribution approach to studying the arousal properties of dissonance. *Journal of Personality and Social Psychology, 29,* p. 706. Copyright © by the American Psychological Association. Adapted by permission.

FIG. 11.1: From Miller, G. R. (1987). Persuasion. In C. R. Berger & S. H. Chaffee (Eds.), *Handbook of communication science* (p. 472). Copyright © 1987 Sage Publications, Inc. Reprinted by permission of Sage Publications, Inc.

FIG. 12.1: From McGuire, W. J. Theoretical foundations of campaigns. In R. E. Rice & C. K. Atkin (Eds.), *Public information campaigns* (2nd ed., p. 45). Copyright © 1989 Sage Publications, Inc. Reprinted by permission of Sage Publications, Inc.

FIG. 12.2: From Meyer, A. J., Nash, J. D., McAlister, A. L., Maccoby, N., & Farquhar, J. W. (1980). Skills training in a cardiovascular health education campaign. *Journal of Consulting and Clinical Psychology, 48,* 137. Copyright © 1980 by the American Psychological Association. Reprinted by permission.

"McGruff" and "Recruiting New Teachers" public service announcements: Reprinted by permission of the Advertising Council, Inc.

PART I
FOUNDATIONS
OF PERSUASION

1
Introduction:
A Case Study in Persuasion

There is general agreement that persuasive communications exert a strong impact on attitudes and behaviors. Consider the following diverse examples of persuasion in action:

Some years ago, Ron Jones, a high school history teacher, conducted a week-long experiment to show how easy it is for a charismatic leader to mobilize support for his cause. Jones ordered his students to take a new seating posture, to carry paper and pencils for note-taking, and to stand at the side of their desks when asking questions. Subsequently, Jones introduced a class salute, which he called the Third Wave salute.

Jones then announced "the Third Wave is a nationwide program to find students who are willing to fight for political change in this country."[1] In an effort to simulate the mass rallies that the Nazis organized during the 1930s, Jones announced that there would be a rally at noon on Friday for Third Wave members only. On the day of the rally, a feverish excitement could be felt around the school. Jones stood up to speak and gave the Third Wave salute, which "was followed automatically by two hundred arms stabbing a reply." Then Jones broke the news. "There is no such thing as a national youth movement called the Third Wave," he told the crowd. "You have been used, manipulated, shoved by your own desires into the place you now find yourself. You are no better or worse than the German Nazi we have been studying." The class was silent as it began to grasp the reality of what had happened.

Three educational researchers, suspecting that professional educators could be "seduced into feeling satisfied that they (had) learned despite irrelevant, conflicting, and meaningless content conveyed by the lecturer," conducted an unusual experiment using teachers as their guinea pigs.[2] The researchers recruited a professional actor "who looked distinguished and sounded authoritative," gave him a name and title (Dr. Myron Fox), and directed him to present a talk to a group of educators

3

"with an excessive use of double talk . . . non sequiturs, and contradictory statements . . . all . . . interspersed with parenthetical humor and meaningless references to unrelated topics."[3] The educators evaluated Dr. Fox favorably on six items, including use of examples, arousal of interest, and stimulation of thinking.

Wendy's, the fast-food hamburger chain, wanted to increase its sales. The company decided it was time to change its approach to advertising, so it hired advertising whiz Joe Sedelmaier to develop a series of television commercials. The commercials featured an elderly woman pulling up to the drive-through window of a competing hamburger chain, taking a look at the hamburger she received, and then crying out "Where's the beef?" Within months after the ad had aired, Wendy's reported that sales had shot up dramatically.[4]

A group of Finnish public health experts noted that Finland had an extremely high rate of coronary heart disease. To help reduce the incidence of heart disease, the researchers developed a national campaign to induce people to quit smoking. The campaign included a series of television programs that were broadcast over the national television network in Finland. Newspapers and local radio stations promoted the series, and national health centers were contacted to recruit individuals to serve as leaders of self-help groups.
    A systematic evaluation of the campaign revealed that approximately 100,000 smokers (10% of all smokers in Finland) closely followed the programs, 20,000 (2% of smokers) quit smoking with the assistance of the TV program, and "some 10,000 succeeded for a period of at least six months and possibly permanently."[5]

These examples are a testament to the powerful impact that persuasive communications can have on attitudes and behavior. In this book, we explore persuasion, focusing on the effects that persuasive communications have on individuals and the processes by which they achieve their effects. We approach the issue from a scientific perspective, reviewing the many studies in communication, psychology, consumer behavior, and public health that have examined how persuasive communications influence attitudes and behavior.

To many people, persuasive messages have magical, subliminal effects. When trying to explain some dramatic instances of real-life persuasion, many people allege that the persuaders employed "mind control techniques" or that they "brainwashed" people into yielding to their messages. Yet these metaphors create a misleading impression of how persuasion works. In fact, persuasion involves a complex assortment of techniques, strategies, and mental maneuvers. It is best understood by examining the theories and findings of social science research.

To demythologize the persuasion process and to illustrate how scientific principles can aid in the understanding of persuasion phenomena, I present an in-depth look at how communications influenced attitudes in one historical context. I deliberately chose a context that conjures up myths and emotional images to illustrate that psychological and communication factors (and not magic) undergird the persuasion process.

I focus on the Unification Church (i.e., the Moonies), a religious sect that gained thousands of adherents in the 1960s and 1970s. The Moonies provide an excellent window on persuasion. The Moonies are one of the many religious cults that have surfaced over the past several decades (Shupe & Bromley, 1980; Zimbardo, Ebbesen, & Maslach, 1977). Soon after joining the Moonies, young people frequently announced that they had been spiritually reborn, and began acting and dressing in decidedly different ways than they had before. Some observers concluded that the Moonies had "brainwashed" these young people into joining; others claimed they physically forced individuals into joining the Church. As we shall see, neither brainwashing nor physical force constitute adequate explanations of the decision to join the Unification Church. To adequately understand the process by which young people became full-fledged members of the Unification Church, we need to examine the issue from the vantage point of social influence theories; viewing the phenomenon as one involving the exercise of social influence provides a fresh and interesting way of examining this issue.

BECOMING A MEMBER OF MOON'S RELIGIOUS ARMY: A CASE STUDY

Like many of her peers, Shelley Liebert traveled abroad, hoping to find herself. "When I returned home," she said, "I decided that I wanted to lead the life of a normal, average girl. I didn't want to be a gypsy anymore. So I got a job as a secretary, and I lived at home, and I was making an effort to be as normal as I could."[6]

"It was the last day of the year," she recalled, "and on the last day of each year, all the secretaries take those little flip calendars out of their holders and let them drop from the office buildings. I was feeling very melancholy, just watching the whole year at my feet. I thought to myself: 'This is my life every year. This is the last day of the year. I have to do one thing or another.' And that's when I met them."

A member of the Unification Church approached Shelley that day. Shelley had not heard anything about the Reverend Sun Myung Moon's religious movement, which had spread from Korea to the United States in the 1970s and which claimed to have thousands of members or witnesses all over the world. "They invited me to a weekend retreat," Shelley recalled. "In that one weekend, I made up my mind to join," she said. It

seemed like the perfect answer. Joining offered her a sense of purpose—
one that her monotonous job as a secretary lacked.

The leader of the movement that would profoundly influence Shelley's
life was a Korean-born evangelist who said that on Easter morning in 1936,
when he was 16 years old, Jesus Christ appeared and told him that he had
been chosen to complete Christ's unfinished mission. After spending 9
years studying religion, Sun Myung Moon began to preach his revealed
message to others. By the early 1970s, Moon regularly drew large crowds
at rallies, and by the mid-1970s, his Unification Church claimed hundreds
of thousands of members worldwide.

The weekend retreats such as the one Shelley attended were designed to
promote a sense of euphoria and spirituality: One observer commented
that they had the quality of a cheer.[7] Events were preplanned to totally
capture participants' attention.

Trainees woke up at 7:00 a.m., prayed at 7:30, and were expected to be
on the volleyball courts at 8:00 sharp.

"All the physical activity helped to build a sense of group, a 'we' feeling,"
Shelley recalled. "We shared the feeling that we had been misunderstood
by society and now we were among friends. We felt that God understood
us and that He had actually prepared us throughout the course of human
history—prepared our ancestors—that we might come to this point in
history."

Shelley completed a 7-day seminar and attended a 21-day training
program. She joined the Unification Church and became a part of a
fund-raising team that traveled to New Mexico and Arizona.

Shelley recalled that the Moonie leaders put a great deal of pressure on
recruits to raise funds for the Church. "We were told that the best Moonie
fund raiser was a girl whose knees both went out and who lost her voice.
The message was clearly that it didn't matter what your physical condition
was: If you had the correct, prayerful attitude, people would appear out of
nowhere."

At one point, Shelley worked at Moon's Pasadena mansion. One day she
had the opportunity to meet Moon. "Moon had a certain magnificence
about him," she recalled. "When he walked into the room, you felt blown
against the wall. He had an invisible force around him. You felt that if
someone were to shoot him, the bullet would swerve."

For a period of time, the Church was Shelley's life. She was a true
believer, a loyal and obedient soldier in the religious army of Reverend Sun
Myung Moon. At one point, however, things changed. Moon was indicted
for filing false tax returns. Shelley's parents became concerned about the
changes that they had observed in their daughter's attitudes and behavior.
They decided to retrieve Shelley from the cult. They made up a story and
convinced her to leave the Moonie camp. In an interview with a scholar
who was studying religious sects like the Moonies, Shelley acknowledged

that "I would have never left by myself. I was firmly convinced that I was doing the right thing."

Indeed, when Shelley participated in the Unification Church, she loved Reverend Moon and fervently believed in his cause. She was a true and devoted believer in the Church and its theology. As she herself noted, "I was embraced by a new life, a new situation."

Brainwashing in the Cults

Many people believed that the behavior of Shelley and other Moonies was nothing less than bizarre. The fact that a young adult from a middle-class background would suddenly leave college to join a religious movement and then claim she was spiritually reborn seemed unbelievable to many parents; it defied any rational explanation. Outsiders looked at these young people and noted that they wore the same type of clothing, spoke the same type of language, and seemed to share a similar dedication to a new religious philosophy. The common explanation was that young people had been brainwashed into a common mold.

The parents of a young man named David who joined the Unification Church in Britain noted that:

> The Moonies we had met at the camp were robots, glassy-eyed and mindless, programmed as soldiers. . . .
>
> We took comfort in realizing that it was not our son . . . but a diabolical force that had been implanted in his mind. . . .
>
> David's mind, we are convinced, was raped. Few people believe that mind control is possible.
>
> It can happen. It can happen to anybody. David is a strong, intelligent personality. Perhaps he was in the mood, over-tired, ready to flow with the tide. . . . (Barker, 1984, p. 121)

Brainwashing and mind control were typically invoked to explain why many young people left school to join a religious sect. But brainwashing does not explain why individuals choose to join a religious movement. If we restate the brainwashing explanation as a syllogism, we can better appreciate its shortcomings:

1. Shelley is a Moonie.
2. Moonies brainwash their recruits.
3. Shelley must have been brainwashed.

Yet, as Barker (1984), an expert in the sociology of religion, noted, such a syllogism does not demonstrate that an individual like Shelley has been brainwashed; "it simply asserts it" (p. 125). Employing a term like *brainwashing* does not explain why young people come to join religious sects like the Unification Church; typically, such a term is invoked to condemn the participants in a social cause rather than to help explain the sociological or psychological antecedents of their behavior. (See also Exhibit 1-1: The Mythology of Brainwashing, p. 21.)

How then can we explain why Shelley and thousands of other young people joined the Unification Church? One view is that Church leaders used physical force to coerce young people to join the Movement. According to this explanation, young people did not freely join the Church; instead, they were kidnapped or signed on under threat of physical duress.

Barker (1984) spent several years studying the Moonies and she does not believe the Moonies used physical coercion. "Whenever I have visited a Unification Centre," she noted, "I never had any difficulty in slipping out when I wanted to." She acknowledged that in some of the Moonie Churches, members "are expected to sign a book before they go out," but she added that it was "perfectly easy to open the door from the inside, and if it has been locked, I have always found a key hanging on a nearby nail" (p. 141).

If neither physical force nor brainwashing constitutes an adequate explanation for the decision to join the Moonies, then what factors help explain the decision to join the Church? To understand why young people joined the Unification Movement, it is necessary to view this issue as a problem in persuasion and social influence. There were a number of influence strategies that Moonie leaders used to try to convince young people to join the Church. Viewed from the perspective of Shelley and other recruits, the Church had many attractive qualities that made the decision to join quite easy. Here are several factors that accounted for the decision to "become a Moonie":

Youth and Vulnerability.   The Moonies appealed to young people who were particularly vulnerable and who were looking for an alternative to their present routines. Many of these youthful joiners were in college, others had run away from home and were confused and in search of a humane life course. The serene and structured world of the Unification Church offered these young people an answer, a solution, and (most importantly) the promise of an end to their agonizing search.

How satisfying it must have been to have stumbled across the Moonie alternative. One young woman put it this way:

> I was raised back East. We were always moving from one place to another—always uprooting and having to go to another school . . . living in poverty and corruption. I was always afraid of people with hate in their hearts. . . . It's so wonderful to be in a place where you do not have to feel

that fear. It's so hard to explain! (She blushes and is on the verge of tears.) When I first came here, I didn't know what Karen meant when she ran up and hugged me, and said, "At least you're home, welcome!" But now I know what she means. I am home! (Bromley & Shupe, 1979, p. 176)

Credible Communicators. The Moonie leaders had a commanding presence that some young people found appealing. They were highly credible communicators: Young recruits regarded them as kind, attractive, trustworthy, and intelligent people. The Reverend Moon bowled many people over, as Shelley herself observed, although in a way that revealed a great deal about her own perceptions of reality: "Moon had a certain magnificence about him. When he walked into the room, you felt blown against the wall. You felt that if someone were to shoot him, the bullet would swerve" (Enroth, 1977, p. 108).

Simple Messages. There was a beautific simplicity to the Church's philosophy; its theology, unique view of Adam and Eve's fall from grace, and its philosophy of life had an elegant logic and simplicity that even doubters found appealing. "It's so amazing, so scientific, and explains everything," said one young recruit.

Persuasive Appeals. The Moonies developed an entire regimen to "hook" young people into joining (Lofland, 1977). Their approach often seemed to parallel those used by aggressive salespersons who were trying to "psyche out" prospective clients. Indeed, some Moonie organizations gave their fund-raising teams a three-page memorandum that provided suggestions on how to solicit funds from strangers. The fund-raising hints included:

- Love the candy you are trying to sell, unite with it and try to convey this feeling to the customer.
- Always address a person as "Sir" or "Miss"—this is a very subtle form of flattery.
- If possible, try to get the . . . customer to hold a box of candy; many people find it difficult to return the candy once they've had an opportunity to hold it.
- We accept food stamps as payment for our candy. Also, if a person tells you he has no money chances are he has his check book with him. Tell him "We accept personal checks" and [he] may feel compelled to buy a box. (Enroth, 1977, p. 115)

Self-Perception. One persuasion theory emphasizes that people come to know who they are and what they believe from what they do—from how they behave (Bem, 1972). Many young people were confused when they came to the Moonie farms; they were in the throes of an identity crisis.

Gradually, they began to participate in group activities, including praying, cooking meals, helping to construct new facilities, and even recruiting new members. As persuasion theory would suggest, these young people observed that they were doing helpful, religious things. Hence, they inferred that they must be "helpful people" who had a strong commitment to religion. These self-perceptions then guided their behavior in a variety of ways.

Conformity to the Group. The Moonies emphasized collective activities; the group was put ahead of the individual. These activities exerted a subtle impact on an individual's thoughts and actions, as Rick Heller, a college student from Dallas, related:

> I was on my sleeping bag on the floor of a room with about 20 other guys. At about 5:30 in the morning this guy comes in with a guitar and starts playing and singing "You are my Sunshine" and I thought "Oh, brother." I rolled over, buried my face and tried to go back to sleep.
>
> But all of a sudden I realized all the other guys were singing and rolling up their sleeping bags. It was weird, like a private production of *Hair* or something. I thought "they're crazy, a bunch of fanatics." But then I realized that I was the only one in the room who wasn't singing . . . so I started to sing too. (Stoner & Parke, 1977, p. 155)

Commitment and Compliance. Commitment to the Moonies did not happen overnight, but instead evolved over time in a manner that was quite consistent with principles of interpersonal persuasion. Commitment started small; it began with attendance of a rally or a lecture, it gradually became larger, as the young person prayed regularly and made contact with the spirit world, and it finally increased to the point that the person participated in all-day door-to-door recruiting and toured the country on the "God Bless America" team.

Casual observers often took note of these behaviors and concluded that the Moonies must have applied strange mind control techniques to get recruits to do these things. Actually, these actions are explained easily by theories of commitment and compliance. (See chapters 10 and 11.) Researchers have found that once people make a small commitment to a cause (e.g., attending a Moonie rally) they can be persuaded to make ever-larger commitments (door-to-door recruiting and donating material possessions to the Church).

DEFINING PERSUASION

Differentiating Persuasion From Other Concepts

A scientific analysis of a phenomenon ordinarily begins with a clear, broad-based definition of the phenomenon under study. This not only requires that we define what we are studying, but also that we indicate how the concept under investigation differs from related terms or constructs.

In the popular mind, persuasion is associated with a wide variety of phenomena, including brainwashing, mind control, hypnotic suggestion, mass conformity, coercion, and propaganda. However, social scientists have emphasized that there are important differences between persuasion and these other concepts. As I noted earlier, terms like *brainwashing* and *mind control* are negative labels that are used to condemn the recipients of a particular persuasive message rather than to clarify or explain the dynamics of the persuasion process. Because these terms carry such negative connotations, I do not use them to describe the process of persuasion. Instead, I suggest that people typically employ a term like *brainwashing* to put a negative label on an intensive indoctrination situation of which they do not approve. As noted in the discussion of the Moonies, and of brainwashing myths, the term *brainwashing* is invoked to describe (or, more accurately, condemn) a situation in which influence agents employ a combination of coercive influence techniques and persuasive communications. Thus, rather than focusing on brainwashing, it is more useful to differentiate coercion from persuasion.

The relationship between coercion and persuasion has long been of interest to philosophers and to communication scholars (Nilsen, 1974; Smith, 1982). At first blush, it may seem like there are sharp and clear differences between these two terms. However, as Nilsen (1974) observed:

> One of the important ethical problems associated with persuasion . . . stems from the difficulty of deciding where persuasion ends and coercion begins. It is hard to determine whether there are forces operating from the outside or inside that are in a real sense "forcing" a particular choice. If, for example, a man fears reprisal for following a course of action, he may still be "free" to act or not, but it is a moot question whether his decision is a result of free choice or of coercion. (p. 66)

Two contemporary approaches have made particularly useful contributions to the definition of these terms. The first perspective is that of Smith, a communication researcher, the second that of Rosenbaum (1986), a social philosopher.

Smith (1982) argued that the most useful way to approach the persuasion–coercion problem is from the perspective of the recipient of the message. Observing that persuasive communication is only one of many forms of social influence, Smith perceptively noted that, from the perspective of the message recipient, the various modes of social influence can be placed on a continuum that range from relatively "noncoercive" to "highly coercive." Smith then suggested that there are two key differences between persuasive communication and coercive social influence:

First, when a person is exposed to a persuasive message, he or she has a *perception of choice* regarding the acceptance or rejection of symbolic appeals. As we stipulated earlier, whether behavioral options actually are available is not relevant. It is only required that an individual have the perception of free will. Second, if people choose to act on the recommendations made in persuasive messages, it is because they *privately accept* or *internalize* the advocated position. . . .

A further distinguishing mark of coercive social influence is that when people act under duress, their behavior is characterized by public compliance without private acceptance. . . . Again, regardless of the label applied to a form of social influence, so long as the recipient experiences *no choice*, we believe the influence strategy is coercive in nature. (p. 10)

Smith's approach to the persuasion–coercion issue is "subjectivist" or phenomenological. Her main point is that if message recipients perceive that they are free to reject the advocated position, then, as a practical matter, they are free; and the influence attempt is regarded as "persuasive in nature"; on the other hand, if recipients feel that they have no choice but to comply, then the influence attempt is deemed "coercive in nature." The second aspect of Smith's definition emphasizes that persuasion is characterized by private acceptance of the position advocated in the message. By contrast, in the case of coercive social influence, people publicly comply with the behavior urged of them, but, privately, they reject the position advocated in the message.

A different perspective on the coercion–persuasion issue can be gleaned from the work of Rosenbaum (1986). Rosenbaum has contended that: "(Person) Q is coerced by (Person) P when P causes Q to relinquish his or her known and valued autonomy over him or herself in some limited respect . . . (p. 135). Presumably, for Rosenbaum, persuasion requires that the individual be capable of acting as an autonomous agent in a social situation.

Smith's analysis of persuasion and Rosenbaum's definition of coercion help explain the dynamic forces at work in the Unification Church. Potential recruits were first exposed to a variety of persuasive communications—including cogent arguments, authority-based appeals, and appeals based on emotion. During this period, individuals perceived that they were free to reject the Moonies' messages; hence, the communications were persuasive in nature.

Over time, however, a different set of psychological processes took hold. Some young recruits formed strong "affective bonds" with members of the Church (Lofland, 1977). They came to depend on their fellow Moonies for support in times of emotional distress. In a systematic study of the Moonies, Galanter (1989) discovered that those individuals who were most attracted to the Church were those who had previously experienced the greatest amount of emotional distress. Galanter argued that the Church helped these individuals by providing them with a relief from neurotic distress and with an increase in psychological well-being. Galanter noted that:

> If, whenever the member feels close to the group, his or her distress is relieved, the member will tend to stay close, and the feeling of closeness to the group becomes the source of operant reinforcement. . . . Conversely, if they (members) disaffiliate from the group a bit, they are prodded to return by the increased distress they are likely to feel. Thus, zealous group members feel unhappy or dysphoric when removed from their group. (p. 89; p. 88)

In effect, these individuals came to depend on the Church for their material, social, and psychological rewards. This in turn diminished these young people's image of themselves as mature, independent young adults; in a very real sense, these individuals may have felt that they could not reject the pleas and requests made of them by Moonie leaders. They may have feared that if they rejected the appeals made of them, love and emotional support would be withdrawn—and the thought of losing these rewards absolutely terrified these individuals. Thus, it would be fair to conclude, based on Smith's analysis, that these converts to the Church perceived that they had no choice but to comply with the requests made of them. Consequently, we would have to say that (at this stage of the conversion process) the Moonie leaders' messages were not persuasive in nature, but, instead, constituted a coercive form of social influence. Similarly, Rosenbaum might argue that once cult members had become so totally dependent on their fellow Moonies for their rewards and self-esteem, they ceased to function as autonomous individuals; thus, using the criteria set forth in Rosenbaum's definition, it would be fair to label some of the Moonie tactics as coercive in nature.

Notice that, according to this analysis, persuasion and coercion are not "polar opposites"; instead, they "shade into one another." The differences are subtle; often they are not discernible to outside observers who use the term *coercion* to describe a social influence attempt that they disapprove of and employ terms like *persuasion* or *information campaign* to describe influence attempts that are consistent with their values.

Thus, if asked to describe the strategies employed by two contemporary social organizations—the Moonies and Alcoholics Anonymous (AA)—most people would probably say that the Moonies employed only coercive techniques (or worse yet, brainwashing); on the other hand, they would most likely assert that AA employed persuasive communications. However, scholars have noted that both organizations use some of the same social influence strategies (e.g., peer pressure, emotional manipulation, and conformity pressures). The difference is that most observers agree with the goals espoused by AA, so they tolerate its social influence strategies. On the other hand, most people are more critical of the Moonies, hence they employ more judgmental terms to describe the Moonies' attempts to influence their members. The same could be said about a variety of other groups as well: thus, U.S. schools "educate," whereas our enemies "indoctrinate their citizens," the U.S. government provides "information," while Saddam Hussein serves up "propaganda," and one's family and friends have "the facts," whereas one's foes have only their "opinions" (see also Zimbardo, 1972).

Definitions of Persuasion

Over the years, a number of definitions of persuasion have been proposed. A synopsis of the major definitions is provided here. According to contemporary scholars, persuasion is:

> a communication process in which the communicator seeks to elicit a desired response from his receiver (Andersen, 1971, p. 6).
> that activity in which speaker and listener are conjoined and in which the speaker consciously attempts to influence the behavior of the listener by transmitting audible and visible symbolic cues (Scheidel, 1967, p. 1).
> a conscious attempt by one individual to change the attitudes, beliefs, or behavior of another individual or group of individuals through the transmission of some message (Bettinghaus & Cody, 1987, p. 3).
> a symbolic activity whose purpose is to effect the internalization or voluntary acceptance of new cognitive states or patterns of overt behavior through the exchange of messages (Smith, 1982, p. 7).
> a successful intentional effort at influencing another's mental state through communication in a circumstance in which the persuadee has some measure of freedom (O'Keefe, 1990, p. 17).
> communicative behavior that has as its purpose the changing, modification, or shaping of the responses (attitudes or behavior) of the receivers (Bostrom, 1983, p. 11).

Although there is not one definition of persuasion that all scholars accept, there is a general consensus that persuasion is an activity or process in which a communicator attempts to induce a change in the belief, attitude, or behavior of another person or group of persons through the transmission of a message in a context in which the persuadee has some degree of free choice. I briefly examine each of the components of this view of persuasion below.

Activity or Process. Persuasion is not simply the product or outcome of a message sent by a source to a receiver. It is a dynamic activity, a process in which both source and receiver send and receive messages. Thompson (1975) noted:

> Persuasion is not an event in which a sender packages his ideas in a container and forwards a box of fixed and unchanging materials; it also is not analogous to the electric light switch. . . . To the contrary, the message that a sender creates and transmits is only one element in a field of new events and prior attitudes and beliefs. (p. 3)

Attempt to Induce a Change.   Persuasion is characterized by the attempt of one person (source) to change the mental or emotional state of another person (receiver). One way of differentiating persuasion from other forms of communication is that, in persuasion, a source *intends* to influence a receiver. If one does not include the concept of intention in a definition of persuasion, then every communicative activity can legitimately be called persuasion. Such a definition would be too broad and encompassing; it would not allow scholars to set limits on the field of persuasion and on the study of persuasive communication effects.

There has been some disagreement among scholars as to whether persuasion should be defined as a successful attempt at influencing others. On the one hand, some theorists have argued that persuasion can occur, regardless of whether anybody is actually influenced by a message. According to this view, persuasion is a dynamic process, a "manipulation designed to produce action in others" (Lerbinger, 1972, p. 3). On the other hand, other theorists have preferred to build the notion of success into the definition of persuasion. O'Keefe (1990) argued that it does not make sense to state that "I persuaded him but failed" (p. 15). Scholars who prefer a process-oriented view of persuasion have tended to emphasize that persuasion involves an attempt to influence, whereas those who adopt an outcome-oriented approach have emphasized that persuasion involves a successful attempt to influence.

Change in Beliefs, Attitudes, or Behaviors.   One of the main differences between coercion and persuasion is that, in the case of coercion, an individual publicly performs a behavior without private acceptance, whereas in persuasion, as Smith (1982) noted, "if people choose to act on the recommendations made in persuasive messages, it is because they *privately accept* or *internalize the advocated position*" (p. 10). Persuasion therefore involves a change of a cognitive or affective nature.

Simons (1971) has taken this viewpoint even further; Simons has argued that all persuasion is fundamentally self-persuasion. According to this view, which is accepted by many contemporary scholars, it is technically incorrect to state that persuaders "change people's minds." Persuaders can manipulate the facts, associate the message with attractive stimuli, and create a situation in which agreement with the message seems like the only sensible response. However, they cannot change an individual's attitude about an issue. As trite as it may sound, it is the individual who decides whether or not to alter his or her attitude about the issue. The best that a persuasive communication can do is create an atmosphere in which an individual can change his or her own attitude about the issue. This is a subtle point, but one that has important theoretical and practical implications.

Transmission of a Message.   Persuasion involves the transmission of some sort of message. The message may be verbal, or nonverbal; it may be relayed interpersonally or through mass media; it may be logical or illogical. However, for persuasion to occur, a message must be transmitted. In saying that persuasion involves the transmission of a message, it is not implied that persuasion is a one-way unidirectional process in which a sender sends (or injects a message) into the minds of receivers. This "hypodermic needle model" of message effects reflects a simplistic approach to persuasion. In fact, receivers and sources "exchange messages" (Smith, 1982). As Reardon (1981) noted, "persuasion is not something one person does *to* another but something he or she does *with* another" (p. 25).

Free Choice.   A final defining characteristic of persuasion is free choice. At some level, the individual must be capable of accepting or rejecting the position that has been urged of him or her. This aspect of the definition of persuasion is clearly the most complicated. After all, there are hundreds of definitions of freedom and free will. As noted earlier, one way of approaching this problem is to adopt a "subjectivist" approach. Smith, a major proponent of this position, has argued that if individuals perceive that they are free to accept or reject the symbolic recommendation, then, as a practical matter, they are free; on the other hand, if individuals perceive that they have no choice but to adopt the behavior urged of them, then they are not (practically speaking) free, and a coercion model would be a more appropriate way to describe the influence situation.

Having defined persuasion, I now provide an overview of the history of the study of persuasion; subsequently, I discuss the approach to persuasion that I adopt in this book; and finally, I touch on the ethics of persuasive communications.

THE STUDY OF PERSUASION

A Brief History of the Field

Persuasion is one of the oldest fields of academic study. Scholars believe that one of the first essays on the subject of persuasion was written in about

3,000 B.C. Addressed to the oldest son of the Pharoh Huni, the essay contained advice on how to communicate effectively (McCroskey, 1972). About 2,500 years later, the Greek scholars Corax and Tisias composed some of the first known scholarly essays on rhetorical communication. At about the same time (5th century B.C.), a group of teachers called the Sophists wrote and lectured about rhetoric and debate. One of their contemporaries, Gorgias, placed great emphasis on style and appealing to the emotions. Plato lambasted Gorgias in one of his dialogues, and subsequently outlined the requirements for a truly satisfactory theory of rhetoric and public communication (Davis & Kraus, 1982; McCroskey, 1972).

It was Aristotle, however, who made the most significant and lasting contribution to persuasion research. Aristotle devoted three books to the subject of rhetoric, which he defined as "the faculty of discovering in a particular case what are the available means of persuasion." For Aristotle— and the scholars who followed in his footsteps—rhetoric had a specific meaning; today, of course, the term has come to be associated with specious reasoning and overly stylized arguments ("empty rhetoric"). Aristotle argued that there were three means of persuasion: *ethos* (the nature of the communicator), *pathos* (the emotions of the audience), and *logos* (the nature of the message). Aristotle went on to outline a distinctive theory and philosophy of rhetoric.

The next "flourishing of eloquence" (to use McGuire's phrase) occurred in Rome around 82 B.C. Cicero refined Greek theories of rhetoric, whereas Quintilian expounded on the ideal training for an orator. However, the Roman era of persuasion "terminated with the . . . demise of Cicero under the knives of the Triumvirs" (McGuire, 1985, p. 234).

Rhetorical theory flourished again during the Italian Renaissance, with the rediscovery of Quintilian's works. Rhetoric experienced another rebirth during the late-1700s, as Fénelon, a French writer, noted that there was a close relationship between rhetoric and logic, and Blair, a British scholar, contended that rhetoric should be evaluated in terms of whether it satisfied criteria of quality and taste (McCroskey, 1972). There was a resurgence of interest in rhetorical theories during the 1930s and 1940s, as theorists adapted modern approaches to language and identification to the study of rhetoric (Burke, 1969; Korzybski, 1933; Ogden & Richards, 1926).

During the 1940s and 1950s, social science approaches to persuasion began to overtake rhetoric as the dominant paradigm in the field. Social science approaches offered researchers a method of testing hypotheses derived from theory and held out the possibility that a body of knowledge of persuasive communication effects might be established. One of the pioneers in modern persuasion research was Carl Hovland, who, during World War II, helped to evaluate the many communications that the U.S. government developed to influence the beliefs and attitudes of Allied soldiers. After the war ended, Hovland embarked on an ambitious program of experimental research, which laid the foundation for the scientific study of persuasion.

Today, persuasion research is flourishing. Scholars in a variety of disciplines—including communication, psychology, consumer behavior, and public health—are investigating the processes and effects of persuasive messages.

A SCIENTIFIC APPROACH TO PERSUASION

A scientific approach to persuasion is adopted in this book. It may seem strange to approach persuasion from a social science point of view. After all, you may think of persuasion as an art. When someone mentions the word "persuasion," you may think of such things as "the gift of gab," "manipulation," "pulling the wool over our eyes," or "subliminal seduction." You may feel that by approaching persuasion from the vantage point of contemporary social science, we are reducing the area to something antiseptic. However, this is far from the truth. Social scientists who study persuasion are curious about the same phenomena as everybody else is: for example, what makes a person persuasive, what types of messages are most effective, and why do people go along with the recommendations put forth by powerful persuaders. The difference between the scientist's approach and that of the layperson is that the scientist formulates theories about attitudes and persuasion, derives hypotheses from these theories, and puts the hypotheses to empirical tests. By empirical tests, I mean that hypotheses are evaluated on the basis of evidence and data collected from the real world.

The purpose of scientific research on persuasion is to develop principles about the processes and effects of persuasive communications. It is commonly assumed that scientific research discovers a set of facts and that these facts are not susceptible to change. When you read a book on persuasion, you probably expect to discover the "facts" about persuasion (e.g., what types of messages work and what messages do not work).

Most researchers have a more dynamic view of science. They believe that the facts that we have at a certain point in time are subject to change. We do have a body of knowledge about persuasion, and there are a number of theories that have done a pretty good job of explaining the effects of persuasive communications. However, as new studies are conducted, new evidence is obtained and new explanations of persuasion phenomena come to the foreground. What this means is that our knowledge of persuasion is dynamic—always changing, never static (Gergen, 1973). Thus, persuasion texts of the 1960s proclaimed that women were more susceptible to persuasion than men; later studies, conducted during the 1960s and 1970s, failed to find evidence that women were more persuadable than men (Eagly, 1978), so current texts report a different set of "facts" on this issue.

THE ETHICS OF PERSUASION

Persuasion is a pervasive part of our everyday lives. Billions of dollars are spent on advertising, politicians take to the airwaves every 2 years to try to win converts, sales professionals employ a variety of techniques to influence their clients, lawyers ponder whether they should present their strongest arguments first or last in the closing statement, and health care professionals spend considerable time and effort trying to convince people to adopt a healthier lifestyle. For these reasons, persuasion is a popular topic; people hope that a knowledge of persuasion theory and research will help them accomplish their personal and social goals.

Yet precisely because persuasion is believed to be a powerful instrument of social control, it has evoked criticisms. Ever since the time of Plato, concerns have been expressed about whether persuasion is an ethical activity. Some critics have argued that persuasion is immoral because a communicator is trying to induce someone to do something that is in the communicator's best interest, but not necessarily in the best interest of the individual receiving the message (Nilsen, 1974).

Although it may be true that persuasive communication involves a certain amount of manipulation and deception, we should be careful not to be overly judgmental on this matter. It is commonplace for people to conceal their true intentions; in fact, conversations could not proceed very smoothly if people always expressed what was on their minds. Reardon (1991) noted that:

> The disguising of intentions is a prevalent communication behavior in our society. It is an accepted and often expected means of avoiding conflict. Even young children learn that saying what one means can sometimes be a very sure way of not getting what one wants. Recognizing the prevalence of indirectness in communication can be disturbing unless we consider what life would be like if all of us were to say exactly what we think. Economizing of truth is a necessity, especially when the truth might hurt. (p. 5)

Thus, making ethical prescriptions about persuasion is not a simple matter. There are many different philosophical positions on what it means to be ethical and on what morality means (Frankena, 1973). In the realm of persuasion, most scholars would acknowledge that certain persuasive techniques (i.e., deception, manipulation, and verbal abuse) are morally offensive; however, they would also note that there may be circumstances in which the use of such techniques would be defensible on moral grounds. For example, most people would argue that it is morally justified for a counselor to use manipulation or deception to try to get a drug addict off of heroin. They also would agree that a U.S. president should use deception if he thought that it would increase the chances that the other side would agree to nuclear arms reductions. However, there are a variety of circumstances in which certain people would endorse the use of a particular persuasion technique, whereas others would condemn it. This is why it is so difficult to come up with general prescriptions or philosophies of ethics.

Nonetheless, it is important to consider the ethical aspects of persuasion, and I touch on them from time to time in this book. Social science research can shed light on ethical issues by providing us with knowledge about people's susceptibility to persuasive messages. By understanding the techniques persuaders commonly use and the impact that these techniques have on audience members, we can make ethical judgments in a more informed way.

CONCLUSIONS

I have provided a case study example of persuasion to show that persuasive messages can exert a powerful impact on attitudes and behaviors. I have noted that persuasion is popularly associated with a variety of phenomena, including brainwashing, mind control, and coercion. However, terms like *brainwashing* and *mind control* do more to obsfucate and condemn than they do to explain and clarify a particular phenomenon. Following Smith, I have argued that there are subtle (but important) differences between persuasion and coercion. The differences focus on the extent to which message recipients perceive that they are free to accept or reject the symbolic appeal, and on the degree to which the behavior is characterized by "public compliance without private acceptance" (Smith, 1982).

A number of definitions of persuasion have been proposed over the past 25 years. There is a general consensus that persuasion is an activity or process in which a communicator attempts to induce a change in the belief, attitude, or behavior of another person or group of persons through the transmission of a message in a context in which the persuadee has some degree of free choice.

EXHIBIT 1-1   21

* * *

EXHIBIT 1-1
THE MYTHOLOGY OF BRAINWASHING

−"I have been brainwashed."

This was what Michigan Governor George Romney said in 1967 when he discovered that the U.S. government had deliberately misled him about the nature of U.S. involvement in Vietnam.

Romney is one of many people who have used the brainwashing label to describe a seemingly inexplicable conversion or change of heart. Brainwashing also was invoked to explain the strange events surrounding the kidnapping of Patty Hearst in 1974 by a radical terrorist group and Patty's eventual commitment to the group's goal of overthrowing the U.S. "imperialist" government. Brainwashing was also the popular explanation of the Steinberg tragedy, which culminated in 1987 in the death of 6-year-old Lisa Steinberg at the hands of her adoptive father, Joel. Joel Steinberg brutally beat young Lisa and then ordered that his lover, Hedda Nussbaum, not request emergency assistance. Hedda, herself a victim of Joel's physical and mental cruelty, could not bring herself to cry for help, leading observers to wonder if she had not been a victim of brainwashing.

The term *brainwashing* was coined in the 1950s to explain a strange series of events in China and North Korea. After taking control of China in 1949, the Communists embarked on an ambitious program of "thought reform" that was designed to educate the Chinese population about the "evils" of capitalism and the "virtues" of Communism (Lifton, 1961). To accomplish their goal, the Chinese imprisoned Western missionaries living in China and demanded that students and intellectuals enroll for a time in new revolutionary universities that provided instruction in the Communist ideology. Shortly after they had completed their "education," some of the missionaries and students made elaborate confessions of their previous "sins," renounced their upper middle-class upbringing, and extolled the virtues of the new Communist order.

During the Korean War, the North Korean Army captured a number of U.S. soldiers and subjected them to physical and psychological torture. After the war, it was rumored that some of the U.S. soldiers had renounced their values and had become loyal supporters of Communism, North Korean style. These events seemed to defy rational explanation. Edward Hunter (1951), a reporter working for a Miami newspaper, said that the explanation was quite simple. Hunter (1951) wrote that:

> Unrevealed tens of thousands of men, women and children had their brains washed in Red China. . . . (Brainwashing causes) actual damage . . . to a man's mind through drugs, hypnotism, or other means, so that a memory of what had actually happened would be wiped out of his mind and a new memory of what never happened inserted. (p. 4; Hunter, 1956, p. 26)

And so brainwashing was born. It soon became the favored explanation for the events in China and North Korea; it gained respectability when CIA Director Allen Dulles warned that the Communists were capable of washing "the brain clean of the thoughts and mental processes of the past." Unfortunately, brainwashing is not an explanation; it is a pejorative label that does more to mystify a phenomenon than to explain it. Yet, to this day, four myths of brainwashing persist:

Myth 1. Brainwashing is a new technology of mind control that was first developed by the Communists.

To examine this claim, we need to know exactly what brainwashing means. Because brainwashing is not a scientific concept, we will not find it defined in social science textbooks. Instead, we must turn to the dictionary. *Webster's Third International* defines *brainwashing* as "The forcible application of prolonged and intensive indoctrination sometimes including mental torture in an attempt to induce someone to give up basic political, social, or religious beliefs and attitudes and to accept contrasting regimented ideas" (p. 267).

Forcible indoctrination and torture? These are as old as humans themselves. Indeed, the use of torture to extract confessions from suspected criminals has a history that goes back at least to ancient Egypt (Suedfeld, 1990). New techniques of torture were developed during the Spanish Inquisition and during the reign of Pope Innocent III. Torture was used to obtain confessions from so-called witches in the 18th century, and it was later employed by Stalin in the Moscow Show Trials of the 1930s. Clearly, the North Koreans and Chinese did not invent these techniques; they merely adapted them to the 20th century. They employed heavy doses of modern psychology in the service of their cause.

Myth 2. The Communists used hypnosis or drugs to convert individuals to their side.

It is possible that the Communists employed these techniques to extract information from prisoners, but it is naive to think that they were able to change attitudes or personality through drugs or hypnosis. After reviewing studies of the effects of hypnosis, Scheflin and Opton (1978) concluded that "Without trust and willingness to enter into an alternate state of consciousness, the subject will not respond to the hypnotic induction process" (p. 455).

Hypnosis can have important psychological effects, but it is naive to imagine that it can cause people to renounce basic cultural values. For hypnosis to be successful, the individual must be receptive to the hypnotist's suggestions and there must be a high degree of trust between the hypnotist and patient. These conditions were surely lacking in the case of the American POWs and the participants in Chinese thought reform.

It is similarly naive to think that drugs administered by interrogators can change a person's basic values. As Scheflin and Opton (1978) noted: "No drug available can wipe out specific memories nor can any eliminate any memories forever. Drugs help to disable people, not to direct them" (p. 469).

The notion that the Communists relied on drugs and hypnosis is the stuff of Hollywood movies. In fact, they employed far more pedestrian techniques, including torture (e.g., pressing thumbs, pencils, and chopsticks beneath a prisoner's skin), continuous interrogation, sleep deprivation, constant surveillance, public testimonials featuring "confessions" from other prisoners, regular lectures outlining the evils of the American form of government, group pressure, and verbal abuse (Schein, 1961).

Robert Lifton (1961), the psychiatrist who conducted an extensive study of Chinese thought reform, noted that:

> Behind this web of semantic (and more than semantic) confusion lies an image of "brainwashing" as an all-powerful, irresistible, unfathomable, and magical method of achieving total control over the human mind. It is of course none of these things, and this loose usage makes the word a rallying point for fear, resentment, urges toward submission, justification for failure, irresponsible accusation, and for a wide gamut of emotional extremism. (p. 4)

Myth 3. Brainwashing induced lasting changes in captives' attitudes and behavior.

The facts argue otherwise. Of the 3,500 U.S. soldiers who survived the "death marches" following their capture by the North Koreans, fewer than 50 made propaganda statements for the North Koreans, and fewer than 10 failed to return to the United States (Scheflin & Opton, 1978; Wolff, 1960).[8]

Contrary to Edward Hunter's grandiose claims about the impact of Chinese thought reform, Lifton's study revealed that there were three different reactions to the "revolutionary university" experience. A minority became "zealous converts" to Communism; it is likely that these persons were initially sympathetic to Communism and thought reform solidified their support. A second group became "resisters"; shocked and disgusted by what they had experienced, they fled the country. If anything, thought reform strengthened these individuals' resistance to Communism.

The most common reaction was exhibited by those who Lifton called "the adapters." Relieved that the program had come to an end, they looked forward to resuming their jobs and relationships once again. They had not become zealous patriots, but they had a better sense of what Communism was all about and what their government expected of them.

Myth 4. Brainwashing is a technique perpetrated by the enemies of the United States.

This may be the most sinister myth of them all. The idea is that other countries brainwash their citizens, but "we" educate ours. Of course, all societies socialize their citizens into accepting a particular political ideology. By claiming that enemy governments use brainwashing techniques, U.S. officials hoped to harden Americans' attitude toward these countries.

Interestingly, the U.S. government may itself have used some of the brainwashing strategies that it has suggested were the exclusive province of the Communist Chinese. From 1953 to 1964, the CIA is believed to have conducted, under Code Name MK Ultra, a series of classified studies that investigated new techniques to aid in the control and manipulation of human behavior (Scheflin & Opton, 1978). The CIA is thought to have recruited private citizens from prisons, hospitals, and universities, and told them that they were taking in important new medical and psychiatric research. In fact, these recruits were guinea pigs in a series of studies that explored the impact of drugs, hypnosis, and electric shock on human behavior. A number of participants in the studies sued the U.S. government, and they disclosed the horrifying details of the experiments to writers and reporters. On December 23, 1984, the CBS newsprogram "60 Minutes" covered the story. Anchorman Ed Bradley began by noting that:

> "MK Ultra" is not the name of a new James Bond movie. It is, or was, the code word for a secret CIA project which took place between 1953 and 1964 in which unsuspecting people were used in mind control experiments that left them emotionally crippled for life. "MK Ultra" consisted of more than 130 research programs which took place in prisons, hospitals and universities all over the United States. Tonight, we'll look at sub-project Number 68, an experiment conducted in Canada. . . .
>
> Each of the plaintiffs came here to the Allen Memorial Institute in Montreal expecting therapy; instead, what they got was a nightmare of experiments. There were electroshock treatments, many times greater than the norm. They were subjected to sleep therapy, long periods, often up to 60 days, during which they were drugged so much that the better part of each day was spent sleeping. During these periods, they were subjected to what's called psychic driving, the constant repetition of tape-recorded messages, often up to a half-million times. They were also injected with drugs, curare, which brought on temporary paralysis, and LSD, which lead to terrifying hallucinations.

Clearly, then, both the United States and its enemies have employed brainwashing techniques in the service of their political and social goals. *Brainwashing*, alas, is hardly an objective, scientific term. Instead, it is a "devil term" that does more to condemn the views of an institution or a nation than it does to shed light on a complex phenomenon (Weaver, 1953). It is, as Lifton (1961) noted some 30 years ago, "a rallying point for fear, resentment . . . and for a wide gamut of emotional extremism."

2
Defining
and Measuring Attitudes

I like American-made cars. I am disgusted with all the flak American cars have been taking lately. . . .

Many Americans have owned and still own American-made cars and like them and would own nothing else. Let us all get behind the American automobile industry and buy American and drive out the foreign manufacturer. . . .

Remember Pearl Harbor.

— Letter to the Editor, *The (Akron) Beacon Journal*

It is very easy to concern ourselves with the breakup of the Soviet Union, and to not be aware of how this country is falling apart.

There is chronic high unemployment, and each day one reads where major companies are laying off more people, often numbering in the five figures. . . .

When a country is more interested in jingoistic adventures than it is in feeding its hungry (the bulk of them children), educating its people, creating meaningful jobs with decent wages, providing health care for everyone, and housing its citizens, it is already a nation in decline. . . .

Letter to the Editor, *The (Cleveland) Plain Dealer*

The Body Shop is against consumer testing in the cosmetics industry. We believe that animals should not suffer for our vanity. It is neither right, necessary, nor scientifically accurate to test skin and hair care products on animals. WE WILL NEVER TEST ON ANIMALS.

(Brochure for The Body Shop, a soap retail store in Beachwood, Ohio)

As these comments indicate, people have attitudes toward a variety of issues. Indeed, today we take the term *attitude* for granted. Statements like "we have very different attitudes about religion," "you have an attitude problem," and "she has a wonderful attitude toward her work" are common examples of how people use the attitude concept in everyday life. Yet, while most of us are familiar with the term *attitude*, we would be hard pressed to come up with a definition of the concept. Defining concepts clearly and comprehensively is one of the main tasks of social science. Thus, researchers have offered a number of definitions of the attitude concept. In this chapter, I describe the major definitions of attitude. I also discuss attitude structure and function and present an overview of the major techniques that researchers have employed to measure social and political attitudes.

THE CONCEPT OF ATTITUDE

The word "attitude" came into the English language vocabulary in the early 1700s. It came from the French "attitude," which evolved from the Italian "attitudine," which in turn developed from the Latin "aptus," which meant adaptedness or fitness (Fleming, 1967; Petty, Ostrom, & Brock, 1981). The term became popular in social scientific circles during the late-1800s. Social scientists were increasingly dissatisfied with the notion that behavior was a product of heredity and instinct; they had come to believe that "custom and environment" shaped human behavior (Allport, 1935). Yet they also believed that terms such as *custom* and *social force* were too vague and impersonal to capture the dynamic process by which individuals came to acquire social behaviors that were appropriate to their culture. The term *attitude*, which referred to a force or quality of mind, seemed much more appropriate.

During the late-19th century, psychologists viewed an attitude as a physical expression or a motor response. It was Sigmund Freud's disciples who "resurrected attitudes . . . and endowed them with vitality, identifying them with longing, hatred and love, with passion and prejudice" (Allport, 1935). In 1935, psychologist Gordon Allport declared that: "The concept of attitude is probably the most distinctive and indispensable concept in contemporary American social psychology. No other term appears more frequently in experimental and theoretical literature" (p. 798).

In making this statement, Allport, a preeminent psychologist, helped to legitimize the concept of attitude. At the time that Allport was working (in the 1930s and 1940s), behaviorally oriented learning theories dominated the field of psychology. Allport departed from this view by defining attitudes as a mental state that must be inferred from behavior. Indeed, for many years scholars referred to an attitude as a "hypothetical construct" – a concept that could not be observed directly but could only be inferred from people's actions. An exemplar of this approach was the Michigan psychology professor who ran through the halls of his department, shouting (in jest) that "I found it. I found it. I found the attitude." His comment illustrates that attitudes are different from the raw materials that other scientific disciplines examine—materials that can be touched or at least seen, such as a rock, a plant cell, or an organ in the human body.

Although in some sense we do infer a person's attitude from what he or she says or does, it would be a mistake to assume that for this reason attitudes are "not real" or are "mere mental constructs." This is a fallacy inherent in behaviorism—the scientific theory that argues that all of human activity can be reduced to units of behavior. Contemporary scholars reject this notion. They note that people have thoughts, cognitive structures, and a variety of emotions, none of which can be reduced to behavioral units. Moreover, they argue that an entity that is mental or emotional is no less "real" than a physical behavior. As Allport (1935) noted perceptively:

> Attitudes are never directly observed, but, unless they are admitted, through inference, as real and substantial ingredients in human nature, it becomes impossible to account satisfactorily either for the consistency of any individual's behavior, or for the stability of any society. (p. 839)

Numerous definitions of attitude have been advanced over the past 100 years. For example, scholars writing in the late-19th century defined attitude as a motor response. Learning theorists of the 1940s viewed an attitude as an implicit response that mediates the impact of a stimulus on behavior (Doob, 1947). By contrast, contemporary theorists define attitude in more cognitive terms, as, for example, "an object evaluation that is stored in memory" (Judd, Drake, Downing, & Krosnick, 1991). For all the diversity, there are several points on which the different theorists would agree. There is a consensus that an attitude is a learned, enduring, and affective evaluation of an object (a person, entity, or idea) that exerts a directive impact on social behavior. It is useful to briefly examine each of these components of the concept of attitude.

Attitudes Are Learned. Attitudes are learned through the course of socialization. Parents, peers, schools, and mass media all play an important role in shaping social attitudes. Social scientists have developed a number of theories (see chapter 3) to account for how children and adults learn social and political attitudes. For the most part, these theories emphasize that attitudes are learned through conditioning, exposure to novel stimuli, and via modeling of influential others' behavior. Some scholars have argued that attitudes are determined by genetic factors (McGuire, 1985; Schacter, 1982). These researchers have contended that genetic factors predispose individuals toward certain attitudes or channel their preferences toward certain behavioral targets. Although it is possible that there is a genetic component to attitudes, there is little convincing evidence that this is the case. Furthermore, even if genetic factors in some sense predispose individuals to adopt certain attitudes, it is likely that the environment interacts with genetic forces and powerfully determines the shape and structure of the social attitudes that individuals ultimately develop.

Attitudes Are Enduring. Attitudes are not ephemeral phenomena— they do not disappear as soon as we have made a public statement, nor do they wither away as soon as we have told a survey researcher what we think about a contemporary issue. On the contrary, attitudes are stable dispositions that influence our cognitions and behaviors in a variety of ways.

Attitudes Are Affective Entities. Attitudes have a strong affective or emotional component. Possessing a social attitude "means that the individual is no longer neutral toward the referents of an attitude. He is FOR or AGAINST, positively inclined or negatively disposed in some degree toward them" (Sherif, Sherif, & Nebergall, 1965, p. 5). Contemporary scholars have emphasized that attitudes are evaluative labels that individuals employ to categorize social objects as good or bad, strong or weak, active or passive, and so on. Attitudes color our perceptions and guide our interpretations of social objects (Fazio, 1989; Pratkanis, 1989).

Attitudes Exert a Directive Impact on Behavior. Attitudes predispose people to act in particular ways. Attitudes guide and influence behavior. This is not to say, however, that attitudes always predict behavior; indeed, as is discussed in chapter 4, there are a variety of conditions under which people's attitudes do not predict their behavior. Nonetheless, most scholars would agree with Allport (1935) that an attitude exerts "a directive or dynamic influence upon the individual's response to all objects and situations with which it is related."

Muzafer Sherif, a leading persuasion scholar, integrated these various components of attitude rather nicely when he observed that:

> When we talk about attitudes, we are talking about what a person has *learned* in the process of becoming a member of a family, a member of a group, and of society that makes him react to his social world in a *consistent* and *characteristic* way, instead of a transitory and haphazard way. We are talking about the fact that he is no longer neutral in sizing up the world around him: he is *attracted* or *repelled, for* or *against, favorable* or *unfavorable.* (Sherif, 1967, p. 2)

Differentiating Attitude From Related Terms

Attitudes are frequently lumped together with other concepts, such as habits, values, beliefs, and opinions. It is useful to differentiate attitudes from these related constructs.

Habits. Like attitudes, habits are well learned and enduring. However, habits differ from attitudes in three important respects. First, habits are routinized behavior patterns, whereas attitudes are not behavioral entities (Oskamp, 1977). Second, individuals may not be conscious that they have a particular habit, yet they are ordinarily aware that they harbor one or another attitude. Finally, individuals may not be capable of verbalizing the content of a habit, but they are ordinarily quite able to verbally express their attitudes (Scott, 1969).

Values. Values are ideals; they are the overarching goals that people strive to obtain. Kluckhohn (1951) defined *values* as "conceptions of the desirable means and ends of action." Rokeach (1973) differentiated between terminal values (e.g., freedom, equality, and wisdom), and instrumental values (e.g., the importance of being honest, broad-minded, or responsible). Values are more global and general than attitudes; they are, according to Oskamp (1977), "the most important and central elements in a person's system of attitudes and beliefs." Thus, a terminal value (equality) may underlie a number of quite specific attitudes (e.g., attitudes toward African-Americans, Women's Liberation, and affirmative action).

Beliefs. Beliefs are cognitions—the information that individuals have about objects or actions. Fishbein and Ajzen (1975) defined belief as the subjective probability that an object has a particular attribute or that an action will lead to a particular outcome. Thus, beliefs are subjectively held and they can be ordered along a probability distribution (e.g., one person may believe that it is very likely that a regular program of exercise will increase longevity, whereas another person may believe that it is not very likely that an exercise regimen will increase longevity). The main difference between attitudes and beliefs is that attitudes have a strong affective component, whereas beliefs are primarily cognitive; they do not have any affective content (although they may trigger strong affective reactions).

Opinions. Of all the terms we have discussed, opinions have proved to be the most difficult to differentiate from attitudes. Some researchers have employed the two terms synonymously, whereas others have argued that there are subtle differences between the two constructs (Childs, 1965; Osgood, Suci, & Tannenbaum, 1957).

We believe that opinions differ from attitudes in two ways. First, opinions are cognitive judgments (like beliefs), whereas (as we have noted) attitudes have a strong affective component. Thus, the statement that "More and more young women are smoking cigarettes" is an opinion, whereas the statement that "I feel that cigarette smoking is a terrible habit" is an attitude. Second, attitudes are broader in scope than opinions. Attitudes are complex structures that are composed of diverse elements, whereas opinions are simpler and less differentiated entities.

THE STRUCTURE OF ATTITUDES

How are attitudes organized? If we could ever decompose an attitude, what would we find? Three models of attitude organization have been proposed: the tripartite approach, expectancy-value theory, and socio-cognitive theory.

The Tripartite Approach

According to this view, attitudes consist of three subcomponents: cognitions, feelings (affect), and behaviors (Rosenberg & Hovland, 1960). Several studies have obtained support for the model; for example, Breckler (1984), Ostrom (1969), and Kothandapani (1971) found that affect, cognition, and behavior emerged as separate and distinctive components of attitude. However, one problem with the tripartite view is that "it tends to prejudge the attitude–behavior relation, assuming that, almost by definition, such a relation must exist" (Zanna & Rempel, 1988). In other words, the tripartite definition assumes that attitudes are associated with behavior when, in fact, there is evidence that, under certain conditions, attitudes do not predict behavior at all (see chapter 4).

Because of these and other problems, many researchers do not subscribe to the tripartite view of attitude structure (Cacioppo, Petty, & Geen, 1989; Pratkanis, 1989). Instead, they prefer to view an attitude as a global evaluation that is determined by or consists of cognition and affect. The two dominant cognitive–affective models of attitude structure are expectancy-value theory and the sociocognitive approach.

Expectancy-Value Theory

The expectancy-value approach emphasizes that attitudes are affective entities. However, according to the expectancy-value perspective, attitudes are themselves determined by expectations (or beliefs) and evaluations. Thus, an individual's attitude toward an object is a function of: (a) the strength of the person's expectations that the object has a particular set of attributes, and (b) his or her evaluation of these attributes. Similarly, a person's attitude toward a behavior is a function of: (a) the strength of his or her beliefs that the behavior will lead to particular consequences, and (b) his or her evaluation of these consequences. Expectations (beliefs) and subjective values (evaluations) combine to determine attitude toward the object or behavior (Fishbein, 1967; Fishbein & Ajzen, 1975). This is represented by the following formula:

$$A = Sum \; b(i) \times e(i)$$

where b(i) = each belief and e(i) = each evaluation.

There is abundant evidence that attitudes can be predicted by employing Fishbein and Ajzen's (1975) formula. A particularly interesting investigation of the expectancy-value approach was conducted by Jaccard and Davidson (1972). They used expectancy-value theory to explore the dynamics of women's attitudes toward birth control.

Jaccard and Davidson asked 73 female college students to indicate their beliefs and evaluations of the consequences of using birth control pills and their intentions of using birth control pills. As you can see from Table 2.1, women who intended to use birth control pills had somewhat different beliefs about the pill than did women who indicated that they had little or

TABLE 2.1
Beliefs and Evaluations of Women Who Intend and Do Not Intend
to Use Birth Control Pills

Outcome	Beliefs		Evaluations	
	Intends to Use	Intends Not to Use	Intends to Use	Intends Not to Use
Would remove the worry of becoming pregnant	2.37	1.13	2.75	2.19
Is using the best method available	2.04	.88	2.67	2.06
Is using a method of birth control that is convenient	2.56	1.75	2.65	1.69
Would increase my sexual pleasure	.51	−.12	2.21	1.06
Leads to major side effects	−.35	1.19	−2.54	−2.50
Would affect my sexual morals	−1.89	−.44	−1.40	−1.62
Would give me guilt feelings	−2.25	.06	−2.40	−2.44

Note. The higher the number, the stronger the belief and the more positive the evaluation. From Jaccard and Davidson (1972)

no intention of using birth control pills. Women who intended to use birth control pills were more likely to believe that the pills would remove the worry of becoming pregnant, that they constituted the best method of birth control available, and that they represented a convenient method of birth control. They also were more inclined to believe that the pills would increase their sexual pleasure. Women who did not intend to use birth control pills were more likely to believe that the pills led to major side effects, that they would affect their sexual morals, and that they would give them guilt feelings.

Interestingly, the two groups of women evaluated these outcomes somewhat differently. Women who intended to use birth control pills evaluated removing the worry of becoming pregnant, using the best method of birth control available, using a convenient method of birth control, and increasing their sexual pleasure more positively than did women who did not intend to use the pills. Both groups viewed the occurrence of major side effects, the impact on sexual morals, and the production of guilt feelings as negative outcomes, however.

By examining attitudes in this way, we get a richer understanding of the underlying dynamics of attitudes. Thus, two women might hold different attitudes about birth control pills because they had different beliefs about the pill's consequences or because they held the same beliefs, but evaluated these consequences differently.

In general, the expectancy-value approach helps to explain how people integrate (or "put together in their minds") the various bits of information that they hold about the attitude object. It is important to emphasize that the beliefs that determine an attitude may often be in conflict. For example, one may simultaneously believe that capital punishment is inhumane and that it is an effective deterrent against crime. Fishbein and Ajzen's expectancy-value approach contends that people sum up in their heads large numbers of beliefs and evaluations. However, other approaches argue that people average the information (Anderson, 1971), and still other theories make different predictions about how people deal with conflicting information about an attitude object (Heider, 1958; Rosenberg & Hovland, 1960).

Sociocognitive Theory

Sociocognitive theory takes a broader, more holistic approach to the issue of attitude structure. Unlike expectancy-value theory, the sociocognitive model does not assume that cognitive components and affective elements are combined in some algebraic fashion. Instead, it postulates that an attitude is an evaluation of an object that is stored in memory. It further stipulates that an attitude is frequently supported by a unipolar or bipolar knowledge structure or system of beliefs (Pratkanis, 1989; Pratkanis & Greenwald, 1989).[1]

Pratkanis (1989), who helped to formulate the model, has noted that some attitudes are supported by a unipolar knowledge structure, whereas others are supported by a bipolar knowledge structure. A unipolar structure contains information on only one side of the issue, whereas a bipolar structure contains arguments for and against one's position. For example, an attitude toward sports is probably supported by a unipolar structure. Pratkanis (1989) noted that:

> A sports fan typically possesses an elaborate knowledge structure containing technical and esoteric information relative to those with less favorable attitudes. . . . Persons with positive attitudes have a vast amount of knowledge whereas those with less favorable (or neutral) attitudes do not. (p. 86)

Figure 2.1 displays a unipolar knowledge structure that a sports fan might carry around in his head.

By contrast, an attitude toward nuclear power is probably supported by a bipolar knowledge structure. Figure 2.2 displays a bipolar knowledge structure for the topic of nuclear power. According to Pratkanis, people who have strong attitudes on either side of the nuclear power issue should know the arguments that support their side and those that are employed by the opposition. One might not think that people would know the

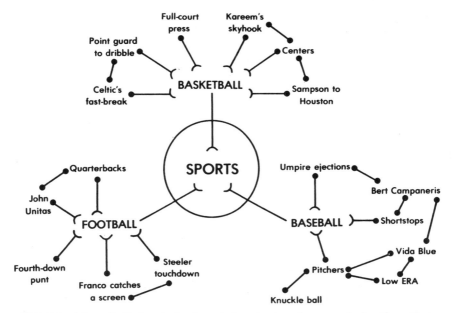

FIG. 2.1 A hypothetical unipolar knowledge structure for a sports fan (from Pratkanis, 1989).

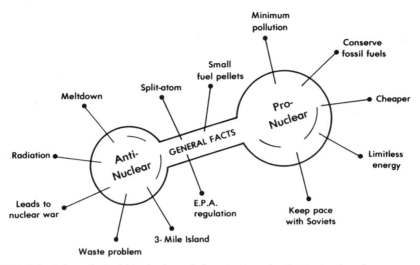

FIG. 2.2 A hypothetical bipolar knowledge structure for the topic of nuclear power (from Pratkanis, 1989).

arguments put forth by the opposition. But attitude scholars argue that, on some (highly controversial) issues, people's knowledge structures contain arguments supporting their position, arguments that are inconsistent with their position, and (in addition) counterarguments that refute their antagonists' position on the issue.

Thus, according to both expectancy-value theory and the sociocognitive perspective, attitudes are global evaluations of social objects. Both theories assume that thoughts and feelings determine (or comprise) people's evaluations. However, it is important to emphasize that some of our attitudes may be based more on feelings than on thoughts, whereas others may be based more on thoughts than on feelings (Millar & Tesser, 1986; Zanna & Rempel, 1988). For example, attitudes toward country or religion may be based almost entirely on affect—on gut level feelings formed at an early age. Such attitudes may have "strong affective components without a large number of beliefs supporting the attitude" (Wilson, Dunn, Kraft, & Lisle, 1989, p. 308). On the other hand, attitudes toward such issues as the federal budget deficit or toward U.S. foreign policy may be based more on cognitions than on affects.

The manner in which an attitude is organized has important implications for persuasion. Clearly, persuasion practitioners should make an effort to understand the type of attitude that most members of the audience have before they devise their communication campaigns. For example, they should determine whether audience members hold an attitude that is based almost entirely on affect; one that reflects a consideration of thoughts and feelings, but only those that support one's own position on the issue; or an attitude that has both cognitive and affective components and reflects instead an awareness of both sides of the issue. Different persuasion strategies will be effective, depending on the nature and content of the attitude.[2]

FUNCTIONS OF ATTITUDES

Have you ever wondered why people hold the attitudes that they do? Ever wondered why some people man the picket lines to protest U.S. policy (such as the Persian Gulf War?) or why other people seem to care so passionately about social causes (like poverty and animal rights), whereas still others hold equally strong attitudes toward social objects, such as fashion, jewelry, or automobiles? The functional approach to attitudes provides useful insights into these questions. The functional approach examines the psychological needs or functions that attitudes serve for different individuals in different contexts (Katz, 1960; Pratkanis & Greenwald, 1989; Shavitt, 1989; Smith, Bruner, & White, 1956). By understanding these functions, we can better understand why people hold certain attitudes and why they avoid others. Scholars have identified five functions that attitudes serve.

Knowledge. Attitudes help people make sense of the world in which they live. In this way, attitudes provide a framework for understanding ambiguous or unpredictable occurrences. For example, religious attitudes perform a knowledge function for many people. Religion provides an explanation of unexpected occurrences; thus, religious attitudes help people understand why "bad things happen to good people." In this way, they help people cope with unexpected events in their lives.

Utilitarian. Attitudes help people obtain rewards and avoid punishments. For example, students often find that it is functional to adopt a positive attitude toward a particularly difficult college class. Adopting a positive attitude toward the class helps students face the material "with a smile," and helps motivate them to spend time studying the material. The attitude, then, directs behavior (studying) that, in turn, helps students to obtain rewards (an "A" in the class).

Social-Adjustive. Attitudes help individuals relate to or "adjust to" their reference groups. Typically, attitudes help cement relationships with important others in a peer group. For example, a male college freshman may adopt a "politically correct" attitude toward national politics in an effort to gain acceptance from his liberal peers. Although the freshman's high school friends may disapprove of his stance, it may be highly functional for the young man in that it helps him adjust to the college environment.

Ego-Defensive. Attitudes can help protect individuals from having to acknowledge unpleasant truths about themselves or about the external world (Katz, 1960). One often finds that immigrants to the United States are extremely patriotic and have extraordinarily positive attitudes toward the United States. The children of these first-generation Americans some-times find themselves embarrassed by their parents' patriotic and zealously pro-American behavior. What the children fail to understand is that these attitudes may serve an ego-defensive function for the parents: They allow the parents to feel good about their identity as Americans, and they help them cope with their ambivalence about the fact that they do not completely "fit into" the homogenized American mainstream.

Value-Expressive. Attitudes help individuals express their central values. Katz (1960) noted that "satisfactions . . . accrue to the person from the expression of attitudes which reflect his cherished beliefs and his self-image" (p. 173). For example, children and adolescents may develop favorable attitudes toward far-out rock groups and MTV to give expression to their central values: autonomy and freedom from restraints.

Contemporary Perspectives

One implication of the functional approach is that different attitude objects serve different psychological functions. For example, some consumer products primarily serve a utilitarian function. Coffee and other caffeinated beverages, for instance, provide drinkers with tangible rewards. Other products are purchased to enhance the self-esteem or social identity of the buyer. For example, men buy cologne and women purchase perfume to make a statement about the kinds of people they are; cologne and perfume help people define and express a social identity.

Shavitt (1990) took this argument one step further by suggesting that the functional approach to attitude objects might be applied in interesting ways to persuasion. Shavitt contended that a persuasive message will succeed in changing attitudes toward a given attitude object to the extent that it engages the function that the object primarily serves. In other words, a communicator who wants to change attitudes toward a particular object (say, a consumer product) must understand the needs that the object fulfills. Shavitt argued that because coffee serves primarily a utilitarian function, messages designed to influence attitudes toward coffee should promise that material rewards will accrue to those who drink coffee; however, because perfume serves primarily a social identity purpose, messages directed at changing attitudes toward perfume should focus on the identity needs of audience members.

To test this notion, Shavitt presented subjects with ads for different products: One of the products (coffee) served a utilitarian function, whereas another product (perfume) fulfilled a social identity need. Shavitt then designed utilitarian and social identity appeals for each product. In the case of coffee, the appeals featured the following arguments:

"The delicious, hearty flavor and aroma of Sterling Blend coffee come from a blend of the freshest coffee beans." (Utilitarian)

"The coffee you drink says something about the type of person you are. It can reveal your rare, discriminating taste." (Social identity)

The perfume ads featured these arguments:

"The fresh, floral scent of Cadeau perfume comes from a balanced blend of oils and essences." (Utilitarian)

"Astoria (perfume) is the sophisticated scent that tells people you're *not* one of the crowd." (Social identity)

Shavitt asked subjects to read each advertisement and to indicate their thoughts and attitudes toward the various products. The results indicated that the utilitarian ad was more effective than the social identity appeal in influencing attitudes toward coffee. However, the social identity appeal was more effective than the utilitarian message in changing attitudes toward perfume.[3] These findings have interesting implications for advertising and persuasion. They suggest that before designing an advertisement, an advertiser must know the particular function that the product serves for most members of the audience. The advertiser is then advised to design the ad so that it engages this particular function.

The preceding discussion has implied that an object (or product) engages a single function or serves a single type of purpose. Although some objects serve a single function, most objects (and attitudes) serve multiple functions. This is a central theme in most of the work on functional approaches to attitudes. The idea is that different people can hold the same attitude toward a person, product, or issue; however, they may differ vastly in the meaning they attach to the attitude object. As Herek (1987) noted, in a discussion of this topic:

Consider, for example, a consumer product such as a particular make of automobile. One person's attitudes toward the automobile may be entirely utilitarian, based on its gas mileage and price. Another's attitudes might be based on reactions to the automobile by significant others (e.g., this particular make is currently fashionable among one's friends). Yet another individual's attitudes may be based on a need to express values implied by owning the auto (e.g., it is manufactured in Detroit and the individual supports the campaign to "buy American"). (p. 300)

Functional theory suggests that a persuasive message is most likely to change an individual's attitude when the message is directed at the underlying function that the attitude serves. Thus, applying the functional approach to the above example of attitudes toward automobiles, we would suggest that a persuasive message directed at the first consumer should focus on utilitarian issues ("The Oldsmobile Cutlass was ranked #1 by Consumer Reports on gas mileage"). On the other hand, a message directed at the second consumer would be advised to adopt a social-adjustive orientation ("The 30-something crowd loves the style and design of the Cutlass"), whereas a message aimed at the third customer would be most likely to succeed if it played on value-expressive needs ("Buy Cutlass and show your support for America").

It should be noted, however, that there have been relatively few tests of hypotheses derived from functional theory. One key shortcoming of the theories developed by Katz (1960) and Smith, Bruner, and White (1956) is that they do not enable investigators to easily determine the particular function that an attitude serves for an individual. In other words, a researcher may know that an individual holds a certain attitude, but the investigator may not be able to determine whether the attitude serves a knowledge, utilitarian, social adjustive, ego-defensive, or value-expressive function. Happily, newer versions of functional theory have made significant progress in this area (see chapter 8).

ATTITUDE MEASUREMENT

Now that we know what attitudes are, how they are organized, and the functions that they serve, we can discuss the "bottom-line" issue of how they are measured. Measurement techniques are of considerable importance to the scholar—and to the persuasion practitioner. For example, advertisers, politicians, community organizers, and health care professionals all are interested in understanding the attitudes of their target audiences; however, they cannot tap into these attitudes unless they have a reliable and valid measuring instrument.

Measurement involves the assignment of numbers to objects on the basis of a set of rules or guidelines (Stevens, 1950). There are a number of different ways to measure attitudes. These include attitude scaling techniques and several indirect procedures that have utility in special circumstances.

Direct Measurement Techniques

Thurstone Scale. The first attitude scales were developed over a half century ago, in the 1920s. In 1928, Thurstone wrote an article entitled "Attitudes Can Be Measured," in which he argued that scientific measurement techniques (specifically, those of psychophysics) could be used to measure social attitudes. The Thurstone method of equal-appearing intervals (as it has come to be called) attempts to determine the exact amount of difference between one individual's attitude and another's (Oskamp, 1977). Because it is a complicated procedure, we have tried to simplify the discussion by presenting a step-by-step description and by providing an example of a Thurstone Scale (see Table 2.2) for measuring sex role attitudes.[4] The eight basic steps that must be followed to construct a Thurstone Scale are listed here.

1. Assemble a large number of opinion statements about a particular topic or issue. For example, if the issue concerns sex roles, the investigator might include items that run the gamut from highly sexist to moderately sexist.

2. Place each statement on an index card.

3. Ask several hundred individuals to serve as judges. These individuals would be asked to sort the cards into 11 equally spaced categories. Category 1 would be used for items that express the most negative attitude toward the issue; Category 11 would be reserved for items that express the most positive attitude toward the issue.

4. Discard all items that are ambiguous or on which there is substantial disagreement among judges.

TABLE 2.2
Sample Thurstone Scale for Sex Roles

Statement		Scale Value
Least favorable	A. Women should be concerned exclusively with being good wives and mothers.	1.0
	B. It is all right for a woman to pursue a career, provided that she does not neglect her husband and family.	2.5
	C. A woman has as much right to a career as a man.	4.0
Most favorable	D. Because society has denied women job opportunities for many years, it should compensate them by adopting affirmative action programs that give preferential treatment to qualified female employees.	5.5

Note. On an actual Thurstone Scale, the values would extend from 1 to 11 and they would not appear on the actual questionnaire. Order of items would also be randomized.

5. Tabulate the judges' ratings. The investigator would examine the ratings of all the judges for a particular item and then calculate the median for that item. This yields the scale value for the particular item.

6. Select 20 or so items that have scale values that fall at equally spaced intervals along the evaluative continuum.

7. Randomize the items and make certain that the scale values do not appear on the final questionnaire.

8. Administer the questionnaire by instructing respondents to check items with which they agree and to leave all other items blank. The respo. lent's score on the scale is calculated by computing the median scale value of all statements that have been checked off.

Likert Scale.   The Thurstone method of equal-appearing intervals relies on judges to determine the scale values. However, the Thurstone technique is cumbersome because it requires the investigator to assemble a large number of judges to establish the values of the various scale items. In addition, it assumes that judges can put aside their individual biases and objectively evaluate the numerous scale items. However, when judges have strong positions on the issue, they are likely to evaluate the items in a biased manner (Hovland & Sherif, 1952). To help remedy these problems, Likert (1932) developed a simpler technique to empirically assess attitudes.

Unlike the Thurstone Scale, which simply asks individuals to indicate whether they agree or disagree with an item, the Likert Scale assesses the extent of agreement with each opinion statement. Thus, respondents indicate on a 5-point scale whether they strongly agree, agree, are neutral, disagree, or strongly disagree with the statement. The Likert Scale makes the important assumption that each statement is measuring (or empirically assessing) the same underlying attitude. Operationally, this means that there should be modest intercorrelations between items, and that there should be a positive correlation between each item and the total score on the scale. A sample Likert Scale for sex roles appears in Table 2.3.

Guttman Scale.   A Guttman Scale (named after psychologist Louis Guttman) is based on the notions of "degree of difficulty" or "passing of lesser hurdles" (Cacioppo, Harkins, & Petty, 1981). Consider as an example the following questions that are designed to measure a child's ability in arithmetic:

1. What is 2 + 3?
2. What is 25 + 38?
3. What is 14 + (38 − 17)?
4. What is 12 divided by (7 + 4 − 5)?
   (Scott, 1969, p. 221).

TABLE 2.3
Sample Likert Scale for Sex Role Attitudes

Please indicate whether you Strongly Agree (SA), Agree (A), are Neutral (N), Disagree (D), or Strongly Disagree (SD) with each of these statements.

1. Women are naturally more emotional than men.	SA	A	N	D	SD
2. When two people go out on a date, the man should be the one to pay the check.	SA	A	N	D	SD
3. Most men are not sufficiently sensitive to the problem of sexual harassment in the workplace.	SA	A	N	D	SD
4. There is no reason why a capable woman should not be elected president of the United States.	SA	A	N	D	SD

A child who is very good in math should be able to correctly answer all the items that the student with a moderate amount of arithmetic skill gets right, plus one or two additional questions. In addition, a child who has a moderate amount of arithmetic ability should be able to correctly answer all the questions that a student with only a little arithmetic skill gets right, plus some additional questions.

A Guttman Scale uses the same logic to measure attitudes. A hypothetical example of a Guttman Scale is provided in Table 2.4.

An individual with a highly favorable attitude on this issue would get a score of 4—indicating that he or she endorses even the most difficult criteria for sex role liberalism. A person with a moderately favorable attitude might accept Items A, B, and C, but might draw the line at Item D. An individual with a mildly positive attitude might accept Item A only. The

TABLE 2.4
Sample Guttman Scale for Sex Roles

Least difficult to accept	A. Fathers should spend some portion of their leisure time helping to raise their children.
	B. Fathers should share in infant care responsibilities, such as getting up when the baby cries at night and changing diapers.
	C. If both parents work, the father and mother should divide up equally the task of staying at home when the child is sick.
Most difficult to accept	D. If both parents work, the father and mother should divide up equally the task of raising the children.

Responses to the items would be scored in the following way:
Endorse no items (Score 0)
Endorse Item A only (Score 1)
Endorse Items A and B only (Score 2)
Endorse Items A, B, and C only (Score 3)
Endorse Items A, B, C, and D only (Score 4)

Guttman Scale is more narrowly focused than other attitude scales; it is based on the assumption that the scale is undimensional or taps only one underlying construct (Guttman, 1944).

Semantic Differential.   The attitude scales discussed thus far assess attitude toward an object by asking respondents to indicate their agreement or disagreement with a series of opinion statements. The semantic differential, which was developed by Osgood, Suci, and Tannenbaum (1957), assesses attitudes by exploring the meanings that people attach to social objects. There are two types of meanings that words can have. The denotative meaning is the direct, specific meaning of a word. The connotative meaning is the meaning that is implied or suggested by the word. Thus, the denotative definition of *country* (according to *Webster's Third New International*) is "the land of a person's origin, birth, residence, or citizenship." However, the connotative definition is different. The word "country" connotes pride, patriotism, love; or perhaps suffering, oppression, and hate. Because connotative meanings are what attitudes are all about, the semantic differential attempts to empirically assess connotative meanings.

The term *semantic* is used because the instrument asks people to indicate their feelings about an object on a pair of bipolar semantic scales. The term *differential* derives from the fact that the measuring instrument attempts to assess the differential connotations available to the individuals evaluating the object.

The semantic differential scale consists of a series of bipolar adjectives; one adjective lies at one end of the scale ("good"), whereas the opposing adjective ("bad") is situated at the other pole. Subjects evaluate a concept that appears at the top of the scale by placing a check mark at the point that corresponds most closely to their own feelings about the concept.

Osgood, Suci, and Tannenbaum (1957) found that people employ three semantic dimensions to rate concepts. Basically, people ask themselves if the object "is good or is it bad for me?" *(evaluation)*, "is it strong or is it weak with respect to me?" *(potency)*, or "is it an active or a passive thing?" *(activity)* (Osgood, 1974, p. 34). We would employ the semantic differential to assess sex role attitudes by listing a generic concept (feminism) and then asking an individual to rate the concept along a series of dimensions (see Table 2.5).

Single-Item Rating Scale

In some situations, it is not feasible to administer a Thurstone, Likert, Guttman, or Semantic Differential Scale. These scales contain a large number of items, and in some contexts (such as telemarketing studies or public opinion surveys) a researcher can only ask respondents a single question. In these situations, investigators rely on single-item scales to

TABLE 2.5
Sample Semantic Differential Scale

Feminism		
Good	--------------------------------------	Bad
Pleasant	--------------------------------------	Unpleasant
Strong	--------------------------------------	Weak
Heavy	--------------------------------------	Light
Active	--------------------------------------	Passive
Fast	--------------------------------------	Slow

Note. Numbers do not appear underneath the dashes. However, for each item an individual is assigned a score from +3 to −3, with a +3 assigned to the blank closest to the positive pole and a −3 assigned to the blank nearest the negative pole.

assess attitudes. However, it should be noted that, precisely because they contain only one item, these scales are considerably less reliable than the standard attitude scales that were discussed earlier. Nonetheless, single-item scales are used widely, and a single-item scale for sex role attitudes can be seen in Table 2.6.

Problems With Questionnaire Measures of Attitude

An attitude scale is designed to provide a valid, or accurate, measure of an individual's social attitude. However, as anyone who has ever "faked" an attitude scale knows, there are shortcomings in these questionnaire measures of attitudes. Scholars have noted that four problems affect the validity of attitude scales[5] (Dawes & Smith, 1985; Scott, 1969):

1. *Carelessness.* Carelessness of responses is a common problem in attitude research. Subjects may read the questions hastily, misunderstand items, or fail to use all of the responses available on the questionnaire.

2. *Extremity.* Some subjects may select the extreme-most responses on an attitude scale (e.g., the numbers 1 or 5 on a 5-point scale). Thus, these individuals' responses may suggest they have extreme views on the issue

TABLE 2.6
Single-Item Scale for Sex Role Attitudes

On a 9-point scale, where 9 means "very sympathetic with feminist goals" and 1 means "not at all sympathetic with feminist goals," where would you place your own attitudes?

Not at all sympathetic with feminist goals	1	2	3	4	5	6	7	8	9	Very sympathetic with feminist goals

when, in fact, their replies indicate only that they prefer to use the extreme ends of the scale.

3. *Acquiescence.*   Some respondents may have a tendency to agree with an item, regardless of its content. They may see this as a way of gaining the experimenter's approval. Needless to say, such responses are problematic because they do not reflect the individual's actual evaluation of the attitude statement.

4. *Social desirability.*   A related problem is social desirability—the tendency for people to give "socially appropriate responses" to the questionnaire items. As Cook and Selltiz (1964) have pointed out, people often are motivated to give replies that make them appear "well adjusted, unprejudiced, rational, open minded, and democratic" (p. 39). Questionnaires that tap attitudes toward racial, ethnic, and religious minorities often are hampered by a social desirability bias. Respondents who harbor negative attitudes toward a particular group may not wish to admit to the experimenter (or to themselves) that they have these feelings. Consequently, they may avoid giving answers that would make them look like bigots (although bigotry is their actual state of mind).

Indirect Measures of Attitude

To minimize the problems discussed here, investigators have developed several methods to measure attitudes indirectly. Indirect measurement techniques do not involve the completion of a paper-and-pencil questionnaire; instead, they involve a series of more subtle (even deceptive) techniques.

Three indirect strategies for measuring attitudes have been developed. Dawes and Smith (1985) have noted that these strategies involve:

> 1. Observing subjects without their awareness of being observed.
> 2. Observing aspects of subjects' behavior (usually physiological reactions) over which they presumably have no control.
> 3. Successfully duping subjects—either into believing that the questioner is observing something that has nothing to do with their attitudes or into believing that they have no control over their responses. (p. 543)

Observing Subjects Without Their Awareness.   One method of observing subjects without their awareness of being observed is to employ unobtrusive measures of behavior (Webb, Campbell, Schwartz, & Sechrest, 1966). For example, suppose that an investigator wanted to tap attitudes toward rock and roll among teenagers in an Eastern European country. Assuming that it was impossible to administer attitude scales to these young people, the researcher might use a series of unobtrusive measures, such as counting sales of rock albums or examining the amount of wear and tear on rock albums sold in record stores. Although unobtrusive techniques would provide useful information in a situation like this one, they have obvious limitations. For example, a particular rock album might have a great deal of wear and tear, but not because consumers liked the group or harbored a positive attitude toward its music. Instead, the wear and tear might reflect curiosity about a racy photo that appeared on the album's cover.

A second technique for observing individuals without their awareness of being observed is the lost-letter procedure, developed by Milgram, Mann, and Harter (1965). Milgram et al. (1965) noted that:

> The technique consists of dispersing in city streets (and other locations) a large number of unmailed letters. The letters are enclosed in envelopes that have addresses and stamps on them but that have not yet been posted. When a person comes across one of these letters on the street, it appears to have been lost. Thus he has a choice of mailing, disregarding, or actively destroying the letter. By varying the name of the organization to which the letter is addressed and distributing such "lost letters" in sufficient quantity, it is possible to obtain a return rate specific to the organization. (p. 437)

Investigators have used the lost-letter technique to determine whether community attitudes are more favorable to one group than another. In one study, Bolton (1974) probed attitudes toward busing by dispersing stamped letters that bore the return address of two fictitious organizations: Citizens Committee for Busing and Citizens Committee Against Busing. Post office boxes were purchased to receive mail for these two groups. The number of letters that were received at the two post office boxes served as the indicator of community attitudes toward busing.

The lost-letter procedure is an innovative method to assess community attitudes when there is reason to suspect the validity of self-report measures of attitude. It is particularly useful in Third World countries where individuals are discouraged or prohibited from publicly expressing their attitudes on attitude surveys. Nonetheless, there are several disadvantages with the approach. First, a large number of letters must be returned for the investigator to meaningfully interpret the results. Second, individuals may return a letter not because they agree with the organization's position on the issue, but because they have heard of the group. Thus, organizations that are better known may get a higher proportion of returns than lesser known groups, which would give the misleading impression that their cause was more favorably evaluated than that of the lesser known organization. Third, the technique fails to provide an accurate reflection of community sentiments on an issue when attitudes about the issue are highly polarized (Dawes & Smith, 1985).

Observing Behaviors That Elude Conscious Control. Another way to assess attitudes indirectly is to observe behaviors over which subjects do not have conscious control. Indirect measurement techniques of this kind have focused on subjects' physiological reactions to social stimuli.

One well-known physiological technique involves the measurement of pupil dilation. According to popular folklore, people's pupils dilate when they gaze at someone they like or love. Dawes and Smith (1985) noted that "When people look at something that interests them, their pupils have a tendency to dilate. . . . That has been known for years by jewel salespeople, by able seducers, and by magicians" (p. 544).

Hess (1965) was among the first to suggest that pupillary response measures could be used to measure attitudes. Hess argued that stimuli that aroused positive feelings would result in pupil expansion or dilation, and that stimuli evoking negative feelings would result in pupil constriction. Atwood and Howell (1971) provided evidence that supported this notion. They studied the pupil dilation of 20 prisoners: 10 were pedophiliacs (child molesters) and 10 were normal prisoners (they had been convicted of nonsexual crimes.) The prisoners viewed pictures of nude or partially nude adult women or young girls. All but one of the pedophiliac prisoners dilated more to pictures of young girls, whereas all but one of the normal prisoners dilated more to pictures of adult women. Unfortunately, the bulk of the evidence on pupillary response is less convincing (Cacioppo & Sandman, 1981). Pupil dilation may not reflect liking or positive evaluation of a stimulus; indeed, there is evidence that pupils dilate in response to interesting and arousing (but not necessarily positively valued) stimuli (Libby, Lacey, & Lacey, 1973).

Another physiological reaction over which people have little or no control is galvanic skin response (GSR). GSR is a change in the electrical resistance of the skin. Typically, GSR levels decrease when sweating increases. Because people often sweat when they are anxious or emotionally aroused, researchers have hypothesized that the GSR might provide a behavioral indication of a person's attitude about a sensitive issue. Once again, the evidence is equivocal. Although some studies have found that GSR predicts racial prejudice (Westie & DeFleur, 1959), other experiments have found that GSR does not predict whether a subject will evaluate a stimulus positively or negatively (Dysinger, 1931). A major problem with the GSR measurements is that they fail to indicate the directionality of an attitude: Sweating may accompany the presentation of stimuli an individual dislikes, as well as those he or she likes.

Clearly then, GSR and pupil dilation provide rather crude assessments of social attitudes. On the other hand, measurements of facial electromyographic activity (i.e., assessments of the movements of the facial muscles, particularly the brow, cheek, and eye regions) have provided more useful information about the directionality and intensity of affective reactions to social stimuli (Cacioppo, Petty, Losch, & Kim, 1986).

Duping the Subject. In 1989, Douglas Wilder, a Democrat and a Black political leader in Virginia, defeated Marshall Coleman, a White Republican, by less than one percentage point. Yet an exit poll conducted by a major polling organization shortly before the election predicted that Wilder would win the election easily, by a margin of 55% to 45% (Traugott & Price, 1991). One explanation for the discrepancy between the poll results and the election is that White voters were reluctant to publicly admit that they harbored negative attitudes toward a Black candidate.

This example underscores the difficulty of obtaining accurate information when the questions focus on prejudiced attitudes. One way to get around this problem is to use an indirect measuring technique called the *bogus pipeline* (Jones & Sigall, 1971). The procedure works in the following way.

Subjects report to the experiment and indicate their attitudes toward such topics as film, music, and sports. The experimenter then tells subjects that questionnaire measures of attitudes have a variety of problems, and that scientists have recently developed an elaborate device called the adapted electromyograph (EMG), which (the experimenter claims) permits "direct, accurate, physiological measurement of attitudes" (Sigall & Page, 1971).

The experimenter informs subjects that the machine can determine their true feelings about an issue and that he or she would like to give them a demonstration of how it works. Subjects are brought over to the EMG and are told that the steering wheel of the machine is connected to a pointer, which registers their feelings on an attitude scale. They are then asked to respond to the attitude questions that they completed earlier. Subjects are informed that electrodes will be attached to their wrists so that the machine can record their EMG reactions to the questions.

The experimenter then runs over to the spot where the original questionnaires were placed. He or she takes a quick look at the questionnaire for a particular subject, marks down the subject's answers, and makes sure that the machine provides output that is in perfect correspondence with the responses that each subject gave to the original questionnaire items. Having convinced subjects that the EMG can read their minds, the experimenter then asks subjects to complete some additional attitude questions while on the EMG. Of course, these are the real items of interest. The assumption is that subjects would prefer to honestly report their own attitudes on the EMG than to distort their answers and be "found out" later on.

Several studies have found that subjects are more likely to admit to socially undesirable feelings when on the EMG than when completing standard attitude scales (Gaes, Kalle, & Tedeschi, 1978; Quigley-Fernandez & Tedeschi, 1978; Sigall & Page, 1971). For example, White students revealed more negative attitudes toward Blacks under bogus pipeline conditions than when under normal rating scale conditions (Sigall & Page, 1971).

The bogus pipeline is a useful method to tap subjects' attitudes on sensitive issues. However, it has several drawbacks (see Ostrom, 1973). First, it obviously cannot be employed to assess opinions of large masses of people; its use is limited to experimental settings. Second, it requires that subjects believe the experimenter's bogus story. Given people's increasing skepticism about research and other institutions, it is questionable whether all or most subjects will believe the cover story. Third, and most important, it requires that the experimenter dupe the subject into believing something that is not true; clearly, ethical issues are raised when an experimenter dupes subjects into believing that a machine has the ability to read their minds.

Attitude Scales Versus Indirect Procedures

Although indirect measurement techniques may appear to be "pure" and "objective," they introduce biasing factors themselves, and (as we have seen) they have important shortcomings. Indirect procedures frequently tap responses other than attitudes, and they do not always provide a clear measure of the directionality of attitude. They are most likely to yield useful information when respondents are unable or unmotivated to report their attitudes on a paper-and-pencil instrument. However, in most cases, an attitude scale or questionnaire provides a more sensitive measure of an individual's attitude. Moreover, in recent years, researchers have devised methods to reduce the impact that carelessness, extremity, acquiescence, and social desirability have on responses to attitude scales (Oskamp, 1977; Petty & Cacioppo, 1981). These methods include building rapport between respondents and the interviewer (to reduce the impact of carelessness), using items with only two alternatives, such as Agree–Disagree (to reduce the influences of extremity), reversing the wording of items so that statements take both the positive and negative alternatives on an issue (to minimize acquiescence), and employing personality scales that identify respondents who are particularly likely to provide socially acceptable responses (in an effort to reduce the impact of social desirability). These methods are not foolproof, and attitude scales will always be susceptible to biasing factors and "faking." Nevertheless, paper-and-pencil measures have provided a wealth of useful information about the dynamics of social attitudes. Therefore, we can expect that they will continue to be used (and refined) in the years to come.

CONCLUSION

An attitude is a complex entity. Numerous definitions of attitude have been proposed over the years. Yet there is general agreement that an attitude is a learned, enduring, global evaluation of an object (person, entity, or idea) that exerts a directive impact on social behavior. A variety of models of attitude structure have been proposed; the dominant models are the tripartite perspective (which asserts that an attitude has a cognitive, affective, and behavioral component), expectancy-value theory (which emphasizes that an attitude toward an object is a function of the strength of the individual's beliefs and the evaluation of these beliefs), and the sociocognitive approach (which assumes that an attitude is an evaluation that is stored in memory and which is frequently supported by an extensive system of beliefs).

Attitudes serve a variety of functions for individuals, including knowledge, utilitarian, social adjustment, ego-defensive, and value-expressive. Applied to persuasion, the functional approach suggests that communicators need to take into account the function that a particular attitude serves for an individual. Indeed, there is some evidence that a message is more likely to change an individual's attitude if it is directed to the underlying function that the attitude serves.

A number of techniques have been developed to empirically assess attitudes. These techniques include attitude scales (Thurstone, Likert, Guttman, and the semantic differential) and a variety of indirect techniques, including the lost-letter procedure, physiological techniques, and the bogus pipeline.

3
Attitude Formation: Myths, Theories, and Evidence

How are attitudes formed? How do people acquire attitudes toward consumer products and toward issues like religion, politics, and sex roles?

In this chapter, I discuss these questions as I focus on the major theories of attitude formation. First, however, I want to address a question that frequently comes up in discussions of attitude formation: namely, are attitudes formed through subliminal persuasive techniques? It is commonly believed that advertisers employ subliminal techniques and that these techniques profoundly influence attitudes (Zanot, Pincus, & Lamp, 1983). Most persuasion instructors find that they cannot get through a course without receiving at least one question about subliminal ads. Ever since the 1950s, when enormous concerns were expressed about the power of subliminal ads, the possibility of subliminal persuasion has aroused enormous interest and has evoked a great deal of controversy. As is seen here, much of this concern is misdirected and reflects myths about "subliminal seduction" (Key, 1974) rather than facts about persuasive communication effects. In view of the popularity of the subliminal notion, however, the question of subliminal persuasion seems to be a good place to begin the discussion of attitude formation.

SUBLIMINAL PERSUASION: MYTH OR REALITY?

The day started like any other for James Vance. He was getting ready for work at a Sparks, Nevada, department store, but when his ride didn't show up, he decided to make other plans. James called up his friend Ray Belknap, the two talked a bit, and figured they'd do something together.

Ray and James were friends: Ray was 18 and James was 20; both had dropped out of high school and had experimented with drugs. Both young men were also heavy metal devotees, with a particular fondness for the rock group Judas Priest. On this day, December 23, 1985, Ray gave James an early Christmas present—the latest Judas Priest album, Stained Class. For hours the two listened to the record in Ray's room, all the while drinking and smoking marijuana. They talked about the songs, and were particularly enamored with the lyrics in Beyond the Realms of Death, especially the line "Keep the world with all its sin, it's not fit for living in."

Later when Ray's mother came home, the two young men dashed out, taking Ray's shotgun with them. The two men made their way to a nearby church playground. It was there that Ray took out the shotgun, put it to his head and pressed the trigger. He died instantly.

Recalling the incident later, James said he too felt he had no choice but to commit suicide. "It was like I didn't have control," he said in a court deposition. "Like my body was compelled to do it and I went ahead and shot." So on that December afternoon, James aimed the gun at himself and pulled the trigger. He survived the injury, but he died 3 years later from complications arising from the injuries he sustained that day (Keen, 1990).

What caused these young men to end their own lives in this way? Lawyers for the two men's families claimed that the Judas Priest album was the culprit. They alleged that the words "Do it, Do it" had been subliminally inserted underneath the lyrics and that these words had unleashed a self-destruct button in the two men's minds.

This is not the first time that subliminal messages have been the focus of controversy. Fears about the powers of subliminal communications date back to 1957, when a drive-in movie theater in Fort Lee, New Jersey, flashed the words "Drink Coca-Cola" and "Eat Popcorn" every few seconds during the showing of the movie Picnic. Marketing researcher James Vicary, who conducted the study, immediately proclaimed success. He reported that Coke sales had increased 18% and popcorn sales had risen more than 50%, as compared with an "earlier period." As news of the experiment spread across the country, commentators were outraged. This is the "most alarming and outrageous discovery since Mr. Gatling invented his gun," The Nation (October 5, 1957) warned. Minds have "been broken and entered," The New Yorker (September 21, 1957) penned.

Like brainwashing, subliminal persuasion conjures up strong images. It is commonly believed to be a powerful force capable of penetrating the deepest impulses of the unconscious mind. Partly as a result of popular books like Wilson Bryan Key's Subliminal Seduction (1974), the term subliminal has become widely known. Many people assume that all communications are subliminal. One study found that a majority of respondents believed that subliminal ads are used in advertising today and that they constitute an effective sales device (Zanot et al., 1983).

Defining Subliminal Perception

Subliminal literally means "sub limen" or below the threshold of conscious awareness. Specifying just where this mental threshold is located has turned out to be a matter of scholarly debate. A useful perspective on this issue has been offered by Dixon (1971), who has argued that the term *subliminal perception* be employed to refer to these three situations:

1. The subject responds to stimulation the energy or duration of which falls below that at which he *ever* reported awareness of the stimulus in some previous threshold determination.
2. He responds to a stimulus of which he pleads total unawareness.
3. He reports that he is being stimulated but denies any awareness of what the stimulus was. (p. 12)[1]

Notice that this definition excludes many of the terms popularly associated with subliminal persuasion. Appeals based on sex, repetition, association, or other subtle psychological influence techniques are not properly called subliminal unless the communicator has embedded within the message a stimulus that the individual cannot (on a conscious level) recognize. Many people commonly assume that advertisements that feature sexy models are subliminal; in making this statement, they are confusing sexual or association-type appeals with subliminal messages. Unless it can be demonstrated that the ad contains a stimulus that eludes conscious recognition, it is a mistake to call it subliminal. In all but the most unusual cases, the viewer is readily aware that the ad depicts a sexy model, hence the subliminal label is inaccurate.

Now that we have defined what we mean by subliminal perception, we can turn to the question of whether advertising and other real-world communications subliminally influence attitudes and behavior. A convincing case for subliminal persuasion would require: (a) the presentation of evidence that most mediated messages contain a subliminal stimulus, and (b) data that these stimuli exert an impact on cognitions, attitudes, or behavior. The first condition concerns message content, the second focuses on message effects.

Content

You cannot pick up a newspaper, magazine, or pamphlet, hear radio, or view television anywhere in North America without being assaulted subliminally. . . . Incredulous though you might be at this point, these subliminal SEXes are today an integral part of modern American life—

even though they have never been seen by many people at the conscious level. (Key, 1974, p. 5)

In his book *Subliminal Seduction,* Key (1974) claimed that erotic pictures are embedded in advertisements for liquor, cigarettes, and perfume products. Is Key right? Two researchers informally tested Key's claim that the phrase "u buy" is embedded in a particular brand of rum. They reported that "neither we nor any of the dozens of others to whom we have shown this ad could find the message" (Vokey & Read, 1985, p. 1233). In a similar fashion, for the past 5 years I have asked students in my persuasion classes to examine the ads that, according to Key, contain subliminal messages. Students invariably report that they cannot see the pictures or the verbal messages that Key claimed are embedded in the ads. Indeed, there have been no scientific studies that have found support for Key's claims.

Although Key's contentions probably tell us more about his sexually oriented imagination than about the content of media ads, the claims that he made should not be rejected entirely. There is a small—perhaps it would be more accurate to say very small—kernel of truth in his argument. There has been a dramatic rise in the number of self-help cassette tapes that claim to have embedded a message (for example "quit smoking" or "believe in yourself") in the audiotapes. Undoubtedly, there *are* a handful of media messages that do contain subliminal embeds. This brings us to the second question—do such messages (as few and far between as they may be) have any effect on attitudes and behavior in real-world persuasion situations?

Effects

You may be surprised to learn that there is abundant evidence that stimuli perceived without awareness can (under certain conditions) influence cognition and affect. After reviewing the many studies of subliminal perception, Moore (1982) concluded that, "Today, the notion that people can respond to stimuli without being able to report on their existence is accepted and well-documented" (p. 39).[2] Some of the most impressive evidence that subliminal stimuli can influence affective preferences has been reported by Bornstein and his colleagues (Bornstein, 1989a; Bornstein, Leone, & Galley, 1987).

In one study, Bornstein and his colleagues (1987) exposed subjects to five presentations of abstract geometric figures at a subliminal (4 milliseconds) exposure duration. Bornstein et al. found that affective evaluations of the geometric figures became more favorable with repeated exposure. The researchers concluded that

[S]ubjects' preferences for abstract geometric shapes may be significantly influenced by subliminal presentation of these stimuli, using exposure

durations so brief that subjects are unable to recognize the polygon figures
and are in fact unaware of having been exposed to any stimuli at all. (p.
1072)

These findings indicate that it is theoretically possible for a stimulus that
has been subliminally embedded in an advertisement to influence an
individual's affective preferences. However, it is extremely unlikely that
such a stimulus would exert a significant impact on the individual's
judgments, attitudes, or behaviors regarding the product. This is because
the laboratory environments in which these findings were obtained differ
in several important ways from real-world communication settings.

In the first place, subjects in laboratory experiments generally devote a
great deal of attention to the experimental stimulus; however, when
viewing media advertisements, people devote considerably less attention
to the stimuli to which they are exposed. Therefore, it is doubtful that a
subliminal stimulus that is (supposedly) embedded in an ad would ever get
noticed. Second, in contrast to laboratory experiments, advertisements
include a good deal of vivid, arousing "supraliminal" stimuli (stimuli that
can be perceived at the level of conscious awareness). These stimuli, Dixon
(1971) pointed out, "almost certainly will swamp any effect by a simulta-
neous stimulus below the awareness threshold. . . . The potential effects
of one stimulus may be completely negated by the presence of another"
(pp. 175–176). As an example, people may pay so much attention to an
attractive model (the supraliminal stimulus) that they may not even "see"
the subliminal stimulus that is (supposedly) embedded in the ad.

There are also a number of practical limitations to the commercial use of
subliminal persuasion techniques. Bornstein (1989a) noted that:

[I]t is not clear that television sets can present visual stimuli for the very
brief exposure durations required to ensure undetectability. In addition,
thresholds for stimulus awareness–both between subjects and within an
individual subject over time–vary widely, so that stimuli that are not
consciously detected by some people would be clearly recognized by
others. Furthermore, television sets are adjusted to different screen
illuminations, and the background (room) illumination differs significantly
from household to household. . . . All of these are critical parameters
which, if not taken into account, would interfere with the use of television
as a medium for the large-scale presentation of subliminal propaganda. (p.
254)

Given these limitations and caveats, it is not surprising that experimental
and field studies of subliminal advertising effects have provided relatively
little convincing evidence that subliminal stimuli influence attitudes or
behaviors. It is instructive to briefly review the findings from these field
studies and experiments.

Advertising Research.   The first study of subliminal advertising was conducted by Vicary in 1957; recall that the investigator reported that Coke and popcorn sales shot through the roof after "Drink Coca-Cola" and "Eat Popcorn" messages were displayed on the screen. However, the study was flawed methodologically. In a review of the study, McConnell, Cutler, and McNeil (1958) noted that there were no "reports of even the most rudimentary scientific precautions, such as adequate controls, provision for replication, etc. which leaves the skeptical scientist in a poor position to make any judgment about the validity of the study" (p. 230). The key point is that the study failed to employ a control group. Thus, it was entirely possible that viewers happened to be hungry at the time that the subliminal messages were presented and that this hunger – rather than the subliminal stimulus – led them to "drink Coca-Cola and eat popcorn." Moreover, the movie *(Picnic)* concerned food; it seems reasonable that people might purchase more food and drinks after viewing a film that involved eating.

Several years after the results of Vicary's experiment had been reported, DeFleur and Petranoff (1959) conducted a more systematic and controlled field investigation of subliminal advertising effects. Working in conjunction with an Indianapolis television station and a local grocery store chain, the researchers arranged to have a series of subliminal and ordinary (supraliminal) ads broadcast over a period of several weeks. During the first week, the station ran a subliminal ad for a food product. During the second week, the station presented the subliminal message in combination with an ordinary advertisement for the product. As a further control, the investigators examined the effects of ordinary advertisements for other products without any subliminal ads in combination.

To determine the effects of the ads, the investigators compared sales figures during the test period with the average number of products sold per week for a normal 6-week period. The subliminal message alone produced a 1% increase over normal sales; the subliminal ad, coupled with the ordinary commercial for the product, increased sales by 282%. This may seem impressive until you take a look at the figures for the control products. The ordinary advertisements shown without subliminal messages increased sales (on the average) by a whopping 2,509%. "There was *absolutely no evidence whatever,*" the authors concluded, "that the subliminal messages broadcast in the present experiment had the slightest effect in persuading the mass audience" (p. 180).

Several experiments also have examined subliminal message effects (Cuperfain & Clarke, 1985; Hawkins, 1970; Kilbourne, Painton, & Ridley, 1985). These experiments have (typically) exposed one group of subjects to an advertisement for Product X, which contains a subliminal message, and then presented the same ad to a different group of subjects, minus the subliminal embed. The investigators have reasoned that if subliminal messages exert an impact on attitudes, experimental group subjects should exhibit greater attitude change than controls. The results of these studies have been equivocal at best. Although several studies reported that the subliminal embed exerted a greater impact on experimental group subjects than on controls, there were methodological shortcomings in these investigations (Moore, 1982; Saegert, 1979). Moreover, other experiments have found that exposure to the subliminal embed did not significantly influence attitudes toward the product (Kelly, 1979).

Similarly, there is little evidence that subliminal stimuli that have been embedded in self-help tapes exert any impact on cognitions or attitudes. Greenwald, Spangenberg, Pratkanis, and Eskenazi (1991) conducted an elaborate study to determine whether self-help tapes that promised to enhance self-esteem or memory abilities had any impact on self-esteem levels or memory skills. The manufacturers claimed that subliminal messages on the topics of self-esteem ("I have high self-worth and high self-esteem") and memory ability ("My ability to remember and recall is increasing daily") had been inserted into the tapes. During the first portion of the experiment, subjects completed several measures of self-esteem and memory ability. Half of the subjects then received an audiotape that had been incorrectly labeled. Some of these subjects received a self-esteem tape, but were led to believe that it was supposed to improve memory, whereas other subjects received a memory tape, but believed that it was supposed to improve self-esteem. The other half of the subjects received tapes that had been labeled correctly.

Subjects were instructed to take their tapes home and to listen to them every day for a period of 5 weeks. Five weeks later, subjects completed various memory and self-esteem measures. They also indicated whether they thought the tapes had been effective. Interestingly, the audiotapes did not improve self-esteem or memory. However, subjects who thought they had been listening to a self-esteem tape believed that their self-esteem had improved, whereas those who thought they had been listening to a memory tape were convinced that their memory had gotten better. The results suggest that whatever effects subliminal messages have on attitudes is more likely to be due to individuals' expectations (their desire "to get better") than to any subtle impact that the subliminal embed has on affective preferences (Pratkanis & Aronson, 1992).

Summary. Subliminal perception *is* a bona fide phenomenon: Individuals can perceive stimuli at subthreshold levels (provided their attention is directed exclusively at the stimuli); subliminal exposure to social stimuli can influence gut-level affective preferences (although the effects are short-lived and, so far, restricted to laboratory settings). Moreover, the question of whether messages presented at subliminal levels can influence affective preference is an important issue to discuss inasmuch as it forces scientists to confront the possibility that communications can change attitudes at preconscious levels. Indeed, there has been a resurgence of interest in the question of perception without awareness—or implicit perception (Kitayama, 1990; Niedenthal, 1990). However, there is nothing in these points or in the literature on subliminal persuasion to suggest that subliminal messages achieve the kinds of effects that critics like Key have alleged. The idea that subliminal ads seduce consumers into buying products, or that subliminal messages embedded in rock music drive young men to commit suicide, is (to say the least) ludicrous.

Perhaps the most interesting aspect of the subliminal persuasion controversy is that so many people believe that people are susceptible to "subliminal seduction" and can be driven to buy products and commit horrific acts as a result of exposure to hidden subliminal messages. The notion that subliminal messages drive people to do things (i.e., buy products or give up smoking) is a major persuasion myth; like brainwashing, it is a rather grandiose and simplistic notion; like brainwashing, it does more to mystify persuasion phenomena than it does to explain them.[3] Thus, to understand how social attitudes are acquired, we need to examine other theoretical approaches. The remainder of this chapter discusses four perspectives on attitude formation: mere exposure, classical conditioning, operant conditioning, and modeling.

MERE EXPOSURE

On February 27, 1967, the Associated Press transmitted the following story to its affiliates all across the country:

> A mysterious student has been attending a class at Oregon State University for the past two months enveloped in a big black bag. Only his bare feet show. Each Monday, Wednesday, and Friday at 11:00 A.M. the Black Bag sits on a small table near the back of the classroom. The class is Speech 113—basic persuasion. . . . Charles Goetzinger, professor of the class, knows the identity of the person inside. None of the 20 students in the class do. Goetzinger said *the students' attitude changed from hostility toward the Black Bag to curiosity and finally to friendship.* (Zajonc, 1968, p. 1)[4]

This story illustrates a fundamental postulate of Zajonc's (1968) mere exposure theory: Through repeated exposure to a stimulus, an individual comes to evaluate the stimulus more favorably. According to the theory, all that is necessary is repetition: The more an individual is exposed to a particular object, the more favorably he evaluates it. There is no stipulation that the object must be associated with an appealing image or that individuals must be rewarded for their use of the object.

Notice that mere exposure makes a prediction opposite to that suggested by various "axioms of common sense." You have probably heard that "familiarity breeds contempt" or that "absence makes the heart grow fonder." Mere exposure theory argues that, on the contrary, familiarity breeds liking and absence promotes negative affect. As it turns out, repeated exposure to social stimuli does enhance positive affect—but (as is seen later) provided certain conditions are met.

The first studies of mere exposure examined responses to nonsense words, Chinese characters, and photographs—all of which were totally unfamiliar to the student participants. Zajonc and his colleagues deliberately chose to manipulate exposure to unfamiliar stimuli to provide as pure a test as possible of mere exposure theory. In this way, they could be sure that whatever differences they obtained were entirely due to the manipulation of repeated exposure.

In a classic study (Zajonc, 1968), subjects were asked to pronounce a variety of nonsense words (e.g., afworbu, civrada, jandara, nansoma, iktitaf). Frequency of exposure was varied, and order was counterbalanced so that each word was pronounced 20, 10, 5, 2, 1, or 0 times. The results provided clear support for mere exposure: The more frequently a word was pronounced, the more positively it was evaluated. Incredibly, although these words were absolutely incomprehensible to the subjects, by the fifth or tenth repetition, the words (like the student encased in the black bag) came to elicit a positive reaction (see Fig. 3.1).

Other studies obtained similar findings: Subjects gave more favorable

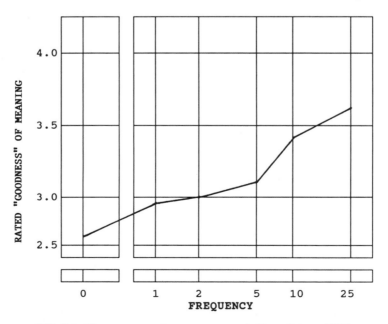

FIG. 3.1 Mere exposure to nonsense words (from Zajonc, 1968).

evaluations to Chinese characters, men's graduation pictures, and even Pakistani music the more frequently they saw or heard these stimuli (Heingartner & Hall, 1974; Zajonc, 1968). Moreover, studies that have been conducted outside university laboratories have also obtained mere exposure effects (Crandall, 1972; Rajecki & Wolfson, 1973). For example, Rajecki and Wolfson (1973) mailed University of Michigan students pairs of IBM cards for 10 days as part of a study of communication and attitude formation. Each card had a different nonsense word (e.g., afworbu) printed in the first seven columns; words were presented 10, 6, 3, or 1 times, respectively. The researchers then asked subjects to evaluate the words on 11-point semantic differential scales. There was a significant relationship between frequency of exposure and evaluation: Words presented 10 times got higher evaluations than words presented 6 times, words presented 6 times got higher ratings than words printed 3 times, and words transmitted 3 times received more favorable evaluations than words presented 1 time.

When Does Mere Exposure Influence Attitudes?

Mere exposure is a strong, robust persuasion phenomenon. Yet there are certain conditions under which repeated exposure is particularly likely to enhance attitudes. First, repetition exerts a stronger effect on attitudes when the target stimulus is presented in a heterogeneous, rather than a homogeneous, exposure context (Bornstein, 1989b). In other words, when the stimulus (e.g., afworbu) appears with different types of words, it is evaluated more favorably than when it repetitively follows itself. This has interesting implications for advertising, as we discuss shortly.

Second, the mere exposure effect is enhanced when the stimuli are presented at brief exposure durations. Stimuli presented for an exposure duration of less than 1 second exert stronger effects on affective evaluations than stimuli presented for longer exposure durations (Bornstein, 1989b).

Third, repeated exposure exerts a somewhat stronger effect on attitudes when the stimuli are complex than when they are simple. To explain these findings, researchers have argued that people are naturally curious about novel stimuli—and that they are particularly curious about complex stimuli. Consequently, over the course of a number of exposures, complex stimuli gain in "hedonic valence"—or perceived attractiveness. By contrast, simple stimuli begin to bore people after only a moderate number of exposures.[5]

A fourth factor moderating the mere exposure effect is the number of exposures. Repeated exposure to a stimulus enhances positive affect up to a point; however, after a certain number of exposures, ratings of the stimulus begin to decline (Bornstein, 1989b). Advertising researchers call this *wear-out*. Apparently, many exposures to a stimulus induce boredom and tedium; this leads to a reduction in positive evaluations of the stimulus.

Finally, exposure effects depend on the familiarity of the stimulus. Harrison (1977) noted that "manipulating the exposure of an already familiar stimulus is unlikely to enhance attitudes" (p. 51). For example, the overwhelming majority of American citizens are already familiar with the flag and have positive attitudes toward it. Showing Americans the flag many times would probably do little to enhance their affective evaluations of the flag.

Explanations of Mere Exposure

Several theories have been advanced to explain why mere exposure induces liking. One explanation emphasizes a process called response competition. According to this view, an unfamiliar stimulus elicits a number of different, often incompatible, responses. For example, afworbu, one of the words Zajonc (1968) presented subjects, might call to mind "word," "if," and "boo;" in addition, the word might also bring to mind an image of a primitive Aborigine tribe. On the first occasion that you saw this word, it is likely that all these thoughts and images would come to your mind. According to response competition, the resultant mental noise would make you feel irritated and annoyed. However, with repeated exposure to "afworbu," you would probably settle on one response to the word. Perhaps "word" would keep coming to your mind every time you saw "afworbu." By the final repetition in the series, you would no longer experience that "unpleasant feeling" you had at first when the many images and thoughts competed against each other for your attention. The reduction in this response competition, and the sense of peace and order you felt when you saw the word, would lead you to evaluate the word positively.

Although response competition provides a compelling explanation of the mere exposure effect, it cannot account for all the findings in this area. Consequently, other theories have been advanced. Berlyne (1970) has proposed that two processes underly the mere exposure effect: habituation and tedium. Berlyne (1970) suggested that early in the exposure sequence, habituation will predominate. The idea is that the stimulus is at first new and threatening, but with exposure it becomes more familiar and less threatening (i.e., people habituate to the stimulus). Over time, tedium sets in. People get bored with the stimulus and evaluate it less positively. Berlyne has argued that the relationship between frequency of exposure and affect resembles an inverted U; according to this view, affective evaluations rise until tedium sets in, at which point they drop back down to their initial level (see, also, Stang, 1974).

Berlyne's two-factor theory helps to explain a variety of the findings on mere exposure. It offers a particularly compelling explanation of the findings that repeated exposure has stronger effect on evaluations for complex than for simple stimuli. Presumably, people habituate to simple stimuli sooner; thus, tedium sets in with fewer repetitions. On the other hand, complex stimuli continue to positively arouse people; hence, the frequency of exposure-affect curve rises to a higher apex in the case of complex stimuli. Nevertheless, the two-factor theory has limitations. Berlyne suggested that the frequency of exposure-affect curve resembles an inverted U, and there is little evidence to support this prediction. As we noted earlier, there is evidence that, after a point, repetition ceases to have an effect and can cause evaluations to decline. However, Berlyne's theory made the additional prediction that affective evaluations drop to their preexposure levels and there is little evidence to support this view.

At present, no theory can account for all of the findings on mere exposure. Contemporary scholars emphasize that both response competition and Berlyne's two-process approach must be modified to take into account that a great deal of learning occurs without conscious awareness, deliberate effort, or higher level cognitive processing (Bornstein, 1989b, p. 282).[6]

Exposure Effects in Real-World Settings

Mere exposure helps explain a variety of real-world phenomena. Consider how Parisians' repeated exposure to the Eiffel Tower may have increased their affection for the monument:

> Announcing the tower's completion in 1889, the journal *de Natuur* noted that its construction took place despite a storm of protest from Frenchmen who considered it an unforgivable profanation of the arts and a slap in the face for a nation which had previously upheld the banner of civilization and refinement. . . . This early condemnation bordered on the universal and, in the early 1900s, almost led to the tower's demolition. . . .
>
> What might account for the seemingly massive shift in attitudes from condemnation and rejection to acceptance and liking? Some attitudes may have changed as engineering feats gained in vogue; some as the result of new contrasts provided by a changing Paris skyline; and some following disconfirmation of the prediction of a major financial disaster. There is, however, a factor that may have affected the attitudes of technophiles, aestheticians, and financiers alike. Because of its tremendous height, the tower was ubiquitous and inescapable and hence was likely to be seen day after day. According to one long-standing hypothesis, familiarity leads to liking, and perhaps attitudes towards the tower changed simply because it became a familiar part of the landscape. (Harrison, 1977, p. 40)

In a similar vein, advertisements for new products (such as the now-familiar Charmin bathroom tissues) owe some of their success to mere exposure principles. Similarly, mere exposure helps us understand why people tend to evaluate first names they have heard frequently (e.g., Jason, Brian, Jennifer) more favorably than those they have heard less often (e.g., Oscar, Bentley, Penelope). On a broader level, the common tendency to positively evaluate the presidency, the flag, and the United States can be explained, in part, by the repeated exposure that the American people have had to these stimuli (Sears & Whitney, 1973).

Of all these areas, perhaps the one that most lends itself to a mere exposure explanation is television advertising. Bornstein (1989b) noted explicitly that:

> [T]elevision advertising has already incorporated certain principles of the exposure-affect relationship in designing and presenting their messages: Television advertisements are typically fairly complex and interesting (albeit with relatively simple messages), fairly brief, and presented in a heterogeneous exposure sequence (i.e., interspersed with other advertisements and episodes of the television programs themselves). (p. 283)

Grush, McKeough, and Ahlering (1978) demonstrated that mere exposure theory could explain the effects of one type of advertising—political advertising in which "political newcomers and individuals holding low-visibility state offices . . . competed." Grush and his colleagues argued that candidates who spent the most money on advertising should have bought themselves the most exposure. This exposure, they contended, should lead to increased liking, as measured by the bottom-line variable of voting behavior. In other words, candidates who spent the most money on advertising should be most likely to win the election. Noting that mere exposure exerted particularly strong effects when the stimuli are neutral or unfamiliar, Grush et al. predicted that advertising should exert an especially powerful impact on voting when the candidates were unknown or unfamiliar (as is the case with many candidates running for House and Senate primaries). Consistent with their hypothesis, the researchers found that in elections involving either political newcomers or persons holding low-visibility government posts (lieutenant governor, secretary of state), the leading spender won nearly 60% of the time. This far exceeded the proportion that one would expect on the basis of chance alone.

The findings by Grush et al. (1978) indicate just how powerful an impact mere exposure exerts on behavior. Prior to the election, few if any of the voters had heard of the candidates running for the various offices. And I would be willing to bet that if you asked voters whether they were aware of the ads for one or the other candidates running for office, they would have said "What candidate?" or "What office?" Like most of us, they probably did not pay much attention to the many political commercials that dominate the airwaves during election campaigns. But, apparently at some level of their minds, the advertisements made an imprint and influenced their gut-level affective reactions toward the candidates.[7]

CLASSICAL CONDITIONING

Mere exposure theory helps to explain how people acquire strong gut-level feelings toward social objects. However, attitudes consist of more than gut feelings; they are complex, global entities that consist of both cognitions and affects. To gain additional perspectives on how people acquire global social attitudes, we need to discuss learning theory approaches to attitude formation. Our discussion begins with classical conditioning.

One of the most powerful ways that attitudes are formed is through association with positive and negative images. Association is the core notion in one of the oldest theories of human learning—classical conditioning. Conditioning is a "form of learning in which a neutral stimulus, when paired repeatedly with an unconditioned stimulus, eventually comes to evoke the original response" (Gardner, 1982, p. 594). The father of classical conditioning was Ivan Pavlov, the Russian psychologist who, in the early days of the 20th century, had the (then-revolutionary) idea that the environment (and not heredity) shaped behavior. Pavlov developed the theory of classical conditioning to explain how higher organisms can learn basic, reflexive responses.

Pavlov began with the knowledge that a hungry dog salivates when it smells food. Salivation occurs automatically (no learning or conditioning is necessary). The food is called the unconditioned stimulus (UCS) and salivation is the unconditioned response (UCR). In his experiment, Pavlov jingled a bell every time he gave the dog food, thereby pairing the bell (conditioned stimulus or CS) with the food. After many trials in which the food appeared at the same time that the bell was rung, the bell was able to elicit salivation on its own, in the absence of the food. The new salivation response is called the conditioned response (CR) because it resulted from the repeated pairing of the CS with the UCS, which automatically elicited a UCR (see Fig. 3.2).

Other studies have demonstrated that humans can be conditioned in much the same way. In one study, John Watson, the celebrated psychologist who declared in the early 1900s that he could mold an individual's personality through behavioral engineering techniques, used classical conditioning principles to induce an infant to fear a white rat. An 11-month-old boy named Albert was chosen for the experiment because he had few fears and responded with friendship when he saw a dog, rabbit, monkey, or rat. Young Albert did exhibit an intense fear reaction when an iron bar was struck behind his head. Watson showed Albert a white rat (CS) and as soon as he started to reach for the rat, Watson struck the iron bar (UCS). After seven pairings of the rat and the noise, Albert began to cry and crawl away (CR) when he saw the rat.

Although classical conditioning was originally invoked to explain the learning of reflexive responses, it has also proved capable of explaining the

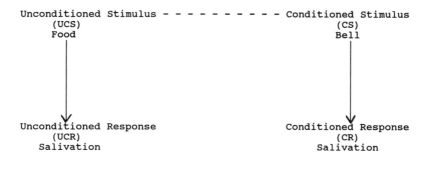

- - - Signifies pairing of UCS and CS

A UCS (food) automatically elicits a UCR (salivation). After repeated pairings of the CS (bell) with the UCS, the bell comes to elicit salivation (CR).

FIG. 3.2 Classical conditioning.

formation of social attitudes. The first study that showed attitudes could be learned through classical conditioning procedures was published by Razran (1940). Taking his cues from the intense political climate of the 1930s, Razran showed students a number of political slogans, including Workers of the World Unite!, Down with War and Fascism!, and America for Americans! One group of slogans was presented while subjects enjoyed a free lunch, whereas another set was shown while students inhaled "putrid odors." The slogans that were associated with the lunch were rated more positively, whereas slogans paired with unpleasant odors were evaluated more negatively (see also, Janis, Kaye, & Kirschner, 1965).

Staats, Staats, and Crawford (1962) demonstrated classical conditioning effects using a more controlled experimental procedure. Staats et al. paired a word with shocks and loud noises, which automatically elicited a strong physiological reaction in subjects as measured by Galvanic Skin Response (GSR). The word "large" functioned as a conditioned stimulus; the shocks and noises were the unconditioned stimuli. Through repeated pairing with the shocks and noises, the word came to evoke a strong physiological reaction; the word "large" also was evaluated more negatively by subjects for whom it had been associated with a UCS than by control group subjects. Thus, simply through association with an unconditioned stimulus, a word acquired a meaning that it did not have before.

In real life, however, it is unusual for an attitude object to be associated with a stimulus that is capable of evoking an automatic response in a person. It happens from time to time. An example is the business lunch in which a business executive hopes that the pleasant responses evoked by the meal will be transferred over to the corporate deal that is being discussed. Typically, conditioning effects are more symbolic: The attitude objects are associated with words and symbols that conjure up good or bad feelings. The responses that these words and pictures call up have been learned. When a conditioned stimulus that is paired with a social symbol comes to elicit the same responses as the symbol evokes, a process of *higher order conditioning* can be said to have occurred.

Higher order conditioning was first demonstrated in a study conducted by Staats and Staats (1957). Using a simple, but elegant, procedure, the experimenters paired certain nonsense syllables ("yof") with words that had positive connotations (gift, happy, beauty); they associated other nonsense syllables ("xeh") with words that had negative evaluative meanings (bitter, sad, ugly). Syllables paired with pleasant words were evaluated favorably, whereas syllables associated with unpleasant words were evaluated negatively.

In a second study, Staats and Staats (1958) paired two nationality groups, toward which individuals had a relatively neutral affect (Swedish and Dutch), with a number of positively valued and negatively valued words. For one group of subjects, the word "Dutch" was paired with words that had positive connotations (gift, sacred, happy) and the word "Swedish" was paired with words that had negative connotations (bitter, ugly, failure). The order was reversed for the second group of subjects: For this group, "Dutch" was associated with negatively valued words and "Swedish" was paired with positively valued words. As Table 3.1 shows, the first group of subjects evaluated "Dutch" positively and "Swedish" negatively, whereas the second group rated "Dutch" negatively and "Swedish" positively.

A large number of our attitudes are formed through higher order conditioning. Children develop positive attitudes toward Christianity in part through association of the Christian religion with warm family get-togethers in which presents are opened around the Christmas tree. Conversely, unfavorable attitudes toward religion can have their roots in negative emotional associations, such as unpleasant experiences with stern and strict parochial school instructors. In the political sphere, candidates

TABLE 3.1
Means for Conditioning Attitude Scores

| Group | Nationality | |
	Dutch	Swedish
1	2.67	3.42
2	2.67	1.83

Note. Lower scores mean more positive attitudes. From Staats and Staats (1958)

for public office often try to use higher order conditioning principles to their advantage by surrounding themselves with American flags. Advertisers constantly make use of conditioning principles by devising ads that associate their product with pleasant imagery.

Vicarious Classical Conditioning

One variant of classical conditioning that has particular application to the formation of social attitudes is vicarious classical conditioning. This occurs when an observer develops a conditioned response to a stimulus simply by watching a model exhibit a classically conditioned reaction to the stimulus. This was first demonstrated experimentally by Berger (1962). Subjects in the experimental group were told they would watch another person receive a series of electric shocks in the last portion of the experiment. Unbeknownst to subjects, the other person actually worked for the experimenter, and no electric shocks were administered. A buzzer (CS) preceded the onset of each supposed electric shock (UCS), and it was accompanied by an arm movement on the part of the model, which presumably reflected a pain response (UCR). Over the course of the experiment, subjects came to exhibit a strong physiological reaction (as reflected by a change in GSR) every time they heard the buzzer go off. Specifically, these experimental group subjects were significantly more likely to exhibit this reaction than a series of control group subjects who did not observe the conditioning of the buzzer to pain. In short, merely watching someone else get conditioned caused subjects to become conditioned themselves.

Application. Vicarious classical conditioning goes a long way toward explaining the development of racial and ethnic prejudice. It helps us understand how children can develop prejudiced attitudes from observing their parents, although the parents may never tell the child that she should avoid such-and-such group. All that is necessary is for the child to observe a parent repeatedly associate the ethnic group with a negative label. As Allport (1935) observed:

> Even before he has an adequate background of appropriate experience a child may form many intense and lasting attitudes toward races and professions, toward religion and marriage, toward foreigners and servants, and toward morality and sin. A parent's tone of voice in disapproving of the ragamuffins who live along the railroad track is enough to produce an uncritical attitude in the child who has no basis in his experience for the rational adoption of the parent's point of view . . . In such cases every contact is prejudged, contradictory evidence is not admitted, and the attitude which was borrowed second-hand is triumphant. (p. 811)

Such was the case in Nazi Germany, where the mere mention of Jews was accompanied by a derisive voice, a grimace, or a hateful stare. It also typifies many families in our own society in which the parents unknowingly communicate prejudiced attitudes to their children.[8]

Alternative Views. So far, we have accepted without question the conclusions reached by researchers studying classical conditioning effects. However, in scientific research it is considered fair game to raise questions about the validity of the research findings. This is exactly what Page (1969) did in a series of studies that critiqued the early classical conditioning experiments.

Page's point was quite simple. He believed that the experiments by Staats and Staats did not demonstrate classical conditioning; instead, Page argued, they merely showed that subjects were able to guess the experimenter's hypothesis and that they were more than willing to comply with the experimenter's demands. This alternative explanation of the research findings is called demand characteristics. Demand characteristics are "the totality of cues which convey an experimental hypothesis to the subject" (Orne, 1962, p. 779). Page argued that, after watching a nonsense syllable repeatedly paired with the words "happy" and "sad," subjects figured out what the experimenter expected of them. In Page's view, it was as if subjects thought to themselves: "Now I see why he keeps putting these two things together. He wants me to rate the syllables positively when they're with 'happy' and negatively when they're with 'sad.' "

To test his hypothesis, Page (1969) carefully replicated Staats and Staats' (1957) procedures. He paired nonsense syllables with words that had positive and negative evaluative meanings. Then he asked subjects a series of questions to probe their awareness of the purpose of the experiment. In particular, Page asked subjects if they had been aware, prior to marking the rating scales, "of how the experimenter expected (them) to rate the syllables." Page found that subjects who indicated that they were aware of how the experimenter expected them to evaluate the syllables were the ones most likely to exhibit the classical conditioning effect.

At one level, Page is correct. Demand characteristics are a chronic problem in studies of human behavior. Research participants will inevitably be curious about the true purposes of a study, and their guesses about the study design may influence their responses to the experimenter's questions (Sawyer, 1975). Page was also correct that the early studies of classical conditioning were subject to alternative explanation. However, it would be a mistake to conclude that all the findings on classical conditioning of attitudes are artifacts of demand characteristics.

In the first place, more recent conditioning experiments that have taken precautions to guard against demand characteristics (e.g., by carefully separating the conditioning trials from the assessment of subjects' attitudes) have found strong evidence of classical conditioning (Zanna, Kiesler, & Pilkonis, 1970). In addition, it is hard to explain the evidence of conditioning of physiological reactions on the basis of demand characteristics. You may recall that Staats et al. (1962) demonstrated that a GSR could be classically conditioned to the word "large." It seems unlikely that the increase in sweating was caused by a desire to comply with the experimental demands.

If demand characteristics do not provide a compelling explanation for the bulk of the research on classical conditioning, then how can we account for the development of conditioned responses? In other words, why (or through what psychological processes) does classical conditioning occur? There are two schools of thought on this question. One view is that conditioning in humans requires the operation of *higher cognitive processes*. According to this account, people must be aware of the association (or contingency) between the unconditioned stimulus and the conditioned stimulus to be classically conditioned (Brewer, 1974). A second view is that conditioning occurs without awareness. According to this theory, the association between the unconditioned stimulus and the conditioned stimulus is "stamped in automatically" (Staats & Staats, 1957).

Both sides can marshal arguments and evidence to support their positions. Proponents of the *higher cognitive processes* school contend that classical conditioning works through different processes in different animals species. Proponents note that, in the case of a rat or a dog, the association between the UCS and the CS may be mechanically "stamped in;" however, in the case of human beings, more complex processes are involved (see Allen & Madden, 1985). Advocates of *higher mental processing* (Brewer, 1974) have argued that people are not passive automatons, but, in fact, are aware that a conditioned stimulus (a soft drink in a TV ad) is being associated with an unconditioned or higher order stimulus (a beautiful nature scene). Furthermore, they have noted that awareness is necessary for conditioning to occur. Stuart, Shimp, and Engle (1987) obtained evidence that supported this view. Stuart et al. paired a consumer product (CS) with pictures of beautiful nature scenes (higher order stimuli). The researchers not only found that subjects evaluated the consumer product favorably as a result of the conditioning procedures (see Exhibit 3-1: Advertising the Association, p. 75); they also discovered that 48% of their subjects reported they were definitely aware that the study had something to do with how pictures influence the development of positive attitudes toward different brands.

On the other hand, proponents of the conditioning-without-awareness school have noted that a great deal of learning occurs automatically — without conscious thought (Kihlstrom, 1987). These scholars have cited evidence that subjects can develop positive evaluations of words that have been presented at levels that elude conscious recognition. Stuart et al.

(1987), who found that 48% of their subjects were definitely aware that the study had something to do with the effects of pictures on liking for different brands, also reported that less than 1% of the subjects mentioned the name of the brand that served as the conditioned stimulus.

The awareness issue is all the more vexing because it is difficult to clearly assess awareness of the CS–UCS contingency (McSweeney & Bierley, 1984). Suppose a researcher conducts a conditioning experiment and later assesses awareness by asking subjects to list the syllables that were paired with words of pleasant and unpleasant meaning. Let us say the researcher finds that subjects who indicated they were aware of the association—those who could remember the names of the syllables—were more likely to show conditioning effects. This could indicate that awareness is necessary for conditioning to occur, but it could also be that subjects were conditioned without awareness, but when they were asked to reflect on the study, they were able to remember the stimuli that were presented. Thus, until researchers reach a consensus on how awareness is to be measured (and, more importantly, defined), there will continue to be debate about the role that awareness plays in classical conditioning.

In summary, there is a good deal of evidence that attitudes can be classically conditioned. Although some of the early findings were susceptible to a demand characteristics explanation, later studies have avoided this problem (see Stuart et al., 1987). Interestingly, recent studies have suggested that attitudes toward products *can* be learned by exposure to television advertisements (Allen & Madden, 1985; Gorn, 1982; Stuart et al., 1987). Nevertheless, there is an important shortcoming in the conditioning approach to attitudes. Conditioning uses a language—featuring terms like *extinction, discrimination,* and *inhibition*—that is somewhat removed from the rich, dynamic arena of social attitude formation. The theory does not deal at all with the cognitive underpinnings of attitudes—with the processes by which people mentally make associations between attitude objects and emotionally laden stimuli (Fazio, 1990; Sears, Huddie, & Schaffer, 1986). Nor does it deal with the processes by which people learn to conceptualize social symbols (such as the flag, the Cross, or the Star of David).

Classical conditioning rightly calls attention to the powerful impact that associations between attitude objects and cultural images exert on attitude formation. However, it pays insufficient attention to the ways in which people form mental associations between objects and emotionally laden stimuli.

OPERANT CONDITIONING

A therapist nods approvingly when a troubled patient at last says something positive about her intellectual abilities. A Moonie leader tells a young student she is recruiting that "you seem like a smart person, I can just tell from talking to you." Upon learning that his son has dropped out of college to join a rock band, a father criticizes him severely, telling him he will never amount to anything.

These are all examples of operant conditioning. Operant conditioning is learning the response (or operation) to perform to receive a reward or avoid a punishment. Operant conditioning differs from classical conditioning in an important respect. In classical conditioning, the conditioned response automatically occurs after it has been paired repeatedly with the UCS. In operant conditioning, the organism's behavior is instrumental in determining whether it gets a reward or avoids a punishment.

In an early study, Greenspoon (1955) demonstrated that operant conditioning principles could be applied to the study of verbal behavior. Greenspoon used verbal reinforcement to condition the use of plural nouns. In the experimental group, the experimenter approvingly said "Mmm-hmm" whenever a subject pronounced a plural noun, whereas in the control group, he did not say anything. Later, observers recorded the frequency with which subjects used plural nouns in a conversation. They found that experimental group subjects used plural nouns more frequently than controls.

Two other studies attempted to make a more direct linkage between operant conditioning theory and persuasive communication. These studies also obtained support for hypotheses derived from operant conditioning theory. Bostrom, Vlandis, and Rosenbaum (1961) reported that students changed their attitudes more in the advocated direction when they were given "As" for writing counterattitudinal essays than when they were given "Ds."

Scott (1957) used a "debate scenario" to study the effects of reward on attitude development. He asked pairs of students to participate in a debate on a controversial issue; the debate outcome was rigged so that one of the students was told that he or she had won the debate, whereas the other student was informed that he or she had lost. Posttests revealed that "winners" changed their attitudes in the direction of their debates, whereas "losers" showed no significant change in attitudes.

Finally, Insko (1965) used a somewhat different procedure to study the operant conditioning of attitudes. Insko had callers telephone University of Hawaii students to probe their beliefs about establishing a Springtime Aloha Week Festival. The callers read students a series of statements. Some statements suggested that the festival would have positive effects (bringing in more tourist dollars), whereas others argued that the impact would be negative (increasing traffic congestion). For half of the subjects, the callers responded positively whenever subjects agreed with a statement that endorsed the festival, whereas for the other half of the subjects, the callers responded positively when subjects endorsed a statement that was critical of the festival. One week later, Insko assessed subjects' attitudes toward the festival. He found that students who had been rewarded for endorsing positive statements about the Aloha festival displayed a more positive attitude toward the festival than those who had been rewarded for making negative statements.

To account for the effect of verbal reinforcement of attitudes, Insko and Cialdini (1969) proposed a two-factor theory of verbal conditioning. They argued that rewards do two things: They provide cognitive information and foster emotional rapport. First, Insko and Cialdini noted that rewards provide the subject with information about the persuader's attitude about the issue. The information that a persuader shares one's point of view may suggest that one has adopted the "correct" position on the issue. Second, rewards increase the rapport between the subject and interviewer; specifically, they tell the subject that "the interviewer approves of or likes the agree–disagree responses and thus by implication approves of or likes the subject himself" (Insko & Cialdini, 1969, p. 334). The resultant good feelings provide the individual with an increased incentive to exhibit the desired response. Insko and Cialdini conducted two experiments to test the two-factor theory of operant conditioning; both experiments provided support for the theory (Cialdini & Insko, 1969; Insko & Cialdini, 1969).

Unfortunately, only a handful of studies have explored the operant conditioning approach to attitudes. Few studies have probed operant conditioning of attitudes in real-world settings, partly because it is difficult to get reliable measures of persuaders' use of reward and punishment in everyday interactions. Research on socialization has strongly suggested that verbal reward and punishment play an important role in how children acquire social attitudes (Mischel, 1966). For example, parents and peers often reward (or do not punish) boys for committing aggressive acts, whereas they are more apt to discourage girls from responding in an aggressive manner. These differences in parental rewards may help explain why males tend to value aggression more than females.

MODELING

In an interesting paper, Beuf (1974) told the story of a young girl who confessed that when she grew up she wanted to fly like a bird. "But I'll never do it," she quietly acknowledged, "because I'm not a boy." Beuf asked the girl why she felt that way. The girl replied that she got the idea from watching a television cartoon program. Beuf noted that "I could not help wondering how many little children believe that only males are capable of something as grand as flight" (Beuf, 1974, p. 143).

Many of our beliefs and attitudes are learned in this way—through observation of role models. Modeling theory stipulates that individuals can learn new attitudes and behaviors simply by observing live or symbolic models. Unlike operant conditioning, modeling theory asserts that individuals can learn novel behaviors in the absence of direct reinforcement (reward or punishment). In his critique of traditional learning theory approaches (e.g., operant conditioning), Albert Bandura (1971) argued that people do not have to be directly rewarded or punished to learn new behaviors. After all, he intimated, children do not get an M&M every time they sit down to watch television, yet children manage to accumulate vast amounts of information from the many hours they spend watching TV.

Bandura argued that four subprocesses govern modeling phenomena: attention, retention, motor reproduction processes, and motivation. To acquire new attitudes or behaviors, an individual must first take notice of (or attend to) what the role model says or does. A father cannot influence a child's attitude toward drugs if he cannot get the youngster to sit down and listen to a rap on the subject. Social learning theorists tell us that people are especially likely to pay attention to modeled behavior that is distinctive and is of high personal relevance for the observer.

Second, an individual must symbolically encode and retain the modeled behavior. This is the key "mental step" in modeling theory. Observers are more likely to acquire new information if they verbally encode (preferably in their own words) the modeled information than if they are distracted from engaging in this mental task (Bandura, Grusec, & Menlove, 1966; Perloff & Brock, 1980). For example, an educator who is trying to convince young people not to experiment with drugs might pause for a moment at several points in the speech and ask audience members to imagine how they would feel if an older brother or sister were strung out on drugs and seemed utterly helpless and destitute.

The third aspect of modeling phenomena involves the physical or motoric reproduction of the modeled behavior. Many intravenous drug users know that by using bleach to clean drug-infected needles, they can kill human immunodeficiency virus (HIV); however, they may fail to use bleach because they lack the physical stamina and "wherewithal" to act on this knowledge.

The fourth component of modeling is reinforcement (reward and punishment). Bandura (1971) emphasized that behavior is controlled not only by "directly experienced consequences arising from external sources, but also by *vicarious reinforcement* and *self-reinforcement*" (p. 46, italics added). That is, reinforcement can be direct—as when a peer role model criticizes a fellow student for bragging about how he experimented with drugs. However, it can also be indirect or vicarious—as when a child watches as his favorite same-age television character stands up to the local drug dealer and wins the respect of the rest of the kids in the school.

There is abundant evidence to support hypotheses derived from modeling theory. Bandura and his colleagues have shown that children can learn new behaviors simply by observing live or symbolic models (Bandura, 1965; Bandura, Ross, & Ross, 1963). They also have demonstrated that children do not have to be rewarded to learn these behaviors.

In our society, parents, peers, schools, religious institutions, and the mass media are influential models and powerful teachers. One would think that parents are the most influential of all these models: They are powerful, nurturant, and highly available (Maccoby & Martin, 1982). Although children acquire a great deal of information from observing their parents, it would be a mistake to conclude that parents are the most influential socialization agent for all children. Interestingly, research on childhood socialization has failed to find strong relationships between parents' personality characteristics and those of their children. In a review of the modeling literature, Maccoby and Martin (1983) observed that "Within a given social class, ethnic group and sex, it has proved extraordinarily difficult to show that children are any more similar to their own parents than they are to other children's parents" (p. 8).

Thus, it is important to examine the impact that other socialization agents exert on children's attitudes and values. One influential socialization agency is the peer group. Peers influence attitudes on a variety of issues. One area in which they have a particularly strong impact is drug use and drug prevention. Oetting, Spooner, Beauvais, and Banning (1991) noted that:

When adolescents use drugs, it is almost always in a peer context. Even when they use drugs alone, it usually reflects the conviction of a group of peers that using drugs alone is "the way to go." Peers provide drugs. Peers initiate each other into drug use. Peers discuss drugs and model drug use, shaping both drug attitudes and drug behaviors. (p. 240)

In addition to live models, such as parents and peers, mediated models exert a profound impact on children's attitudes and values. Children spend more time watching television than any other activity outside of school or sleep. Mass communication research has found that television portrayals of violence, sex, sex roles, politics—you name it—exerts a significant impact on children's attitudes and behavior (Comstock, Chaffee, Katzman, McCombs, & Roberts, 1978; Kraus & Davis, 1976; Liebert, Sprafkin, & Davidson, 1982; McLeod, Atkin, & Chaffee, 1972).

One of the most interesting issues in modeling theory concerns the ways in which children integrate information they get from different socialization agents. When all the socialization agents (parents, peers, schools, media, etc.) convey the same message, then the situation is rather simple: the child will probably internalize the position advocated by the different influence sources. But what happens when socialization agents present conflicting information? Suppose, for example, a girl is urged by her mother, a doctor, to pursue an achievement-oriented career; at the same time, the girl's friends tell her that she should spend less time studying and more time partying; and, in addition, the girl is exposed to a constant barrage of television advertisements that make the point that beauty, not brains, is what matters in life.

Gerbner, Gross, Morgan, and Signorielli (1980) argued that television is particularly influential in such cases. They contend that television exerts a "mainstreaming impact" whereby it brings those who hold nontraditional values into the cultural mainstream.

Morgan (1982) tested this notion by examining the impact of heavy television viewing on adolescents' sex role attitudes. Morgan measured teenagers' sex role attitudes and television viewing at two points in time; he also obtained measures of respondents' IQs and their socioeconomic status (SES). Morgan found that heavy viewing led to significant increases in sexist attitudes for girls who had high IQs and who were from high SES backgrounds. Apparently, the constant exposure to televised sex role stereotypes—in ads, children's programs, and in adult dramas like "Charlie's Angels"—left an imprint on these young women. It led them to reevaluate their "nontraditional views" and to decide that it would be safer to adopt a more conservative course in the area of gender roles.

CONCLUSIONS

People are not subliminally seduced into adopting social and political attitudes. On the contrary, attitudes are formed through repeated exposure to novel social objects, through classical conditioning, operant conditioning, and through exposure to live and symbolic models. One of the classic issues in attitude research concerns the extent to which attitudes that have been formed at an early age are susceptible to change. Some of our attitudes—notably, those that bear on the self, such as attitudes toward politics, race, and religion—are remarkably resistant to change. In many instances, these attitudes serve important functions for the individual; for example, they preserve self-esteem and they allow the individual to express underlying values. Thus, there are good reasons why individuals might hold onto attitudes that they acquired at an early age (although these attitudes may be dysfunctional for individuals in other respects). On the other hand, some attitudes do change. Clearly, over the past 20 years, Americans have changed their attitudes about a number of things, including large cars, fatty foods, and cigarette smoking. There is no simple formula for determining which attitudes will persist and which will change. Life is too complicated for that. We can say, however, that early socialization experiences do shape attitudes. In addition, we can also conclude, from a review of the research in this area, that attitudes that

EXHIBIT 3–1   75

serve important functions for the individual or that are linked to core aspects of the self-concept are likely both to endure and to influence the individual's reactions to social influence attempts.

* * *

EXHIBIT 3–1
ADVERTISING THE ASSOCIATION

A classic ad for Marlboro cigarettes shows a Macho-looking cowboy smoking a Marlboro. A soft drink ad shows attractive young people whooping it up on a beautiful summer beach while the voice-over sings the praises of the beverage. An ad portrays a perfume product alongside the depiction of a man and woman embracing one another. These are not subliminal ads. Instead, they illustrate how advertisers use classical conditioning techniques to promote products.

There is evidence that attitudes toward products can be classically conditioned through advertising. Gorn (1982) paired the slide of a blue or a beige pen with pleasant or unpleasant music. He then asked subjects to choose one of the two colored pens. Gorn found that 79% of the subjects selected the pen associated with the pleasant music, whereas only 30% chose the color of the pen paired with the unpleasant music.

Stuart, Shimp, and Engle (1987) provided even stronger support for the classical conditioning view of advertising in an elegant study that included four separate experiments. In the first experiment, the researchers showed subjects a neutral conditioned stimulus ("Brand L toothpaste") and a higher order stimulus (e.g., a mountain waterfall or a sunset over an island). For experimental group subjects, the toothpaste and beautiful nature scenes were paired together over the course of a number of conditioning trials. For control group subjects, the toothpaste and nature scenes were presented in random order with respect to each other. (This elaborate control procedure was employed to make certain that it was the contingency—or causal relationship—between the CS and the higher order stimulus that was responsible for the conditioned response.) Stuart and her colleagues found that subjects exposed to the conditioning trials in which the toothpaste was paired with the beautiful nature scenes exhibited significantly more positive attitudes toward Brand L toothpaste than did control group subjects.

Consumer behavior scholars have argued that the findings obtained from these and other studies have a number of practical implications for advertising. Five implications are listed here.

1. Conditioned Responses Are Hard to Change. Coca-Cola discovered this in 1982 when it introduced a new brand of Coke that had a sweeter aftertaste than the time-honored Coke formula. Unfortunately, Coca-Cola grossly underestimated the loyalty that consumers felt to the old Coke.

The company was besieged by letters, phone calls, even protests demanding a return of the old Coca-Cola. The company's marketing manager in Roanoke, Virginia, received a letter from a woman who said "There are only two things in my life: God and Coca-Cola. Now you have taken one of those things away from me."

Wrote another disgruntled customer, "Changing Coke is like making the grass purple or putting toes on our ears and teeth on our knees" (Greenwald, 1985).

For years, Coke had been associated with some of the most powerful higher order stimuli in our culture. (In classical conditioning terms, Coke was a CS that had acquired a positive evaluation as a result of having been paired for years with powerful higher order stimuli.) Indeed, since the early 1900s, advertisements have linked Coke with all things "genuinely American"—the flag, the fighting troops, baseball, motherhood. "It is the American character in the can," a *Newsweek* magazine writer proclaimed. "Friendly, frisky, fizzy with a little kick. Dark, full of empty calories—a lot of gas in a glass." A *Time* magazine writer noted that "changing the taste of the real thing was like tampering with motherhood, baseball and the flag" (Gelman, 1985).

Echoing these sentiments, a number of individuals launched (humorous) protests against the company. Faced with these grassroots responses to their decision to introduce a new Coke product, the company backed down and brought back the old Coca-Cola.

2. One Repetition Is Not Enough. Studies indicate that the CS and the higher order stimulus must be paired several times before conditioning can occur. According to consumer behavior researchers McSweeney and Bierley (1984), "presenting a commercial once will not be enough to substantially alter consumer preferences. Instead, an advertisement containing a soft drink and a jingle must be presented several times to insure that a change in preference occurs" (p. 626).

3. Images Should Be Crafted Carefully. Research indicates there should be a good fit between the higher order and conditioned stimuli. A stimulus that is too sexy may cause people to forget the product. In addition, if the higher order stimulus blends into the background of the ad—as when the image of a sunset is blurry and dark—the association will not be stamped in.

McSweeney and Bierley suggested that advertisements should try to create situations that resemble the situations in which the person finds the advertised product. "If this setting (e.g., an exotic resort) is very different from the one in which the person encounters the product (e.g., the supermarket), then very little generalization (very little preference) may carry over the from the advertisement to the situation in which the product is actually sold," (p. 627) they pointed out.

4. Celebrity Endorsements Must Be Used With Care. A celebrity endorser functions as a higher order stimulus that can transfer a warm glow of pleasure to an advertised product. The problem is that if the celebrity's reputation gets tarnished, the product represented by the celebrity can also suffer a kind of guilt by association. When John McEnroe got thrown out of a tennis tournament a few years ago, his credibility as a spokesman for Bic shavers was also tarnished. Advertisers also worry that endorsers can create the wrong kind of associations. The manufacturer of Diet Coke canceled a series of ads featuring Madonna because they felt her new hit song was too sexy and controversial. All this suggests that celebrities must be used carefully in advertisements.

EXHIBIT 3-1   77

5. *Conditioning Principles Can Be Used in Comparative Ads.* One principle of classical conditioning, discrimination, occurs when a conditioned stimulus is paired with an unconditioned stimulus, whereas another CS is not paired with the UCS. Conditioning effects will emerge for the CS that is paired with or followed by the unconditioned stimulus, but it will not occur for the other CS. McSweeney and Bierley (1984) suggested, based on this principle, that advertisers might wish to play music after their product, but present a rival product not followed by a musical number. This strategy might help consumers "develop a preference for the first product and prevent a preference from developing for the rival product" (p. 627).

4
Attitudes and Behavior

The movie *Guess Who's Coming to Dinner* provides film buffs with a glimpse into the dynamic—and highly complicated—relationship between attitudes and behavior. The film begins as Joanna Drayton returns home to California with her fiancee, John Prentice, a debonair and distinguished African-American physician. Joanna has invited John to meet her parents. Joanna's father, Matthew Drayton, is a zealous newspaper publisher. In his daughter's words, he is a "life-long fighting liberal who loathes race prejudice and has spent his whole life fighting against discrimination." His wife, Christina, is a sensitive woman who shares her husband's commitment to social causes.

Joanna feels that she knows her parents' attitudes toward racial issues. She expects that they will accept John without hesitation. But this is not exactly what happens. Her mother is so upset at first that John suggests that she sit down before she falls down. Joanna translates: "He thinks you're going to faint because he's a Negro." Joanna's father has more serious reservations. "I am not going to try to pretend that I'm happy about the whole thing because I'm not," he says.

Joanna's mother eventually sees her daughter's point of view, and she attempts to persuade her husband to support their daughter's decision. Christina tells her husband that:

> (Joanna is) 23 years old and the way she is is just exactly the way we brought her up to be. We answered her questions, she listened to our answers. We told her it was wrong to believe that the White people were somehow essentially superior to the Black people or the brown or the red or the yellow ones for that matter. People who thought that way were wrong to think that way—sometimes hateful, usually stupid, but always, always wrong. That's what we said. And when we said it we did not add, but do not ever fall in love with a colored man.

78

Ultimately, Matthew Drayton comes to terms with his anger. He thinks through his attitudes about the issue and decides that he was wrong to oppose his daughter's decision to marry John Prentice. In the last scene of the movie, he delivers a stirring speech about racial equality (one that seems to jibe with his strong attitudes on the issue). Drayton then gives his strong support to his daughter's decision to marry John Prentice.

The nature of the relationship between attitudes and behavior has long intrigued observers of the social scene. Scholarly interest in this topic dates back to 1935, when Allport argued that attitudes exert "a directive or dynamic influence upon the individual's response to all objects and situations with which it is related." Allport assumed that attitudes influenced or guided behavior. However, subsequent studies that have tested this assumption have indicated that the relationship between attitudes and behavior (A & B) is far more complex than Allport and early scholars suggested in their writings.

The nature of the relationship between attitudes and behavior is of considerable importance to persuasion scholars and practitioners. Many definitions of attitude have assumed that attitudes guide or influence behavior. If this belief turned out to be incorrect—if attitudes did not predict behavior—then there would be less reason to study and examine the attitude concept. From a practitioner's perspective, attitudes are important to study only insofar as they predict behavior. After all, the bottom line for advertisers, politicians, and other professional persuaders is influencing behavior. If it turned out that attitudes had no bearing on behavior, then serious questions could be raised about the need to study attitudes in a variety of real-world settings. Finally, the attitude–behavior issue deserves scholarly attention for the simple reason that it is a topic that engages many people in everyday life. Indeed, we all can probably think of a person who has displayed a very favorable attitude toward a group or issue, but then does something that seems completely at variance with this attitude. "That hypocrite," we think to ourselves. The term *hypocrite* is, of course, one of those persuasion devil terms, in the same league with *brainwashing* and *propaganda* (see chapter 1). I refrain from using this term, because it is a highly pejorative label. Instead, I examine the "consistency question" from a scientific perspective by reviewing the literature on attitude–behavior relations.

This chapter is organized into three sections, based on Zanna and Fazio's (1982) organization of the research in this area. The first section reviews early research on the topic, which was primarily concerned with determining whether there was a relationship between attitudes and behavior. The second section focuses on the "when" question: When do attitudes accurately predict behavior, and when don't they? The third section examines the "how" issue: How do attitudes guide behavior, or what are the psychological processes that underlie the relationship between attitudes and behavior?

DO ATTITUDES PREDICT BEHAVIOR?

The first study of the relationship between attitudes and behavior was conducted by LaPiere (1934). LaPiere, accompanied by "a personable Chinese student and his wife," stopped at a number of restaurants, auto camps, and hotels in the United States. The researchers wanted to know whether the proprietors would serve the couple; the man and woman, after all, were Chinese, and many Americans harbored negative attitudes toward persons of Chinese ancestry during this period. As it turned out, the couple had no trouble getting served:

> In something like ten thousand miles of motor travel, twice across the United States, up and down the Pacific Coast, we met definite rejection from those asked to serve us just once. . . . To provide a comparison of symbolic reaction to symbolic social situations with actual reaction to real social situations, I "questionnaired" the establishments which we patronized during the two year period. . . . To the hotel or restaurant a questionnaire was mailed with an accompanying letter purporting to be a special and personal plea for response. The questionnaires all asked the same question, "Will you accept members of the Chinese race as guests in your establishment. . . . 92% of the (cafes and restaurants) and 91% of the (autocamps, tourist homes and hotels) replied "No." The remainder replied "Uncertain; depend on upon circumstances." (LaPiere, 1934, pp. 232–234)

The results suggested that employees were behaving in a way that was inconsistent with their attitudes. All but one of the hotel and restaurant employees served the Chinese couple, yet over 91% of those surveyed indicated on a questionnaire that they personally would not accept members of the Chinese race as guests in their establishments. LaPiere's results were widely interpreted as indicating that there was little or no relationship between attitudes and behavior. However, there are several methodological problems with LaPiere's study, which cast doubt on the validity of this conclusion (Campbell, 1963; Kiesler, Collins, & Miller, 1969). The problems include the following:

1. It is not clear that the person who waited on the Chinese couple was the same as the one who filled out an attitude questionnaire. Conceivably, one person served the couple at the hotel or restaurant, whereas another filled out the mail questionnaire.

2. LaPiere's questionnaire measure ("Will you accept members of the Chinese race as guests in your establishment?") did not assess attitude toward the Chinese. An attitude, as you may recall, is a global evaluation, a general feeling about a person, group, or issue. The questionnaire measure did not tap feelings; at best, it assessed respondents' intentions to serve Chinese people. Thus, the inconsistency was not between attitude and behavior, but between behavioral intention and behavior.

3. In a sense, it was an unfair test. LaPiere and a Chinese couple entered the establishment and asked to be served. By LaPiere's own admission, the Chinese student and his wife were "personable," "charming," and "skillful smilers." However, the questionnaire measure did not ask respondents whether they would accept a White man and a charming Chinese couple as guests in their establishment. Instead, the survey asked whether patrons would "accept members of the Chinese race as guests in your establishment."

LaPiere's study, flawed though it may have been, stimulated a great deal of empirical research. As it turned out, some of these investigations found significant associations between attitudes and behavior (Warner & De-Fleur, 1969), whereas others did not (Corey, 1937; Kutner, Wilkins, & Yarrow, 1952; see, also, Calder & Ross, 1973; Schuman & Johnson, 1976; Wicker, 1969). Researchers concluded that it was unrealistic to expect attitudes to guide behavior under all conditions. Consequently, scholars reformulated the research question. Instead of asking "Do attitudes predict behavior?", they asked instead, "When do attitudes predict behavior and when don't they forecast behavior accurately?"

WHEN DO ATTITUDES PREDICT BEHAVIOR?

Three general factors determine the strength of the attitude–behavior relationship: (a) situational factors, (b) individual difference variables, and (c) measurement (research methods) issues.

Situational Factors

Situations exert a powerful impact on behavior. Roles, norms, and a desire to be accepted by the group are among the many aspects of a situation that place pressure on the individual to adopt a particular behavior. As Kiesler, Collins, and Miller (1969) noted, these variables often vary, "while the attitude remains constant." A number of studies have demonstrated that situational factors moderate the attitude–behavior relationship. Warner and DeFleur (1969) provided particularly strong evidence that situational forces influence attitude–behavior consistency. As you read over the description of this study, keep in mind that it was conducted in the 1960s—an era in which there was little interaction between Black and White college students.

Subjects were White college students at a western university. Students completed a "Public Information Questionnaire," which included 16 items that assessed attitudes toward civil rights issues. Based on their scores, subjects were divided into two groups: those high and low in racial prejudice. Subjects were then asked whether they would sign a pledge to participate in some type of activity involving Blacks. Half of the subjects received a private form of the letter, which promised the student anonymity in the later activity, and half received a public form, which "advised the subject that his pledged actions would be disclosed to others via the campus newspaper and other media" (p. 158).

The nature of the setting strongly influenced willingness to comply with the request to write a letter. Subjects in both groups were significantly more likely to comply with the requested behavior when they were promised anonymity than when they believed that their actions would be made public. This, of course, demonstrates the powerful impact that norms—in this case, racist norms—exert on social behavior.

Warner and DeFleur also found that the setting interacted with prejudice level to determine the degree of A–B consistency. In the public setting, there was a high degree of consistency between attitudes and behavior for highly prejudiced individuals. Apparently, the knowledge that their pledge to participate in an activity involving Blacks would be made public touched a nerve in these highly prejudiced persons. Thus, they uniformly rejected the request for compliance in this context. In the private setting, there was a high degree of A–B consistency among low-prejudiced individuals. In this context, Warner and DeFleur noted, "the protections of anonymity permitted the least-prejudiced subjects to act more favorably toward the attitude object" (p. 164). Sadly, it was only when these low-prejudiced individuals were certain that their action would not be made public that they felt comfortable translating their attitudes into action.

The conclusion that situational factors moderate the A–B relationship is useful, but (from a scientific perspective) it is not satisfactory. It is important to specify the types of situational factors that influence attitude-behavior consistency. Abelson (1982) argued that to understand the impact that situational factors exert on the attitude–behavior relationship, it is necessary to categorize situations according to whether they are (a) individuated, (b) deindividuated, or (c) scripted.

Individuated Situations. Individuated situations heighten self-awareness; they call on the individual to focus inward and to access his or her own feelings and relevant attitudes. In these situations, the individual is aware of what his or her attitude toward the issue is, and this increases the likelihood that he or she will translate his or her attitudes into action. In such situations, there is a strong relationship between attitudes and behavior (Carver, 1975; Pryor, Gibbons, Wicklund, Fazio, & Hood, 1977; Snyder & Kendzierski, 1982). For example, a special seminar devoted to racism on campus would be classified as an individuated situation. Such a seminar would encourage a White student to focus on his or her attitude toward Blacks and other minority groups. Such intense self-focus should increase the salience (or prominence) of the attitude. This in turn should increase the chances that the seminar participant would behave in a way that is consistent with his or her attitude.[1]

Abelson (1982) emphasizes that it is only in individuated situations that we should expect attitudes to predict behavior. He reminds us that many situations do not encourage people to focus on their attitudes. In these contexts, individuals may not know what their attitude toward the issue is. If they do know their attitude, they may not be sufficiently in touch with their feelings to translate their attitude into action.

Deindividuated Situations. These situations "focus the individual away from him/herself and provide anonymity" (Sherman & Fazio, 1983). These situations "deindividuate" the individual; they strip the person of his or her personal identity and give the individual a new role and outlook—one based on the philosophy of the group. In these situations, an individual's private attitudes are unlikely to forecast his or her public behavior. Sherman and Fazio (1983) observed that:

> Rioters riot, looters loot in mobs, and cult members may be driven to suicide not because they have positive attitudes to rioting, looting, or suicide but because these acts are meaningful in the context of group identity and help to establish and preserve the relationship between the individual and the group. (p. 317)

Deindividuation helps us understand the form that the attitude–behavior relationships takes in extreme cases, such as the Jonestown Massacre of November 1979. On November 19, 1979, the Reverend Jim Jones, the spiritual leader of a strange religious cult, the People's Temple, gathered his followers together in a grassy field at the cult's home in Guyana, South America. Calmly and with apparent conviction, Jones ordered the members of the Temple to drink from a vat of strawberry-flavored poison. The overwhelming majority of the people there (some 910 individuals) followed Jones' directive and committed suicide. There are a variety of explanations for this bizarre and tragic event (Cialdini, 1984), but what concerns us is the relationship between cultists' attitudes and behavior. There is no reason to believe that cult members harbored a positive attitude toward suicide.

Hence, on the level of their private attitudes, their behavior was quite inconsistent with their attitudes. However, the action becomes more explicable when one considers that members strongly identified with the People's Temple and had a deep commitment to Jones and his teachings. By committing suicide, members may (on some strange and symbolic level) have believed that they were solidifying their relationship to Jones and to God.

Scripted Situations.   Consider this scenario. Anne is a graduate student in communication at an urban university. To save money, Anne regularly takes the subway to work. Knowing that the subway is not safe, Anne tries to get where she has to go as quickly as she can, and she steadfastly avoids contact with strangers. On one occasion, a scruffy looking young man approaches Anne and asks her if she would mind filling out a questionnaire. Although Anne likes to help out others who (like herself) use survey instruments, she refuses and brushes past the young man.

Anne has employed what Abelson (1982) called a script, or a "knowledge structure governing perceptual and cognitive processes (or) an organized bundle of expectations about an event sequence" (p. 134). The action rule of Anne's script for answering requests in the subway is "Ignore all requests; just go your own way." According to Abelson, when a situation involves scripted behavior, people mindlessly play out standard script scenes, that is, they use the script to guide their behavior and they do not consult their attitudes when trying to decide on a course of action. In scripted situations, attitudes are not likely to be particularly good predictors of behavior. Thus, although Anne has a positive attitude toward completing questionnaires, she does not translate this attitude into behavior because the attitude is not relevant to the scripted action.

Script theory helps us understand the behavior of the hotel and restaurant proprietors in LaPiere's famous study. Abelson (1982) noted that:

> In script terms, we would say that when the Chinese arrived, the management representatives played standard script scenes from their role perspectives. In the restaurant, the crucial scene is "seating the customer"; in the hotel, "registering the guest." Given very well-practiced scripts, the action rules—the policies for whether to enter the scripts—are presumably very well learned. What a hotel manager is likely to check before registering a guest is whether a room is available and the guest looks able to pay. Hotel managers (and clerks) are very well practiced at going ahead if the answers are yes, but refusing the guest politely if either answer is no. On the other hand, it seems quite unlikely that managers would ask themselves, "Do I feel favorable towards these potential guests?" (p. 135)

In summary, situational factors moderate the attitude–behavior relationship. However, the type of situation matters a great deal. There is some evidence to support the notion that in scripted and deindividuated situations, specific attitudes are not highly correlated with behavior, whereas in individuated situations, the correlation between attitudes and behavior is considerably higher.

Individual Differences

Individuals differ in the extent to which they display consistency between attitudes and behavior. Some individuals exhibit a high degree of correspondence between attitudes and behavior. If these individuals have a strong attitude on an issue, you can be sure that they will express this view in public. Other individuals are less concerned with maintaining a consistent image. They may have a strong attitude about an issue, but they will keep their opinion to themselves, or they may even argue for the opposite point of view. In this section, two representative individual difference variables that moderate the relationship between attitudes and behavior are discussed: self-monitoring and direct experience.[2]

Self-Monitoring. Self-monitoring is a personality trait that has been shown to have a rather strong impact on A–B consistency. According to Snyder (1987), who developed the concept, self-monitoring is: "The extent to which people *monitor* (observe, regulate, and control) the public appearances of *self* they display in social situations and interpersonal relationships" (pp. 4–5). Snyder (1987) has developed a scale to measure self-monitoring. He has found that people can be classified, based on their scores on the scale, as high self-monitors or low self-monitors.[3]

High self-monitors are adept at controlling the images of self they present in interpersonal situations, and they are highly sensitive to the social cues that signify the appropriate behavior in a given situation. High self-monitors agree with statements like these:

"I'm not always the person I appear to be."
"In different situations and with different people, I often act like very different persons."
"When I am uncertain how to act in a social situation, I look to the behavior of others for cues."

By contrast, low self-monitors are less concerned with conveying an impression that is appropriate to the situation. Rather than relying on situational cues to help them decide how to act in a particular situation, low self-monitors consult their inner feelings and attitudes. They endorse statements like these:

"My behavior is usually an expression of my true inner feelings, attitudes, and beliefs."

"I have trouble changing my behavior to suit different people and different situations."

"I would not change my opinions (or the way I do things) in order to please someone else or win their favor."

Valuing congruence between their expressive public self-presentations and their private selves, low self-monitors frequently "say what they feel," even if such statements are situationally inappropriate. Whereas the typical high self-monitor would agree with Jacques in Shakespeare's "As You Like It" that "all the world's a stage" or that life is theater, the archetypical low self-monitor would find greater comfort in the injunction, "To Thine Own Self be True" (Snyder, 1974, 1987).

Snyder has argued that the self-monitoring construct has interesting implications for the issue of attitude–behavior consistency. According to the self-monitoring formulation, high self-monitors rely on situational cues to help them decide on a behavioral choice. They select behavioral strategies on the basis of whether the strategies fit or are congruent with the demands of the situation. By contrast, low self-monitors are considerably less sensitive to situational cues. They are primarily concerned with "being themselves"; thus, as Snyder (1982) argued, low self-monitors "monitor or guide their behavioral choices on the basis of information from relevant inner states" (p. 107). According to the self-monitoring formulation, low self-monitors should be more likely than high self-monitors to "say what they think"—that is, there should be a higher correlation between attitudes and behavior for low self-monitors than for high self-monitoring individuals.

A number of studies have obtained support for this hypothesis. These studies have found that the correlation between attitudes and behavior is statistically significant for low self-monitors, but not for high self-monitors (Snyder & Swann, 1976; Snyder & Tanke, 1976; see, also, Ajzen, Timko, & White, 1981). It turns out, however, that although (as a general rule) low self-monitors exhibit greater attitude–behavior consistency than high self-monitors, the impact of self-monitoring on A–B consistency depends in important ways on other characteristics of the person and the situation.

One person factor that interacts with self-monitoring to influence A–B consistency is the variability of the behavior under investigation. Zanna, Olson, and Fazio (1980) observed that an individual cannot exhibit A–B consistency in a behavioral domain if his or her previous behavior within that domain has been highly variable. Take religion, which was the subject of the study by Zanna et al. (1980). Suppose an individual *rarely* prays, *sometimes* attends classes on religious holidays, and *frequently* gives money to religious institutions. This person clearly exhibits a great deal of variability in religious behavior. Zanna et al. noted that if an individual displayed this much variability across religious situations, he or she would have difficulty figuring out just what his or her attitude was on the subject of religion. On the other hand, an individual whose behaviors were relatively invariant (e.g., he or she prayed frequently, never attended classes on religious holidays, and gave a lot of money to religious institutions) should have no trouble figuring out where his or her heart was on the subject of religion.

Furthermore, Zanna and his colleagues argued that only individuals who "employ their past behaviors as critical inputs from which to infer their attitudes" (in other words, low self-monitors) will exhibit A–B consistency under conditions of low behavioral variability. The investigators predicted that when low self-monitors and high self-monitors both exhibited a great deal of variability in their religious behavior, lows would be no more likely than highs to exhibit attitude–behavior consistency. However, the authors contended that when both groups showed relatively little variability across religious situations, low self-monitors would exhibit more attitude–behavior consistency than high self-monitors. The study's findings strongly supported the researchers' hypotheses.

Snyder and Kendzierski (1982) took these findings one step further by noting that there are two psychological requirements that must be met if attitudes are to predict behavior. The first is *availability* (individuals must know where they stand on the issue, and they must bring to mind their feelings, beliefs, and behavioral intentions). The second requirement is *relevance* (individuals must regard their attitudes as relevant to the behavioral choices that confront them in a social situation). Snyder and Kendzierski contended that availability and relevance information would be processed differently by high and low self-monitors. They noted that:

> For low-self monitoring individuals, the availability of knowledge of their attitudes ought to be sufficient to prompt them to translate that knowledge into behaviors that meaningfully reflect their attitudes. . . . For high-self monitoring individuals, who claim that what they do may not always reflect what they believe, available knowledge of their attitudes may not be sufficient to guarantee correspondence between attitude and behavior. Nevertheless, situations that provide clear specifications that attitudes ought to be relevant guides to action should induce high-self monitoring individuals, who claim to be creatures of their situations, to be responsive to this situational information and to studiously use their attitudes as guides to action. (p. 168)

To test these hypotheses, the investigators examined the relationship between attitudes toward affirmative action and behavioral verdicts rendered in a mock court case involving a charge of sex discrimination. Subjects first completed the self-monitoring scale and then indicated their attitudes toward affirmative action. Subsequently, subjects rendered judgments in a mock court case—that of Ms. C. A. Harrison versus the University of Maine. Students read the resumes of two biologists: Ms. C. A. Harrison and Mr. G. C. Sullivan. Both individuals were candidates for a faculty position in biology at the University of Maine. The resumes detailed the candidates' qualifications, and both Ms. Harrison and Ms. Sullivan were described as having excellent qualifications for the job.

The brief indicated that the university named Mr. Sullivan to the faculty position. Ms. Harrison then filed a lawsuit charging the university with sex discrimination. Subjects were instructed to read arguments for both sides and then render a verdict.

In the basic scenario situation, students received only these instructions. In the attitude *available* situation, subjects were given a few minutes "to organize your own thoughts and your own views on the issue of affirmative action." This manipulation was designed to make students more aware of their own attitudes toward affirmative action. Finally, in the attitude *relevant* situation, subjects were told that their decision will "have implications for the parties involved, but it may also have implications for affirmative action programs. . . . That is, what you decide about this case may help determine how other court cases may be decided." By encouraging students to believe that their verdicts would have an important impact on the future course of affirmative action, the experimenters hoped that students would regard their own attitudes toward affirmative action as relevant guides for action.

As Table 4.1 shows, in the basic situation the correlations between attitude and behavior were minimal for both low and high self-monitors. (Even so, the A–B correlation was higher for low self-monitors.) In the attitude-available situation, the relationship between attitude and behavior was substantial for low self-monitoring individuals, but it remained minimal for high self-monitoring individuals. In the attitude-relevant situation, both high and low self-monitors displayed substantial A–B consistency.

The study demonstrated that situational factors interacted with self-

TABLE 4.1
Correspondence Between Attitude and Behavior

	Basic Situation	Attitude Available Situation	Attitude Relevant Situation
Low self-monitors	.18*	.47**	.45**
High self-monitors	−.17	.18*	.60**

*Minimal correspondence
**Substantial correspondence
From Snyder and Kendzierski (1982)

monitoring to influence attitude–behavior consistency. A situation that encouraged individuals to thoughtfully consider their own attitudinal position (attitude-available condition) exerted a particularly strong impact on low self-monitors. Low self-monitoring individuals believe that their behavior reflects their inner feelings and attitudes; consequently, a situation that put them in touch with these feelings and attitudes encouraged them to translate this attitude into action. By contrast, high self-monitors exhibited A–B consistency only when the situation suggested that attitudes were a relevant guide to action. High self-monitors, being creatures of the situation, were likely to translate attitudes into action only when they believed that the situation required that they take their attitudes into account.

Clearly, then, an adequate explanation of the effects of self-monitoring on attitude–behavior consistency must take into account the nature of the situation (i.e., does it encourage the individual to focus on his or her attitudes or does it emphasize that attitudes are a relevant guide for action?).

Direct Experience. Another person variable that influences the A–B relationship is the amount of direct experience that the individual has had with the attitude object. Individuals differ in the extent to which their attitudes have been formed on the basis of direct experience with the attitude object. Consider formation of attitudes toward drugs. One person may have formed a negative attitude toward drugs as a result of some very unpleasant experiences with marijuana in high school. Another person also may have a negative attitude toward drugs, but his or her attitude may have been formed through indirect experience (e.g., by reading magazine stories that discuss the harmful effects of hallucinogenic drugs). Fazio and Zanna (1981) argued that attitudes based on direct experience "are more clearly defined, held with greater certainty, more stable over time, and more resistant to counterinfluence" than attitudes formed through indirect experience (p. 185). Thus, Fazio and Zanna contended that attitudes based on direct experience should predict behavior better than attitudes formed through indirect experience.

The researchers tested this hypothesis by examining whether the relationship between attitudes toward psychological experiments and willingness to sign up for a psychological study was moderated by the number of experiments in which a student had previously participated (Fazio & Zanna, 1978). Subjects first completed a series of background questions, including a question that asked them to specify the number of psychological experiments in which they had previously participated. Students then indicated their attitude toward psychological research by completing several attitude scales. Finally, students were told that the psychology department was setting up a subject pool; they were also informed that the typical experiment lasted 30–60 minutes and that students were paid $2–$3 for their assistance. Subjects were then asked to indicate the number of experiments in which they would like to participate.

Consistent with the authors' hypothesis, the correlation between attitude toward research and willingness to participate in psychological experiments varied as a function of direct experience. For subjects who had a great deal of experience volunteering for psychological research, the A–B correlation was .42; for moderate experience subjects, it was .36; and for low experience subjects, the correlation was −.03. Thus, the more experience an individual had with the attitude object, the stronger was the relationship between attitudes and behavior.

These findings have interesting implications for persuasion in everyday situations. For example, a teenager may tell someone that he or she personally opposes the use of marijuana, and yet the same individual may agree to smoke some marijuana at a party the next day. Such an action may baffle an observer. However, it may be that the adolescent has formed an attitude toward drugs from reading magazines and from watching television documentaries about drugs. Fazio and Zanna's research suggests that attitudes formed on the basis of indirect experience with the attitude object rarely predict behavior. These attitudes are defined rather vaguely in the individual's mind, and, as a consequence, these attitudes are quite susceptible to being influenced by persuasive communications.[4]

Measurement Issues

Measurement factors also determine the strength of the attitude–behavior relationship. Fishbein and Ajzen have conducted much of the research on measurement aspects of attitudes and behavior. They began their work on this topic in the late-1960s and early 1970s. At this time, there was considerable controversy about the status of attitudes in psychology and communication. Wicker (1969) had suggested that, in view of the small correlations between attitudes and behavior, it might be wise to abandon the attitude concept completely. To a new generation of persuasion researchers, who were disenchanted with the old "behaviorist" theories and who strongly believed that thought influences action, the idea of abandoning the concept of attitude was deeply unsettling.

Over the course of the 1960s and 1970s, Fishbein and Ajzen conducted a series of studies that breathed new life into the attitude concept. They argued that the failure to find significant relationships between attitudes and behavior did not mean that attitudes did not predict behavior or that people were hopelessly inconsistent. Instead, they argued that the failure to obtain strong A–B relationships was attributable to poor measurement techniques and a refusal to measure attitudes and behavior at the same level of specificity. Fishbein and Ajzen contended that a strong relationship between attitude and behavior could be obtained if the attitudinal predictor "corresponded with" the behavioral criteria. By "corresponded with" they meant that the attitudinal and behavioral entities were measured at the same level of specificity. This is called the compatibility principle.

Ajzen and Fishbein (1977) differentiated between *attitude toward a behavior* (highly specific attitude) and *attitude toward the object* (the familiar broadly based attitude). For example, in the area of religion, an attitude toward prayer is an example of an attitude toward a specific behavior, whereas attitude toward religion is an example of an attitude toward an object. The researchers also differentiated between *single acts* (specific behaviors that are directed at a target and take place in a particular context at a particular time) and *behavioral categories*, or multiple acts, that "involve sets of actions rather than single action" (Ajzen & Fishbein, 1980). A single act might involve praying in the church chapel right before a chemistry test; a behavioral category would include all behaviors involving religion — for example, praying, attending religious services, reading the Bible, and dating a person from outside the faith. The compatibility principle suggests that attitudes toward an object (the general attitude measure) should predict behavioral categories or broad classes of behavior that cut across different situations. Specific attitudes (attitude toward the behavior) should only predict single acts. To help explain these concepts, I discuss the findings of two representative studies. The first focuses on the prediction of specific behaviors, and the second focuses on the prediction of behavioral categories.

Predicting Specific Behaviors. Ajzen and Fishbein (1977) argued that attitudinal and behavioral entities consist of four elements: "the *action*, the *target* at which the action is directed, the *context* in which the action is performed, and the *time* in which it is performed" (p. 889). An attitude will predict a behavior to the extent that it corresponds with (is identical to) the behavior in terms of action, target, context, and time.

Suppose, for example, a researcher wanted to predict family planning behavior — specifically, a woman's intention to have a child in the next 2 years and her intention to use birth control pills. According to the compatibility principle, the more specific the attitude measure, the higher the correlation between attitude and behavior. Davidson and Jaccard (1975) tested this hypothesis by asking a sample of women to complete a questionnaire that assessed their attitudes on the subject of family planning, their intention to have a child in the next 2 years, and their intention to use birth control pills.

Davidson and Jaccard predicted that the correlation between attitude and intention to have a child in the next 2 years would be lowest when the attitude was general (attitude toward children), somewhat higher when the attitude corresponded to the behavior in terms of target and action (attitude toward having children), and much higher when the attitude corresponded to the behavior in terms of target, action, and time (attitude toward having a child in the next 2 years). Similarly, they expected that the correlation between intention to use birth control pills and attitude would be lowest when the attitude was general (attitude toward family planning), slightly higher when the attitude was more specific (attitude toward birth control), somewhat higher when the attitude corresponded to the behavior in terms of target (attitude toward birth control pills), and highest when the two entities corresponded in terms of target and action (attitude toward using birth control pills).

Table 4.2 shows that these hypotheses are strongly supported. The findings make sense. A woman might have a very positive attitude toward children, yet have no intention of having children in the next 2 years because she wants to devote her full energies to her career. On the other hand, a woman might wholeheartedly agree that (in general) family planning was a good idea, yet, because she wanted to get pregnant, she might have little intention of using birth control pills. Thus, general attitudes were weakly associated with behavioral intentions. In contrast, specific attitudes that corresponded to the behavior in terms of target and action were strongly associated with behavioral intentions. The lesson is that attitudes can predict specific behaviors, provided the investigator tailors the attitude measure to the behavior he or she wants to predict.

Predicting Broad Classes of Behavior.   The compatibility principle suggests that a general attitude (attitude toward the object) should accurately forecast behavior when the behavioral criteria consist of broad classes of behavior that cut across situations. The general attitude measure "corresponds with" the general, cross-situational behavioral measure. Weigel

TABLE 4.2
Correlations Between Selected Attitudinal Variables and Behavioral Intentions

Attitudinal Variable	
Using birth control pills	
Attitude toward using birth control pills	.778
Attitude toward birth control pills	.497
Attitude toward birth control	.202
Attitude toward family planning	.109
Having a child in the next 2 years	
Attitude toward having a child in the next 2 years	.798
Attitude toward having children	.225
Attitude toward children	− .038

Note. The higher the correlation, the stronger the relationship between attitude and behavioral intention.
From Davidson and Jaccard (1975)

and Newman (1976) provided support for this hypothesis in a study of the relationship between environmental attitudes and environmental protection behavior.

Weigel and Newman measured general attitudes toward the environment by asking subjects to indicate where they stood on 16 conservation and pollution issues. Three months after the questionnaire data had been collected, subjects were contacted on three separate occasions and asked if they would participate in a variety of environmental protection projects. First, they were asked if they would sign three petitions (one opposed drilling oil off the New England coast, a second opposed construction of nuclear power plants, and a third recommended harsher sentences for individuals who removed air pollution devices from their automobile exhaust systems). Subjects also were asked if they would distribute the petitions to family members and friends to obtain more signatures on the petitions. Six weeks later, subjects were contacted again. This time they were asked if they would participate in a roadside litter pick-up project. Approximately 2 months later, subjects were again contacted. On this occasion, they were asked if they were willing to participate in a recycling project in which they would bundle their papers, take metal rings from their bottles, and place recycleables outside their homes for a period of 8 weeks.

To obtain a cross-situational measure of behavior, the investigators summed responses to the petitioning, litter pick-up, and recycling items. They constructed an even broader index of environmental behavioral by incorporating these scales into a comprehensive behavioral index. Table 4.3 shows the correlations between subjects' environmental attitudes and the behavioral criteria. The correlations between attitude and behavior were higher when broad categories of behavior were employed than when single behaviors were analyzed; the correlation was still higher when the comprehensive behavioral index was the criterion variable.

These findings indicate that general attitudes were strongly associated with behavior. As a general rule, so long as the breadth of the behavioral index matches that of the attitudinal measure, attitudes will accurately forecast behavior. In Weigel and Newman's study, an individual who had a positive general attitude toward the environment would be expected to engage in environmental protection behaviors "under most circumstances" (i.e., most of the time). However, the same individual might not perform an environmental protection behavior in a particular situational context. This point was nicely illustrated by the comments that one subject made about an apparent discrepancy between her attitude and her behavior. Weigel and Newman related her observation:

> A subject who scored high on the environmental concern scale initially agreed to participate in the litter pick-up project but later reversed her

TABLE 4.3
Correlations Between Subjects' Environmental Attitudes and Behavioral Criteria

Single Behaviors		Categories of Behavior		Behavioral Index	
Offshore oil	.41				
Nuclear power	.36	Petitioning behavior			
Auto exhaust	.39	scale (0–4)	.50		
Circulate petitions	.27				
Individual		Litter pick-up		Comprehensive	
participation	.34	scale (0–2)	.36	behavioral	
Recruit friend	.22			index	.62
Week 1	.34				
Week 2	.57				
Week 3	.34				
Week 4	.33	Recycling behavior			
Week 5	.12	scale (0–8)	.39		
Week 6	.20				
Week 7	.20				
Week 8	.34				

Note. The higher the correlation, the stronger the relationship between attitude and behavior.
From Weigel and Newman (1976)

decision. In reneging on her offer, she told the confederate that she would have liked to participate, but her husband had asked her not to do so. She explained that her husband opposed her participation because he had hopes of organizing the Boy Scouts in a similar project and felt that the current project could undermine the realization of those hopes. (p. 800)

As this example illustrates, other variables besides attitudes influence behavior. However, this does not mean that attitudes do not predict action. It simply means that a general attitude measure will not predict behavior in each and every instance. However, as Ajzen and Fishbein (1977) pointed out, if a researcher samples a wide variety of situations, he or she should find that general attitudes predict behavior.

On a broader level, the Ajzen–Fishbein model suggests that one should not assume that a discrepancy between attitudes and behavior means that an individual is "inconsistent." Suppose someone with an extremely patriotic, pro-American attitude bought a Japanese car. Some observers might call the consumer a hypocrite or label his or her behavior as inconsistent. However, the research on attitude–behavior relations should give these observers pause. In the first place, Ajzen and Fishbein's model suggests that a general attitude (attitude toward America) will not predict a specific behavior (purchasing a Japanese car). Their research also suggests that if we sampled enough attitudinally relevant behaviors (for example, displaying the flag on Flag Day and supporting the president in times of crisis), we would find a high degree of correspondence between attitudes toward America and behavior. Moreover, one can easily imagine that our hypothetical consumer would argue that he or she did not think that holding a pro-American attitude meant that you had to engage in behaviors that ran counter to your self-interest (such as purchasing a gas-guzzling American car when a Japanese car would save you money on gasoline). This illustrates the difficulty of making simple judgments about the level of inconsistency between attitudes and behavior. Some researchers have argued that consistency is a label that observers apply to an actor's behavior—and the label, they have suggested, probably tells us more about the observer than it does about the actor (Craig, 1980; Salancik, 1982).

The Theory of Reasoned Action

Another perspective on the "when do attitudes predict behavior?" question is the theory of reasoned action, also proposed by Fishbein and Ajzen (1975). The theory has generated voluminous amounts of research in a variety of social science disciplines, and has exerted an important impact on the area of attitude–behavior relations. The theory assumes that people rationally calculate the costs and benefits of engaging in a particular action and think carefully about how important others will view the behavior under consideration. The hallmark of the model is its emphasis on "conscious deliberation."

There are four components of the theory of reasoned action: *attitude toward the behavior* ("the person's judgment that performing the behavior is good or bad, that he is in favor of or against performing the behavior"), *subjective norm* ("the person's perceptions of the social pressures put on him to perform or not perform the behavior in question"), *behavioral intention* (the intent to perform a particular behavior), and actual *behavior* (Ajzen & Fishbein, 1980, p. 6) (see Fig. 4.1).

Attitude. Attitude toward the behavior consists of two subcomponents: (behavioral beliefs) (beliefs about the consequences of the behavior) and (outcome evaluations) (affective evaluations of the consequences). For example, suppose we wanted to predict whether a person will adopt a low-cholesterol diet. We would assess the individual's attitude toward adopting a low-cholesterol diet by obtaining a measure of his or her salient beliefs about the consequences of adopting such a dietary regimen and his or her evaluation of these consequences. We might assess beliefs and evaluations by using these items:

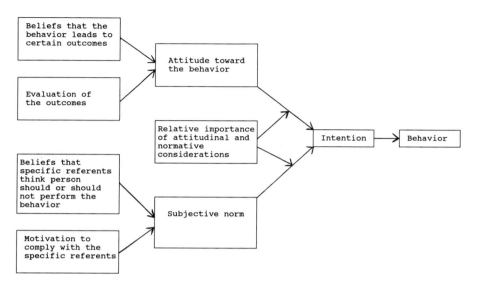

FIG. 4.1 Theory of reasoned action: Schematic diagram (adapted from Ajzen & Fishbein, 1980).

Behavioral Beliefs

1. Adopting a low-cholesterol diet will reduce my risk of suffering a heart attack.
   Likely 1 2 3 4 5 6 7 Unlikely
2. Adopting a low-cholesterol diet will control my caloric intake.
   Likely 1 2 3 4 5 6 7 Unlikely

Outcome Evaluations

Reducing my risk of suffering a heart attack is:
   Good 1 2 3 4 5 6 7 Bad
Controlling my caloric intake is:
   Good 1 2 3 4 5 6 7 Bad

An individual's attitude toward the behavior (adopting a low-cholesterol diet) would be computed by multiplying the score on each behavioral belief (b) by its corresponding evaluation (e) and then summing for all the items. The formula, which is essentially the same as the one we presented in chapter 2, is: AB = Sum b(i) × e(i). (Note: AB = Attitude toward the Behavior, b(i) = each behavioral belief, and e(i) = each evaluation.)

Subjective Norm. The second component of the model, subjective norm, also consists of two subcomponents: normative beliefs ("the person's beliefs that specific individuals or groups think he should or should not perform the behavior") and motivation to comply (the individual's motivation to go along with these significant others) (Ajzen & Fishbein, 1980). We might assess these components in the following way:

Normative Beliefs

My father thinks that I:

Definitely should adopt a low-cholesterol diet.	1 2 3 4 5 6 7	Definitely should not adopt a low-cholesterol diet.

My best friend thinks that I:

Definitely should adopt a low-cholesterol diet.	1 2 3 4 5 6 7	Definitely should not adopt a low-cholesterol diet.

Motivation to Comply

In general, how much do you care about what each of the following think you should do:

Care Very Much   *Do Not Care at All*

| My father | 1 | 2 | 3 | 4 | 5 | 6 | 7 |
| My best friend | 1 | 2 | 3 | 4 | 5 | 6 | 7 |

The subjective norm is computed by multiplying the normative belief score by the corresponding motivation to comply score, and then summing for all the items. The formula is: SN = Sum NB(i) × MC(i). (Note: SN = Subjective Norm, NB(i) = each normative belief, and MC(i) = each motivation to comply.)

Behavioral Intention. As the name suggests, behavioral intention is the intention to perform a particular behavior. Intention to adopt a low-cholesterol diet would be assessed in the following way:

I intend to adopt a low cholesterol diet.

| 1 | 2 | 3 | 4 | 5 | 6 | 7 |
| Likely | | | | | Unlikely | |

The theory of reasoned action stipulates that intention is a joint function of attitude toward the behavior and subjective norm. That is, both attitude and subjective norm are assumed to predict intention to perform a particular behavior. Under some conditions, a person's attitude predicts his or her intention to perform a behavior. In other circumstances, subjective norm (one's desire to comply with the views of important others) predicts intention. Both attitude and subjective norm receive an empirical weight, based on their ability to predict behavioral intention (BI). The formula is: $BI = AB(w1) + SN(w2)$. (Note: BI = Behavioral Intention, AB = Attitude toward the Behavior, SN = Subjective Norm, and $w1$ and $w2$ are the empirical weights for each component.)

Behavior. Fishbein and Ajzen (1975) argued that most social behavior action is under the volitional control of the actor. Consequently, the intention to perform a particular behavior should predict the actual performance of the act. An intention is most likely to predict behavior when the measure of intention corresponds to the behavior in terms of target, action, context, and time. In sum, attitude toward the behavior and subjective norm determine intention to perform a behavior, and intention "is the immediate determinant of the action" (Ajzen & Fishbein, 1980).

Predicting Behavior from Attitudes. The theory of reasoned action makes allowance for the fact that attitudes do not always predict behavior. When normative influences are salient, they (rather than attitudes) may influence behavior. That is, there may be times when perceived pressures from significant others exert a stronger influence on behavior than do attitudes. For example, an individual's attitude toward adopting a low-cholesterol diet may fail to predict his or her behavior. However, the subjective norm (the desire to comply with the recommendations of important others) may accurately forecast the decision to adopt a low-cholesterol regimen. Whereas earlier researchers might have thrown up their hands and concluded that because attitudes do not always predict behavior, behavior is unpredictable, Ajzen and Fishbein contended that behavior is predictable, provided you take both attitudes and norms into account.

As noted earlier the theory of reasoned action emphasizes that attitudes influence behavior via behavioral intentions. The assumption is that attitudes (and subjective norms) influence behavioral intentions, and that intentions influence behavior. These predictions are based on Ajzen and Fishbein's (1980) assumption that "human beings are usually quite rational . . . (and) consider the implications of their actions before they decide to engage or not engage in a given behavior" (p. 5).

The ultimate test of a theory is whether the empirical evidence confirms its core hypothesis. Using this criterion as a guide, the theory of reasoned action has fared reasonably well. A number of studies have found that behavioral intentions can be predicted from measures of attitude toward the behavior and subjective norm. The list of behaviors for which attitudes and subjective norms predict intentions is long and diverse. It includes consumer product preferences (Fishbein & Ajzen, 1980), voting in presidential elections (Fishbein & Ajzen, 1981), eating meals in fast-food restaurants (Brinberg & Durand, 1983), women's occupational preferences (Sperber, Fishbein, & Ajzen, 1980), family planning (Fishbein, Jaccard, Davidson, Ajzen, & Loken, 1980), and breast-feeding newborn infants (Manstead, Proffitt, & Smart, 1983). Given that one of the goals of social science research is to predict behavior, the finding that behavioral intentions can be predicted from measures of attitude and subjective norm is noteworthy. It is even more significant when one considers that intentions have been found to predict actual behavior in a variety of circumstances.

Not all the evidence is consistent with the theory, however. For example, some studies have found that intentions are influenced by variables other than attitudes and subjective norms (e.g., by previous behavior) (Bentler & Speckhart, 1979; Manstead et al., 1983). Other studies have found that, contrary to the assumption that the impact of attitudes on behavior is mediated by behavioral intentions, attitudes exert a direct impact on behavior (Bentler & Speckhart, 1979; Zuckerman & Reis, 1978). In addition, critics have questioned the assumption that people "consider the implications of their actions before they decide to engage or not engage in a given behavior" (Ajzen & Fishbein, 1980, p. 5).[5] Fazio (1990), among others, has noted that people frequently make behavioral decisions without carefully considering the consequences of their actions. He has noted that whereas the theory of reasoned action does an excellent job of predicting behaviors that are planned and deliberate, it provides a less satisfactory account of behavioral decisions that are made spontaneously and "automatically."

HOW DO ATTITUDES INFLUENCE BEHAVIOR?

The research discussed so far makes it clear that under some circumstances (and for some people) attitudes predict behavior, whereas under other conditions (and for other people) attitudes do not accurately forecast behavior. However, these studies do not tell us why attitudes predict behavior under some conditions and not under others. Fazio (1989) explored this issue for over a decade and has developed a processing model of the attitude–behavior relationship.

The core concept in Fazio's model is *accessibility*. Attitudes, he argued, can influence behavior only if they are accessible—that is, if they can be activated from memory). As Fazio (1989) noted:

Unless the attitude comes to mind when the individual encounters the attitude object, the individual may never view the object in evaluative terms. It is the chronic accessibility of an attitude from memory, i.e., the likelihood that the attitude will be activated from memory upon mere exposure to the attitude object, that determines the power and functionality of an attitude. (p. 154)

In other words, unless the individual knows what his or her attitude is and (to put it colloquially) "is in touch with his feelings about the issue," the individual's attitude will not predict his or her behavior. The flip side of this is that attitudes will strongly predict behavior if the individual knows what his or her attitude is, has accessed it from memory, and (in the common parlance) "is in touch with his feelings about the issue."[6]

The accessibility construct explains a number of findings in the attitude–behavior area. For example, recall that Fazio and Zanna (1978) found that the relationship between attitude toward psychology experiments and willingness to participate in a psychological study was stronger among students who had a great deal of direct experience with psychology experiments than among students who had relatively little experience with psychological research. One reason why direct experience subjects were more likely to translate their attitudes into action was that they could retrieve their attitudes rather quickly from memory. "Oh, yes," they could think to themselves, "I know about psych experiments. They're kind of weird—but interesting. I always learn something new about myself after I participate in one of them." On the other hand, students who had formed their attitudes toward psychological research through indirect experience (say, by reading *Psychology Today*) probably found it a bit difficult to retrieve their attitudes from memory. These students might have evaluated psychological research just as positively on a semantic differential scale as did direct experience subjects. However, their attitudes probably did not come as quickly or as vividly to mind.

In a similar fashion, the accessibility notion helps explain why low self-monitors typically show greater attitude–behavior consistency than high self-monitors. Low self-monitors attach considerable importance to "being themselves." Consequently, they typically are more aware of what their attitudes about an issue are, and (as a result) they are probably better able to retrieve them from memory than high self-monitors.

Of course, these examples do not prove that accessibility mediates (or explains) the attitude–behavior relationship. To provide a more compelling demonstration of the mediating impact of accessibility on A–B relations, Fazio and his colleagues conducted two studies in which they measured accessibility directly (Fazio, Powell, & Williams, 1989; Fazio & Williams, 1986). Let us examine the study by Fazio et al. (1989) in detail.

Fazio and his colleagues examined attitudes and behavior toward 10 products. The products included Fritos corn chips, Planters peanuts, Sun-Maid raisins, and V-8 juice. The investigators first measured accessibility of attitudes. They did this by asking subjects to respond to the names of 100 products (including the 10 target items) by pressing one of two keys ("like" or "dislike") on a microcomputer. Subjects were told to indicate their feelings about each product, and to "respond as quickly and as accurately as possible." The way it worked was that a product name would appear on the screen (e.g., "Fritos"), and an individual would respond as quickly as possible to the name by pressing the appropriate button ("like" or "dislike"). Then there would be a 3-second pause, and the next name would appear.

The experimenter recorded the response (either "like" or "dislike"); she also measured the latency of response, or the amount of time that it took an individual to press one of the buttons. The latency of response constituted the measure of accessibility.[7] The investigators reasoned that individuals whose attitudes toward a product were highly accessible should know immediately whether they liked or disliked the product. Fazio and his colleagues argued that these individuals should press the button immediately upon seeing the product's name. By contrast, the investigators contended that individuals whose attitudes were less accessible would need more time to decide how they felt about the product and would, therefore, take longer to push the "like" or "dislike" button. Subjects then indicated their attitude toward each of the 100 products. During the final phase of the experiment, individuals' behavioral preferences were assessed. Ten of the products were arrayed in two rows of 5 on a table. The experimenter told subjects that, as a token of the researchers' appreciation for their time and effort, they could take 5 of the 10 products. Unbeknownst to subjects, the experimenter made note of which products had been selected.

The researchers then examined whether subjects who had more accessible attitudes toward a given product exhibited greater A–B consistency than students who had less accessible attitudes toward the product. For example, if the researchers were right, then a subject who had a highly favorable and accessible attitude toward Sun-Maid raisins would be more likely to choose Sun-Maid raisins than an individual who had an equally favorable attitude toward Sun-Maid raisins but whose attitude was less accessible. The results confirmed the researchers' hypotheses. For high accessible subjects, the correlation between attitude and behavior was .62, whereas the A–B correlation was .54 and .50 for moderate and low accessible subjects, respectively.

You may recall that the experimenters arranged the 10 products in two rows. They did this for a reason. They noted that when an attitude is low in accessibility, it is unlikely to be retrieved from memory upon exposure to the object. Quite obviously, if an attitude cannot be retrieved from memory, it cannot guide or influence behavior. Thus, under these circumstances, an individual's behavioral choices should be influenced by salient aspects of the situation. Fazio and his colleagues argued that subjects whose attitudes were relatively inaccessible should be influenced by "momentarily salient features of the object," such as whether the product was placed in the front or the back row. The researchers predicted and found that product selection was more influenced by product positioning when attitudes were low, rather than high, in accessibility. Snickers, Planters peanuts, Dentyne gum, and Star-Kist tuna had been placed in the front row. The investigators found that subjects with less accessible attitudes toward these products were more likely to choose these products than subjects with highly accessible attitudes.

IMPLICATIONS FOR PERSUASION

The attitude–behavior literature has interesting and important implications for the study of persuasion. Ultimately, most persuaders want to change behavior, and they hope to influence behavior by changing attitudes. Thus, it behooves persuasion specialists to understand the conditions under which attitudes do and do not predict behavior. Furthermore, persuasion specialists may wish to develop messages that enable people to more easily translate their attitudes into action. The research discussed in this chapter is obviously relevant to these issues.

Fazio's Model

Fazio's work suggests that communicators should employ different message strategies, depending on whether the targeted attitudes are strongly held (strong association between the object and evaluation in memory) or weakly held (weak association between object and evaluation in memory). If communicators want to influence strongly held attitudes, they will be more successful to the extent that they induce the individual to retrieve these attitudes from memory.

Political consultants frequently employ this strategy when they devise political commercials. Tony Schwartz, a consultant based in New York, has long been an advocate of an attitude-accessibility approach to political ads, although he does not use this terminology. Schwartz (1973) has argued that:

> Political advertising involves tuning in on attitudes and beliefs of the voter and then affecting these attitudes with the proper auditory and visual stimuli. . . . Commercials that attempt to *tell* the listener something are inherently not as effective as those that attach to something that is already in him. We are not concerned with getting things *across* to people as much as *out* of people. Electronic media are particularly effective tools in this regard because they provide us with direct access to people's minds. (p. 96)

In 1988, George Bush tried to "access" voters' fears that his opponent, Michael Dukakis, would be "soft on crime." Bush succeeded in bringing these fears to the foreground by developing the now-famous Willie Horton spots. The ads told the true story of how convicted felon Willie Horton had been released from a Massachusetts prison under then-Governor Duka-kis's furlough program. After leaving Massachusetts, Horton moved to Maryland, where he raped a woman. The ads aroused voters' fears that Dukakis would initiate a similar program that would have similar effects on a national level. According to Fazio's research, the ads helped to "access" voters' attitudes toward crime. By associating a negative attitude object (a convicted felon who raped a woman) with Dukakis, the ads succeeded in increasing voters' antipathy toward the Massachusetts governor. From an attitude–behavior perspective, these ads may have increased attitude–be-havior consistency among voters who already disliked the Massachusetts governor. By accessing not only their fears but their negative attitudes toward Dukakis, the ads helped to ensure that these voters would translate their attitudes into action at the voting booth.

On the other hand, Fazio and his colleagues' research suggests that a different message strategy should be employed to influence weakly held attitudes. You may recall that Fazio, Powell, and Williams (1989) found that a salient visual cue—the row in which the product was located—promoted attitude–behavior consistency among low attitude accessible subjects. This finding has interesting implications for politics. It suggests that, when appealing to voters who really do not care much about politics, candidates should not even try to "access" these voters' attitudes. Instead, they should develop messages that use striking images and attention-grabbing cues— for example, appealing photographs of the candidate or catchy music.[8]

The Ajzen–Fishbein Model

Although Fazio's research suggests that communicators should focus on the accessibility of attitudes, Ajzen and Fishbein's theory of reasoned action emphasizes that communication specialists should target attitudes and subjective norms. Suppose, for example, that a congressman wanted to induce voters to support a proposal for national health insurance. The theory of reasoned action offers several directions for a persuasion cam-paign. First, the congressman might try to change attitudes by inducing a change in behavioral beliefs or outcome evaluations. Ajzen and Fishbein emphasize that the communicator should first determine respondents' salient beliefs about the issue at hand (see also Cronen & Conville, 1973). Thus, if preliminary tests revealed that most voters believed that national health insurance would result in lengthy waiting periods and extensive delays in medical service, the campaign commercials might counterargue this point by noting that in some cases national health insurance has actually reduced the time patients had to wait to see a family doctor. The campaign might also target evaluations of salient beliefs. If pilot tests indicated that most voters liked the fact that national health insurance would cut medical costs, the ads might remind voters that they would enjoy saving money on medical expenses.

The campaign might also focus on the subjective norm component of the Ajzen–Fishbein model. Once again, the theory emphasizes that communicators should identify respondents' salient beliefs—in this case, their beliefs about the reference groups that exert the strongest impact on their intentions to support a national health care bill. If pilot tests revealed that most voters strongly believed that family members thought they should support a health care bill, advertisements might feature family members in "honest, frank" discussions on the subject of national health insurance. The campaign might also target the motivation to comply subcomponent of subjective norm. TV ads might remind viewers that they often find their loved ones' advice on health matters to be particularly useful.

Remember that attitude and subjective norm are weighted according to their empirical contributions to behavioral intentions. Thus, if attitude makes a stronger contribution to behavioral intentions, the campaigner may wish to focus on changing behavioral beliefs and evaluations. If the subjective norm makes a stronger contribution, the communicator may wish to emphasize the views held by important others.[9]

CONCLUSIONS

Do attitudes predict behavior? As we have seen, there is no simple answer to this question. The relationship between attitudes and behavior depends on the type of situation, the personality and background of the person, and on the ways in which the researcher measures attitudes and behavior. Under some conditions, for some people, with attitudes measured in a particular way, attitudes do predict behavior. Under different conditions, for different people, with attitudes measured in a different way, attitudes will not predict behavior particularly well. Although some individuals might be dismayed that the answer to the question we posed at the beginning of this chapter ("Do attitudes predict behavior?") is so complex, we believe that human behavior is (by definition) complex. Hence, it is only fitting that we obtain complex answers in the area of attitude–behavior relations.

Contemporary research has focused on the "how" and "why" of the attitude–behavior relationship. Studies have shown that an attitude is more likely to influence behavior to the extent that the attitude can be accessed from memory. We have noted that studies of attitude–behavior relations have a number of interesting implications for the persuasion practitioner who wishes to encourage individuals to translate their attitudes into action.

PART II
CHANGING ATTITUDES
AND BEHAVIORS

I t is September 1976, and a 15-year-old boy from Trenton, New Jersey has just been arrested for robbery. Instead of being taken to a standard juvenile detention home, he goes to Rahway State Prison to participate in a novel program to curb juvenile crime.

The young man is transported to the prison facility and, with the other juvenile offenders, he is led through the dank halls of the prison to a large room. It is there that he encounters the "Lifers": men who have been sentenced to life imprisonment for armed robbery, murder, and other crimes. The Lifers are big and brawling. One convict orders the young man to sit up straight. Another hurls verbal epithets at the youngster. Then each of the convicts explains the horrors of prison life, complete with vivid personal anecdotes.

The 15-year-old boy has just participated in the Juvenile Awareness Project that was initiated by the Rahway State Prison in the late-1970s. By 1978, the program had begun to attract national attention. A story appeared in *Reader's Digest* in January 1978. Then on November 2, 1978, a documentary entitled "Scared Straight," narrated by actor Peter Falk, was shown on KTLA in Los Angeles. Within a few years, "Scared Straight" was shown on local TV stations all over the country.

The Rahway project is a classic example of a persuasive communication that is designed to change attitudes—in this case, attitudes toward crime. Although scientific studies have questioned the long-term effects of the program (Finckenauer, 1982; Rajecki, 1990), it remains an excellent example of a modern persuasion campaign.

In Part II of this book, I discuss research on persuasive communication and attitude change. I begin by discussing contemporary cognitive processing models of attitude change. Then I discuss the role that source, message, channel, and receiver variables play in the persuasion process (chapters 6, 7, and 8). Chapter 9 summarizes the social judgment theory of attitude change, and chapter 10 focuses on research generated by a classic theory of attitudes: cognitive dissonance.

5
Cognitive Processing Models of Persuasion

Let's begin with a mental exercise. Read this excerpt from George Bush's State of the Union address, which was delivered on January 29, 1991, 2 weeks after the start of the Gulf War. As you read, make a mental note of the thoughts that cross your mind.

> Halfway around the world we are engaged in a great struggle in the skies and on the seas and sands. We know why we're there. We are Americans, part of something larger than ourselves. . . . Most Americans know instinctively why we are in the Gulf. They know we had to stop Saddam now, not later. They know that this brutal dictator will do anything, will use any weapon, will commit any outrage, no matter how many innocents suffer. They know we must make sure that control of the world's oil resources does not fall into his hands only to finance further aggression. . . . The winds of change are with us now. The forces of freedom are together, united. And we move toward the next century more confident than ever that we have the will at home and abroad to do what must be done: the hard work of freedom.

This speech probably evoked some thoughts and mental reactions. The thoughts may have been favorable ("We did the right thing in Iraq."), unfavorable ("I do not feel the United States should have gone into Kuwait"), neutral ("The United States sent thousands of men and women to Kuwait"), or totally irrelevant to the message ("I'm not interested in politics").

The theoretical approaches described in this chapter assign central importance to thoughts and mental reactions. The theories do not assume that people's thoughts are always logical, internally consistent, or devoid of emotion. However, they insist that people think about persuasive communications. I begin by describing the cognitive response approach to persuasion; then I discuss the elaboration likelihood model, a theoretical approach that evolved from the cognitive response perspective.

THE COGNITIVE RESPONSE APPROACH TO PERSUASION

As the name suggests, the cognitive response approach emphasizes the thoughts and ideas that occur to people as they attend to a persuasive communication. Cognitive responses refer to "all the thoughts that pass through a person's mind while he or she anticipates a communication, listens to a communication, or reflects on a communication" (Petty, Ostrom, & Brock, 1981, p. 7). (See Exhibit 5–1: Measuring Cognitive Responses, p. 133.) Unlike early approaches, such as the legendary hypodermic needle model that assumed audience members were essentially passive, the cognitive response approach assumes that receivers play an active part in the communication process. Festinger and Maccoby (1964) articulated the main assumption of the cognitive response approach when they observed that the listener:

> does not sit there listening and absorbing what is said without any counteraction on his part. Indeed, it is more likely that under such circumstances, while he is listening to the persuasive communication, he is very actively, inside his own mind, counterarguing, derogating the points the communicator makes and derogating the communicator himself. In other words, we can imagine that there is really an argument going on, one side being vocal and the other subvocal. (p. 360)

Think of how you react to a persuasive message. Do you sit there, taking in everything that the speaker says? Are you so mesmerized by the source that you stifle any thoughts or mental arguments? Hardly. You actively think about the speaker, the message, or some aspect of the persuasion context. Moreover, if the message touches on an issue that is close to your heart, you are likely to pay more attention to what the communicator says. If the speaker says something with which you disagree, you probably formulate arguments to rebut the communicator's position.

The cognitive response approach was developed by a group of persuasion researchers working at Ohio State University during the 1960s and 1970s. Prior to the Ohio State program of research, there had been only a handful of studies exploring people's cognitive responses to persuasive messages. The lion's share of persuasion studies had focused on the effects of variables external to the person, such as the source, message, and channel. To be sure, there had been a great deal of research concerned with cognitions—for example, explorations of cognitive dissonance, attitude structure, and belief change. However, few studies had attempted to articulate the cognitive processes or the thoughts that lie behind attitudes (Brock, 1981; Petty, Ostrom, & Brock, 1981).

By the late-1960s, there was a growing recognition that persuasion research had failed to identify the processes by which communications change attitudes. Also during this period, psychology was becoming increasingly cognitive. More and more studies were examining cognitive structure and cognitive processes. These developments paved the way for the focus on cognitive responses to persuasion.

The cognitive response approach argues that thoughts mediate the impact that a persuasive message exerts on attitudes. The idea is that a message will not change attitudes unless it induces positive cognitive responses, or reduces negative cognitive responses (see Fig. 5.1).

The next section discusses four major streams of research that can be placed loosely under the cognitive response heading. Some explanations as to why cognitive responses help to facilitate persuasion are then offered.

Counterattitudinal Role-Playing

Janis and King (1954) proposed that individuals are more likely to change their attitudes on an issue when they actively participate in the persuasion process than when they passively receive information. The researchers argued that one way to get people involved is to have them extemporaneously compose or improvise a persuasive message.

In one particularly effective demonstration of the improvisation procedure, Janis and Mann (1965) asked a group of young women who were heavy smokers to imagine that they had developed a bad cough and had gone to the doctor to obtain the results of a series of x-ray tests. Subjects also were asked to make believe that the experimenter was the physician who was treating her for her cough. Women expressed their thoughts out loud while waiting for the doctor's diagnosis and then again when they were told that they had a small malignant tumor in the right lung that required immediate surgery. A control group of subjects listened to a tape recording of the improvisation session. The results indicated that role-playing subjects were significantly more likely than controls to express negative attitudes toward smoking and to report that they had reduced their daily cigarette consumption.

The differences persisted over an 18-month period. Although there are

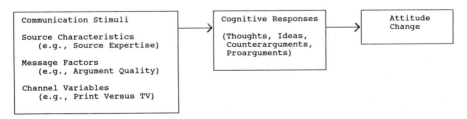

FIG. 5.1 The cognitive response approach to persuasion.

many reasons why the role-playing procedure was successful, one explanation is that it stimulated smokers to cognitively rehearse the reasons why
smoking is detrimental to their health. As one smoker noted:

> The (Surgeon General's) report did not have much effect on me. But I was
> in this other study. A professor was doing this psychological thing and I
> was one of the volunteers. . . . I got to thinking, what if it were really true
> and I had to go home and tell everyone that I had cancer. And right then
> I decided I would not go through this again, and if there were any way of
> preventing it I would. And I stopped smoking. . . . (Mann & Janis, 1968,
> p. 342)

Inoculation Theory

There was great concern in the 1950s about the susceptibility of American
soldiers to Communist propaganda. Remember that in the early 1950s, the
public had the impression that thousands of American soldiers had been
brainwashed in Communist North Korea. Recall also that this was the era
of the Cold War. There was enormous concern about the threat that
Communism posed to the nations of the free world. These developments
did not go unnoticed in the social science community. Persuasion scholars
who came of age during this era were interested in developing techniques
to help individuals better resist persuasive communications.

It was during this historical era that William McGuire developed his
novel inoculation approach to persuasion. McGuire began with a biological
analogy. He noted that some individuals had grown up in such a sterile
and protective environment that they had failed to develop appropriate
mechanisms to ward off infection. McGuire noted that there were two
ways that such individuals could increase their resistance to bodily
infection. They could be given a large dose of "supportive therapy"—a
healthy diet, plenty of exercise, more sleep; or these individuals could be
given a dose or inoculation of the attacking virus. Preexposure to the virus
in a weakened form would then stimulate the body's defenses, leading to
increased production of antibodies; this in turn would help the body fight
off the disease.

McGuire argued that the biological analogy could be usefully applied to
the realm of persuasion. He suggested that there were two techniques that
American authorities could use to bolster their citizens' psychological
defenses. They could develop a regimen of supportive therapy by asking
that schools, religious institutions, and families spend more time teaching
children about the virtues of the American way of life. Alternatively, they
could inoculate children by providing them with a weakened dose of
counterarguments against the American political and economic system.

McGuire reasoned that just as the provision of a dose of an attacking virus stimulates the body to fight off the disease, so too would the presentation of arguments against American values motivate the individual to bolster his beliefs about America (McGuire & Papageorgis, 1961). Just as inoculation worked better than supportive therapy in the health arena, so too should it prove to be a superior treatment in the persuasion realm. While McGuire (1970) believed that the inoculation approach had implications for the bolstering of morale during wartime, he also saw it as a more general theory of resistance to persuasion. He noted that: "We can develop belief resistance in people as we develop disease resistance in a biologically overprotected man or animal: by exposing the person to a weak dose of the attacking material, strong enough to stimulate his defenses, but not strong enough to overwhelm him. (p. 37)

To test the inoculation theory approach, McGuire (1970) chose to focus on beliefs that had been maintained in a "germ-free ideological environment," that is, beliefs "that are so generally accepted that most individuals are unaware of attacking arguments" (p. 37). Cultural truisms ("You should brush your teeth three times a day" and "People should get a yearly check-up") were excellent examples of these beliefs.

McGuire and Papageorgis (1961) gave subjects a supportive and a refutational (inoculation) defense to resist persuasion. For one truism, they received a supportive defense—a series of arguments that defended a particular truism (e.g., "Everyone should get a chest x-ray each year in order to detect any possible tuberculosis symptoms at an early stage"). For a second truism (e.g., "Everyone should brush their teeth after every meal if at all possible"), subjects received a refutational defense. This treatment consisted of arguments against the notion that you should brush your teeth after every meal, together with a refutation of these arguments.

Two days later, subjects read three essays. The first essay attacked the truism that had received the supportive defense, the second essay presented arguments against the truism that had received the refutational defense, and the third essay attacked a truism that had received no defensive treatment. Subjects then indicated their attitudes toward all three truisms. They also indicated their views about a fourth truism for which neither a defensive pretreatment nor a subsequent attack was provided.

The results strongly supported the inoculation theory predictions. As Fig. 5.2 shows, both the supportive and the refutational (inoculation) defense helped subjects resist the counterattitudinal arguments. However, the refutational treatment was significantly more effective. In fact, there was almost as much agreement with the truism that had received the refutational defense as with the truism that had received no attack at all.

In the study just described, the investigators used in their attacks the *same* counterarguments as had been previously refuted during the first session. McGuire argued that prior refutation of counterarguments against

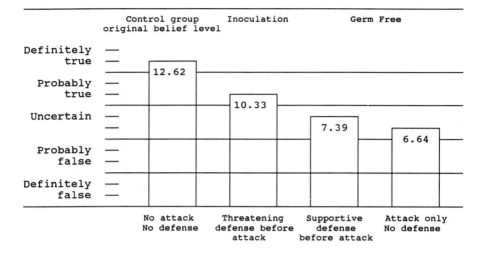

FIG. 5.2 Resistance to persuasion conferred by supportive and refutational treatments (from McGuire, 1970).

a truism should also increase resistance to *other* counterarguments that were directed at the belief. Thus, refutation of the argument that "Too frequent brushing tends to damage the gums and expose the vulnerable parts of the teeth to decay" should not only confer resistance to the belief that frequent brushing damages the gums, but also the belief that frequent brushing does damage to the inner lining of the mouth. A *refutational-same defense* is when the arguments employed in the counterattitudinal attack were the same arguments as had been previously refuted in the defensive pretreatment. A *refutational-different defense* is when arguments other than those employed in the subsequent attacking message are refuted. Papageorgis and McGuire (1961) found that the refutational-same and refutational-different treatments were of approximate equal effectiveness in conferring resistance to persuasion.

As we have seen, the refutational-same treatment motivates the person to defend his or her belief. But this treatment depends on the subject's ability to remember the arguments used in the refutational defense. Because memory of these arguments should fade, the resistance conferred by the refutational-same treatment should decrease as time passes. By contrast, the theory stipulates that resistance produced by the refutational-different treatment should persist over time. The latter defense works by teaching the individual how to rebut a variety of different arguments that bear on the belief.

McGuire (1962) tested these predictions by providing subjects with supportive, refutational-same, and refutational-different defenses. In some cases, he attacked the truisms immediately after providing the defensive pretreatments, whereas in other cases he waited two days before attacking the truisms; in still other cases he waited a week before attacking the truisms. Resistance conferred by the supportive and refutational-same treatments decreased from the first to the second measurements, while resistance produced by the refutational-different treatment increased. Although agreement levels decreased from the first to the third measurements, in all three groups, there was still greater agreement with the truisms in the refutational-different condition than in the other two groups. In summary, just as the body produces antibodies to fight off a virus, so too does the mind generate counterarguments to fight off attacks on deeply rooted beliefs.

Application. Inoculation theory has interesting implications for political campaigns. One political consultant has noted that "inoculation and preemption are what win campaigns;" other campaign experts have suggested that incumbents must "anticipate negatives and preempt them" (see Pfau & Kenski, 1990). Pfau and his colleagues have examined the implications of inoculation theory for the development of political campaigns. In one study, Pfau and Burgoon (1988) developed a series of political messages for a senatorial campaign in South Dakota (refutational-same defense, refutational-different, and a noninoculation control). Interviewers asked a sample of adult residents in Sioux Falls, South Dakota, to read one of the messages; a couple of weeks later, interviewers asked the same individuals to read a message that attacked the candidate described in the previous message. Subjects in the refutational-same and refutational-different groups exhibited significantly greater resistance to persuasion than subjects who did not receive an inoculation pretreatment.

These findings have intriguing implications for real-world politics. They suggest that a candidate could use inoculation theory to preempt an opponent's plan to sponsor a series of attack commercials. For example, suppose that a Republican candidate for Senate learned that the Democratic opponent planned to attack the candidate's position on Social Security. Rather than waiting until the Democratic candidate's ads aired to broadcast his or her counterattack, the Republican candidate would be better advised to develop an ad in which he or she presented, then refuted, his or her opponent's charges. This ad would help to deflect the impact of the opponent's subsequent attack.

Bill Clinton was apparently aware of this approach when he accepted the Democratic party nomination for president in 1992. Clinton anticipated that the Republicans would attack his record as governor of Arkansas. Clinton attempted to preempt the anticipated attacks by acknowledging that "there is no Arkansas miracle." He then alluded to the benefits he had provided the people of his state while governor.

Forewarning

What happens when people expect to receive a communication on a particular topic? If people are warned that a communicator is going to try to persuade them, do they bolster their psychological defenses? Is there any truth to the expression "Forewarned is Forearmed?"

These questions focus on the effects of forewarning. Forewarning is similar to inoculation in that it is a device communicators can use to confer resistance against persuasion. However, it differs from inoculation in that the pretreatment does not involve exposure to a weakened dose of counterarguments. Instead, forewarning is the general process of informing individuals that they soon will be exposed to a particular message. There are actually two types of forewarning: *forewarning of persuasive intent* and *forewarning of message content* (Cialdini & Petty, 1981; Papageorgis, 1968). In a forewarning of persuasive intent, the communicator informs subjects that an attempt will be made to influence their attitudes. The statement "And now a word from our sponsor" is a classic example of such a forewarning. Several studies have found that forewarning people that a speaker intends to change their attitudes increases their resistance to persuasion (Kiesler & Kiesler, 1964).

A forewarning of message content is more subtle. In this case, subjects are informed only that they will receive a communication on a particular topic. Expecting to be exposed to a counterattitudinal message increases resistance to persuasion, particularly when the message topic is highly involving (Apsler & Sears, 1968; Brock, 1967). For example, suppose you warn someone that you want to talk with them about a new plan to balance the federal budget. The budget deficit is a low-involving issue for most people, hence the warning should not stimulate much counterarguing with the message. If anything, the forewarning should lead to increased persuasion.

Now consider a highly involving issue. Suppose you tell your best friend that you want to talk with him or her about his or her decision to drop out of college. The warning should bolster your friend's resistance and strengthen his or her resolve. Research shows that when the issue is highly involving, forewarnings strengthen resistance to persuasion (Cialdini & Petty, 1981).

What are the psychological processes that mediate the impact of forewarning on resistance to persuasion? A possible answer to this question is suggested by the old saying, "Forewarned is Forearmed." Warning someone that you are going to deliver a counterattitudinal message on an involving issue may stimulate the other person to formulate counterarguments against the discrepant position and to generate supportive thoughts in favor of his or her own position.

Petty and Cacioppo (1977) conducted a study to test this explanation, which was based on the cognitive response approach. They found that subjects who were warned that they would hear a counterattitudinal message on an involving topic were more likely to list counterarguments on the topic than subjects who did not receive this warning. A second experiment offered stronger support for the cognitive response view. Thus, expecting to receive a discrepant message on an involving topic causes the individual to generate arguments opposing the other position on the issue. This anticipatory counterargumentation strengthens the person's position prior to the communication, thereby inhibiting subsequent persuasion (Cialdini & Petty, 1981).

Distraction

You're sitting around at a friend's house, sipping wine and listening to a mutual acquaintance explain why she believes that the government should ban the sale of rock albums that contain violent and suggestive lyrics. You do not think that even the most obscene rock albums should be banned, so you're challenging the arguments that are being put forth by your opinionated acquaintance. Suddenly, there is a loud noise. Someone has run into the punch bowl and has knocked over the assortment of liquor, soft drinks, and food. There is a lot of commotion and you keep glancing over to the table to see what is going on. Meanwhile, your friend does not miss a beat. She keeps talking, offering more arguments to support her position. You listen politely, but you find it hard to devote your full attention to the conversation.

A cognitive response analysis of this situation would begin by noting that, under normal conditions, you would be silently challenging the allegations made about the effects of rock music. But the commotion over at the punch bowl has disrupted your normal process of counterarguing against discrepant messages. Given that you have formulated relatively few counterarguments, you should find that you are more sympathetic than usual with your acquaintance's argument that violent rock music should be banned. This is the essence of the distraction hypothesis, the notion that distraction facilitates agreement with a counterattitudinal message by interfering with the production of counterarguments.[1]

A number of studies have investigated the effects of distraction on persuasion. There is general agreement that for distraction to facilitate persuasion, two conditions must be met:

1. The message must evoke counterarguments. If the message does not stimulate counterarguing under normal conditions, then distraction cannot block counterarguments, and, therefore, it cannot facilitate message acceptance.

2. Subjects must attend primarily to the message and not to the external distraction. If the distraction becomes so absorbing that it totally diverts attention from the message, then the message arguments cannot be learned, processed, and integrated into the person's cognitive system.

In addition, Buller (1986) argued, based on a meta-analysis (or statistically based analysis) of the distraction research, that different types of distractors have different effects on attitude change. For example, a distractor that is intentionally manipulated by a source (such as a nonverbal gesture whose meaning conflicts with the spoken message) may have a different impact on attitudes than a distractor that is not controlled by the communicator (such as a loud noise in the auditorium).

A number of theories have been advanced to explain the distraction effect (Buller, 1986; Petty & Brock, 1981). However, the cognitive response model provides the most parsimonious interpretation of the results.[2] A particularly strong demonstration of the mediating impact of cognitive responses was provided by Osterhouse and Brock (1970).

Osterhouse and Brock instructed subjects to listen to a message that advocated an increase in quarterly tuition at Ohio State University under conditions of high, moderate, or no distraction. Highly and moderately distracted subjects were seated before a panel of lights and were asked to call out the number of a series of flashing lights while they listened to a message recommending a tuition increase. Nondistracted subjects listened to the same speech on earphones.

After listening to the speech, subjects completed a questionnaire that assessed attitudes toward the proposed tuition increase. Subjects also listed their thoughts (e.g., counterarguments) on the topic of raising quarterly tuition at Ohio State University.

Highly and moderately distracted subjects had more favorable attitudes toward the tuition increase than did nondistracted subjects. They also generated fewer counterarguments against the tuition increase than did nondistracted subjects. Moreover, the investigators reported that when they statistically eliminated the effects of counterargument production, the relationship between distraction and attitude change was significantly reduced. This suggested that distraction facilitated persuasion by inhibiting the production of counterarguments.[3]

Application. Advertisers regularly try to distract consumers from counterarguing with the claims made in the commercial. They use all sorts of techniques, including sex, humor, and speed of speech. The research that we have reviewed suggests that distraction can facilitate persuasion if it is used wisely and subtly. Distraction should work if the ad ordinarily generates counterarguments, and if the distraction does not prevent people from attending to the message (e.g., people sometimes remember the joke, but forget the product).

As an example, consider the television ads for Miller Lite beer ("Tastes Great–Less Filling"). When the ads first appeared, many consumers probably disputed the notion that a light beer tastes great. Thus, the Miller ads should have evoked counterarguments. Second, the commercials used compelling, but not totally absorbing, distractions (humorous skits involving sports personalities). We do not know for sure what impact the campaign has had on sales of Miller Lite beer. However, advertising experts strongly believe that the ads have helped to make Miller Lite a leader in the light-beer market.

Explanatory Mechanisms

A number of studies, such as the ones we have discussed, have demonstrated that cognitive responses mediate the impact that persuasive communications exert on attitude change. These findings stand in opposition to Hovland, Janis, and Kelley's (1953) contention that message reception (or recall) is a critical mediator of persuasive communication effects. Additional evidence in support of the cognitive response approach comes from studies that have compared the size of the correlation between cognitive responses and post-message attitudes, on the one hand, and recall of message arguments and message attitudes, on the other. Most studies have reported that cognitive response measures are more closely correlated with post-message attitudes than are indices of message recall. What this means is that attitudes toward a message are better predicted by the number of arguments individuals generate in response to the message than by the number of message arguments they can remember.[4]

Several studies have explored the reasons why cognitive responses appear to be so influential. One explanation suggests that people process their own arguments more deeply and extensively than those that are contained in the message. As a result, own arguments are better remembered than message arguments (Greenwald, 1968; Slamecka & Graf, 1978). A second explanation emphasizes that people are more impressed by their own arguments than they are by those contained in the message. Pascal observed that "we are more easily persuaded, in general, by the reasons we ourselves discover than by those which are given to us by others." Perloff and Brock (1980) have suggested that people may regard their arguments as more original and more cogent simply because they are "theirs." These authors argued that:

> Aspects of one's personal space are valued even though these aspects may not be otherwise distinguishable. We prefer our own bed, even though it

is the same as other beds in the barracks or dormitory. We prefer our own place or chair at table. We prefer our towel, although it is identical to your towel. If *external* objects associated with the self can become so coveted, it is not surprising that internal extensions of the self, such as thoughts, dreams, fantasies and the like, can be accorded special value. (p. 82)

In support of this notion, Shavitt and Brock (1986) found that thoughts that implicated the self predicted post-message opinions better than message-related cognitive responses that were not self-relevant.[5]

THE ELABORATION LIKELIHOOD MODEL

Contemporary persuasion research is process-oriented. Scholars believe that if they can understand how a person cognitively processes a message, they can better understand the impact that the message has on the individual's attitudes and behavior. Two cognitive processing models have dominated the field: the Heuristic Model of Persuasion (Chaiken, 1987) and the Elaboration Likelihood Model (ELM) (Petty & Cacioppo, 1986). This section focuses on the ELM because it has generated relatively more research across a variety of social science disciplines. I first discuss the ELM's basic principles and then I examine the research that it has generated.

The ELM evolved from a decade of research on cognitive responses to persuasion. Petty and Cacioppo (1986), who developed the ELM, noted that there was an important shortcoming in the cognitive response approach: It failed to consider the enormous variability in the extent to which people engage in message-relevant thinking. For example, in some situations, people are active message processors: They counterargue vociferously with the message and formulate abstract, complex issue positions. In other contexts, people are more passive: Although they cognitively respond in some way to the message, their thinking is far more superficial. Yet because the cognitive response approach was primarily concerned with explaining the mediating role that cognitions played in the persuasion process, it did not specify the conditions under which issue-relevant thinking was likely and the situations in which it was unlikely.

In an effort to develop a more comprehensive model of the persuasion process, Petty and Cacioppo (1986) developed the Elaboration Likelihood Model. Elaboration refers to "the extent to which a person thinks about the issue-relevant arguments contained in a message" (Petty & Cacioppo, 1986, p. 128). Elaboration can be viewed as falling along a continuum. At one end of the continuum, there is virtually no thinking about the issues discussed in the message, whereas at the other end there is an enormous amount of mental activity, as the individual mulls over and cognitively elaborates on message arguments.

The interesting thing about the ELM is that it postulates that a message can change attitudes or produce resistance to change in one of two ways: by getting the person to do a great deal of thinking about the message, or by inducing the individual to focus on simple, but compelling, cues that are peripheral to the message content. This has led to the assumption that there are two "distinct routes to attitude change," or two very different processes by which a message can influence attitudes. The first pathway is called the *central route,* and the second is termed the *peripheral route.*[6]

Central route processing is characterized by cognitive elaboration. Under this route, individuals engage in a great deal of thinking about the message, and they ultimately incorporate these thoughts into their attitudinal schema. This is the thinking person's route to persuasion inasmuch as messages that trigger central processing require the person to do a great deal of cognitive work. The peripheral route to attitude change could not be more different. Attitude changes that occur under this route do not require any substantive consideration of the message arguments.

Instead, peripheral processing is characterized by an association of the advocated position with positive values or pleasant images. The person accepts the advocated position because the images evoke pleasant memories. Peripheral processing is also typified by the use of simple decision rules, also called heuristics or scripts, such as "The expert is to be believed," "Men are usually right on political issues," or "The message that has a lot of arguments is invariably correct." Notice that reliance on these rules requires very little thought.

Under what conditions will a person centrally process a message? When will a person process a message peripherally? The ELM stipulates that an individual's motivation and ability to process the message will influence his or her choice of processing strategy (see Fig. 5.3). In the next sections, I discuss the impact that motivation and ability exert on processing strategy.

Motivation to Process

Involvement. Can you think of an issue that has important implications for your own life? Perhaps it is a university proposal to raise tuition by 10%, or a state government plan to raise the drinking age to 21. Now think of an issue that has little impact on your day-to-day routines. This might be a proposal to change the language requirement at a local high school or a plan to use a different weed spray in a farm community. Researchers use the term *high-involvement* to describe the first two issues, and the term *low-involvement* to describe the second two concerns. More formally, individuals are said to be high in involvement when they perceive that an issue is personally relevant (i.e., when they believe that the issue bears

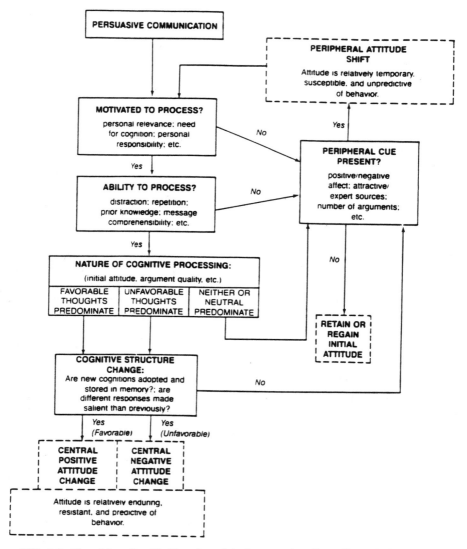

FIG. 5.3 The elaboration likelihood model of persuasion (from Petty & Cacioppo, 1986).

directly on their own lives). Individuals are said to be low in involvement when they believe that the issue has little or no impact on their own lives.

By defining involvement in this manner, ELM researchers were able to generate an interesting hypothesis. They argued that when individuals perceive that an issue has important consequences for their own lives (high-involvement), they will be motivated to engage in a great deal of issue-relevant thinking. Individuals will perceive that it is in their own best interest to carefully consider the arguments in the message. Moreover, even if message recipients oppose the advocated position, they may change their attitudes if the arguments are sufficiently strong and compelling to convince them that it is in their self-interest to adopt the advocated position. Under high-involvement, then, individuals should process a message through the central route—paying careful attention to the message arguments and engaging in a great deal of cognitive elaboration.

On the other hand, under low-involvement, message recipients should have little motivation to attend to the message arguments. Given that the issue is of low personal relevance, they should adopt a relatively simple strategy for processing the message. For example, they should focus on peripheral cues or rely on simple decision rules to help them decide whether to accept the advocated position.

Petty, Cacioppo, and Goldman (1981) conducted an experiment to test the hypothesis that, under high-involvement, individuals thoughtfully process message arguments, whereas under low-involvement they attend to peripheral cues. Students were told that the university was currently reevaluating its academic programs and was soliciting recommendations about prospective changes in policy. Furthermore, they were told that the administration had asked several groups to develop policy statements, that the statements had been tape-recorded for possible use on the university radio station, and that the psychology department was helping the administration by having the statements evaluated for their broadcast quality. Subjects then listened to a tape recording in which a speaker recommended that seniors be required to take a comprehensive examination in their major area of study. Three variables were manipulated: personal involvement, argument quality, and source expertise.

Half of the subjects were told that academic policy changes would be put into effect the following year (high-involvement). The remaining half of the subjects were informed that the changes would take effect in 10 years (low-involvement). Thus, highly involved subjects perceived that the comprehensive exam requirement would affect them directly, whereas low involved subjects did not believe that the academic policy change would have any impact on their own lives.

Half of the subjects read strong arguments on behalf of the advocated position. The arguments employed statistics and evidence ("institution of the exams has led to a reversal in the declining scores on standardized achievement tests at other universities"). The other half of the subjects read weak arguments ("a friend of the author's had to take a comprehensive exam and now had a prestigious academic position").

In addition, half the subjects were led to believe that the policy report had been prepared by a class at a local high school (low expertise), whereas the remaining half of the subjects were told that the report had been developed by the Carnegie Commission of Higher Education, which had been chaired by an education professor at Princeton University (high expertise). After listening to one of the versions of the speech, subjects rated the comprehensive exam on a series of semantic differential and Likert scales.

Under high involvement, argument quality exerted a significant impact on attitudes toward the comprehensive exam. Regardless of whether a high school class or a Princeton professor was the source of the message, strong arguments produced more agreement with the message than did weak arguments. Under low-involvement, the opposite pattern of results emerged. A highly expert source induced more attitude change than did the low expert source, regardless of whether the arguments were strong or weak (see Fig. 5.4).

The ELM provides a parsimonious interpretation of the findings. Under high-involvement, students believed that the institution of a senior comprehensive examination would affect them directly. This heightened motivation led them to pay particular attention to the quality of the arguments. Strong arguments, therefore, exerted a greater impact on their attitudes than did weak ones. Under low-involvement, the students possessed little motivation to process the message arguments. The requirement was 10 years away, they must have thought, and by the time it was instituted they would have long since graduated. Having little reason to devote their full energies to the message, they focused only on the peripheral cue—the expertise of the source.

Other Peripheral Cues. One might summarize the findings by Petty et al. (1981) by noting that, under high-involvement, "what is said" is more important than "who says it," whereas under low-involvement the reverse is true. However, we need to be careful in taking this summary statement too far. The point is not that message appeals are more effective under high-involvement and that source appeals are more impactful under low-involvement. The principal finding is that people engage in issue-relevant thinking under high-involvement, whereas under low-involving conditions they focus on simple cues that are peripheral to the message.

Petty and Cacioppo have argued that under low-involvement conditions a simple message cue (as opposed to a source cue) could exert a significant impact on persuasion. One example of such a message cue is the number of arguments in the message. For example, suppose you were asked to read two persuasive messages, one containing nine arguments, the other containing three arguments. If you did not give the messages much thought, you might conclude that the first message was more persuasive than the second. You might assume that "more arguments are better arguments" or "length means strength" (Eagly & Chaiken, 1984). The problem with this "psychologic" is that it ignores the possibility that the

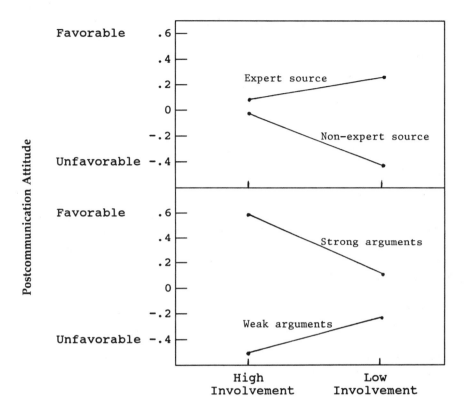

Top panel: Interactive effect of involvement and source expertise on postcommunication attitudes.
Bottom panel: Interactive effect of involvement and argument quality on postcommunication attitudes.

FIG. 5.4 Effects of involvement, source expertise, and argument quality on attitudes (from Petty, Cacioppo, & Goldman 1981).

nine arguments might be all shoddy, whereas the three arguments might be strong. The ELM suggests that people are particularly likely to employ this specious reasoning under low-involvement conditions. Under high-involvement, however, people should give more careful consideration to the quality of the message arguments. Therefore, highly involved subjects should be more persuaded by three strong arguments than by nine weak ones. Petty and Cacioppo (1984) conducted an experiment to test this hypothesis. The results provided strong support for the hypothesized impact of involvement on processing strategy. The authors noted that:

> If college students were evaluating a relatively low-involvement proposal to raise tuition at a distant university . . . or to institute comprehensive

exams at their own university 10 years in the future, the students found the proposal to be more acceptable the more arguments that were presented in support of it. The quality of the arguments didn't have much impact. On the other hand, when the proposal concerned a relatively immediate increase in tuition or the institution of senior comprehensive exams at their own university, acceptance of the proposal depended more on the quality than on the number of issue-relevant arguments provided. (pp. 77–78)

These findings have important implications for the practice of persuasion. They suggest that a persuader needs to modulate his or her approach to fit the involvement level of the audience. If audience members do not perceive that the message will have a direct effect on their own lives, a persuader would be ill-advised to try to coax receivers into attending closely to the message arguments. Instead, he or she should try to focus their attention on simple, but highly persuasive, cues such as the message has many arguments, the speaker is an expert, most people in the audience agree with the speaker, or the message has long been associated with "honest American values."

Such an approach would be doomed to failure under high-involvement. Under this condition, message recipients are highly motivated to carefully examine the message arguments. Consequently, a message emphasizing peripheral cues would be viewed as superficial at best or insulting at worst by highly involved receivers. Under high-involvement, a persuader would be strongly advised to develop a message that taps into receivers' motivation to thoughtfully elaborate on message arguments. Persuaders should either present compelling message arguments or provide receivers with the opportunity to extensively elaborate on the message.

Need for Cognition.   The foregoing research has examined the impact of a situational determinant of motivational level: involvement. Cacioppo and Petty (1982) and Cacioppo, Petty, and Morris (1983) have argued that there are also individual differences in processing strategies. One such personality variable is the need for cognition (NFC).

The need for cognition is "a need to structure relevant situations in meaningful, integrative ways. It is a need to understand and make reasonable the experiential world" (Cohen, Stotland, & Wolfe, 1955, p. 291). People who are high in the NFC are apt to say they "prefer complex to simple problems" and that they "enjoy thinking about an issue even when the results of (their) thought will have no effect on the outcome of the issue." By contrast, individuals who are low in the NFC cognition "feel relief rather than satisfaction after completing a task that required a lot of mental effort" and "would rather do something that requires little thought than something that is sure to challenge (their) thinking abilities"

(Cacioppo & Petty, 1982, pp. 120–121). As you might expect, need for cognition is associated with verbal intelligence. People who are high in NFC also perform well on standardized intelligence tests. However, there is a difference between the NFC construct and intelligence. A person might be highly intelligent, yet not particularly enjoy thinking about issues or problems.

Cacioppo and his colleagues argued that because individuals who score high in need for cognition enjoy tasks that require thinking, they should be likely to expend considerable cognitive effort in evaluating a persuasive message. The authors' data supported this hypothesis (Cacioppo, Petty, & Morris, 1983). Individuals high in NFC reported that they put more effort into evaluating a communication, recalled more message arguments, and made more discriminating judgments of message arguments than did persons low in NFC.

The ELM also stipulates that different types of persuasive appeals will be effective among high-NFC and low-NFC subjects. For high-NFC subjects, messages that encourage issue-relevant thinking should be maximally effective. Consistent with this hypothesis, Cacioppo et al. (1983) reported that argument quality exerted a greater impact on message evaluations and attitudes of individuals high in need for cognition than on those low in NFC (see also, Miller, White, & Boone, 1990).

The ELM also stipulates that peripheral cues should carry more weight among individuals low in need for cognition. Axsom, Yates, and Chaiken (1987) found that a peripheral cue enhanced persuasion among low-NFC subjects, but only under low-involvement conditions. To understand the full implications of these findings, we need to discuss the methodology in detail.

In the study, college students were asked to listen to a tape-recorded segment from a debate on whether probation should be instituted as an alternative to imprisonment. Involvement, argument quality, and audience response (peripheral cue) were manipulated, and need for cognition was measured. Subjects in the high-involvement condition were led to believe that the probation debate had important implications for their own community. Low-involvement subjects were told that the debate had taken place in a different region of the country. Argument quality was varied by providing subjects with either strong or weak arguments in favor of probation as an alternative to imprisonment.

An interesting twist to the experiment was the manipulation of audience response. Previously recorded audience responses were edited into the different versions of the debate. For one group, the audience responded with "five enthusiastic bursts of clapping and cheers of approval, and (the speaker's) concluding statement was met with a sustained round of loud applause." For the other group, the audience gave "only one or two tentative clappers and an occasional cry of derision, and his concluding statement was met with an indifferent, barely polite smattering of applause" (Axsom et al., 1987, p. 33).

The investigators predicted that, under high-involvement, both subjects high in NFC and those low in NFC would be motivated to carefully scrutinize message arguments. Axsom et al. also predicted that, under low-involvement (when the issue was of little personal relevance), low-NFC subjects would be especially likely to take "the easy, lazy way out." That is, under low-involvement, low-NFC subjects were expected to accept the message recommendation when they thought the audience enthusiastically supported the speaker and to reject it when they believed the audience was less than enthusiastic about the speaker's position. The results supported these predictions.

Ability to Process Information

A second determinant of processing strategy (besides motivation) is the individual's ability to process the message. When individuals are able to process the message, they should (everything else being equal) engage in considerable issue-relevant thinking. When they lack this ability, they should rely instead on peripheral cues.

A number of variables influence ability to think about a message, including distraction (individuals are less able to process message arguments when they are distracted) and message repetition (the more frequently a message is repeated, the greater the opportunity to ponder the major arguments in the message). One of the most interesting determinants of ability to process the message is a person's knowledge about an issue.

Think of an issue you know a lot about (let us say, contemporary movies). Now think about an issue about which you know very little (let us say, high-speed printers). The ELM suggests that you would process persuasive messages on these topics very differently, and that persuaders would be advised to use different techniques to change your attitudes on these issues. Given your expertise on the subject of modern films (you know all about different film techniques and you know the strengths and weaknesses of the famous directors), there is every reason to believe you would systematically process a message that argued that today's movies are worse than those produced in the 1960s. The only way that a message could change your attitude on this issue would be to provide message arguments that were highly cogent and that addressed your perspective on contemporary film.

Yet this approach would be ineffective on the subject of high-speed computer printers. Given your ignorance of high-speed printers, you would have difficulty following highly technical arguments concerning the advantages and disadvantages of various printers. On the other hand, the salesperson who used a peripheral approach might be more effective. You might be impressed if the salesperson noted that "I've been working with computers for 10 years and I've never seen a better printer than Epson" (expertise) or proceeded to give you 10 arguments why Epson is better than Toshiba (number of arguments). Consistent with this line of reasoning, Wood, Kallgren, and Preisler (1985) demonstrated that argument quality had a stronger impact on attitudes among individuals with a great deal of knowledge about an issue, whereas message length exerted a stronger influence on those with little knowledge about the topic.

Persistence of Persuasion

The ELM also provides a cognitive interpretation of why some attitudes persist over time, whereas others show less temporal stability. The ELM stipulates that attitude changes based on issue-relevant thinking (central route) should show long-term persistence and should be highly resistant to counterpersuasion. By contrast, opinion changes that result from peripheral cues are expected to show less persistence of persuasion.

The idea is that when people think deeply about an issue (as they do in central route processing), they frequently access their thoughts and rehearse mental arguments. The effect of this is to increase the internal consistency of an attitudinal schema and to make it more resistant to counterpersuasion. By contrast, attitudes changed through the peripheral route do not receive this extensive cognitive elaboration. Consequently, these attitudes are more difficult to defend when they come under attack, and they are more likely to fade away when the peripheral cues become less salient.

A variety of studies have found that attitudes based on issue-relevant thinking persist for a longer period of time, are more resistant to counterpersuasion, and show greater attitude–behavior consistency than attitude changes induced by peripheral cues.[7]

Once again, these findings have interesting implications for real life. They provide a novel explanation of why strongly held attitudes on such topics as religion, abortion, and politics persist over time, whereas other attitudes (such as those that concern convenience goods) have less temporal stability. The former attitudes have received a great deal of cognitive elaboration: People have thought a great deal about their views on these issues. The effect of this thinking is to make these attitudes highly resistant to change (see, also, Tesser, 1978). Of course, this is our common experience: Attempts to influence attitudes about religion or abortion meet with ferocious resistance and are frequently accompanied by strong counterarguments. By contrast, attitudes formed through peripheral cues are likely to be less temporally stable.

Affect and the ELM

The thrust of our discussion so far has been on the role that cognitive factors play in message processing. Recently, researchers have observed that affective factors—particularly mood states—also exert an important impact on the likelihood of message elaboration (Gleicher & Petty, 1992; Schwarz, Bless, & Bohner, 1991; Sypher & Sypher, 1987; Worth & Mackie, 1987).

Petty, Gleicher, and Baker (1991) argued that affect should interact with involvement to influence persuasion. Petty et al. (1991) showed subjects an advertisement for a new pen. The ad was shown in the context of a situation comedy (which induced a positive mood) or a documentary (which produced a neutral mood). High-involvement subjects were told that they could select a free pen at the end of the experiment, and that the pen to be advertised would soon be test marketed in their home town. Low-involvement subjects were informed that the pen would be test marketed in a city far away from their own home town, and that they could select a free gift from a variety of brands of coffee. Cognitive responses and attitudes were then measured.

Interestingly, subjects who were in a pleasant mood evaluated the pen more favorably than those in a neutral mood. Thus, positive mood state influenced attitudes toward the product. Additionally, mood manipulation influenced high- and low-involvement subjects for different reasons. Under low-involvement, mood exerted a direct impact on attitudes; in this condition, mood operated as a peripheral cue. The mere association of the product with the good feelings evoked by the comedy enhanced affective evaluations of the pen. On the other hand, under high-involvement, the effect of mood on attitudes was mediated by thought production. As Petty et al. (1991) noted, "when subjects were motivated to think, positive affect increased the proportion of positive thoughts generated." These findings are generally consistent with the ELM prediction that, like other persuasion variables, affect can serve in different roles in different situations.

Thus, it is simpleminded to assume that an advertisement can change attitudes simply by putting people in a good mood. The ELM suggests that this technique may work under low-involvement (or for low-involvement products like soft drinks). But it is unlikely to suffice when the individual is moderately or highly involved in the product. Under these conditions, affect may exert a powerful impact on attitudes, but the impact is likely to be mediated by thoughts, ideas, and other cognitive processes.

Complicating Factors

Up to this point, the predictions made by the ELM have been elegant and straightforward. However, when we look at the model in more depth, we find that there are several intricacies and complications that require further explanation. The first involves the biased processing of message arguments, and the second issue concerns the ability of the same variable to perform different functions under different conditions.

Biased Processing. We have emphasized that when people process messages through the central route, they carefully examine the arguments in the message. We have noted that people will even change their attitudes on the issue, provided that the message provides cogent arguments in support of the advocated position. The research has provided us with a positive view of human nature; it has suggested that if people are motivated to think about an issue, they will look objectively at the evidence and may even change their minds about an issue if the evidence is strong and compelling.

Unfortunately, things are not this simple. There are a variety of situations in which people stubbornly refuse to look at facts supporting the other side and maintain, even when the evidence is equivocal, that they are right and the other guy is wrong (see chapter 9). To account for these perceptual tendencies, Petty and Cacioppo have argued that there are conditions under which individuals can be expected to process information through the central route in a highly biased, "ego-defensive" fashion.

What conditions facilitate biased processing? A key factor is extremity of initial position.[8] When people have extreme views on an issue (e.g., abortion or gun control), they will process the message deeply, centrally, and stubbornly; they will be highly critical of arguments that do not support their point of view. When people have extreme views on an issue, they are inclined to reject information that is inconsistent with their attitudinal schema, and they are likely to accept facts that are schema-consistent (Cacioppo, Petty, & Sidera, 1982).

Multiple Functions. Up to this point, we have emphasized that a given variable serves as a persuasive argument or a peripheral cue. However, it turns out that the *same* variable can serve as an argument or a cue, or it can instigate issue-relevant thinking, depending on the person and the situation.

Consider the case of George Bush's 1988 presidential campaign. Bush developed a number of patriotic appeals that associated him with the flag and other value-laden American symbols. For low-involved voters who did not care much about politics, these symbols probably functioned as peripheral cues; the association of Bush with the flag aroused positive emotions, and the mere association was enough to get them to vote for Bush on election day. However, these symbols probably exerted a different effect on life-long Republicans who actively participated in political activities. For these individuals, the association of Bush with the flag may have instigated a great deal of cognitive activity—it may have helped to remind them that the United States had an obligation to defend freedom and democracy and to continue to build up its military forces. Notice that for some voters, the flag served as a simple, peripheral cue, whereas for others it stimulated a great deal of cognitive elaboration.

In a similar fashion, source attractiveness can serve as a peripheral cue under some conditions and as a persuasive argument in other situations (DeBono & Harnish, 1988; Kahle & Homer, 1985). Under low-involvement, physical attractiveness may serve as a peripheral cue. A low-involved receiver, lacking the motivation to carefully process message arguments, may fall back on the fact that the source is physically attractive as a way to help decide whether to accept the message. The receiver may focus on the messenger rather than the message; accordingly, he or she may decide to accept the message recommendation because he or she likes or identifies with the communicator.

In other situations, physical attractiveness can function as a persuasive argument. For someone trying to decide between two brands of shampoo, the information that an attractive model uses the shampoo is not peripheral to the message—it is central. As Kahle and Homer (1985) said, "if a stunningly attractive person claims to use a beauty product, that product may be assumed to be an element of the beauty formula" (p. 959).[9]

Some scholars have been critical of the notion that the same variable can perform multiple functions. Stiff and Boster (1987) claimed that this ambiguity allows the ELM "to explain all possible outcomes, rendering it practically impossible, in principle, to falsify and of little value for making a priori predictions of experimental outcomes" (p. 251).[10] In response to this, Petty, Cacioppo, Kasmer, and Haugtvedt (1987) have suggested that a careful reading of the ELM makes it possible to make a priori predictions about the effects that situational and individual difference variables exert on message processing. They have emphasized that, depending on the individual and the circumstances, a particular variable can serve as a persuasive argument or a peripheral cue, or it can instigate issue-relevant thinking.

APPLICATIONS: ELECTIONS AND POLITICAL ADVERTISING

Perloff (1984) noted that the ELM has intriguing implications for political advertising. The ELM suggests that different advertising strategies will be effective on high- and low-involvement voters and in elections that arouse a great deal of interest (high-involvement) or little interest (low-involvement). Consider the typical high-involvement election: a school levy. The levy is highly relevant to most voters because it usually involves an increase in property taxes and because it bears on an issue of intense personal concern—the education of their children. Therefore, most voters will systematically process the arguments contained in political commercials. This suggests that advertising strategists need to construct arguments that will be perceived as strong and compelling by the voters in the district. A strategist who is working for a group that supports the levy might emphasize that if the levy fails teachers will be fired, and class sizes will increase. If the consultant is working for a group that opposes the levy, he or she might want to emphasize that monies collected from previous levies have done nothing to improve the quality of local schools.

Consider an election that is low in involvement: a state referendum on government regulation of the insurance industry. Although voters are concerned about the cost of their own insurance premiums, they probably have little interest in whether the insurance industry should be regulated. Messages that contain complex arguments or that require extensive cognitive activity are likely to fall on deaf ears. Although these types of messages would probably exert a large impact in a high-involvement campaign, they are likely to be ineffective in a low-involvement election. In a low-involvement race, the key word is *simplicity*. Thus, advertisements in favor of insurance regulation might depict insurance companies as "rich fat cats" who do not care about "the little guy." This type of appeal is easy for most people to understand, and it employs the popular caricature of businessmen as "rich fat cats." Ads that oppose regulation might invoke the "length means strength" script: They might run a long list of prestigious groups (American Bar Association, Better Business Bureau) that oppose regulation of the insurance industry. People might not know who the groups are, but the fact that so many groups oppose the referendum would be a powerful argument for low-involvement voters.[11]

Just as advertising strategists need to consider the voters' level of involvement, so too do they need to adapt their strategies to individuals who are high and low in the need for cognition. Voters who are high in the need for cognition are likely to process political information more systematically and deeply than their counterparts who are low in the need for cognition.

Ahlering (1987) found that voters high in the need for cognition were more likely than lows to follow the 1984 presidential and vice-presidential debates. High-NFC voters also held more beliefs about the presidential and vice-presidential candidates than did their low-NFC counterparts. Cacioppo, Petty, Kao, and Rodriguez (1986) examined the relationship between need for cognition and consistency between political attitudes and voting behavior. These investigators assessed students' attitudes toward the 1984 presidential and vice-presidential candidates 8 weeks before the election. Following the election, the researchers obtained a self-report of actual voting behavior. The relationship between preelection attitudes and postelection voting behavior was stronger among high-NFC subjects than among lows. To explain this finding, Cacioppo et al. (1986) argued that high-NFC voters were more likely to have thought about the campaign issues than their low-NFC counterparts. Attitudes formed on the basis of issue-relevant thinking persist for a longer period of time and exert a stronger impact on behavior than do attitudes formed by means of peripheral cues.

CONCLUSIONS

In this chapter, I have discussed two contemporary cognitive models of persuasion: the cognitive response approach and the Elaboration Likelihood Model (ELM).

The cognitive response approach has advanced research on persuasion by showing how thoughts and self-generated mental reactions influence recipients' evaluations of messages. This approach served as a needed corrective to earlier theories, which assumed that individuals passively and mindlessly processed persuasive messages. Research has demonstrated that cognitive responses help to mediate the impact that role-playing, inoculation, forewarning, and distraction exert on persuasion.[12] One of the hallmarks of the cognitive response approach is its emphasis on self-persuasion. The core notion is that messages succeed in changing attitudes to the extent that they induce receivers to favorably elaborate on message arguments. Cognitive response research has forced us to revise the notion that persuasion is something that a persuader does "to" an audience. Instead, persuasion is more properly viewed as the attempt to convince an individual to change his or her own attitudes about an issue or person.

The ELM and other contemporary models of persuasion (Chaiken, 1987) focus on the cognitive processes by which communications achieve effects. The ELM emphasizes that messages can change attitudes by instigating extensive issue-relevant thinking (central processing) or by inducing the individual to focus on simple, but compelling, peripheral cues. Motivation and ability factors determine whether an individual will engage in central or peripheral processing.

By emphasizing the psychological processes that underlie persuasion effects, the ELM has provided a fresh perspective on a variety of classical persuasion phenomena. Basically, the ELM suggests that there are no hard and fast rules about the impact that a given variable exerts on the persuasion process. In contrast to earlier theories, which suggested that a particular variable had a constant and predictable effect on persuasion, the ELM stipulates that the effect that a given variable exerts on the attitude change process depends on the message recipient's motivation and ability to process the message. Thus, the ELM argues that it is impossible to say

EXHIBIT 5-1   133

that source credibility or factual evidence has "this or that effect" on the audience. Instead, it emphatically asserts that the effects depend on the person's motivation and ability to process the message.

The ELM has generated numerous studies; most have supported the model's fundamental postulates. Nevertheless, a number of issues require further consideration. For example, how do people simultaneously process central and peripheral information.[13] Can clearer a priori predictions be made concerning the processing implications of a particular variable? How do situational and personality factors interact to influence processing strategy?

From a practitioner's point of view, the ELM has enormous implications. It provides guidance regarding the types of strategies persuaders should use on high- and low-involvement audiences, and on audiences that differ in their ability to process communications. From the perspective of the receiver, the ELM helps to demystify portions of the persuasion process. It offers a clear and compelling explanation of why people will sometimes accept a message recommendation without engaging in any apparent thought, and why, under other conditions, people will change their attitudes only after they have thought long and hard about the message arguments.

* * *

EXHIBIT 5-1
MEASURING COGNITIVE RESPONSES

"How does one study objectively something as unobservable as a cognitive response to a stimulus?" This question, raised by Cacioppo, Harkins, and Petty (1981), points up the difficulty of scientifically measuring thoughts and mental reactions to persuasive messages.

Like attitudes, cognitive responses are hypothetical constructs that cannot be observed directly. Consequently, researchers have had to devise a variety of methods to measure cognitive responses (e.g., Miller & Baron, 1973; Wright, 1981). The most common method has been to ask subjects to write down their thoughts following exposure to a persuasive message.

I illustrate the thought-listing methodology by drawing on actual comments made about the Gulf War. Most of the comments that appear were made by American teenagers in the winter of 1991 in response to questions posed by two professional interviewers: Marian Salzman and Ann O'Reilly. For the present purposes, I ask the reader to imagine that these comments were made in response to George Bush's speech announcing that the United States was at war with Iraq. To illustrate the thought-listing methodology, I reprint Bush's speech, which you read earlier. Then I categorize the thoughts using the classification scheme developed by Cacioppo et al. (1981).

Halfway around the world we are engaged in a great struggle in the skies and on the seas and sands. We know why we're there. We are Americans, part of something larger than ourselves. . . . Most Americans know instinctively why we are in the Gulf. They know we had to stop Saddam now, not later. They know that this brutal dictator will do anything, will use any weapon, will commit any outrage, no matter how many innocents suffer. They know we must make sure that control of the world's oil resources does not fall into his hands only to finance further aggression. . . . The winds of change are with us now. The forces of freedom are together, united. And we move toward the next century more confident than ever that we have the will at home and abroad to do what must be done: the hard work of freedom.

In a typical study, subjects would read or listen to this message and would then receive the following instructions:

We are interested in your thoughts about George Bush's speech. Please write down the first idea that comes to your mind on the first line, the second idea that occurs to you on the second, and so on. Please put only one idea or thought on a line.

Coding Procedure

Category 1: Polarity. A thought can be favorable to the advocated position, unfavorable to advocacy, or neutral. Favorable thoughts are frequently called *proarguments,* and unfavorable thoughts are called *counterarguments.*

Favorable Thought: "I completely support President Bush's actions. He is helping Kuwait because Saddam should not have been there in the first place."[14]

Unfavorable Thought: "I do not agree with President Bush's actions, because I feel there could have been other ways to solve the problem."[15]

Neutral Thought: "I'm ambivalent about what the President said."

Category 2: Origin. A cognitive response can originate with the message and simply restate a message argument (message-originated), offer a reaction to or an illustration of the message arguments (modified message-originated), or mention ideas and arguments that cannot be directly traced to the message itself (recipient-generated).

Message-Originated: "I support President Bush because I think that Saddam was wrong and we had to stop him."[16]

Modified Message-Originated: "I support President Bush completely. . . . He decided to act before Saddam got a chance to really take over. And Saddam Hussein needed to be stopped before he could use nuclear weapons."[17]

Recipient-Generated: "I do not think there will ever be peace in the Middle East because of the oil and so many countries involved with it. All the countries will never agree on anything."[18]

Category 3: Target. Thoughts can focus on the message topic itself, the source, the audience, or the channel of communication.

EXHIBIT 5-1   **135**

Message-Topic: "I support President Bush because America had a responsibility to stop Iraqi aggression."

Source-Oriented: "I feel that perhaps he (Bush) knows more information compared to what the rest of America knows.[19]

Audience-Centered: "I do not think the public will buy this speech."

Channel-Oriented: "It was a good speech for television."

6
"Who Says It":
Source Factors in Persuasion

Ⅰt was summer 1963, and hundreds of thousands of people converged on Washington, DC, to protest racial prejudice in America. Their inspirational leader was Reverend Martin Luther King, the civil rights leader who had organized so many protests during the 1950s and early 1960s. Later in the day, after the march had culminated at the Lincoln Memorial, King spoke, delivering one of the most eloquent and impassioned speeches in the history of American public address. Here is how his wife, Coretta Scott King (1969), recalled the audience's reaction to her husband's speech:

> Two hundred and fifty thousand people applauded thunderously, and voiced in a sort of chant, *Martin Luther King*. . . . He started out with the written speech, delivering it with greater eloquence. . . . When he got to the rhythmic part of demanding freedom *now* and wanting jobs *now,* the crowd caught the timing and shouted *now* in a cadence. Their response lifted Martin in a surge of emotion to new heights of inspiration. Abandoning his written speech, forgetting time, he spoke from his heart, his voice soaring magnificently out over that great crowd and over to all the world. It seemed to all of us there that day that his words flowed from some higher place, through Martin, to the weary people before him. Yea— Heaven itself opened up and we all seemed transformed. (pp. 238–239)

Coretta King's description captures many of our most vivid images of persuasive speakers. The word often used to describe these speakers is *charisma*. Charisma is used to describe the qualities exhibited by communicators ranging from John Kennedy to Jesse Jackson to Billy Graham. To many of us, it seems to capture the essence of the most persuasive speakers of an era. It is a quality that many people wish they could grab onto and possess for themselves.

What is charisma? Coined over a century ago by German sociologist Max

Weber (1968) charisma is: "a certain quality of the individual personality by virtue of which he is set apart from ordinary men and women and treated as endowed with supernatural, superhuman, or at least exceptional powers and qualities" (p. 240).

Weber was careful to qualify his definition by noting that these exceptional individuals do not become powerful leaders unless the situation is right (Riggio, 1987). A leader must attract followers, and the followers must be supremely devoted to the cause. Yet, despite Weber's attempt to qualify his definition, charisma continues to call to mind simple images. It is a "god term," in the terminology of Weaver (1953)—a concept that evokes so many positive images that we do not subject it to critical scrutiny.

From a scientific perspective, charisma is a difficult concept to define. It encompasses so many different aspects of the persuasion situation— including the qualities of the source, the verbal style of the message, and the channel used to communicate the message—that it is difficult to operationalize. Perhaps charisma involves some dynamic combination of source, message, and channel attributes, coupled with a keen appreciation of how to fine-tune these variables to reach a particular audience at a particular time. We do not know for sure. What we do know is that a scientific analysis requires a systematic examination of each variable, one step at a time. We begin with the source. The remainder of this chapter reviews research on the role source factors play in the persuasion process.

SOURCE CREDIBILITY

In October 1991, Americans were glued to their television sets. They were not watching the World Series; instead their attention was riveted on the Senate hearings for Supreme Court nominee Clarence Thomas. However, it was not Thomas' positions on social issues that fascinated the viewing public; it was the controversy surrounding the charge, leveled by one of his former employees (Anita Hill), that Thomas had sexually harassed her. Hill described the details of the alleged harassment luridly to the members of the Senate Judiciary Committee. Thomas vehemently denied that he had sexually harassed Anita Hill.

Everywhere, it seemed, people were asking each other: Who do you believe, Thomas or Hill? Which one is telling the truth? Because only the accuser and accused knew the truth, viewers had to rely on their interpretations of the evidence and their judgments of what they saw. To many people, this came down to a question of credibility: Which person was the more credible witness?

Communicator credibility is probably the oldest concept in persuasion research. It dates back to Aristotle, who wrote in the 4th century B.C. that:

Of the modes of persuasion furnished by the spoken word there are three kinds. The first kind depends on the personal character of the speaker. . . . We believe good men more fully and more readily than others; this is true generally whatever the question is, and absolutely true where exact certainty is impossible and opinions are divided. . . . It is not true, as some writers assume in their treatises on rhetoric, that the personal goodness revealed by the speaker contributes nothing to his power of persuasion; on the contrary, his character may almost be called the most effective means of persuasion he possesses. (Roberts, 1954, pp. 24–25)

Aristotle lay the groundwork for the scholarly study of persuasion. Yet his approach gave rise to several questions. Contrary to Aristotle's argument, we can think of a number of speakers who were not "good," who possessed little character, and yet were enormously persuasive. Adolf Hitler, Joseph Stalin, and Ayatollah Khomeini are among the many examples of history's villains who have been highly effective persuaders. We also do not know what Aristotle meant by character, or what it is about "good men" that makes them more believable. In addition, Aristotle did not supply us with any empirical evidence that people actually believe "good men" more than others.

Building on Aristotle's theory, contemporary researchers have employed two different approaches to study source credibility. Hovland et al. (1953) took a deductive approach, defining credibility a priori or on logical grounds. They viewed credibility as consisting of two components: expertise and trustworthiness. Communication researchers adopted a different strategy. Defining credibility as "the attitude toward a speaker held by a listener" (McCroskey, 1966), they reasoned that it was more useful to investigate how message recipients perceived a particular communicator than to simply assume that credibility consisted of x or y components. Their approach was inductive. They sought to explicate credibility by obtaining information from the external world—specifically, from recipients of persuasive messages. As we shall see, this approach produced useful insights. However, it also was vulnerable to methodological criticisms.

One of the classic studies that explored the dimensions of source credibility was conducted by Berlo, Lemert, and Mertz (1969). Berlo et al. asked subjects to evaluate a number of different sources who (they were told) were speaking on various issues. The sources and contexts were:

1. Public source, speaking in a relevant context: Former United Nations Ambassador Adlai Stevenson speaking on the United Nations; former Chinese Premier Mao Tse-Tung talking on China's domestic problems.

2. Public source, speaking in an irrelevant context: baseball player Mickey Mantle speaking on organized crime; ex-Teamsters boss Jimmy Hoffa talking about abstract art.

3. Public source, with no context specified: John F. Kennedy; Cuban Premier Fidel Castro.

4. Interpersonal sources: "Each respondent was asked to recall the names of three people he knew well: one whose opinion he respected highly, one whose opinion he did not respect, and one whose opinion he neither respected nor lacked respect for" (p. 566).

Subjects rated each of the sources on 35 semantic differential scales that included "informed–uninformed," "just–unjust," and "active–passive." The researchers then employed a statistical technique called *factor analysis,* which determines whether large amounts of data can be reduced to a common set of factors. Berlo et al. found that three credibility factors emerged from their factor analysis of subjects' responses. Specifically, they discovered that credibility consisted of three dimensions: *safety, qualification,* and *dynamism.* Safe communicators were perceived to be kind, friendly, and just. Qualified communicators were viewed as trained, experienced, and informed. Dynamic sources were seen as bold, active, and energetic.

Berlo and his colleagues found that source credibility was a multidimensional concept, consisting of many dimensions rather than one. These dimensions were also independent: A communicator could be viewed as safe, but unqualified, or as dynamic, but dishonest. (This is, of course, our experience in everyday life: Few speakers get high ratings on all dimensions; instead, they are evaluated positively on some traits, and negatively on others.)

Other studies also have found that credibility consists of several dimensions (Markham, 1968; McCroskey, Holridge, & Toomb, 1974; Whitehead, 1968). Expertise and trustworthiness have emerged consistently, whereas other factors (notably dynamism and sociability) have emerged in particular studies (Miller, 1987).

Critique

Although these studies have enriched our understanding of the dimensional structure of source credibility, they have been criticized on several grounds. In a 1976 article, Cronkhite and Liska identified a number of shortcomings in the source credibility studies. In essence, they argued that the way in which a researcher frames the question determines the answer he or she gets. They noted that different researchers have asked different questions, using very different procedures to measure source credibility. Some investigators asked subjects to assess the credibility of famous persons supposedly giving speeches on particular topics, others asked subjects to watch a newscast and rate the newscasters' credibility, whereas still other researchers instructed students to evaluate hypothetical communicators solely on the basis of tape-recorded introductions. The use of such different procedures, coupled with wide variation in investigators' choice of scales and rating procedures, made it difficult to generalize the results beyond the individual studies.

One particularly glaring problem noted by Cronkhite and Liska in their critique of the factor-analytic studies was the confounding of the source and the rating scale (i.e., the tendency for subjects to interpret a scale of credibility questions differently when rating different sources).

For example, in one study discussed by Cronkhite and Liska, subjects were asked to rate the credibility of a variety of different sources, ranging from the U.S. government to sources they knew (such as their parents). Cronkhite and Liska observed that a scale assessing the "maturity" of a source meant very different things, depending on the source that subjects were asked to evaluate. For example, when evaluating the maturity of the government, subjects may have had responsibility and efficiency in mind, but when rating their father they may have been thinking of something quite different, possibly their father's morality or generosity. Yet researchers frequently lumped ratings of government together with ratings of father without considering the fact that the two ratings meant very different things to subjects. In the final analysis, Cronkhite and Liska pointed out:

> The particular factor structure which an investigator finds will depend on the rating scales he chooses, the speakers he chooses, the raters he chooses, the function the raters perceive themselves and the speaker to be performing vis-a-vis each other and vis-a-vis the speech topic or the circumstances in which the speech is delivered, and the structure depends finally upon the investigator's choice of a particular method of factor analysis. (p. 92)

Contextual Influences

Cronkhite and Liska emphasized that an adequate conceptualization of credibility must take into account the functions a source performs for a receiver in a particular context. Different attributes will be salient, depending on the function the communicator performs for the individual (see also, Liska, 1978). Consider a therapist who helps a person cope with his or her job and personal life. In this case, credibility may involve composure and sensitivity. Think about the biologist who gives a talk on new developments in genetic engineering. An audience will probably evaluate the speaker on his or her knowledge and cognitive skills: expertise (not composure) may be the critical dimension.

In addition to function, time also determines which dimension of credibility will be most important. This is particularly true in politics, where cultural changes make different components of credibility salient (Kinder & Sears, 1985). For example, in 1976, the memory of Watergate lingered in voters' minds. Consequently, honesty and trustworthiness were regarded as particularly important qualities for a president to posses. Jimmy Carter seemed to embody these qualities more than Gerald Ford, and (for this reason, as well as many others) Carter was elected president. Four years later, it was a different story. With inflation hovering above 15%, and Americans held hostage in Tehran, voters valued "leadership" and "authority." Ronald Reagan, not Jimmy Carter, seemed the embodiment of these traits, and Reagan was elected by a wide margin.

Culture also influences credibility judgments. One study found that American students evaluated political leaders on the basis of their competence and character, whereas Japanese students employed two additional factors: consideration and appearance (King, Minami, & Samovar, 1985).

Size of the audience also makes a difference. When a politician speaks before a large rally, audiences may ask "Was he or she dynamic?" But if the setting is a small-group question-and-answer session, they may query instead "Does he or she care?"

Although context influences credibility judgments, we should not push context effects too far. Although individuals do use different criteria to evaluate speakers in different situations, they also use some criteria more than others. Expertise and trustworthiness are apt to be highly salient criteria for most message recipients (Miller, 1987). Thus, although Hovland et al. (1953) probably oversimplified things when they declared that expertise and trustworthiness were the fundamental dimensions underlying credibility, they also were on target in identifying these particular factors as components of the credibility construct.

Now that we have discussed the nature and structure of source credibility, we can move on to a central issue in persuasion research: the impact that source attributes exert on the persuasion process. Four key source dimensions are discussed: expertise, trustworthiness, similarity, and physical attractiveness.

EXPERTISE

Although many people believe that all you have to do to persuade someone is to declare yourself an expert, the fact is that expertise is not a panacea. Some studies have found that expertise enhances persuasion, whereas others have found that expertise has relatively little persuasive impact (see, e.g., Benoit, 1991; Harmon & Coney, 1982; Hovland & Weiss, 1951; Johnson & Scileppi, 1969; Rosnow & Robinson, 1967; Sternthal, Dholakia, & Leavitt, 1978). Indeed, when individuals have strong positions on the issue or are distracted from attending to the message, expertise is likely to have minimal effects. Think of an issue that you care a lot about: for example abortion, the environment, your career priorities. Now suppose an expert argued for a position with which you disagreed. Do you really think that you would change your mind about the issue "just because an expert said so?"

Instead of asking "Do expert sources change attitudes?", we should ask "When do expert sources change attitudes," and "Why?" We obtain a useful perspective on these latter questions by examining the Elaboration Likelihood Model (ELM).

According to the ELM, communicator expertise is particularly effective when individuals lack the motivation or ability to process the message. For example, suppose you are listening to a speaker discuss the problem of the nation's budget deficit. Let us assume the deficit is not one of your favorite topics—in fact, it is a subject about which you know very little. The ELM suggests that you would be unlikely to devote much cognitive energy to the message. Instead, the model predicts that you would seek out a simple strategy for making the decision. One convenient rule of thumb would be the notion that "Experts know their stuff."

On the other hand, if you were interested in the budget deficit, or were somewhat knowledgeable about the topic, source expertise would have a considerably different impact. The fact that the source was an expert might draw you into the message; you might pay more attention to the message than if the source was described as someone who had little training in the area (Petty & Cacioppo, 1986). However, source expertise in and of itself would not be enough to swing your position on the issue.

Source expertise is probably most effective when our psychological defenses are down—when we do not care about the issue or do not think we have the ability to counterargue the message arguments. Thus, low-involved, low-ability receivers are likely to be easy prey for clever persuaders who can claim to have developed expertise in the particular issue under consideration. (See also Exhibit 6-1: Timing the Expert's Identification, p. 153.)

TRUSTWORTHINESS

It was often said that Walter Cronkite was "the most trusted man in America." Cronkite anchored the CBS evening news for more than 20 years, and in the eyes of many viewers he could be relied on to bring a truthful account of the day's events. Some observers went so far as to say (only partly in jest) that if Walter wanted to run for president of the United States, he could have the nomination hands down.

What was it about Walter Cronkite that engendered such respect? What causes people to trust some communicators and to distrust others? These questions strike at the heart of source trustworthiness, perhaps the most important source attribute (Sereno & Hawkins, 1967). A communicator is perceived as trustworthy to the extent that the audience has confidence "in the communicator's intent to communicate the assertions he considers most valid" (Hovland, Janis, & Kelley, 1953, p. 21). The critical factor in source trustworthiness is the audience's perceptions of the source's intentions or its attributions of the communicator's behavior.

Eagly and her colleagues have developed an attribution-based theory of source credibility, and particularly of source trustworthiness. Eagly, Wood, and Chaiken (1978) argued that people want to understand why a communicator takes a particular position. Consequently, they are motivated to make attributions about why the speaker advocates a particular position on an issue (e.g., Why did my friend the athlete say such great things about the university's intramural facility? Is it because she's a jock herself or because she's getting paid by the athletic office?). Eagly and her colleagues contended that these causal attributions—or explanations for the communicator's behavior—influence the judgments that message recipients make about the source's credibility. Perceptions of communicator credibility are (in theory) diminished when audience members infer that the speaker possesses either a *knowledge bias* or a *reporting bias*.

Knowledge Bias

Suppose you were told that a liberal young female professor was going to talk to your class about affirmative action for women. Suppose you learned that a Hispanic social worker was scheduled to give a talk on "Issues in Recruitment of Minorities at the Workplace." What if you heard that a 70-year-old city councilman planned to make a speech on catastrophic health insurance for elderly citizens? In all probability, you would hazard some guesses, or develop some expectations, about what each speaker was going to say on each issue. Most of us might expect that the young liberal woman would speak in favor of affirmative action for women, the Hispanic social worker would push for more aggressive recruiting of minority employees, and the 70-year-old city councilman would argue for an increase in catastrophic health insurance for senior citizens.

If the speakers confirmed your expectations, you would conclude that they possessed a *knowledge bias*. That is, you would assume that their background (gender, ethnicity, age) and knowledge about the topic had prevented them from looking objectively at the various sides of the issue. You would not regard them as particularly credible sources of information. Now suppose the speakers disconfirmed your expectations—suppose they surprised you.

Suppose the young female professor argued against affirmative action for women, the Hispanic social worker roundly rejected the need for increased recruitment of minorities, and the 70-year-old councilman lambasted health insurance policies that put elderly persons ahead of other needy members of the population. You might wonder why the speakers took these unexpected positions. In the absence of other explanations, you might conclude that the arguments for these positions were so compelling that they overrode the three speakers' personal biases. That is, you might assume that the speakers had no choice but to disregard their biases in light of the superior truth value the arguments possessed. Consistent with these speculations, Eagly, Wood, and Chaiken (1978) found that subjects displayed greater attitude change when they believed that the communicator had taken a position that did not reflect a knowledge bias.

The knowledge bias helps us understand many instances of real-life persuasion. As an example, consider the case of a public service announcement (PSA) that former President Ronald Reagan made on AIDS in the late-1980s. Reagan urged compassion and tolerance for persons with AIDS; he noted that anyone can get AIDS, even children. The PSAs attracted considerable attention and (in my view) were highly credible. The knowledge bias helps us understand their probable effects. One would not have expected Ronald Reagan to have taken a strong position on behalf of persons with AIDS. As president, he took a very conservative position on the AIDS issue. In fact, he gave AIDS a rather low priority on the national agenda. How can one explain Reagan's change of heart? One explanation is that the message that persons with AIDS deserve compassion is so strong and so compelling that even Ronald Reagan was forced to acknowledge its validity. (See also, Exhibit 6-2: The Convert Communicator, p. 154.)

Reporting Bias

Message recipients frequently infer that the pressures of a situation have compromised a communicator's willingness to be open and honest. When audience members believe that situational pressures have caused a speaker to withhold (or not report) certain facts or interpretations, they have (in Eagly's terminology) concluded that the speaker is guilty of a reporting bias.[1]

Evidence for this notion was provided in a study conducted by Eagly, Wood, and Chaiken (1978). Subjects were told that an aluminum company had been dumping industrial waste into a local river. Students then read a speech in which mayoral candidate Jack Reynolds took a strong proenvironmental position on the waste-disposal issue. Reynolds argued that the company should be forced to stop production and institute a major overhaul of its waste-disposal system. One group of subjects was told that Reynolds had taken this stand in a talk before an audience concerned with environmental issues; a second group was told that Reynolds had presented his argument to an audience concerned with business issues, particularly the continued operation of the aluminum company. When subjects believed that Reynolds had delivered the speech to a proenvironmental group, they regarded Reynolds as "insincere" and "manipulative." When they were led to believe that Reynolds had made the speech to a group concerned with business issues, they regarded him as more sincere and less manipulative. In addition, subjects displayed more attitude change when they believed that Reynolds had given the speech to a group concerned with business issues.

How can we explain these findings? Apparently, people assume that speakers feel constrained to tell an audience what they think the audience wants to hear. Thus, when they were told that Reynolds had given a proenvironmental speech to a group concerned with environmental issues, they assumed that he had taken this position to please the audience. Consequently, they perceived Reynolds to be insincere and even manipulative. On the other hand, when subjects believed that Reynolds had delivered the same speech to a group concerned with business interests, they had a much different reaction. In this case, they could not conclude that he had taken the proenvironmental position to please his audience. Instead, they had to come up with a different explanation. A plausible explanation was that the proenvironmental message was so compelling and "obviously correct" that Reynolds felt he had an obligation to present this view, even at the risk of offending his audience. This made Reynolds a more trustworthy speaker and it increased confidence in the validity of his message.

The reporting bias helps us understand why voters often react with skepticism when they hear politicians promise elderly citizens that they will not cut social security or when they read that two candidates for the U.S. Senate told auto workers that they will work to block imports of Japanese cars. Voters assume that these statements reflect a situational factor—a desire to get elected. Politicians whose statements are thought to reflect such a reporting bias are quickly disbelieved and distrusted. (In 1984, this belief plagued Walter Mondale, the Democratic presidential candidate. Many voters believed that Mondale told every special interest group that he would give them what they wanted, and this perception dogged Mondale throughout the campaign.)

SIMILARITY

During the summer of 1992, Bill Clinton and Al Gore launched their presidential campaign by embarking on a bus trip across Middle America. Clinton and Gore wore short sleeve shirts and Levis. They threw the football around an open field. They talked about their small town backgrounds. The candidates were trying to accentuate their similarity with the voters. In doing so they were trying to capitalize on a classic finding in persuasion research: Communicators are more likely to change attitudes if they are believed to be similar rather than dissimilar to those they seek to influence. A number of studies have found that similarity between source and receiver enhances persuasion.

In an early study, Brock (1965) chose a real-world locale (the paint department of a retail store) to explore the impact that similarity exerts on the persuasion process. The experimenter approached customers who were about to purchase some paint. For some of the customers (similarity condition), he told them that he had just bought the same amount of paint as they planned to purchase. The experimenter added that he had bought a different brand of paint than they intended to buy "and it worked out beautifully." Then he commented that he had also bought some of the paint that they planned to purchase, and "honestly it didn't turn out as well at all." For other subjects (dissimilarity condition), he gave the same spiel, but he noted that he had bought 20 times as much paint as they planned to buy. In both cases, the experimenter recommended that the customer purchase the brand of paint that had worked out so well in his own case.

Sixty-four percent of the subjects in the similarity condition followed the experimenter's recommendation and purchased the recommended brand of paint, compared with only 39% of those in the dissimilarity condition. Similarity led to significantly more compliance with the experimenter's recommendations than dissimilarity, even when the experimenter urged that the customer buy a more expensive brand than he or she originally had intended to buy.

One of the persistent issues in attitude research is the type of similarity that exerts the greatest impact on receivers' judgments. McCroskey, Richmond, and Daly (1975) argued that there are four critical dimensions of perceived similarity: *attitude, morality, background,* and *appearance.* According to McCroskey and his colleagues, message recipients ask if a communicator shares their attitude ("does he think like me?"), morality ("are his morals like mine?"), background ("is his social class similar to mine?"), and appearance ("does he look like me?"). Of the four components, perceived similarity in attitudes and morals are probably most important. Indeed, source–receiver similarity along these dimensions exerts the greatest impact on persuasion (Simons, Berkowitz, & Moyer, 1970).

Understanding Why

There are two reasons why people go along with the views espoused by similar others. The first view emphasizes liking. People like those who share their attitudes (Byrne, 1971) and liking enhances persuasion (Wright, 1966). (See Exhibit 6-3: The Power of Liking, p. 155.) A second explanation emphasizes social comparison processes. In his social comparison theory, Festinger (1954) argued that people tend to compare themselves to similar others. These comparisons then set in motion cognitive processes that facilitate persuasion. Consider the following example.

Let us say you plan to work as a newspaper reporter after you graduate. Suppose you also have a very positive attitude toward the media and the First Amendment. Suppose you get to know the student sitting next to you in an upper level communication class, and you find out she is like you in all these respects. One day your new acquaintance starts talking about a topic you're not familiar with—mandatory drug testing for professional athletes. Chances are you will react positively to what she has to say about this issue—or at least more favorably than if the acquaintance did not share your attitudes and values. Given that she agrees with you on the other issues, you probably will assume that the acquaintance uses the same criteria as you do to make up her mind about the drug testing issue (Freedman, Carlsmith, & Sears, 1970).

Limits

Similarity is not a panacea. It does not always induce attitude change. Under some conditions, similarity induces persuasion; in other cases, it has very little impact on attitudes. Two important determinants of the impact of similarity on attitudes are the relevance of the similarity and the factual basis of the decision.

Source–receiver similarity is more likely to affect attitudes when the similarity is relevant to the message. When the similarity is irrelevant to the communication, it will have little or no impact on attitudes (Berscheid, 1966). Thus, computer salespeople are likely to be more effective if the sales reps confide that they share the customer's view that many word processing packages are difficult to follow than if they acknowledge that they share the customer's distrust of both Democratic and Republican politicians.

The second delimiting factor concerns the factual basis of the decision. Goethals and Nelson (1973) hypothesized that when the issue concerns potentially verifiable facts, a dissimilar source will induce greater persuasion than a similar source.

Subjects in Goethals and Nelson's study were students who had just graduated from high school and who planned to attend college in the fall. The experimenter informed the students that a state university was reassessing its admission criteria and that it had decided to obtain the ideas and views of high school students. Students were told that they would watch excerpts from interviews with two applicants to the university. Both applicants, they were told, had been accepted and had just now completed their junior year. Half of the subjects were instructed to try "to decide which student has made the better academic record at the university." The other subjects were asked "to decide which of the two students you personally like better. That is, which of the two would you prefer to have as a close friend or fellow student if you were also going to be a freshman there?" (p. 119).

After subjects in each condition indicated their preferences, they were handed a comparable evaluation from another subject who either shared or did not share their values. Then they were asked to say how confident they were that their initial judgment was correct.

When subjects were trying to decide which of the two applicants had the stronger academic record, they felt more confident about their evaluation when they were told that a dissimilar other agreed with them. By contrast, a similar other bolstered their confidence more when they were struggling to decide which applicant they would like to have as a close friend.

How can we explain these findings? The unifying principle is that different situations require the use of different social comparison criteria. When asked to make an academic evaluation, subjects put on their intellectual hats. Here, their own feelings were irrelevant: They had to make a hard-headed decision based on the academic data. What better confirmation of their own interpretation of the data, subjects reasoned, than to learn that someone completely different from themselves — someone who did not share their own pet peeves or private predilections — came to exactly the same conclusion as did they. In contrast, when they were trying to decide if the applicant would make a good friend, they applied a different set of criteria. Here, their own feelings and personal assessments were of central importance; and they assumed that a similar other would be more likely than a dissimilar other to employ the same yardstick for evaluating friends that they employed.

In sum, dissimilar others carry more weight when the source is trying to influence perceptions of factual matters or cognitions about an issue (Hass, 1981). On the other hand, when the issue is more affective and more personal, similarity exerts a greater impact. On a broader level, these findings raise the question of when communicators should emphasize expertise (dissimilar other) and when they should stress similarity. Cantor, Alfonso, and Zillmann (1976) broached this issue and obtained findings consistent with those reported by Goethals and Nelson (1973).

Subjects were students at Indiana University. They listened to a message that claimed the IUD birth control device was superior to other methods of birth control. For some subjects, the message was attributed to a same-age peer (high similarity), and for others it was attributed to a 39-year-old woman (low similarity). In addition, half of the subjects were led to believe that the speaker had expertise in the field of medicine, whereas the other half was led to believe that the communicator had no previous experience in the medical field. Subjects who heard a peer give a favorable evaluation of the IUD were more likely to indicate that they would choose the IUD as a method of birth control than subjects who heard the nonpeer present the same evaluation. Expertise did not exert a significant impact on intentions to use the IUD. These findings are consistent with those obtained by Goethals and Nelson (1973). The decision to use an IUD is highly emotional and personal. Thus, based on Goethals and Nelson's results, we would expect that the endorsement of the IUD by a same-age peer would carry considerable weight.

The question of whether a communicator should emphasize expertise or similarity comes up in many real-life persuasion situations. Politicians, advertisers, and salespeople are often faced with deciding whether to emphasize their experience or the fact that they are "just plain folks." In sales, for example, Weitz (1981) emphasized that if persuaders expect the relationship to last for a long time, they are better off emphasizing similarity than expertise. Ultimately, the determination of whether to use similarity or expertise will depend on the context, the persuader's goals, and a message recipient's attitudes about the issue.

PHYSICAL ATTRACTIVENESS

Flip through any issue of *GQ* magazine and chances are you will come across an advertisement that features a sensationally attractive male model sporting a fashionably tailored suit or sportcoat. Turn on the TV and you will see a beautiful female model promoting perfume or a new line of clothing for women. Advertisers obviously believe that attractiveness sells products. Social science studies also find that physical attractiveness enhances persuasion, but the effects are more complicated than these examples from advertising suggest.

Early studies employed a simple set of procedures to study attractiveness effects. Subjects were asked to read a persuasive message on a relatively low involving issue, such as lowering the speed limit by 10 or 15 miles an hour. Attached to the message was a photograph of the person who had supposedly written the message. Some photographs were of highly attractive men and women, others depicted persons of relatively average looks, and other photos depicted people low in physical attractiveness. Subjects were then asked to indicate their opinion on the issue. Invariably, subjects who read the essay paired with the attractive photo changed their attitudes on the topic significantly more than subjects in the other conditions (Horai, Naccari, & Fatoullah, 1974; Snyder & Rothbart, 1971; see, also, Patzer, 1983).

Unfortunately, these early studies were all conducted in laboratory settings, and most manipulated attractiveness by means of photographs of individuals of different attractiveness levels. Chaiken (1979) lamented that these studies used highly artificial procedures to study attractiveness effects. Noting that attractiveness should be studied in real-life settings, Chaiken (1979) designed an experiment in which individuals who were high and low in physical attractiveness approached passers-by on the University of Massachusetts campus and asked them to complete a short questionnaire. Students who agreed to fill out the questionnaire then were told that the communicator was in a campus group that believed the university should stop serving meat at breakfast and lunch at all dining commons; the communicator backed up this position with two arguments. Students exposed to the attractive communicators changed their attitudes and behaviors more in the direction of the advocated position than did those who heard the unattractive speakers.

Understanding Why

Several explanations for the attractiveness effect have been advanced. The first explanation emphasizes attention. People are more likely to pay attention to an attractive than an unattractive speaker, the argument goes, and this then makes it more likely that they will remember the arguments in the message. There is only limited support for the learning/attention view of source effects. The fact that people attend to an attractive model does not guarantee that they will remember what the model said, or that they will change their attitudes to conform with the advocated position. Therefore, processes other than attention must be invoked to adequately explain attractiveness effects.

A second explanation emphasizes classical conditioning. According to this view, exposure to a physically attractive speaker elicits a pleasant reaction; this positive response becomes associated with the message, which in turn leads people to evaluate message arguments more favorably. Advertisers try to take advantage of this association when they devise advertisements that pair sexy models with various products. One study found that male subjects who saw an automobile advertisement that featured an attractive female model rated the car as better designed, more expensive looking, and more appealing than did male subjects who did not see a model promote the car (Smith & Engel, 1968). Apparently, the mere association of the attractive model with the car enhanced its appeal.

A third interpretation stresses communication skills. Chaiken (1979) found that attractive speakers were judged to be more fluent than their less attractive counterparts. In addition, attractive communicators made more positive self-evaluations than did unattractive speakers: Attractive-speakers were more likely to describe themselves as being attractive, interesting, and persuasive. Thus, another reason why attractive communicators affect greater attitude change is that they are more effective and more confident public speakers.

A fourth view is that attractiveness facilitates attitude change through the processes of liking and identification. This interpretation stresses that people like and identify with attractive communicators and that liking enhances persuasion. At some level, people may feel that they can improve their own self-image by adopting the attitudes held by attractive others or by associating themselves with the attractive communicator, if only vicariously. Clearly, this is why many advertisers hire movie stars (e.g., Madonna, Prince, Michael J. Fox) to represent their products; they are hoping that audience members' identification with the stars will lead them to buy the products.

Generally speaking, attractiveness works through different mediators than does source credibility. Norman (1976) demonstrated this by asking subjects to read a counterattitudinal message that was attributed to either an expert or an attractive source. Subjects read a message arguing that people get too much sleep. The message was attributed to either a professor of physiology who had recently co-authored a book on the functions of sleep (expert) or a smiling, physically attractive young man (attractive source). Half of the subjects read an essay that simply stated the writer's opinion that, in general, people sleep too much. Other subjects read six carefully crafted arguments that supported the writer's opinion on the issue.

Subjects only accepted the expert's view when he supported it with arguments. However, they agreed with the attractive source, regardless of whether he furnished supporting arguments. The results supported Kelman's (1958) model of source attractiveness. Kelman argued that credible sources induce persuasion through a process of internalization (i.e., by getting people to incorporate the speaker's arguments into their belief systems). In contrast, Kelman contended that the persuasive impact of attractiveness has its roots in the listener's identification with the speaker.

Other studies also make it clear that attractive communicators do not induce attitude change because they get people to think carefully about the arguments in the message. Pallak (1983) made a source's physical attractiveness either highly salient (by providing a vivid photograph of an attractive male communicator) or not at all salient (by providing a degraded copy of the photograph). When the communicator's attractiveness was made highly salient, subjects were apt to agree with the communicator, regardless of whether he presented strong or weak arguments. What seemed to underly their change in attitude was their perception of the communicator, not their evaluation of his message. Pallak argued that the increased salience of the communicator's attractiveness led subjects to invoke the decisional rule, "I generally agree with people I like."[2]

Limits

There are several limits to the persuasive impact of physical attractiveness. When a communicator is extremely attractive, persuasion may actually be reduced (Maddux & Rogers, 1983). Exposure to an exceptionally attractive speaker may distract people from paying any attention to the message. They may also be jealous of the attractive communicator, and this may interfere with reception of the message.

Attractiveness can also fail when it violates people's expectations of what is appropriate for a particular role or job (Burgoon, 1989). You probably expect that the spokesperson for a new shampoo will be physically attractive; the endorser's attractiveness (particularly his or her hair) is an important selling point for the shampoo. However, in other contexts, attractiveness is not relevant to the persuasive message and you would not expect the communicator to be particularly attractive. Most people would not expect their family doctor to be sensationally attractive; and so the doctor with exceptionally good looks may find that physical attractiveness is not necessarily a persuasive asset.

Finally, attractiveness effects tend to be rather short-lived. Kelman (1958) noted that opinions changed through a process of identification are not particularly well integrated within the person's value system. Because people go along with attractive communicators without giving their arguments much thought, "they may lack the bolstering topic-relevant cognitions that may be a prerequisite for enduring opinion change" (Chaiken, 1986, p. 154). Remember that people go along with attractive communicators largely because they like and identify with them. But likes and dislikes can be ephemeral, changing with the wind. Once an individual ceases to identify with the attractive communicator, the entire basis for opinion change collapses. In the case of advertising, for example, once an attractive celebrity model loses his or her lustre, or becomes less popular, the opinion changes that he or she induced are apt to disappear as well.

In sum, just as there is a myth that attractive people are "good" and "kind," so too is there a myth that attractive speakers always get their way. Being attractive helps; it provides the speaker with a slight advantage. Everything being equal, the attractive speaker is more likely than a less attractive counterpart to change attitudes. However, there are a number of factors that complicate things: The effects of attractiveness depend on the topic of the message, the audience member's involvement, and the level of speaker attractiveness. Furthermore, because attractive speakers rarely get receivers to internalize their message, the effects of attractiveness are likely to be short-lived.

EXHIBIT 6–1   153

CONCLUSIONS

What makes a communicator persuasive? What are the characteristics that individuals should possess if they wish to convince others to change their minds about issues and ideas?

Scholars have been asking these questions for thousands of years. Much of the current debate about this subject has focused on source credibility. Studies have found that credibility consists of several dimensions; expertise and trustworthiness have consistently emerged, whereas other factors, such as dynamism, have emerged in particular investigations.

The effects of communicator characteristics, such as expertise, trustworthiness, similarity, and attractiveness, vary with the person and the situation. It is not possible to say that "an expert will always persuade an audience" or that "an attractive communicator will exert a powerful effect on the audience." Much depends on the biases and beliefs that audience members bring to the persuasion situation, and the extent to which receivers are motivated and able to process the message. It should be noted that different processes underlie the effects of expertise, trustworthiness, similarity, and attractiveness. In addition, the same source characteristic can influence different people for different reasons. This is not to say that source variables exert a negligible influence on persuasion; on the contrary, under certain conditions source factors contribute a great deal to persuasive impact. Our point has been that context matters, and that persuaders must take context into account when they are planning a persuasion campaign.

* * *

EXHIBIT 6–1
TIMING THE EXPERT'S IDENTIFICATION

You are trying to persuade an audience to change its position on an issue. Should you identify your credentials before presenting the message, or would you be better advised to deliver the message first and then tell the audience about your background in the area? The answer depends on whether your audience perceives that you are an expert in the area.

If you think the audience will view you as an expert, you should describe your background before you talk. There is some evidence that highly expert sources are more likely to change attitudes if they identify their credentials before rather than after they present their message (Mills & Harvey, 1972). In this way, they bolster the audience's confidence that their message is correct. The opposite holds for sources low in expertise. Consequently, if you think your audience will perceive that you lack knowledge of the topic area, you are better off giving your speech first and then describing your background in the area. If you tell listeners at the outset that you are a novice, they are likely to derogate your arguments and ignore what you have to say (Greenberg & Miller, 1966; Ward & McGinnies, 1974).

* * *

EXHIBIT 6-2
THE CONVERT COMMUNICATOR

Tommy used to drink heavily—for years he had a problem with alcohol. But now he is speaking at an Alcoholics Anonymous (AA) meeting and he has a story to tell. It is his own. He begins with the sentence that all AA members use to introduce themselves at meetings. "My name is Tommy and I'm an alcoholic. And let me tell you, it's been a bitch." Empathic laughter from the audience follows. Everyone relaxes.

Tommy is one of the alcoholics whose story is profiled by Nan Robertson in *Getting Better: Inside Alcoholics Anonymous (1988).* As Robertson told it, Tommy confides to the AA audience that he used to go "drinking and drugging" with his friends from the rock music circuit, until his life took a turn for the worse.

"For eleven years, I wanted drugs and booze to take me somewhere, but I never got there," he says. One day he realized his life was a shambles. He went out to a bar, and "A guy asked me as we were standing there, 'What's your name, man?' " Tommy recalls that, "I thought and I thought and I couldn't remember. I couldn't remember the name I was born with." Later that day, he picked up the phone and called AA.

Tommy looks up, and decides it is time to complete his story. "I can't tell you how to fix your life," he says. "I *can* tell you how to stay sober. I've been here for 5 years. I should be okay by now. Sometimes I'm not okay. But it's better than it was—a lot better. I owe you people plenty. Thank you." Tommy stops. Loud applause follows.[3]

Tommy is one of many people who has given up drinking and now dedicates his energy to spreading the word that alcohol is a killer. Communicators like Tommy wield considerable influence—precisely because they are alcoholics who have gone straight. They are what Levine and Valle (1975) called "convert communicators"—individuals who have converted from one lifestyle and ideology to a totally opposite set of beliefs. Convert communicators often lack status and frequently do not occupy prestigious positions in society, and yet they can be extremely credible communicators.

Levine and Valle (1975) demonstrated this by having students listen to either a reformed alcoholic (convert communicator) or a lifelong abstainer from alcohol explain the perils of consuming alcohol at even moderate levels. As they expected, subjects perceived that the convert communicator was more credible than the speaker who was described as a lifelong abstainer from alcohol.

The convert is not a new phenomenon. Levine and Valle noted that the biblical prophet Paul was a convert communicator who converted from Judaism to the new and radical religion of the day, Christianity. Paul, they noted, was among the "weary pilgrims" who walked the long road from sin to salvation. Two thousand years later, converts are ubiquitous. Rock musician David Crosby, of Crosby, Stills, Nash, and Young, used drugs when he was a young singer; after giving up drugs, he decided to devote his energies to lecturing about the terrible effects drugs have on people's lives. Similarly, some scholars think that intravenous drug users perceive an ex-drug user to be more credible than a variety of more established

EXHIBIT 6-3   **155**

sources, such as a doctor, a "straight" community organizer, or the surgeon general of the United States (Perloff & Pettey, 1991).

There are two explanations for the convert communicator effect. First, the convert plays on feelings of similarity between source and receiver; second, the convert is believed to have overcome a knowledge bias, which in turn enhances his or her credibility. The only proviso is that the convert must be seen as having freely made the decision to convert. A Mafia hit man who goes straight may lack credibility because he is seen as having made this decision to save his own skin. He may not be the most effective spokesperson for an anticrime campaign.

* * *

EXHIBIT 6-3
THE POWER OF LIKING

Likability plays an important role in the persuasion process, as was illustrated by Wright (1966). Subjects first indicated their opinions on the value of intercollegiate athletics. Then they were assigned to a group discussion in which they were asked to discuss this topic by exchanging written notes with other students. Unbeknownst to subjects, one of the members of the group was a confederate of the experimenter who behaved in either a friendly or unfriendly manner.

In the friendly condition, the confederate disclosed that: "I'd sure like to get acquainted with you at least a little before we start the game. . . . I'm glad I can communicate directly to you; you seem like a good guy to talk to. . . ."

In the unfriendly condition, the confederate revealed that: "I do not like the idea of conversing with virtual strangers, so I have really nothing to say to you. This note is just for the sake of practice, and doesn't mean I really want to communicate to you."

After exchanging the notes, the confederate attempted to convince the subject to reduce his support for intercollegiate athletics. The confederate in the friendly condition induced the greatest amount of attitude change. Wright concluded that persuaders should "make sure the person you are trying to persuade likes you in the first place, or your efforts are likely to be in vain" (p. 210; see, also, Karlins & Abelson, 1970).

7
Message Effects

S hould you present just your side of the argument or would it be better to present both sides? Should you include facts and figures or would that just bore people? Do scare tactics work? These questions all focus on the *message*, the centerpiece of many contemporary theories of persuasion.

The first scholarly essay on the persuasive message was written more than 2,500 years ago. Two Greek scholars, Corax and Tisias, developed a theory of argumentation during 5th century B.C. (McCroskey, 1972). A century later, Aristotle wrote the *Rhetoric*, perhaps the greatest book ever written on the subject of rhetorical communication. Over the past 2,500 years, rhetoricians, philosophers, politicians, and (most recently) behavioral scientists have theorized about the types of messages that are likely to achieve the greatest effects on audience members. In this chapter, I summarize what is known about message effects. The discussion focuses on three categories of message variables: (a) those pertaining to message content, (b) those focusing on the style in which the message is delivered, and (c) those focusing on the language of the message.

MESSAGE CONTENT VARIABLES

Evidence

It is commonly believed that evidence helps to strengthen a persuasive message. Advertisers use evidence-based appeals regularly (e.g., "Studies conducted at a leading medical school show that aspirin reduces pain and inflammation"; "9 out of 10 dentists say that regular flossing prevents tooth decay"). Similarly, a wide variety of persuasion practitioners—ranging from attorneys to health care practitioners—make sure they support their arguments with evidence.

The research literature strongly supports the notion that evidence enhances persuasion. After reviewing the research on the effects of evidence, Reinard (1988) declared that "there actually may be more consistency in evidence research than can be found in almost any other area of persuasion. Evidence appears to produce general persuasive effects that appear surprisingly stable" (p. 46).

Evidence has been broadly defined as: "Factual statements originating from a source other than the speaker, objects not created by the speaker, and opinions of persons other than the speaker that are offered in support of the speaker's claims" (McCroskey, 1969, p. 170).

Thus, evidence includes testimonial assertions ("Tommy Lasorda says Slimfast works best"), eyewitness reports ("An eyewitness to the crime testified that the defendant was wearing horn-rimmed spectacles"), factual statements ("Institution of senior comprehensive exams has led to a marked improvement in students' performance in graduate degree programs"), and statistics. Given this broad definition of evidence, it is not surprising that researchers have found that the use of evidence enhances persuasion.

Certain factors can enhance the impact of evidence on persuasion. These factors can be either internal or external to the information contained in the message (Reinard, 1988). Internal factors include the credibility of the source of the evidence, evidence quality, and novelty. As the source expertise literature suggests, evidence is more persuasive when attributed to a highly credible communicator than to a low-credible source (this is one reason why journalists are always careful to quote "White House officials" or "high administration sources"). Evidence is also more likely to change attitudes if it is of high quality (Luchok & McCroskey, 1978), is plausible, and is novel rather than "old hat" (Morley & Walker, 1987). Clearly, communicators who know the rules of good evidence can use evidence to their advantage.

Factors external to the evidence include the credibility of the speaker, message delivery, and the subject's familiarity with the evidence. By credibility, we mean the credibility of the individual who delivers the message, not the sources quoted in the message. McCroskey (1969) has found that the use of evidence enhances attitude change when the communicator is perceived to be moderate or low in credibility. On the other hand, evidence has little or no impact when the communicator is believed to be highly credible. However, it should be noted that this conclusion applies primarily to efforts to induce short-term changes in attitude. When the goal of the communicator is to effect long-term changes in attitude, evidence can also benefit the highly credible communicator (Burgoon & Burgoon, 1975).

In addition, evidence has relatively little impact when it is included in a speech that is delivered poorly, when the audience is familiar with the topic, and when the data presented are inconsistent with individuals' initial attitudes (Brilhart, 1970; Lord, Ross, & Lepper, 1979; Wall, 1972).

We gain additional insights into the role that evidence plays in the persuasion process by examining Petty and Cacioppo's Elaboration Likelihood Model (ELM). The ELM reminds us that evidence will have different effects, depending on the involvement and ability of the audience. When message recipients lack the motivation or ability to process a message, they will rely on simple cues to help them decide whether to accept the recommendation contained in the message. One such cue is the sheer amount of evidence. Messages that contain a great deal of evidence will persuade low-involvement, low-ability receivers, even when that evidence is shoddy (Petty & Cacioppo, 1984). Thus, advertisers can bamboozle low-involved consumers by devising ads that contain many arguments, numerous facts, and lots of high-tech flow charts. (See Exhibit 7–1: Can You Lie with Statistical Evidence?, p. 180.)

On the other hand, when individuals are highly involved in the message or are highly capable of processing message arguments, they are unlikely to be persuaded by simple evidentiary cues. In these situations, the content of the evidence matters more. Strong, specific, and—above all—high-quality evidence is likely to carry more weight with individuals who are high in involvement or cognitive ability.

Vividness

Evidence-based arguments are often pitted against vivid, graphic message appeals, and the two could not be more different. Although evidence typically contains facts and numerical data, vivid messages use colorful pictures, concrete descriptions, jarring images, and personal anecdotes to make their points. A picture of a starving child is used to induce viewers to donate money to a charity, graphic language is used to make the case against a defendant in court, and personalized anecdotes are related to persuade a customer to buy a car. More formally, vivid information is that which is "likely to attract and hold our attention and to excite the imagination"; it is "emotionally interesting, concrete and imagery-provoking, and proximate in a sensory, temporal, or spatial way" (Nisbett & Ross, 1980, p. 45).

It is commonly assumed that vivid and graphic messages are enormously powerful. However, this assumption is not borne out by the research literature. In their review of the vividness literature, Taylor and Thompson (1982) noted that concrete descriptions do not exert a greater impact on judgments than do abstract summaries, and that pictorially illustrated information has no consistent impact on beliefs compared with equivalent information that is not illustrated with pictures. Consequently, we need to be careful about blithely assuming that vivid and graphic displays of information will always change attitudes and behavior. We all have seen memorable pictures of airline disasters, yet few of us stop flying.

On the other hand, certain types of vivid messages *do* exert a strong impact on attitudes. In particular, case history information has been shown to exert a stronger impact on judgments than statistical (base-rate) information. This is interesting because case histories are based on the reports of a relatively small number of persons, whereas statistics reflect the experiences of a large, representative sample of individuals. It is likely that case studies capture more attention and have certain tangible qualities that make them easier to remember than statistical facts (Bell & Loftus, 1985). Case histories also have a certain reality and immediacy that enhance their believability.

These findings have important implications for practitioners. Consider the communication educator who is trying to convince young people to engage in safe sex practices to protect themselves from AIDS. The educator could present young adults with hard facts about the spread of AIDS, including new statistics that show that AIDS is increasingly spread through heterosexual sex. The vividness literature argues for a more personalized approach, which is illustrated by the following (actual) case study account:

> Her date came with champagne, roses, . . . and AIDS. Eight years later, Ali Gertz, 24, is fighting for her life and warning women that, yes, it *can* happen to you. . . .
>
> At 24, pretty, poised and privileged, Gertz is an unlikely candidate for the disease. She lives on Manhattan's fashionable Upper East Side, not in the inner city, and she has never had a blood transfusion or been an intravenous drug user. In her case, AIDS comes down to a simple situation: one night with the wrong man.
>
> The night that took away the promise of Ali Gertz's life was in the summer of 1982, when the disease was little more than a whisper in New York City. Gertz, a precocious 16-year-old, was infatuated with an older man named Cort Brown, whom she had met a year earlier at Studio 54, the flashy New York City club where he was a bartender. . . .
>
> His name didn't come up again until the summer of 1988. . . . That August, unable to shake a low-grade fever and chronic diarrhea, she was hospitalized. . . . Finally, after more than two weeks of painful tests, she developed pneumonia—and a bronchoscopy solved the mystery. As Ali lay half-conscious, an oxygen mask covering her face, her family doctor came to her bedside with tears in his eyes and told her she had AIDS. (McMurran & Neill, 1990, p. 62)

Fear

A presidential candidate suggests that if elected, his opponent will start a third world war. . . . A deodorant ad intimates that if you do not use the

Lady Killer

Smoking is deadly. For help in quitting, please call us.

AMERICAN CANCER SOCIETY®

The American Cancer Society used fear appeals such as the one shown here to induce smokers to give up the habit. Research indicates that several conditions must be met in order for fear messages to successfully change attitudes and behavior.

product, people will shun you because you have body odor. . . . A driver's education film shows pictures of car crashes and mutilated bodies to convince young people to buckle up their seat belts. . . . A preacher intones that a life of "hell and damnation" will follow those who sin against the Lord.

These are all fear appeals—communications that use fear to induce individuals to accept the message recommendations. It is commonly believed that fear appeals work. It is a rather simple matter (the argument goes): scare people enough and they will do what the persuader wants. Of course, it is not that simple. A variety of theories have been proposed to explain the effects of fear appeals on attitudes, and hundreds of studies (some of which have obtained conflicting results) have explored these issues. Indeed, if there is one word that characterizes the research on fear appeals, it is "complex." Researchers have examined the effects of fear messages across many different contexts (Higbee, 1969). Topics have included cigarette smoking, tetanus shots, dental hygiene, use of seat belts, and fallout shelters.

To make matters more complicated, some researchers have found that a high fear message is more persuasive than a low fear message, whereas other investigators have reported that, on the contrary, a communication is more likely to change attitudes if it arouses a small, rather than a large, amount of fear. For many years, the consensus among researchers was that the findings on fear appeals were so inconsistent and so hard to synthesize that it was not possible to make any general statement about the effects of fear-arousing messages on attitudes.

Over the past several years, a new consensus has emerged. The results of two systematic reviews of the research literature have forced researchers to revise their earlier agnosticism. Boster and Mongeau (1984) and Sutton (1982) used meta-analytic procedures to review the fear appeals literature. Meta-analysis is a statistical procedure that allows researchers to assess the strength of the findings in an area. Three general conclusions have emerged from these reviews of the fear appeals literature.

First, although it may seem axiomatic, many experiments have failed to manipulate fear successfully. As Boster and Mongeau (1984) noted: "Manipulating fear does not appear to be an easy task. What appears to be a highly-arousing persuasive message to the experimenter may not induce much fear into the recipient of the persuasive message" (p. 375).

This is an important point. Studies that find that fear appeals fail to change attitudes are often interpreted as meaning that fear *cannot* change attitudes. Boster and Mongeau's research suggested that this conclusion is incorrect. It is quite possible that these fear-arousing messages failed not because fear is a weak psychological weapon, but because the researcher did not successfully manipulate fear. For example, many driver's education films may fail to change attitudes toward drunk driving because their appeals are so farfetched (bodies strewn all over the road) that no one believes them. Had they used a more realistic manipulation of fear, they might have been more successful.

Second, provided that the researcher has manipulated fear successfully, there is compelling evidence that high-fear appeals are more effective than low-fear appeals. Given the choice, it is better to arouse more fear than less.

Third, personality factors set limits on the impact of fear appeals. In particular, anxiety level moderates the effects of fear messages on attitudes. Persons low in anxiety, who can presumably tolerate threats to their well-being, are more influenced by high-fear messages than by low-fear communications. On the other hand, low-fear appeals tend to be more effective among individuals high in chronic anxiety (Goldstein, 1959; Wheatley & Oshikawa, 1970). These persons like to avoid threatening information, and messages that arouse relatively little fear are less threatening to highly anxious persons.

Theoretical Approaches.   Several theories of fear appeals have been proposed. The first theory is that fear operates as a drive. According to this view, the persuasive message arouses fear; fear is an unpleasant drive-state that audience members are motivated to reduce. Drive theory suggests that to reduce the fear, individuals change their attitudes and behaviors in the direction advocated by the message. However, there are two problems with the drive theory explanation.

First, as Sutton (1982) noted, drive reduction theory has received little support from the fear appeals literature. Second, the theory presents a rather simplistic, mechanistic conceptualization of fear. As Reardon (1989) pointed out, "the fear-drive model is an 'odd mixture' of fear arousal, which involves higher mental processes, and fear reduction and resultant behavior change, which involve low-level, animal-like processes" (p. 284).

A second approach holds that there is a curvilinear relationship between fear arousal and attitude change (Janis & Leventhal, 1968; McGuire, 1968). According to this view, the slope of the fear/attitude change curve is positive and linear as fear increases from zero to moderate levels. At a certain point, however, the message arouses too much anxiety, and this results in a negative relationship between fear and attitude change. Although the curvilinear hypothesis is intuitively appealing, it has not · been supported by the research on fear appeals (Boster & Mongeau, 1984; Sutton, 1982). Everything being equal, the greater the arousal of fear, the greater the attitude change.[1]

In contrast to these early theories, contemporary approaches emphasize that fear appeals change attitudes to the extent that they trigger the appropriate cognitive mechanisms. The current view is that it is less important for a message to arouse fear than to induce individuals to change their beliefs and expectations regarding the problematic behavior (e.g., smoking, eating fatty foods, practicing unsafe sex).

In an influential paper, Leventhal (1970) proposed a parallel response model of fear appeals. He argued that a fear-arousing message triggers two responses: emotional (fear control) and cognitive (danger control). Fear control occurs when individuals turn their attention inward and attend to their fearful responses. Danger control occurs when individuals turn their attention outward and appraise the external danger. Fear control may help individuals reduce their fear, but it will not help them deal with the danger that a particular behavior presents.

Building on this notion, Rogers (1975) proposed a protection motivation theory of fear appeals. He argued that a fear message works to the extent that it motivates individuals to protect themselves from danger. The emphasis is not on whether the message reduces fear, but on whether it gets the individual to take the steps necessary to deal with the danger at hand. Rogers (1975) argued that a fear appeal must contain three components if it is to succeed in changing attitudes or behavior. Listed here are the three components of protection motivation theory, coupled with an example of how a fear appeal on the topic of cocaine might employ these components.

1. *Magnitude of Noxiousness.* Information about the types of consequences that can occur if the problematic behavior is not modified. ("Cocaine kills; it fries your brain and burns your future.")

2. *Probability of Occurrence.* Information about the probability that these consequences will occur, given that no modifications are made in the individual's current behavior patterns. ("Cocaine doesn't make exceptions. People who use cocaine are putting their body and mind in grave jeopardy.")

3. *Efficacy of Recommended Response.* Information about the effectiveness of a protective response that can help avert the danger. ("Cocaine treatment programs save lives. People who enter these programs can rehabilitate their bodies and minds and return to a normal lifestyle and routine.")

Rogers also noted that each of these three message components triggers a cognitive reaction in the individual. Thus, magnitude of noxiousness information should (theoretically) convince the person that there are negative consequences associated with the problematic behavior, probability of occurrence information should persuade the person that there is a high probability that the consequences will occur if the individual maintains the present behavior, whereas information about the efficacy of the recommended response should convince the individual that these consequences can be avoided if he or she changes the problematic behavior.

Rogers and his colleagues have conducted several studies to test protection motivation theory. In one study, Rogers and Mewborn (1976) manipulated the three protection motivation components by asking subjects to watch a film and then read a message on the topic of cigarette smoking. Low-noxiousness subjects watched a film that told the story of a man who learns that he has gotten lung cancer and then is informed by his doctor that one lung must be removed; high-noxiousness subjects saw the same film, plus an additional segment that presented the operation for removing the lung.

In the case of probability of occurrence, low-probability subjects read a message that argued that "the chances of any given smoker actually developing cancer are very small"; high probability subjects read a communication that used facts and statistics to support the argument that smoking causes lung cancer.

For low-efficacy subjects, the message provided little reassurance that, by quitting smoking, an individual could reduce the risk of contracting lung cancer. For high-efficacy subjects, the message argued that smoking cessation significantly reduced the risk of getting cancer.

Subjects were smokers who indicated that they had smoked at least 10 cigarettes a day for the past year. Following exposure to the messages, subjects indicated their intention to quit smoking.

Information about the effectiveness of the recommended action had a particularly strong impact on intentions. As Rogers and Mewborn (1976) noted:

> Regardless of . . . how noxious (the threatened event) was, or how likely it was to occur, the stronger the belief that a coping response could avert a danger, the more strongly people intended to adopt the communicator's recommendations. (p. 59)

Moreover, effectiveness interacted with the other protection motivation variables in interesting ways. For example, smokers who were led to believe that there was a high probability that smoking causes cancer only changed their intentions if they believed that the recommended practice (quitting smoking) was highly effective.

The Role of Self-Efficacy.   Rogers expanded his model in 1983 to incorporate another variable: self-efficacy (Maddux & Rogers, 1983). Self-efficacy refers to the perception that one is capable of performing the recommended action. The idea is that individuals may know that a behavior has bad consequences, realize that the consequences are likely to occur if the behavior is not modified, and recognize that there are coping responses that can help avert the danger. However, the fear appeal may fail to influence attitudes or intentions because individuals perceive that they are not capable of modifying the problematic behavior. Thus, to change attitudes, the message must convince individuals that they are psychologically capable of performing the recommended action (see Fig. 7.1).

Two social psychologists, Beck and Lund (1981), provided strong support for the self-efficacy view of fear appeals. The investigators exposed dental patients to messages that "described the cause of periodontal disease, the areas of the gums affected by it, the progress of the disease, and its eventual outcome (tooth loss)" (p. 406). The messages also described methods for preventing periodontal disease, such as special brushing techniques and flossing between the teeth.

After listening to one of the messages, subjects completed a series of items tapping beliefs and affects on the topic of periodontal disease. Of particular interest was the question, "How effective do you think *you* will be in flossing your teeth properly?" Intentions to engage in the recommended behaviors, as well as self-reported behavior, were also assessed. Self-efficacy proved to be the best predictor of intention to floss and of actual flossing behavior. Thus, the fear appeal persuaded individuals to floss their teeth by convincing them that they were personally capable of performing the recommended action successfully.

The studies that we have reviewed make it clear that the term *fear appeal* is actually a misnomer. "Fear appeal" implies that a message changes behavior by employing fear. However, protection motivation theory suggests that fear arousal is only part of the story. Yes, communicators

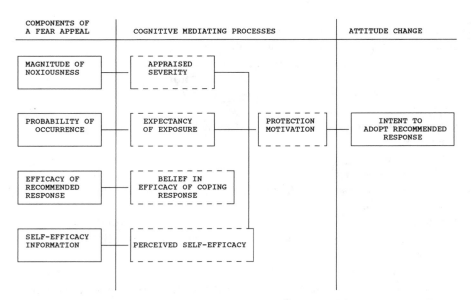

FIG. 7.1 Schema of the protection motivation theory (adapted from Rogers, 1975).

should devise appeals that get respondents scared: The more frightened individuals feel, the more likely they are to respond positively to the advocated position (Sutton & Eiser, 1984). However, fear arousal is not enough. Communicators must also convince individuals that the negative outcome is likely to happen, that there are steps they can take to ward off the danger, and that they are personally capable of performing these preventive behaviors. Needless to say, it is often difficult to persuade individuals to change their beliefs in these ways.[2]

You may recall that I began the discussion of fear appeals by emphasizing that the research in this area is complex. Although recent meta-analytic reviews and Rogers' programmatic research on protection motivation have provided us with some generalizations and prescriptions, they have not altered this basic assessment. Fear is a complex emotion, and the issue of how cognitions and emotions interact is even more complicated. No wonder, then, that the effects of fear appeals on persuasion have turned out to be so complex, and that fear has emerged as a particularly tricky variable to manipulate successfully.

MESSAGE STRUCTURE

One- Versus Two-Sided Messages

Illinois Power was in trouble. "60 Minutes" had just done a story that charged that the nuclear power company had seriously mismanaged its finances, to the point of running up thousands of dollars in cost overruns. In this age of corporate public relations, the company knew it had to do something. One solution was to write a press release that described all of the positive accomplishments the company had made in the areas of nuclear power and financial management. Another possibility was to take on "60 Minutes" directly by developing a message that outlined each of the charges by "60 Minutes" and then explained why each charge was false. If you were working for Illinois Power, which message strategy would you select?

Hold onto your solution for the time being—at least until we have reviewed the research that bears on the dilemma that the Decatur, Illinois, power company actually faced in 1980. The research focused on the question of whether it is more effective to develop a one-sided message, which gives arguments in favor of the persuader's position on the issue, or a two-sided message, which gives arguments for both sides of the controversial issue.

Two-sided messages tend to be more persuasive when individuals initially disagree with the persuader's position. Giving both sides is also more effective when audience members are likely to have information about opposing arguments (Burgoon, 1989). By giving both sides, "the communicator is saying he is aware of the (opposing) information, has taken it into account, and still finds that the weight of the evidence favors his position" (Hass & Linder, 1972, p. 227). On the other hand, one-sided messages tend to be more effective when individuals initially agree with the position advocated in the message (Hovland, Lumsdaine, & Sheffield, 1949). When addressing an audience of true believers, persuaders are not likely to win many points by acknowledging that there is another position on the issue.

In most situations, people are likely to have some information about opposing sides of the issue. Thus, a two-sided message is the better bet in most persuasion contexts. There is some debate about the best method for dealing with opposing information. A message can first refute opposing arguments and then give the pro-arguments in support of the speaker's position (refutation-pro), or it can begin with the supportive arguments and follow them up with refutation of the opposition's point of view (pro-refutation). Some studies have found that the refutation-pro order is more effective (Hass & Linder, 1972), whereas others have reported that the pro-refutation strategy induces the most persuasion (Burgoon, 1989).

There are two reasons why a two-sided message is more effective among individuals who disagree with the persuader's position and who are likely to be exposed to opposing arguments. First, a message that gives both sides respects the receiver's intelligence. It says: "We think you're smart enough to know that there are two sides to any issue, and we're going to give you both sides, even though we think one is better than the other." Second, a two-sided message allows the persuader to develop counterarguments against the opposing position, which, according to the cognitive response approach, should stimulate counterarguing activity on the part of the receiver.

Armed with these facts and ideas, let us return to the dilemma faced by the executives at Illinois Power. Given the popularity of "60 Minutes," it would be a good bet that many members of the target audience were familiar with the charges leveled against Illinois Power. Thus, a two-sided message would clearly be preferable. Illinois Power, as it turns out, devised a high-quality, two-sided message. The company developed a videotape that went through each of the charges presented on the "60 Minutes" broadcast; for each charge, Illinois Power presented the "60 Minutes" footage first, and then provided its own rebuttal to the charge (refutation-pro order).

Illinois Power then made the videotape available to its stockholders and to colleges and universities across the country. How effective was the message? Clavier and Kalupa (1983) conducted an experiment to examine the effects of the videotape. The investigators found that the subjects who saw the Illinois Power videotape perceived that "60 Minutes" was less credible and that representatives of the nuclear power industry were more credible than did subjects who saw only "60 Minutes' " side of the story.

Order Effects

A classic issue in persuasion research is the order of presentation of message arguments. There are two subissues here: the ordering of strong and weak arguments when only one side of the issue is presented, and the order of arguments when one set of arguments advocates one position on an issue and the other takes the opposite point of view. The first is a question of ordering of message arguments with regard to strength, whereas the second concerns the question of primacy versus recency.

Ordering of Message Arguments. Is it better to give your strongest arguments first, putting your best foot forward? Or would you be better off ending with your strong arguments, building to a crescendo of argumentation and debate? Starting with strong arguments and ending with the weak ones is called an anticlimax order. Beginning with weak arguments and ending with the strong ones is called a climax order. Putting the strongest arguments in the middle is called a pyramidal order. The pyramidal order is least effective: There is no evidence that it facilitates comprehension or attitude change. By contrast, both the anticlimax and climax orders have been shown to facilitate attitude change (Gilkinson, Paulson, & Sikkink, 1954; Gulley & Berlo, 1956). In courtroom settings, where organization of closing arguments is of particular interest, research has supported the climax ordering. Walker, Thibaut, and Andreoli (1972) varied the order of strong and weak evidence for the prosecution and defense in a mock jury trial. They found that the weak followed by strong ordering was typically more effective than the strong followed by weak organization.

Primacy Versus Recency. Candidates frequently must decide whether to speak first or second in a political debate. Sales representatives often have to decide whether they should present their case before or after their leading opponents. Both of these situations involve issues of primacy and recency.

A primacy effect occurs when early information on an issue exerts a greater impact on attitudes than later information. Recency occurs when later information exerts the stronger impact. The evidence on this question is mixed. Some studies have found primacy effects, others have found recency effects, and still others have found that order of presentation does not make a difference (Hovland et al., 1957; Miller & Campbell, 1959; Rosnow & Robinson, 1967). Presumably, the impact of order of presentation on persuasion depends on a host of contextual factors, including the amount of attention audience members devote to the message, the audience's familiarity with the issue, and the amount of time that elapses between messages. Given the equivocal nature of the research findings, the best advice we can give persuaders is that order of presentation probably does not make that much difference in most persuasion situations. Rather than worrying about whether they should speak first or second, persuaders would be better advised to work on developing a message that addresses audience members' salient concerns.

Implicit Versus Explicit Conclusions

We have reviewed the major stylistic variables that must be considered in constructing a persuasive message. The last step in the process is formulating an appropriate ending to the message. There are two possibilities: A communicator can soft-pedal things by letting the audience draw its own conclusion, or the speaker can take a more hard-hitting approach, explicitly drawing the conclusion for the audience.

It is possible to make good arguments for each position. On the one hand, some scholars have contended that it is more effective to let listeners draw their own conclusions than to draw it for them explicitly. Proponents of nondirective psychotherapy have argued that: "No conclusion drawing by the communicator would make for greater attitude change, since decisions are said to be more effective when reached independently by the client than when suggested by the therapist (Thistlethwaite, de Haan, & Kamenetzky, 1955, p. 107).

Legal experts also have contended that when compared to explicit conclusion drawing:

> Subtle understatement is always more effective. A stark naked woman (or, one might suppose, a man as well) walking into the room suddenly has great shock value, but it really does not appeal to many people's prurient interest. If she (or he) is partially clothed, however, and leaves a little for the imagination, the prurient effect is much better. So, too, with argument. It is far better to let the jury's imagination do a little work. Give them the basic information. . . . Make them think they have arrived at the conclusion independently. (Smith, 1991, p. 1.31)

On the other hand, McGuire (1969) has argued that it is more effective to draw the conclusion explicitly for the audience:

> It may well be that if the person draws the conclusion for himself he is more persuaded than if the source draws it for him; the problem is that in the usual communication situation the subject is either insufficiently intelligent or insufficiently motivated to draw the conclusion for himself, and therefore misses the point of the message to a serious extent unless

the source draws the moral for him. In communication, it appears, it is not sufficient to lead the horse to the water; one must also push his head underneath to get him to drink. (p. 209)

As with other issues, the answer to the conclusion-drawing question depends on a host of other variables in the persuasion situation. When the message is difficult to comprehend or the receiver is not motivated to draw the appropriate conclusion, it is more effective to draw the conclusion explicitly (Fine, 1957; Hovland & Mandell, 1952). Under these circumstances, receivers are likely to miss the main point of the message unless the communicator explicitly draws the conclusion for them.

In other contexts, drawing a conclusion explicitly has definite drawbacks. When individuals are motivated and able to reach the appropriate conclusion independently, it is more effective to "leave the conclusion open and leave it to the audience to draw its own conclusions from the message" (Sawyer, 1988, p. 160). In these situations, a message that explicitly draws the conclusion for receivers may insult their intelligence or cause them to feel pressure to conform with the communicator's position. A message that leaves the conclusion open benefits from greater liking, due to the perception that the communicator respects the audience. It may also generate more vivid and personal responses to the message (Sawyer, 1988).

Applying these ideas to the advertising domain, Sawyer (1988) hypothesized that when receivers are highly involved in an advertisement, they should be more persuaded by a message that leaves the conclusion open than by one that draws the conclusion explicitly.

Sawyer argued that, under high-involvement, individuals should be motivated to carefully process the message, regardless of whether the message draws the conclusion explicitly for the audience. Sawyer (1988) manipulated involvement in an advertisement for a razor ad and developed two versions of the advertisement. One version drew the conclusion explicitly, noting that: "Now That You Know the Difference Shave with Edge – The Disposable Razor That is Best for You." The other ad left the conclusion open: "Now That You Know The Difference, Decide for Yourself Which Disposable Razor You Should Shave with." Among highly involved subjects (who were motivated to think carefully about the advertisement), the open-conclusion ad exerted a more positive impact on beliefs, attitudes, and purchase intentions than did the explicit conclusion advertisement. The findings suggest that when advertisers are deciding how to close a commercial, they should consider a consumer's level of interest and involvement in the product.

LANGUAGE STYLE

You landed a job working as an assistant to the director of public relations at a big consulting firm downtown. One morning your boss tells you he is shorthanded and needs your help. He would like you to give a short presentation to the director of the local United Way chapter on the firm's plans for the fall campaign. With this person, he tells you, how you say things is as important as what you say. Should you talk quickly, or make your pitch in a slower, more painstaking fashion? Should you be careful to qualify your statements, or would it be better to avoid qualifying phrases? Should you use figurative, graphic language, or opt instead for a less strident approach?

These questions focus on the role that language plays in persuasion. Language variables are also called *speech markers* or *noncontent cues*, because they do not focus on the content of what is said, but on how that content is spoken.[3] Three major language variables are discussed here: speed of speech, speech style, and language intensity.

Speed of Speech

A TV advertisement for Federal Express depicts a harried businessman, apparently facing an urgent deadline. The man is giving orders to two subordinates, and he is speaking in a staccato voice at a lightning quick speed:

> *Businessman:* You did a bang up job. I'm putting you in charge of Pittsburgh.
> *Employee:* Pittsburgh's perfect.
> *Businessman:* I know what's perfect, Peter. That's why I picked Pittsburgh. Pittsburgh's perfect, Peter. Can I call you, Pete?
> *Employee:* Call me Pete.

It was an ear-catching ad. Its claim to fame was the speed at which the actor playing the businessmen delivered his message. Speed of speech is a noncontent linguistic cue that is believed to enhance communicator credibility and message acceptance. A number of studies have examined the effects that speech rate exerts on persuasion, typically by having speakers deliver the same persuasive message at a slow, moderately fast, and extremely fast rate of speech (Miller, Maruyama, Beaber, & Valone, 1976; Street & Brady, 1982; see also LaBarbera & Maclachlan, 1979).

The main conclusion from these studies is that speed of speech enhances perceptions of credibility. Moderately fast and fast speakers are perceived to be more intelligent, more confident, and more effective than their slower-speaking counterparts. Faster speakers are also seen as more socially attractive (friendlier, kinder, nicer) than slower speakers. After a certain point, the effects of speech rate level off: Extremely fast speakers do not get higher competence ratings than moderately fast speakers. Clearly, however, a slow speaking rate is a persuasive liability. In most cases, slower speakers are perceived to be less fluent, less active, less persuasive, and even of lower social status than their faster talking counterparts.

A gender bias also seems to be at work here. Male communicators who speak quickly are rated as more competent and more socially attractive than males who speak slowly. On the other hand, fast-talking female speakers are perceived to be more competent than females who talk slowly, but they are not perceived to be more attractive (Street, Brady, & Lee, 1984). Perhaps women who speak quickly are perceived to be more aggressive and dominant than women who speak slowly; aggressiveness and dominance, in turn, may be viewed as undesirable traits in women.

Although there is strong evidence that speed of speech enhances credibility judgments, there is somewhat less support for the idea that it leads to attitude change. In fact, the effects of speech rate on persuasion depend on a host of other factors, of which the most important are the listener's own speaking rate, the topic of the message, and issue involvement.

First, there is some evidence that listeners who speak fast themselves evaluate faster talking communicators more positively than do individuals who speak at a slower clip (Street & Brady, 1982). This is, of course, another illustration of the similarity effect that we discussed in chapter 6. Not only do people prefer others who share their attitudes, but they also gravitate to speakers who speak at the same rate as they do.

Second, research suggests that, on intimate topics, slow speech will be more effective, whereas on nonintimate topics, fast speech will exert a greater impact (Giles & Street, 1985). For example, when the message concerns medical problems, sex, or a personal dilemma, slow speech may be more preferable. In these situations, slow speech may convey communicator concern and empathy, thereby enhancing credibility judgments.

Third, there is some evidence that speed of speech exerts a greater impact when receivers are low in involvement. Miller et al. (1976) found a speech rate effect, using a low-involving topic (the dangers of hydroponically grown vegetables), whereas Woodall and Burgoon (1983) failed to find an effect, using a highly involving topic (tuition increase). Once again, the Elaboration Likelihood Model (ELM) provides a useful framework for understanding these findings. When individuals lack the motivation to process a message, they are likely to look for simple cues in the persuasion situation to help them decide whether to accept the message recommendation. One such cue is speech rate. Under low-involvement, receivers are likely to invoke the decisional rule that "Fast speakers know what they're talking about"; although this notion amounts to a cultural myth, low-involved receivers will often use this heuristic to help them make a quick decision about the message. On the other hand, under high-involvement, receivers will carefully scrutinize message arguments. Consequently, under highly involving conditions, speed of speech will have little or no effect on message evaluations or on attitudes.[4]

Speech Style

The style in which a speech is delivered also influences credibility judgments and message evaluations. Consider the difference between these two versions of court testimony:

Version 1:

Johnson: . . . But . . . I . . . uh . . . well . . . I thought he had insulted my friend. I felt you know really very embarrassed. Then we . . . uh . . . we began shouting at each other. It happened kind of quickly. We both sort of shouted obscenities. I was very mad. Really mad, you know? Well, the bartender apparently said to stop it but we were both . . . uh . . . furious and you know didn't hear him very well at the time. Let us see . . . well, I guess . . . well that's about it up to. . . .

(Q.: Then Mr. Zander hit you?) or,

(Q.: Then you hit Mr. Zander?)

Johnson: Yes, sir, he (I) definitely did.

Version 2:

Johnson: . . . but I thought he had insulted my friend. Felt rather embarrassed. Then we began shouting at each other. It happened quickly. We both shouted obscenities. And I was mad. Quite mad. The bartender apparently said to stop it, but we were both furious. We didn't hear him well at the time. . . . And that's all there is up to. . . .

(Q.: Then Mr. Zander hit you?), or

(Q.: Then you hit Mr. Zander?)

Johnson: Yes.

(Bradac, Hemphill, & Tardy, 1981, p. 330)

The content of both messages is the same. However, the two versions differ dramatically in how the content is expressed. The first version is an example of powerless speech, and the second exemplifies powerful speech. There has been a great deal of interest on the part of researchers in determining the impact that a powerless or powerful speaking style has on attitudes toward the speaker.

First, let us define what we mean by powerless and powerful speech. Powerless speech, as conceptualized by Lakoff (1975) and other sociolinguists, includes the following language forms:

Hedges or Qualifiers. "Sort of," "kinda," "I guess" are phrases that "blunt the force or definitiveness of an assertion" (Newcombe & Arnkoff, 1979).

Hesitation Forms. "Uh," "well, you know" communicate a lack of certainty or confidence.

Tag Questions. "That plan will cost us too much, don't you think?" according to Bradley (1981) "is a declarative statement without the assumption that the statement will be believed by the receiver" (p. 77).

Disclaimers. "This may sound a little out of the ordinary, but," and "I'm not an expert, of course" are introductory expressions that ask the listener to show understanding or forbearance (Eakins & Eakins, 1976).

Intensifiers. "so," "very surely," and "really" are thought to display formal, bookish grammar.

Polite Forms. "I'd really appreciate it," "please," "if you wouldn't mind," and "if you please?" are often used to express deference to authorities.

Researchers have argued that a powerless speaking style reduces communicator credibility. For example, a tendency to hedge and qualify one's statements may suggest that the speaker lacks knowledge, and this may reduce perceptions of expertise. Listeners may also assume that a powerless style reflects low social status, and this may cause them to derogate the speaker. Consistent with these speculations, there is strong evidence that the use of a powerless speaking style is perceived to be less credible and less competent than a powerful speaking style (Erickson, Lind, Johnson, & O'Barr, 1978; Newcombe & Arnkoff, 1979).

These findings have interesting implications. They suggest that, in real life, many communicators may be downgraded not because of what they say, but because of how they say it. In academic settings, students (and professors) sometimes will preface a question with the phrase, "I know this sounds stupid, but. . . ." People use this phrase because they are afraid that the authority figure will ridicule them for asking a dumb question. The irony is that, by using this disclaimer, speakers undercut their own credibility and tarnish their image in the eyes of the authority.

Research on speech style also has interesting implications for jury decision making. Two scholars interested in the relationship between psychology and the law reviewed the research in this area and concluded that:

> The attorney should, whenever possible, come directly to the point and not hedge his points with extensive qualifications. The same holds for witnesses whom the attorney calls to the stand. Each witness should be encouraged to answer questions in the most direct and powerful way possible. (Linz & Penrod, 1984, pp. 44–45)[5]

Complicating Factors

Initially, researchers viewed speech style as either powerless or powerful. Therefore, they lumped a number of language forms (e.g., hesitation, intensifiers, politeness, tag questions) under the rubric of powerless speech. However, as several scholars have noted, this may oversimplify matters inasmuch as there are likely to be important differences between the various types of powerless language features (Bradac & Mulac, 1984; Hosman, 1989). As Bradac et al. (1981) observed:

> It may well be the case that with regard to certain judgments, e.g., communicator competence, low hesitancy and high politeness produce a rather positive attribution, perhaps especially when the communicator is a female, whereas high hesitancy and low politeness produce a relatively negative attribution. (p. 341)

Consistent with this theorizing, several teams of researchers have found that the use of hesitations, hedges, and tag questions reduces communicator credibility (Bradac & Mulac, 1984; Hosman, 1989; Newcombe & Arnkoff, 1979). On the other hand, intensifiers ("very surely," "really") and polite forms ("I'd really appreciate," "Thanks for the advice") can accentuate a speaker's credibility.[6]

The effects of language forms also depend on the speaker's goals. Bradac and Mulac (1984) found that powerful language was more likely to enhance source ratings when the communicator's intention was to appear authoritative rather than sociable. When the communicator wanted to appear sociable, rather than authoritative, polite language forms were more likely to create the desired impression.

The Role of Gender

Powerless speech has different effects, depending on the gender of the communicator.[7] Bradley (1981) designed an interesting study to examine the interaction of gender and communicator style. Bradley arranged for students to participate in a group discussion on the topic of drinking alcoholic beverages in moderation. Unbeknownst to the subjects, one of the group members was an experimental confederate who always opposed moderate drinking of alcohol. In half of the groups, the confederate was male; in the other half, the confederate was female. Half of the confederates used tag questions and disclaimers ("Well, I'm no expert but. . . .") to advance their arguments, whereas the other half did not use these powerless speaking techniques. At the end of the discussion, subjects evaluated the credibility of the confederate. Women who argued with qualifying phrases were perceived to lack knowledge and intelligence. However, men who advanced their arguments with qualifying phrases were not evaluated negatively.

Although in most situations women who use powerless speech forms may be evaluated more negatively than their male counterparts, there appears to be one situation in which powerless speech works to women's advantage. When a female is trying to persuade a male to change his mind on a low-involving issue, it appears as if powerless speech may be a highly effective linguistic device. Carli (1990) noted that:

> In interactions with men, women are not only expected to be less competent, but they are also expected to show relatively little competitiveness or dominance (Meeker & Weitzel-O'Neill, 1977). Exhibiting competitive or dominant behavior can be construed as an attempt to gain status or influence, and such attempts are considered inappropriate in people who are low in external status, regardless of their level of competence. . . . Because women may find it difficult to influence men if they behave too assertively . . . they may instead have to rely on more subtle and less direct strategies to induce influence. . . . One subtle approach to influence may be the use of uncertain or tentative language. (p. 944)

Consistent with these hypotheses, Carli (1990) found that female speakers were more influential with males when they spoke tentatively rather than assertively. On the other hand, women were more influential with other women when they used assertive (powerful) speech forms. By contrast, language made no difference for male speakers. Males were equally influential, regardless of their language or the gender of the receiver.

Clearly, there is a double standard in the area of powerful and powerless speech. Men can use powerful or powerless speech forms and still exert an influence on their audience. However, women have a more difficult time. In some contexts, they may find that powerless speech reduces credibility; in other situations (dominated by men), they may discover that powerless speech enhances credibility. Either way, women are likely to discover that society does not reward them for employing direct and decisive language.

Language Intensity

Intense language encompasses some of the most dramatic instances of social speech: obscenity, political metaphors, graphic language, and highly opinionated statements. Language intensity has been defined more formally as "the quality of language which indicates the degree to which the speaker's attitude toward a concept deviates from neutrality" (Bowers, 1964, p. 416).

Metaphors were among the earliest studied variants of intense language, and for good reason. They have been long invoked by political orators from William Jennings Bryan ("You shall not press down upon the brow of labor this crown of thorns. You shall not crucify mankind upon a cross of gold") to Ronald Reagan ("For those who yearn to be free . . . America is not just a word, it is hope, a torch shedding light to all the hopeless of the world") to Jesse Jackson ("If there were occasions when my grape turned into a raisin and my joy bell lost its resonance, please forgive me"). Metaphors can enhance persuasive message effects, provided that the metaphor is not too intense (or obscene), in which case it can reduce confidence in the speaker (Bostrom, Baseheart, & Rossiter, 1973; Jones & Burgoon, 1975; Mulac, 1976). In addition, receivers must be capable of processing the metaphor. One study found that political metaphors (the United States is hurtling its trade policies "like transatlantic spitwads aimed at the heart of Soviet repression") were only effective among politically sophisticated subjects who, presumably, had the cognitive structures necessary to make sense of the information (Johnson & Taylor, 1981).

On a broader level, language intensity effects are moderated by receivers' initial attitudes about the issue. Intense language enhances the impact of a message that is compatible with an individual's attitude, but reduces the effect of a communication that is discrepant with the person's position on the issue (Bradac, Bowers, & Courtright, 1979). If the listener agrees with the speaker, he or she is apt to feel even stronger about the cause when the speaker invokes another powerful adjective, throws out another epithet, or heaps more verbal fuel on the fire. Each additional use of intense language probably stimulates more favorable thoughts in the listener's mind and causes him or her to feel even more strongly about the issue. On the other hand, if the receiver vehemently disagrees with the communicator, the use of intense language will probably stimulate even more counterarguing, irritate the listener even more, and reduce persuasive message effects. Burke (1969) put it well. He noted that when a speaker addresses an audience that shares his or her point of view, the speaker should "(thunder) about its startling scope." But when speaking to a hostile audience, the speaker should use language that will "soften the effects of the blow" (p. 393).

Expectations also moderate language intensity effects. Burgoon (1989) noted that individuals have developed expectations about what constitutes appropriate communication behavior in a particular situation. In our culture, Burgoon noted, a double standard operates: Men are expected to employ intense, forceful language, but women are discouraged from speaking in more graphic ways. Thus, men can employ intense language and be highly effective in changing attitudes, whereas women are less persuasive when they use intense language (Burgoon & Stewart, 1975).

In politics, intense language can be particularly damaging to female candidates' credibility. Describing a vicious Massachusetts campaign between a male incumbent and a female challenger, one political commentator noted that there were limits to how aggressive the female candidate could be in her response to the opponent's attack ads. "It's sad but true," she wrote. "If you're a man and pull this stuff, you're tough. If you're a woman you're a bitch" (Boston Phoenix, 1982).

CURRENT VIEWS ON LANGUAGE AND PERSUASION

Popular books often warn people not to be taken in by glib speakers who have a "gift for gab." These accounts frequently leave readers with the impression that audience members are helpless at the hands of eloquent communicators who know how to use language to their advantage. These accounts perpetuate two myths about language and persuasion: (a) listeners passively go along with whatever the communicator suggests, and (b) verbal communication is a one-way process proceeding from the speaker to members of the audience (Giles & Street, 1985). Contemporary perspectives on language and persuasion dispute these notions.

Contrary to the "audience is passive" myth, listeners do not approach persuasion situations with a blank mental slate. Long before they sit down to listen to a particular speech, individuals have acquired beliefs about what constitutes effective communication and appropriate language usage. Listeners also have well-developed ideas about the qualities that an effective public speaker should possess. They have a sense of what "a voice of competence" sounds like (Street & Brady, 1982), and some scholars think that listeners compare a speaker with their prototype of an ideal speaker to arrive at a credibility judgment (Ray, 1986). In our culture, the prototypically competent communicator is someone who:

Speaks at a moderately fast rate of speech,
Uses powerful, forceful language,
Varies pitch levels,
Speaks loudly,
Uses a conversational style of speech, and
Speaks in a mainstream American dialect rather than in an ethnic dialect.

Speakers who exhibit these traits are likely to be evaluated positively. Those who depart from them are apt to get downgraded (Apple, Streeter, & Krauss, 1979; Aronovitch, 1976; Burgoon, Birk, & Pfau, 1990; Giles & Street, 1985; Pearce & Conklin, 1971; Scherer, 1979). Thus, far from passively riding the waves of a speaker's oratory, listeners are enormously active. They compare the speaker's linguistic style with their mental template, and, on this basis, decide whether the speaker sounds competent and credible. Little is known about the processes by which this occurs, but there is general agreement that listeners bring a rich storehouse of language beliefs to bear when they evaluate everyday persuaders.

Language effects do not proceed unidirectionally from speaker to audience members. Instead, interpersonal persuasion (as is seen in chapter 11) is fluid, dynamic, and reciprocal. In interpersonal settings, listeners' evaluations of a communicator's speaking style are frequently communicated to the speaker, and the speaker then must process these reactions and decide whether to adapt the message accordingly (Bryant & Street, 1988).

Speech accommodation theory notes that speakers can converge their speaking style so that it is more similar to those with whom they interact, or they can diverge their style so that it differs from the speech style of audience members (Giles & Smith, 1979). Speech accommodation theorists suggest that communicators are more effective when they "converge" or accommodate their style to suit the audience.[8] One study found that speakers who slowed their speaking rate down to match the level of their audience were evaluated more favorably than those who kept speaking at the same fast clip (see Giles & Street, 1985). Thus, smart persuaders adapt their style to fit the needs and perspectives of the audience. They speak quickly when talking to a fast-talking crowd, and slowly when talking about sensitive topics. They use a mainstream American dialect when trying to raise funds from a group of White businessmen, and avoid mainstream phrases like the plague when trying to convince a group of ghetto ministers to donate money to the cause. Volume, pitch, and conversational style are modulated to fit the perceived needs of the audience. Notice that we say perceived needs. Persuaders necessarily rely on their interpretations, filtered through their prototypes and belief systems, of what audience members are thinking. Audience members also filter the persuader's message through their own needs and their stereotypes of a "competent communicator." All of this makes interpersonal persuasion a dynamic process.[9]

CONCLUSIONS

We know a great deal about the types of messages that are most likely to influence an audience. We know that two-sided messages are (under certain conditions) more effective than one-sided messages, that high-fear appeals are more impactful than low-fear appeals, and that moderately fast speech is judged to be more credible than slow speech. What we lack is a comprehensive theory of message effects.

Contemporary scholars are trying to redress this imbalance in the research literature by fusing theories of cognitive processes with studies of message effects (Chaiken, 1987; Petty & Cacioppo, 1986). This is a healthy development. Simply knowing that message factor A has a greater impact on attitudes than message factor B is of little utility in practical situations.

Persuaders must know something about the ways in which an audience processes the persuasive message if they are to devise appropriate and effective communications.

* * *

EXHIBIT 7-1
CAN YOU LIE WITH STATISTICAL EVIDENCE?

Can you lie with statistics?

Darrell Huff thinks you can. In *How to Lie With Statistics,* Huff (1954) presents a variety of examples of how advertisers and persuasion practitioners make deceptive use of the trappings of social science (i.e., graphs, charts, and data). Huff's claim that advertisers "lie" with statistics is open to question. Before one can accept this statement, it must be shown that the information about the product is false. However, there is little question that advertisers freely use (and sometimes abuse) evidence to serve their needs.

One reason why evidence-based claims in advertising may be believed is because consumers do not fully understand the methods by which the data are gathered. For example, there is a principle of statistics that states that the larger the size of the sample, the more likely it is that behavior of the sample reflects the behavior of the larger population. According to this principle (called the *law of large numbers*), an investigator would have more confidence that his or her sample reflected the larger population than if it had a relatively small number of respondents than if it had a relatively small number of respondents. Yet Beltramini and Evans (1985) found that consumers perceived that an advertisement that contained data based on a sample of 10 individuals was more believable than findings obtained from a sample of 100 individuals.

Consumers also may not understand that hypotheses are tested by comparing the obtained results with those that would be expected on the basis of chance alone. Advertisers frequently take advantage of consumers' naivete in this area, as Huff (1954) noted:

> Let any small group of persons keep count of cavities for six months, then switch to Doakes' (toothpaste). One of three things is bound to happen: distinctly more cavities, distinctly fewer or about the same number. If the first or last of these possibilities occurs, Doakes & Company files the figures (well out of sight somewhere) and tries again. Sooner or later, by the operation of chance, a test group is going to show a big improvement worthy of a headline and perhaps a whole advertising campaign. This will happen whether they adopt Doakes' or baking soda or just keep on using their same old dentrifice. (p. 38)

* * *

EXHIBIT 7-2
THE SLEEPER EFFECT

During World War II, psychologist Carl Hovland conducted numerous studies of the impact of persuasive communications on Allied soldiers' beliefs, attitudes, and

EXHIBIT 7–2   **181**

general morale. The communications were documentary films, and they focused on the history of World War II from the rise of fascism in Germany to America's declaration of war against Germany and Japan in December 1941. Typically, Hovland and his colleagues obtained pretest measures of soldiers' beliefs and attitudes on a particular issue. They then assigned subjects to either the experimental group (which viewed the film) or the control group (which did not) and measured their beliefs and attitudes at a second point in time. However, in one study, Hovland et al. (1949) tried something different. For some subjects, they measured attitudes soon after the film had ended (a week later, to be exact), whereas for other subjects they waited 9 weeks until they assessed attitudes. Interestingly, the investigators found significantly more attitude change on the delayed, rather than on the immediate, posttest (Hovland et al., 1949).

The results attracted a great deal of attention because they were "counterintuitive" (i.e., the opposite of what you would expect on the basis of common sense). Intuitively, you would expect that a message would exert its strongest impact immediately after the message was received, or at least 7 days afterward. You certainly would not expect the message to have its greatest influence some 2 months after subjects had been exposed to the communication. Yet this is exactly what Hovland and his colleagues observed. They called this phenomenon the "sleeper effect."

Generally speaking, a sleeper effect occurs when the effects of a persuasive communication increase with the passage of time. In an effort to explain the effect, Hovland et al. invoked what has come to be known as the "discounting cue hypothesis." This interpretation asserts that a message will not change attitudes when a discounting cue is present. A discounting cue is defined as any information that causes an individual to question or summarily reject the position advocated in a persuasive message. Such cues include information that the source is low in credibility, a note that states the message arguments are inaccurate, or a qualifying remark such as "I'm not sure that my facts are correct." When the discounting cue is paired with the message conclusion, it reduces acceptance of the advocated position. This makes sense. If a speaker tells you at the outset that "I'm not sure my facts are correct," you will be more critical of the position that the communicator endorses.

With the passage of time, however, the association between the discounting cue and the message breaks down (i.e., the discounting cue becomes dissociated from the message). In other words, listeners forget that they received information that caused them to discount the message; they forget that the speaker told them at the outset that "I'm not sure my facts are correct." Yet they continue to remember the message arguments. Consequently, they exhibit a more positive attitude toward the advocated position on the delayed posttest than on the immediate posttest.

The discounting cue hypothesis helps explain the findings obtained by Hovland et al. (1949). Cook, Gruder, Hennigan, and Flay (1979) noted that the hypothesis specified that:

(a) the army, which sponsored the film, was seen as a biased and therefore untrustworthy source for war-relevant information; (b) that its sponsorship of the film led the soldiers to initially discount the filmed message, thereby reducing its immediate impact on their beliefs; (c) that as time passed the source of the message was forgotten or dissociated from the message, thereby removing the change-inhibiting force of the untrustworthy source; and (d) that once the source was no longer linked to the message, soldiers' attitudes rose to the residual level of belief change caused by the message alone. (p. 663)

Findings by Hovland et al. (1949) led other researchers to see if they could also obtain a sleeper effect. Some studies found a sleeper effect (Kelman & Hovland, 1953; Watts & Holt, 1979), whereas others did not (Gillig & Greenwald, 1974). Gruder et al. (1978) surveyed the research in the area and proposed that for a sleeper effect to occur, four conditions must be met:

1. The message must have a significant initial impact on attitudes;
2. The discounting cue must be powerful enough to significantly inhibit the attitude change that the message would otherwise have caused;
3. The discounting cue and message must become dissociated before delayed measurement takes place; and
4. The cue and message (must be) dissociated quickly enough so that the message by itself still has some impact when dissociation occurs (pp. 1063, 1074).

Gruder et al. (1978) tested their hypotheses about the sleeper effect by conducting a series of experiments in which subjects were assigned to one of three conditions: (a) a discounting cue/message group in which the cue was initially paired with the message, (b) a message-only group that did not receive the discounting cue, and (c) a no-message control. In one experiment, the message argued that the 4-day work week "produces more problems for the worker than it solves, and thus, is doomed because it will decrease rather than increase worker satisfaction" (p. 1065).

The discounting cue was a "Note to the Reader," which appeared at the end of the message and stated that the message conclusion was false. Attitudes toward the 4-day work week were measured immediately after the message and once again 5 weeks later. As Fig. 7.2 shows, a sleeper effect was obtained. The difference between immediate and delayed attitude in the discounting cue group was significantly greater than the difference between Time 1 and Time 2 attitude change in the no-message control.

One issue left unanswered by Gruder et al. concerns the mechanism by which a sleeper effect is obtained. The discounting cue hypothesis fails to explain why the discounting cue is forgotten over time, whereas the message arguments are remembered. Hannah and Sternthal (1984) proposed an availability-valence hypothesis that argued that people develop more favorable associations to the message than to the discounting cue, and that they mentally elaborate more on the message arguments than on the discounting cue. As a result of this greater cognitive elaboration, message information is "more available in memory" than is the discounting cue. Consequently, when attitudes are assessed after a time delay, the favorable associations people have to the message come to mind and influence their attitudinal judgments. Two studies have obtained evidence consistent with the availability-valence interpretation (Hannah & Sternthal, 1984; Mazursky & Schul, 1988).

EXHIBIT 7–2   **183**

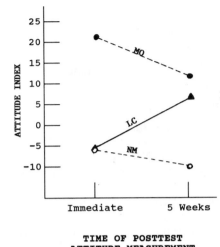

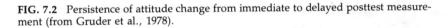

MO = Message-only Group
LC = Low Credibility Discounting Cue Group
NM = No Message Group

FIG. 7.2 Persistence of attitude change from immediate to delayed posttest measurement (from Gruder et al., 1978).

These findings poke another hole in Hovland's theory that persuasion results from learning message arguments. Instead, these latter results suggest that a sleeper effect will be obtained only when an individual cognitively elaborates on—or thinks a lot about—the information in the message. Passive, rote learning of arguments is not enough to ensure that the arguments will be available at a delayed measurement.

Although contemporary studies have identified the necessary conditions for a sleeper effect, they also have demonstrated that a sleeper effect is not nearly as pervasive a phenomenon as was once believed. A sleeper effect is only likely to be obtained if four conditions are met, and few situations in real life meet all four conditions. Moreover, as Hannah and Sternthal (1984) noted, persuaders who try to rely on the sleeper effect to enhance persuasion run the risk that they will make both the discounting cue and message arguments available to individuals at the time that they are pondering a course of action.

On the other hand, sleeper effects *can* occur in real life. Consider the case of Patrick Buchanan, who, in 1992, challenged George Bush for the Republican nomination. During the 1992 primaries, Buchanan charged that Bush had failed to articulate a sensible policy on the economy; Buchanan also criticized Bush for supporting various liberal causes. For many voters, Buchanan was a discounting cue—a low-credibility source who significantly inhibited attitude change. Thus, initially, many voters were not strongly influenced by Buchanan's message. Over time, however, the cue (Buchanan) became dissociated from the message; yet the message left an imprint on voters' attitudes toward George Bush.

* * *

EXHIBIT 7-3
EFFECTS OF HUMOR

Approximately 40% of all advertisements employ humor. Advertising executives believe that humorous ads can help attract attention to a commercial product (Madden & Weinberger, 1984). Public relations consultants suggest that their clients inject humor into their persuasive speeches (Hamlin, 1988). Presidential candidates hire consultants to prepare one-line jokes for use in presidential debates. Indeed, Ronald Reagan's use of one-liners is legendary: When opponent Walter Mondale accused Reagan of "government by amnesia," Reagan replied, "I thought that remark accusing me of having amnesia was uncalled for. I just wish I could remember who said it."

Does humor facilitate persuasion? The answer depends on the type of effect a persuader wishes to achieve (Ray, 1982).

There is strong evidence that injecting humor into a persuasive message helps get people's attention. Experiments have demonstrated that people pay more attention to a humorous message than to a serious communication (Duncan & Nelson, 1985; Markiewicz, 1974; Zillmann, Williams, Bryant, Boynton, & Wolf, 1980). Advertisers often try to cash in on humor's attention-grabbing potential— sometimes with great success. At the conclusion of a humorous ad campaign for Alaskan Airlines, a company official remarked that "our name recognition is so high it's embarrassing."

Besides capturing attention, humor can enhance the image of a communicator. Gruner (1985) found that even when a communicator ridiculed him or herself (as when a psychologist reputedly said, "You know what a psychologist is. That's a guy who would father a set of twins, have one baptized, and keep the other for a control") he or she got higher ratings on "sense of humor" and "wittiness" than a communicator who did not inject humor into the message. Importantly, the use of self-deprecating humor did not reduce evaluations of the communicator's credibility.

On the other hand, there are serious hurdles humor must cross on the road to persuasive effects. Humor frequently interferes with listeners' comprehension of the message (Bryant, Brown, Silberberg, & Elliott, 1981; Cantor & Venus, 1983). In some cases, it is humor's very ability to capture people's attention that acts as a stumbling block to its increasing message comprehension. The jokes are so funny and arousing that they take people's minds away from the message. In commercial advertising, people may remember the slogan, but forget the product.

When it comes to changing attitudes, humor's impact is decidedly mixed. Theoretically, one can argue that humor should facilitate persuasion by distracting people from thinking up counterarguments to the message, by putting them in a pleasant state of mind, or even by increasing their physiological arousal. However, the majority of studies have found that adding humor to a message does not increase its persuasive impact (Markiewicz, 1974). One reason for the null findings is that the jokes often were not sufficiently amusing to exert any impact. In other cases, the humor may have been too distracting, interfering with comprehension of the message. It is also possible that putting people in a good mood is not sufficient to change attitudes, particularly when those attitudes are strongly held.

EXHIBIT 7–3 185

It is often believed that humor can help reduce prejudiced attitudes. By getting people to laugh at themselves, the argument goes, ethnic prejudice can be reduced. The problem is that when the humor concerns ethnic or racial issues, people often perceive the humor selectively so that it reinforces what they already believe. A case in point is the 1970s' television comedy, "All in the Family." Although the show's creators hoped that the comedic portrayal of a bigot might cause people to question their own racial attitudes, it had the opposite effect. Vidmar and Rokeach (1974) reported that people selectively perceived the humor so that it fit their own biases. Highly prejudiced viewers identified with the bigoted views of Archie Bunker, the superpatriotic "hard hat" character. Prejudiced viewers admired Archie and believed that he won his arguments with liberal "hippie" son-in-law, Mike. Yet viewers low in prejudice had a different reaction: They admired Mike and believed that Archie lost the arguments.

There is some evidence that humor exerts a more subtle impact on attitudes, setting up the cognitive environment that facilitates long-term attitude change. One study found that people generated more promessage arguments when they read a humorous message than when they read a serious one, but only when a period of time had elapsed to allow the humorous material to "take hold" (Lammers, Leibowitz, Seymour, & Hennessey, 1983).

In bargaining contexts, humor may help redefine a serious situation into a more relaxed encounter, thereby making it easier for the other party to give in. O'Quin and Aronoff (1981) set up a situation in which the subject played the role of painting buyer and an experimental confederate played the role of seller. Buyer and seller were told that they should try to come to an agreement on the price of a painting. After both parties made a number of bids, they were informed by the experimenter that they had to come to some agreement shortly, and that the seller should make the next offer. The two participants returned to the bargaining table. In the humor condition, the seller quipped, "Well, my final offer is $_____ (one of several possible bids), and I'll throw in my pet frog." In the nonhumor condition, the seller simply said, "Well, my final offer is $_____ ." Buyers made a greater financial concession when the offer was accompanied by humor than when it was made without humor.

In summary, the effects of humor on persuasion depend on the communicator's objectives. If a persuader wants to attract attention to the message, then humor can help accomplish this goal. In competitive market situations, an advertiser may want to draw attention to a product, so as to separate it from the rest of the pack. Here, humor can be an effective tactic. But if the goal is comprehension, then humor may do more harm than good, particularly if the message is complicated (Bryant et al., 1981; Ray, 1982). If the goal is attitude change, then the communicator faces an uphill fight. Although humor can enhance communicator credibility, there is mixed evidence about its effect on attitudes. The research does suggest that before communicators design a humorous campaign, they should ask themselves several questions: (a) Do other people find the jokes funny?; (b) Does the humor offend key portions of the market?; (c) Is the humor relevant to the campaign objectives (Scott, Klein, & Bryant, 1990); and (d) What type of humor are we using—visual? verbal? self-disparagement? disparagement of others? (Eshleman & Neuendorf, 1989).

8
Channel
and Receiver Factors

This chapter focuses on the two other critical aspects of the persuasion process: the channel and the receiver. The channel is the modality in which the message is presented (e.g., face-to-face communication, the written modality, and videotape). The receiver is the audience member to which the message is directed. Studies of the receiver have examined whether certain types of people are more susceptible to persuasion than others. The discussion here focuses on theory and research on three receiver variables: gender, self-esteem, and self-monitoring.

CHANNEL VARIABLES

Literally thousands of studies have examined the impact of channel variables on cognitions, attitudes, and behavior. Most of these investigations have focused on television. Thus, investigators have explored the psychological impact that television entertainment, news coverage, and other events exert on viewers. A review of these studies goes beyond the scope of a book on persuasion, for the simple reason that they have examined the effects of content that is not explicitly designed to change attitudes or behavior. Persuasion, as you may recall, involves the intentional attempt to influence attitudes through the transmission of a message. Yet, the research on television examines the effects of content that was designed to impart information (news), to entertain (television violence), or to accomplish other goals that do not involve persuasion. Therefore, this section focuses rather narrowly on the handful of studies that have examined the persuasive effects of channel variables on attitudes.

Early channel research compared videotaped messages with similar messages presented by other modalities (e.g., audiotape and print) (Frandsen, 1963; Knower, 1935; Wilson, 1974). One might think that messages presented via videotape would be most effective, because the televised version of a current event offers the most vivid and graphic image of the event, and such imagery should enhance persuasion. However, this supposition is not supported by the available empirical data.

Taylor and Thompson (1982) systematically reviewed the research that compared the persuasive effects of videotaped versus oral versus written presentation of information. Taylor and Thompson found there was little evidence to support the view that videotaped presentations were most effective. Instead, the authors suggested that the impact of the channel on persuasion depends on other variables, such as the nature of the message that is transmitted. In other words, it is not possible to make blanket statements about whether one channel (e.g., television) is more effective than another (e.g., print). Instead, one channel may be ideally suited for the presentation of one type of message, whereas a different channel may be appropriate for the transmission of another type of message.

One message variable that interacts with the channel is message difficulty. Chaiken and Eagly (1976) contended that messages that are difficult to understand should be more persuasive when written than when audiotaped or videotaped. On the other hand, they argued that easy messages should be more persuasive when videotaped than when audiotaped, and more persuasive when audiotaped than when written.

Chaiken and Eagly noted that the written modality should help facilitate the comprehension of a difficult-to-understand message. After all, individuals can reread and review a written message. This should be particularly useful in the case of a difficult message whose content may not be readily understandable the first time around.[1] Chaiken and Eagly also argued that an easy message should be most persuasive when delivered through the videotape modality. When the message is easy, people do not have to devote their full energies to the content of the message. Consequently, they may attend more closely to the image of the communicator that they see on the screen. When the communicator projects a pleasant image, this should enhance liking, which in turn should augment message effects. The results supported the investigators' hypotheses: A difficult message was most persuasive when written than when audiotaped or videotaped, and an easy message was more persuasive when videotaped than when audiotaped, and more persuasive when audiotaped than when written.[2]

These findings have interesting implications for real-life persuasion situations, particularly politics (a realm in which the media have a substantial impact on attitudes and behavior). Chaiken and Eagly's results plainly suggest that a president will be more effective on television if he uses simple (easy) messages rather than complex (difficult) ones. If there was one president who used simple, easy-to-understand language, it was Ronald Reagan. Reagan used ordinary language—language that everyone could understand. For example, in a speech on heroism, he commented that: "We have every right to dream heroic dreams. Those who say that we're in a time when there are no heroes, they just do not know where to look. You can see heroes every day going in and out of factory gates . . . (Hart, 1984, p. 228).

By contrast, Jimmy Carter used more complex language. Consider this example:

> In distributing the scarce resources of our foreign assistance programs, we will demonstrate that our deepest affinities are with nations which commit themselves to a democratic path of government. Toward regimes which persist in wholesale violations of human rights, we will not hesitate to convey our outrage, nor will we pretend that our relations are unaffected. (Hart, 1984, p. 189)

Now there are many reasons why Carter lost his bid for reelection in 1980, and why Ronald Reagan was elected twice—once in 1980 and again in 1984. However, one communication-oriented explanation for these outcomes is that Reagan understood the limits and requirements of television and tailored his speeches to meet its needs, whereas Carter did not adapt his messages to fit the special needs of the television medium.

Another stream of research on the channel has adopted a more macro-approach to the communication channel. Researchers have found that individuals and subgroups differ in their uses and perceptions of communication channels. For example, in the area of health communication, certain subgroups (the poor) are likely to get most of their information from television, whereas other subgroups (the elderly) turn to doctors for their health facts (Freimuth & Marron, 1978); still other subpopulations (segments of the adolescent community) rely on peers and media for information about health (DePietro & Clark, 1984). These investigations suggest that persuasion campaigns targeted at these subgroups are most likely to influence attitudes if they direct their messages through the modalities that the subpopulations use and perceive to be the most credible.

For example, an AIDS campaign might want to reach intravenous (IV) drug users inasmuch as IV drug users are at high risk for getting AIDS. However, IV drug users tend to distrust information relayed through established channels, such as television PSAs. On the other hand, they rely heavily on information that is filtered through their interpersonal networks. Thus, to influence this subgroup, campaign planners must make sure that they direct their messages through the interpersonal, as well as the mass media, modality, and that they contact the most influential members of the IV drug use social network. This is an obvious point, but many practitioners tend to neglect it. They assume that television is the most powerful and persuasive medium. Studies of the channel make it clear that a message will not change attitudes unless there is a match between the medium, the message, and the channel preferences of the target audience.

RECEIVER FACTORS

One of the classic issues in persuasion research concerns whether certain people are more susceptible to persuasion than others. Research has focused on three individual difference variables: gender, self-esteem, and self-monitoring.[3]

Gender Differences

Are women more persuadable than men? For many years, the conventional wisdom was that women were, in fact, more susceptible to influence than men. This conclusion turned out to be quite controversial. Feminists and other writers questioned whether the research actually revealed strong evidence of a gender difference in susceptibility to influence (Maccoby & Jacklin, 1974). During the 1970s and 1980s, a number of researchers reanalyzed the literature on sex differences in persuasion using a measurement technique called *meta-analysis* (Cooper, 1979; Eagly & Carli, 1981). Meta-analysis provides a statistically based evaluation of the strength of the findings in a particular area. As is seen here, if there is one conclusion that has emerged from the meta-analyses of the research in this particular area, it is that the relationship between gender and influenceability is highly complex.

Eagly conducted two systematic analyses of the research on gender differences in influenceability (Eagly, 1978; Eagly & Carli, 1981). Eagly divided the research into three general areas: persuasion studies, conformity studies that involved surveillance by other group members, and conformity studies that did not involve surveillance by others members of the group. In the persuasion studies, the influence agent offered arguments supporting a particular position. In the conformity studies, subjects were faced with the task of deciding whether to go along with a view advocated by other members of the group. In some of the conformity studies (surveillance), individuals believed that other group members would see or hear their responses to the experimental questions. In other studies (nonsurveillance), subjects did not believe that their responses were under the surveillance of other members of the group.

Women were more susceptible to influence than men in all three settings. The effects were strongest in the conformity situations in which subjects believed that other group members would see or hear their responses (Eagly & Carli, 1981). However, it should be noted that these differences were relatively small in magnitude. Eagly and Carli (1981) estimated that only 1% of the variability in influenceability was accounted for by gender. Thus, the (relatively small) impact that gender exerts on susceptibility to influence depends, to a considerable degree, on the situation in which the influence induction takes place. Women are particularly likely to yield to the advocated position when the induction takes place in a group pressure situation in which individuals believe that other group members will see or hear their responses.

Several theories have been advanced to explain these findings. One view, expressed by Middlebrook (1974),[4] is that "the feminine role in our society has traditionally emphasized passivity and yielding so that when little girls are socialized into their roles, they may be trained to yield" (p. 190). A second socialization-oriented interpretation, advanced by Eagly, emphasized that women have been taught not so much to be passive, but, instead, to be cooperative and to maintain group harmony. As Eagly (1978) noted:

> Females are generally more concerned with social relational aspects of group situations than males are, and they are especially concerned with maintaining social harmony and insuring smooth interpersonal relations. This approach assumes that yielding to other people's views is a by-product of females' stronger interpersonal orientation. (p. 103)

At this point, we do not know which of these interpretations is correct.[5] However, given that the gender differences in influenceability are relatively small in magnitude, the search for the most parsimonious interpretation is probably of greater interest to the persuasion scholar than to the practitioner. Practitioners who wish to segment their audiences on the basis of psychologically relevant characteristics should probably focus on variables other than biological sex.

Self-Esteem

Research on self-esteem and persuasion has been guided by a communication/persuasion model developed by McGuire (1969). Based on Hovland's early work, McGuire (1969) argued that attitude change is the outcome of sequential steps, including attention and comprehension of the message and yielding to the arguments presented in the message. The communication/persuasion model proposed that these variables mediate the impact that self-esteem (or any personality variable) exerts on attitude change. Specifically, the model predicts that low self-esteem persons will be influenced primarily through the "yielding mediator," whereas high self-esteem individuals will be affected via the "comprehension mediator."

The idea is that low self-esteem persons typically fail to *attend to* or *comprehend* the persuasive message. McGuire was not terribly clear about why this should be the case, but presumably, low self-esteem persons are preoccupied with their own problems. Consequently, they focus their attention on themselves rather than on an external communication. At the same time, persons with low self-esteem also lack confidence in their own opinions. Consequently, the model stipulates that they should accept the position advocated by the communicator (i.e., they should *yield* to the position advocated in the message).

McGuire argued that high self-esteem persons should be more likely than their low self-esteem counterparts to attend to and comprehend the persuasive message. Individuals with high self-esteem should be more inclined to direct their attention outward (to the message) rather than inward (toward their own thoughts and feelings). However, persons high in self-esteem, being confident in their own views, should not *yield* to the views expressed by the communicator. McGuire (1968) also suggested that the failure of low self-esteem persons to comprehend the message and the tendency for high self-esteem individuals to refuse to yield to the message should cancel each other out. This should result in a nonmonotonic, inverted U-shaped relationship between self-esteem and persuasion, with the greatest amount of attitude change occurring among persons who have a moderate level of self-esteem.

The available evidence is consistent with McGuire's theory. Rhodes and Wood (1992) conducted a meta-analysis of the research on self-esteem and influenceability. They found evidence of a curvilinear relationship between self-esteem and persuasion. Specifically, they found that individuals of moderate self-esteem were more susceptible to influence than those of high or low self-esteem.

In addition, there is also empirical support for McGuire's notion that high self-esteem persons change their attitudes through a process of comprehension. Skolnick and Heslin (1971) provided particularly convincing evidence in support of this hypothesis. These authors argued that the relationship between self-esteem and attitude change depends on the quality of the message. They reasoned that low self-esteem persons should be influenced by a message of either low or high quality, whereas high self-esteem individuals should be more persuaded by a high-quality message. Skolnick and Heslin (1971) contended that:

> (low self-esteem) persons have little confidence in themselves and their opinions, do not attend to the quality of the communications and consequently will change their attitudes when faced with almost any influence attempt. Alternatively, for high quality communications, persons with high levels of self-esteem will be most persuaded, since these persons keenly attend to the quality of the communication and are highly persuaded by good, valid, logical arguments. (p. 244)

Skolnick and Helson went back to the original studies of self-esteem and persuasibility and asked students to evaluate the quality of the persuasive messages that were used in the studies. The authors also divided the messages into two groups: those that produced positive or linear relationships between self-esteem and persuasion (the higher the self-esteem, the more the persuasion), and those that found negative relationships (the lower the self-esteem, the greater the persuasion). Consistent with their hypothesis, Skolnick and Heslin (1971) found that messages that produced positive relationships between self-esteem and persuasion employed more cogent arguments than those that uncovered negative relationships between the two variables.

Self-Monitoring

High self-monitors and low self-monitors differ profoundly in their susceptibility to persuasive messages. You may recall from chapter 4 that high self-monitors are adept at controlling the images of self they present in interpersonal situations, and that they are highly sensitive to cues that signify the appropriate behavior in a given situation. High self-monitors use these cues as guidelines for regulating their own behavior. By contrast, low self-monitors are less concerned with conveying an impression that is appropriate for the situation. Low self-monitors, either because they are less able or less motivated to regulate their public self-presentations, are less sensitive to social information about how one should behave in different situations. Instead, low self-monitors look "within themselves" for information about how to behave in a social situation. Their behavior reflects their internal dispositions and beliefs.

One implication of the existence of individual differences in self-monitoring is that high and low self-monitors should react very differently to the same persuasive message. Drawing on functional theories of attitudes, Snyder and DeBono (1985) articulated several hypotheses regarding the impact of self-monitoring on susceptibility to persuasion. In particular, DeBono (1987) argued that, for high self-monitors, attitudes serve primarily a *social-adjustive* function: They help individuals behave in ways that are appropriate to their social circumstances. Given that high self-monitors are concerned with tailoring their behavior to fit the situation, it is reasonable to believe their interpersonal orientations might contain attitudes that have been formed on the basis of how well they serve the needs of fitting into social situations and of interacting smoothly with peers. In contrast, for low self-monitors, attitudes can be expected to serve a *value-expressive* function: They allow the individual to express his or her underlying values and dispositions. Given that low self-monitors "value congruence between who they are and what they do" (Snyder, 1987), their interpersonal orientations should include attitudes formed on the basis of how well they enable the person to communicate underlying values.

DeBono (1987) tested these hypotheses in a laboratory experiment. High and low self-monitoring subjects were informed that the psychology department was sponsoring a mental health week during which psychologists would talk about a number of mental health issues. Students were told that several speakers had sent audiotapes of their lectures to give students a feel for the issues that were to be discussed. Subjects then were informed that they would listen to an audiotape made by Dr. Gregory Stevenson, a leading researcher from the University of Nebraska.

In the social adjustive condition, subjects listened to an audiotaped message in which the fictitious Professor Stevenson discussed the results of a survey he had conducted, which found that 70% of the students polled were in favor of treating the mentally ill in state hospitals and institutions. The message played on social-adjustive concerns by letting subjects know what the majority (socially appropriate) position was on the topic of institutionalization of the mentally ill. In the value-expressive condition, Professor Stevenson discussed research that he had conducted on the values underlying institutionalization of the mentally ill. The professor noted that he had found that the values of responsibility and loving (values that most students had previously rated as important) underlied favorable attitudes toward institutionalizing the mentally ill, whereas the values of imaginativeness and courageousness (values that most students had indicated were relatively unimportant) underlied favorable attitudes toward the deinstitutionalization of the mentally ill. The message played on value-expressive concerns by associating one side of the issue with values that were rated as highly important and associating the other side with values that were rated as relatively unimportant.

After listening to the audiotape, subjects indicated their attitudes toward institutionalizing the mentally ill. (Tests conducted before the experiment had revealed that most students opposed treating the mentally ill in hospitals and institutions.) High self-monitors experienced greater attitude change in the direction of institutionalization of the mentally ill after hearing the social-adjustive message. Low self-monitors experienced more attitude change after listening to the value-expressive speech. For high self-monitors, who tailor their attitudes to fit the situation, the information that the majority of students favored institutionalization was quite useful; it told them what the dominant position on the issue was. Thus, after hearing the social-adjustive message, high self-monitors changed their attitudes in the direction of institutionalization. Low self-monitors, who disdain the idea that one should adopt attitudes to please others, were not influenced by the message that played on social adjustive concerns. Being primarily concerned that their attitudes reflected their underlying values and convictions, low self-monitors were influenced by the message that addressed value-expressive concerns.

Implications for Advertising.   Snyder and DeBono (1985) have suggested that the self-monitoring construct has interesting implications for the development of product advertisements. They argued that *image-based messages* should appeal to high self-monitors, whose attitudes perform a social adjustive function. "Image appeals," they noted, "may allow (high self-monitors) . . . to perceive that a product has the potential to create images appropriate to various social circumstances" (Snyder & DeBono, 1989, p. 345). By contrast, Snyder and DeBono contended that *product-quality messages* should be particularly effective among low self-monitors, whose attitudes perform a value-expressive function. "Information about product-quality," they noted, "may be readily interpreted by (low self-monitors) . . . in terms of underlying values and other evaluative reactions" (p. 345).

To test these hypotheses, the investigators devised three sets of magazine advertisements. One ad emphasized the image associated with the product; the other made claims about the product's quality. The products advertised were whisky, cigarettes, and coffee. The contents of the whiskey ads are summarized here:

> The picture for this set of advertisements prominently displayed a bottle of Canadian Club resting on a set of house blueprints. The written copy for the image-oriented advertisement stated, "You're not just moving in, you're moving up," and the product-quality-oriented advertisement claimed that "when it comes to great taste, everyone draws the same conclusion." (Snyder & DeBono, 1985, p. 589)

Subjects read an image-oriented and a product-quality advertisement for each of the three products. They then indicated their attitudes and behavioral intentions toward the products. High self-monitors responded more favorably toward the image-oriented ads, whereas low self-monitors reacted more favorably to the product-quality ads. High self-monitoring individuals were willing to pay more money for a product if it was marketed with an appeal to its image than if it was advertised with an appeal to its quality. By contrast, low self-monitoring individuals were willing to pay more money for a product if it was advertised with a product-quality orientation than if it was advertised with an image orientation. In addition, high self-monitors were more willing to try a product if it was advertised with an image orientation, whereas low self-monitors were more willing to try a product if it was marketed with a product-quality orientation.

These results have fascinating implications for advertising. They suggest that image-oriented advertisements should be particularly influential with high self-monitors, whereas product-quality ads should be especially effective among low self-monitors. Thus, if advertisers believe that a particular audience (e.g., upwardly mobile Yuppies) consists primarily of high self-monitors, they may wish to emphasize the image associated with the product. On the other hand, if advertisers believe that the target audience consists primarily of low self-monitors, then they may wish to make claims about the product's quality. Or, advertisers may try to have their cake and eat it by developing image- and product-quality ads for the same product; this way they can use the image appeal to draw in the high self-monitors and the product-quality ad to attract the low self-monitors.

Commentary on Personality and Persuasibility Research

Receiver studies debunk the common notion that there are "certain types of people" who are gullible or highly susceptible to persuasion. Forty years of research have failed to uncover a "personality type" (or "demographic category of persons") that invariably falls prey to social influence attempts. Much of the confusion in this area has stemmed from the absence of good theories regarding personality and persuasibility. Researchers have made "stabs in the dark," trying to determine whether this personality variable or that variable influences susceptibility to persuasion. However, studies based on personality variables have met with limited success, because these investigations have not been adequately grounded in cognitive theories of attitude change (Eagly, 1981). By contrast, an interactive approach that combines both personality and attitude change processes has met with greater success.

McGuire's information-processing model stipulated that the impact of a personality factor on persuasibility depends on whether the factor influences the "comprehensibility mediator" or the "yielding mediator." McGuire proposed that the relationship between a personality variable (such as self-esteem) and persuasibility resembles an inverted U, with individuals in the middle of the distribution (e.g., those with moderate amounts of self-esteem) exhibiting the greatest amount of change. The available evidence on self-esteem and influenceability is consistent with McGuire's theory. In addition, the notion that low self-esteem persons change their attitudes through a process of yielding, and that high self-image persons modify their attitudes through a process of comprehension, has received some support from the research literature. In general, McGuire's model has made an important contribution to the field. By calling attention to the fact that the processes by which a persuasive message achieves its effect differ, depending on whether the receiver has low or high self-esteem, McGuire helped stimulate later information processing-oriented research on personality and persuasibility (Cacioppo et al., 1983).

Functional theory, as invoked by Snyder, DeBono, and their colleagues, promises to make an even more substantial contribution to research on personality and susceptibility to influence. The functional approach suggests that for a message to change an individual's attitude, it must be directed at the underlying function that the attitude serves. One of the classic problems with functional theories is that they do not indicate a priori (or in advance) just what function an attitude serves for a particular person. However, this appears to be a nonproblem in the case of self-monitoring, because Snyder's conceptualization allows us to make a priori predictions. Indeed, Snyder and DeBono were able to predict that attitudes would serve a social adjustive function for high self-monitors and a value-expressive function for low self-monitors. This prediction enabled them to hypothesize that different message strategies would have to be employed to reach high self-monitoring and low self-monitoring individuals.

Like McGuire, Snyder and DeBono do not believe that individuals who are at one end of the personality variable are more susceptible to persuasion than those at the other end. They do not believe that high self-monitors are more susceptible to persuasion than lows, or vice versa. Instead, they argue that messages can influence individuals at both ends of the continuum—the key is that messages must play on the appropriate attitudinal function. The implication for persuaders is that if they want to change an individual's attitudes, they must understand "what the attitude does for the person"—that is, they must understand the particular function that it serves.[6]

CONCLUSIONS

Research on channels and receivers has debunked several common myths. It also has demonstrated that an adequate understanding of communication effects requires that we take an "interactive" approach, focusing on the ways in which a particular variable "interacts with" or combines with other contextual or person factors. Studies of the communication channel have found that the impact of a particular channel on persuasion depends on other variables, such as the complexity of the message and the recipient's perceptions of the credibility of the channel.

Research on individual differences in persuasion has found that the relationship between a particular personality (or demographic) variables and persuasion is considerably more complex than has been commonly assumed. Eagly's research has shown that women are not invariably more susceptible to persuasion than men; instead, the (relatively small) effect that gender has on influenceability depends, to a considerable degree, on the situation in which the influence induction takes place. Even here, there is debate about just why it is that women are more likely than men to conform in group pressure/surveillance situations.

Studies of personality and persuasibility have also obtained complex answers to intuitively interesting questions concerning the impact of personality factors on susceptibility to influence (Perloff, 1978). There is some evidence that high self-esteem individuals process messages differently than low self-esteem individuals. This suggests that different message strategies will be effective on high self-esteem and low self-esteem persons. There is also evidence that individuals with moderate self-esteem are more susceptible to influence than those of high or low self-esteem. At the same time, Snyder, DeBono, and their colleagues' research on self-monitoring has demonstrated that a message is more likely to change an individual's attitude when it addresses the underlying function that the attitude serves. Thus, messages that play on social adjustive concerns exert a particularly strong impact on the attitudes of high self-monitors, whereas communications that appeal to value-expressive needs have an especially strong effect on the attitudes of low self-monitors. The functional approach represents a promising direction for future studies of personality and persuasibility.

9
Social Judgment Theory

In a lithograph, "Hand with Reflecting Globe," the Dutch artist Maurits Escher has cleverly depicted the tendency for the individual to be the focus of his world (see next page). In a commentary on Escher's work, Gardner (1966) noted that in this lithograph:

> Escher is seen staring at his own reflection in the sphere. The glass mirrors his surroundings, compressing them inside one perfect circle. No matter how he moves or twists his head, the point midway between his eyes remains exactly at the center of the circle. "He cannot get away from that central point," says Escher. "The ego remains immovably the focus of his world." (p. 121)

These comments aptly describe the social judgment theory approach to persuasion, which is the focus of our discussion in this chapter. It is useful to begin our discussion of social judgment theory by contrasting it with Hovland's theory of message effects. As you may recall, Hovland, Janis, and Kelley (1953) emphasized that communications change attitudes to the extent that they induce receivers to remember the major arguments contained in the message. Hovland and his colleagues focused on the impact of variables that were external to the individual—factors such as source expertise, primary-recency, and message sidedness. By contrast, Muzafer Sherif, Carolyn Sherif, and their colleagues argued that any analysis of communication effects must begin with the receiver. Any attempt to change attitudes, they contended, must begin with a thorough understanding of the beliefs and biases of the target audience that the communicator was trying to reach. As Sherif and Sherif (1967) noted:

> The basic information for predicting a person's reaction to a communication is *where* he places its position and the communicator relative to

"Hand with Reflecting Globe" by Maurits Escher

himself. The way that a person appraises a communication and perceives its position relative to his own stand affects his reaction to it and what he will do as a result. (p. 129)

Thus, social judgment theory emphasizes that receivers do not evaluate a message purely on the merits of the arguments. Instead, the theory stipulates that people compare the advocated position with their initial attitude and then determine whether they should accept the position advocated in the message. Like Escher staring at his own reflection, the receiver is preoccupied with his own attitude about the topic. He can never escape his perspective. He always evaluates the external message in terms of his own "internal" attitude toward the issue.

This chapter is divided into three sections. The first section discusses the core concepts of social judgment theory (the latitudes of acceptance, rejection, and noncommitment) and assimilation and contrast effects. The second section focuses on the impact of message discrepancy on attitude change. The third section describes classic and contemporary studies of ego-involvement.

CORE COMPONENTS OF SOCIAL JUDGMENT THEORY

Latitudes of Acceptance and Rejection

Traditionally, persuasion researchers have defined an attitude as "the stand or position the individual upholds" (Whittaker, 1967). Social judgment theory has a more dynamic view of the concept. It views an attitude as consisting of a continuum of evaluations—a range of acceptable positions, unacceptable positions, and positions toward which the individual has no strong commitment. Think of it this way: If we ever could see an attitude up close, we would discover that it is a large emotion-packed terrain that consists of three separate subdivisions. The *latitude of acceptance* consists of all those positions on an issue that an individual finds acceptable, including the most acceptable position. The *latitude of rejection* includes all those positions that the individual finds objectionable, including the most objectionable position. Lying between these two regions is the *latitude of noncommitment*, which consists of all those positions on which the individual has preferred to remain noncommittal. This is the arena of the "do not know," "not sure," and "haven't made up my mind" responses. Interestingly, the latitudes notion suggests that two people may endorse the same position on an issue, but differ dramatically in their tolerance for other (alternative) positions on the same issue.

A number of early studies found that extremity of position influenced the size of the latitudes (Sherif & Hovland, 1961; Sherif, Sherif, &

Nebergall, 1965). Thus, individuals who advocate an extreme position on an issue typically have large latitudes of rejection relative to their latitudes of acceptance and noncommitment. Individuals who have a strong position on an issue reject nearly all opposing positions and accept only statements that are adjacent to their own stand on the issue. Persons who take a more moderate position tend to be relatively open to new positions; thus, they accept about as many statements as they reject.[1]

Assimilation and Contrast Effects

Assimilation and contrast are judgmental distortions (i.e., perceptual biases that result from the tendency to perceive phenomena from the standpoint of a personal reference point or "anchor"). Assimilation is the displacement of the judgment toward the anchor (i.e., the judgment that the stimulus is more similar to the anchor than it actually is). Contrast is the displacement of the judgment away from the anchor (i.e., the perception that the difference between the stimulus and the anchor is greater than it actually is).

Sherif et al. (1958) first demonstrated assimilation and contrast effects in a study that involved perceptions of simple physical objects. Subjects in the study by Sherif et al. were asked to lift six weights that ranged from 55 to 141 grams and then to sort the weights into six different categories based on how heavy they were. On the first task, subjects were not provided with a reference point, nor a standard for determining what "heavy" meant. As Fig. 9.1 indicates, subjects did a pretty accurate job of sorting the weights into categories, assigning approximately the same number of weights to each category. On the second task, subjects were given an "anchoring stimulus." They were asked to lift a weight of 141 grams. When subjects believed that 141 grams was what the experimenter meant by "heavy," their evaluations of the other weights changed dramatically. They judged more of the other weights to be heavy—an assimilation effect. On the third task, subjects lifted a weight of 347 grams. When subjects were presented with this extreme anchoring stimulus (i.e., when they believed that 347 grams was what was meant by heavy), they judged many more of the weights to be light by comparison. In this case, subjects moved their judgments of heaviness away from the anchor (a contrast effect). One researcher summed up the latter findings by observing that: "If one has been lifting fifteen to twenty-pound turkeys all day, an eight-pound turkey may seem exceptionally light" (Granberg, 1982, p. 308).

A similar process occurs when people evaluate social objects. In the case of persuasive communications, people evaluate a message by comparing the advocated position to their own position on the issue. Their attitudes serve as the reference points or anchors for their evaluations. Specifically, social judgment theory stipulates that positions that fall in the latitude of

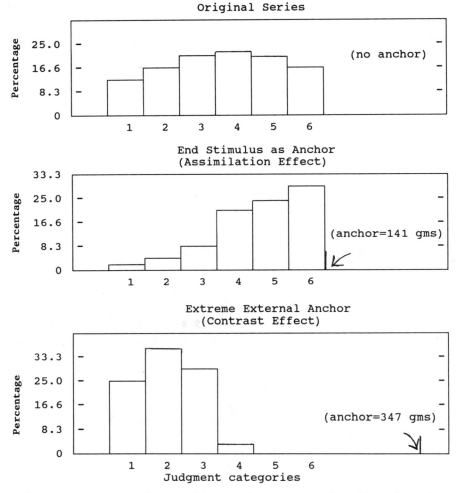

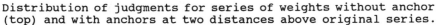

Distribution of judgments for series of weights without anchor (top) and with anchors at two distances above original series.

FIG. 9.1 Assimilation and contrast effects (from Kiesler, Collins, & Miller, 1969, as adapted from Sherif, Taub, & Hovland, 1958).

acceptance are *assimilated* (i.e., judged to be more similar to the individual's own position than they actually are). Communications that fall into the latitude of rejection are *contrasted* (i.e., judged to be more discrepant from the person's own position than they actually are).

As an example, consider the issue of federal spending on defense. Suppose you feel that too much federal money is being spent on defense (and particularly on nuclear weapons) In your view, more money should be spent on pressing social problems, such as AIDS, unemployment, and the deterioration of inner-city neighborhoods. You recognize that some money needs to be devoted to national security needs, so you would not support a cutback on defense spending of more than 70%. On the other hand, you believe that the cutback has to be large enough so that social programs can benefit. You favor a cutback in the range of 30%–70% (see Fig. 9.2).

Now suppose you attend a foreign policy debate between a liberal and a conservative. The liberal emphasizes that federal monies are urgently needed to finance job training programs in depressed areas of the country. She recommends a 60% cutback in funding for defense. The conservative acknowledges that the United States can afford to trim its defense budget, given that it no longer faces serious threats from foreign powers. However, she insists that the United States needs to maintain a strong nuclear defense arsenal. The conservative recommends a 20% cutback in defense spending.

Social judgment theory predicts that you would assimilate the liberal's position to your own, because it falls within your latitude of acceptance. The theory also suggests that you would contrast the conservative's position, because her position falls within your latitude of rejection. Specifically, you should overestimate the extent to which you agree with the liberal speaker on the question of defense (in fact, you are more sympathetic with the prodefense position than is the liberal). In the same fashion, you should exaggerate the differences between your view and the conservative's (in fact, you and the conservative speaker both agree that social programs deserve a significant amount of federal funding). In both cases, the anchor (your attitude toward defense) should serve to distort your judgments about the positions advocated in the message.[2]

Political Applications.   Much of the research on assimilation and contrast has examined perceptions of political communications. (There is a good reason for this, as is discussed in the next section.) Granberg and Brent

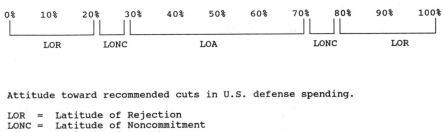

Attitude toward recommended cuts in U.S. defense spending.

LOR   = Latitude of Rejection
LONC = Latitude of Noncommitment
LOA   = Latitude of Acceptance

FIG. 9.2   Hypothetical example of the latitudes.

(1974) conducted one of the first studies of assimilation and contrast of candidates' issue positions. Granberg and Brent focused on voter perceptions of the positions that 1968 presidential candidates Hubert Humphrey, a Democrat, and Richard Nixon, a Republican, took on Vietnam. Granberg and Brent asked respondents to tell them which candidate they voted for and to estimate where the candidate stood on the Vietnam War. They also asked voters to indicate their own position on the Vietnam War. The results indicated that voters overestimated the similarity of their own views on Vietnam and those of their preferred candidate (assimilation effect). Voters who opposed the Vietnam War and voted for Humphrey perceived that Humphrey was more opposed to the war than did Humphrey voters who favored a military solution to the conflict. Similarly, Nixon voters who supported the war were more likely to perceive that Nixon supported the war effort than were the Nixon voters who opposed the Vietnam War.

Interestingly, an analysis of the two candidates' speeches revealed little evidence of actual differences in their positions toward the Vietnam War (Page & Brody, 1972). Thus, voters may have been projecting their own biases onto their preferred candidates. At the same time, Granberg and Brent found little evidence that voters contrasted the position of their nonpreferred candidate from their own position on the Vietnam issue.

Other studies of political perception also have found a stronger tendency toward assimilation than contrast (Granberg, 1982; Granberg & Jenks, 1977; King, 1977–1978). However, the lack of evidence for contrast may be due, in part, to measurement problems. One study suggested that if these problems were corrected, a stronger contrast effect would emerge (Judd, Kenny, & Krosnick, 1983).

Social Judgments and Attitude Change

Now that we have described the ways in which people judge social communications, we can move on to the question of how these judgments influence their susceptibility to persuasion. In general, as we noted at the beginning of the chapter, social judgment theory assumes that an individual's reaction to a communication depends on "where he places its position and the communicator relative to himself" (Sherif & Sherif, 1967). Specifically, the theory stipulates that attitude change occurs when the position advocated in the message is judged to lie within the latitude of acceptance. However, when the advocated position is perceived to fall within the latitude of rejection, little or no attitude change is expected to occur.

Two studies conducted during the 1960s found support for these general propositions (Atkins, Deaux, & Bieri, 1967; Peterson & Koulack, 1969). Eagly and Telaak (1972) argued, based on these findings, that persons who have a relatively wide latitude of acceptance on a particular issue should change their attitudes on that issue following exposure to a persuasive message. However, they contended that individuals with narrower latitudes of acceptance should be more resistant to influence.

Eagly and Telaak (1972) assessed latitudes of acceptance by asking students to complete a Thurstone-type attitude scale for birth control. The scale included statements that were highly favorable to birth control ("Birth control devices should be available to everyone, and the government and public welfare agencies should encourage the use of such devices"), items that were moderately favorable to birth control ("To curtail indiscriminate premarital sex, birth control products should be distributed by doctors to married people only"), and statements that opposed birth control ("All birth control devices should be illegal and the government should prevent them from being manufactured").

Based on their evaluation of these items, subjects were divided into three groups: those with a wide latitude of acceptance (tolerant of a large number of positions on birth control), those with a medium latitude (accepting of a moderate number of positions), and those with a narrow latitude of acceptance (accepting of only a few positions). Subjects then read a persuasive message that took a position on birth control that was either slightly, moderately, or highly discrepant from their own attitudes about the issue. Subjects with wide latitudes of acceptance changed their attitudes to a significantly greater degree than did subjects with medium or narrow latitudes. The interaction between latitude width and discrepancy size was not significant, however.

The findings obtained by Eagly and Telaak, as well as by other researchers, have interesting implications for everyday persuasion situations. Whittaker (1967) noted that research on social judgment theory shows that:

> Communicators *must* know the position or stands of individuals with whom they are communicating, at least if they are interested in changing attitudes. It is not enough to simply present one's own position. In fact, presentation of one's own position without regard for that of the listener may result in convincing the listener that he is right and the communicator is wrong. (p. 175)

Thus, according to social judgment theory, a communicator should avoid making statements that fall into the latitude of rejection of most members of the audience. Under such circumstances, the communicator will induce little or no change in attitude; in fact, he or she may actually produce a "boomerang effect" (attitude change in the direction opposite to that intended). Instead, the speaker should determine where most members of the audience stand on the issue and then tread carefully, trying as much as possible to make statements that are judged to lie within the latitude of acceptance or the latitude of noncommitment.

Social judgment theory has particularly interesting implications for the development of political messages. Political communicators, after all, are faced with the task of tailoring their messages to diverse constituencies. Moreover, their goals differ somewhat from those of other persuaders (O'Keefe, 1990). Candidates for public office generally are not interested in changing voters' attitudes about the issues; they are not trying to convince voters to alter their stands on abortion, environmental pollution, or foreign aid. Instead, politicians typically attempt to convince voters that they share voters' views on the major issues of the campaign (Schwartz, 1973). In social judgment theory terms, the candidate wants to encourage voters to assimilate the candidate's position (i.e., to overestimate the similarity between their own position and that of the candidate).

One way that a candidate can encourage voters to engage in biased assimilation is to present the issues in a vague and diffuse manner. By being very vague and unclear about where he or she stands on the issues, a candidate can encourage voters to conclude that "the candidate really shares our point of view on Issue X." Voters may not change their views about Issue X, but they may decide to vote for the candidate who espouses this position. Granberg and Seidel (1976) aptly noted that:

> Unless a candidate is satisfied with being right rather than President, the attitudes of the electorate and the distance between them and the positions to be taken should be carefully considered. In order to be assimilated and elected, it may be necessary to moderate one's publicly stated positions, especially in a two-party system and on issues on which the opinions of the electorate are normally distributed and centered at some moderate point. . . . (p. 13)

Of course, although moderation may be in the best interest of the presidential candidate, it may not be in the best interest of the voters or of a country that needs radical proposals for social reform.

MESSAGE DISCREPANCY

We have emphasized that an individual appraises a message and judges its position relative to his or her own stand on the issue. Thus, the perceived distance (or discrepancy) between the individual's own position and the position advocated in the message should determine the individual's reaction to the message. Social judgment theory makes a rather precise prediction about the relationship between discrepancy and attitude change. The theory stipulates that the relationship between message discrepancy and attitude change is curvilinear (with the curve resembling an inverted U). Whittaker (1967) summarized the social judgment theory view of discrepancy by noting that: "As discrepancy increases, positive attitude change increases up to a maximum point and then diminishes until, finally, increasingly larger negative changes occur" (p. 175).

According to this view, when the discrepancy between the advocated position and the individual's own stand is zero, there should be no attitude change. Because the message advocates a position with which the individual already agrees, there is no possibility of attitude change. However, so long as the position is perceived to fall within the latitude of acceptance, increasing discrepancy should produce increasing amounts of attitude change. Positive attitude change diminishes as the advocated position moves into the latitude of rejection. As the message position moves farther into the latitude of rejection, discrepancy becomes negatively associated with attitude change.

There is some empirical support for the social judgment view of discrepancy. A number of studies have found that attitude change increases with increasing discrepancy, but only up to a point. When the message becomes too extreme, attitude change drops off significantly (Granberg, 1982; Whittaker, 1967). However, even this conclusion oversimplifies the impact of discrepancy on attitude change. In fact, the shape of the discrepancy/persuasion curve depends on other factors, the most important of which are the credibility of the communicator and the receiver's level of ego-involvement (Insko, 1967). Another way of stating this is that the point at which discrepancy becomes a persuasive liability differs, depending on whether the speaker is high or low in credibility, and the receiver is high or low in ego-involvement.

Turning first to credibility, the research indicates that the apex or peak of the discrepancy-attitude change curve occurs at a higher level of discrepancy for a highly credible source than for a low-credible communicator (Aronson, Turner, & Carlsmith, 1963; Bochner & Insko, 1966). Thus, everything else being equal, a highly credible communicator can induce people to go along with a message that is more discrepant from their attitudes than can a low-credible communicator (see Fig. 9.3).

Another variable that moderates the relationship between discrepancy and attitude change is ego-involvement. An individual may be said to be ego-involved in an issue when the issue touches on strong values or on the person's sense of self (see next section). Social judgment theory suggests that when individuals are highly (ego) involved in an issue, they are quite intolerant of opposing positions on the issue. Specifically, the theory predicts that, under conditions of high ego-involvement, individuals will have a narrow latitude of acceptance and a wide latitude of rejection. They will tend to reject messages that diverge even a small amount from their own point of view. Hence, as Whittaker (1967) noted, "under conditions of higher involvement, the optimal discrepancy (that yielding maximum change) is close to the subject's own position" (p. 174).

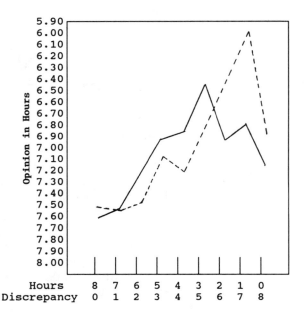

Opinion as a function of discrepancy in both the high credible source (dashed line) and the low credible source (solid line) conditions.

Note: The persuasive message argued for a reduction in the number of hours needed for sleep each night.

FIG. 9.3 Opinion change as a function of discrepancy (from Bochner & Insko, 1966).

On the other hand, under low ego-involvement (when the issue does not touch on central values or on the person's core identity), the individual should be more tolerant of opposing points of view. Consequently, the theory suggests that, under low-involvement, an individual will have a large latitude of noncommitment relative to his or her latitudes of acceptance and rejection. Thus, social judgment theory predicts that, under low-involvement, the optimal discrepancy level should be farther from the individual's own position on the issue. These propositions have received some (although by no means universal) support from the research literature.

There is much more to be said about ego-involvement and the role that it plays in social judgment theory. We discuss ego-involvement in more detail in the next section. (See also Exhibit 9-1: Biased Perceptions of Capital Punishment, and Exhibit 9-2: Pro-Israeli and Pro-Palestinian Partisans React to News Coverage of the Middle East, pp. 215-219.)

EGO-INVOLVEMENT

Some individuals (perhaps you are one of them) have strong feelings about social and political issues. Typically, one issue arouses great passion for such persons, and they devote themselves ceaselessly and tirelessly to the cause. Think for a moment of abortion activists, of proponents and opponents of gun control, of religious zealots and strong-minded atheists. It is quite likely that these individuals are ego-involved in these particular causes.

According to social judgment theory, ego-involvement is "the arousal, singly or in combination, of the individual's commitments or stands in the context of appropriate situations" (Sherif et al., 1965, p. 65). In other words, as we noted earlier, an individual may be said to be ego-involved in an issue when the issue touches on strong values or on the self-system. It is important to emphasize that ego-involvement is situationally aroused. Thus, an issue, topic, or situation that is ego-involving for one person may be uninteresting or psychologically irrelevant to someone else. (Ego-involvement is somewhat different from issue involvement, the focus of our discussion in chapter 5. We discuss the similarities and differences between these terms in the final section of this chapter.)

Social judgment theory stipulates that individuals appraise messages differently when they are high rather than low in ego-involvement. Sherif et al. (1965) argued that:

> In highly ego-involving issues (for example, when the religious beliefs of a devout person are at stake, when the honor of the good father's family is challenged, or when a person dedicated to democracy faces a debate on the democratic way of life versus the totalitarian), the individual's entrenched position is the weighty anchor that *overrides situational concerns* to be tolerant of contrary opinions or to be agreeable. The felt discrepancy in these highly involving issues is never resolved by moving toward the advocated position. The advocated position is invariably felt as an outrage, a violation of what is sacred, as a travesty of human decency in our eyes. In ego-involving issues, therefore, the present approach predicts further displacement of a discrepant position away from the subject's own, unless the exhortation to change is sufficiently camouflaged or otherwise unstructured. (p. 228)

Hovland, Harvey, and Sherif (1957) conducted a study to test these propositions, as well as other hypotheses derived from social judgment theory. The focus of the study by Hovland and his colleagues was an issue of great controversy in the state of Oklahoma: repeal of a law prohibiting the sale of alcoholic beverages. (At that time—the mid-1950s—it was illegal to sell alcoholic beverages in Oklahoma. Several groups opposed to prohibition launched an all-out effort to repeal the law.) The researchers focused on prohibition because it offered an excellent opportunity to test their hypothesis that, on ego-involving issues, own position serves as an anchor against which message arguments are compared.

Hovland, Harvey, and Sherif secured participants from both sides of the controversy. The Women's Christian Temperance Union and the Salvation Army favored prohibition, so the researchers recruited members of both these groups to represent the "dry" side of the controversy. Individuals who opposed prohibition (the "wet" side) were recruited from cases personally known to the researchers or their assistants. To get a sampling of opinion that was neither pro-"dry" nor pro-"wet," the experimenters recruited college students from classes at an Oklahoma university.

Subjects read over nine statements that ranged from extremely "dry" to extremely "wet." They then indicated the position that they found most acceptable, as well as other acceptable positions, and the position they judged to be most objectionable, as well as other objectionable positions. We have reprinted the nine positions here.

1. Since alcohol is the curse of mankind, the sale and use of alcohol, including light beer, should be completely abolished.
2. Since alcohol is the main cause of corruption in public life, lawlessness, and immoral acts, its sale and use should be prohibited.
3. Since it is hard to stop at a reasonable moderation point in the use of alcohol, it is safer to discourage its use.
4. Alcohol should not be sold or used except as a remedy for snake bites, cramps, colds, fainting, and other aches and pains.
5. The arguments in favor and against the sale and use of alcohol are nearly equal.
6. The sale of alcohol should be so regulated that it is available in limited quantities for special occasions.
7. The sale and use of alcohol should be permitted with proper state controls, so that the revenue from taxation may be used for the betterment of schools, highways, and other state institutions.
8. Since prohibition is a major cause of corruption in public life, lawlessness, immoral acts, and juvenile delinquency, the sale and use of alcohol should be legalized.
9. It has become evident that man cannot get along with alcohol; therefore, there should be no restriction whatsoever on its sale and use.

A couple of weeks later, subjects listened to several messages concerning repeal of the prohibition law. The "dry" groups heard an extremely "wet" message, which argued that the law should be repealed, or a moderately "wet" message. The "wet" groups listened to an extremely "dry" message, which opposed repeal of the prohibition law, or a moderately "wet" message. Students with moderate views on the issue listened to all three messages. Subjects then indicated their opinions on the prohibition issue.

Respondents' own positions on the issue exerted a strong impact on their evaluations of the message. When there was a small distance between own position and the position advocated in the communication, the message was judged to be fair and factual. However, when the distance between own position and message position was larger, the message was perceived to be unfair and propagandistic. Thus, persons who favored the extremely "dry" side judged the extremely dry message to be fair, but viewed the "wet" message as propagandistic. Those who strongly opposed prohibition (the extreme "wets") evaluated the extreme "wet" message as fair, yet they viewed the other message as more biased and propagandistic.

In addition, there was some, albeit weak, evidence that individuals whose own positions were close to the position advocated in the message perceived that the communication was closer to their own viewpoints than it actually was. This provided some evidence that an assimilation effect was operating. Hovland, Harvey, and Sherif found stronger evidence that a contrast effect was operating. They discovered that subjects who had extreme positions on the prohibition issue perceived that a discrepant message was further removed from their own position on the issue than it really was.

Consider, as an example, subjects' evaluation of statement 6: "The sale of alcohol should be so regulated that it is available in limited quantities for special occasions." The researchers classified this statement as somewhat "wet"—it was sixth on the list, where the first statement was extremely "dry" and the ninth was extremely "wet." If subjects were fair and objective, they would acknowledge that this statement constituted a moderately "wet" position on the issue. But that is not how these ego-involved subjects reacted.

Individuals who indicated that statement 2 was their most acceptable position on the issue displaced statement 6 to 7; that is, they considered position 6 to be as unacceptable as position 7 ("The sale and use of alcohol should be permitted with proper state controls, so that the revenue from taxation may be used for the betterment of schools, highways, and other state institutions."). Yet, statement 7 clearly advocates a more extreme position on the prohibition issue than does statement 6. In addition, subjects who endorsed position 1 displaced item 6 even further toward the extreme end of their latitude of rejection; they placed position 6 between items 7 and 8. Thus, they considered statement 6 to be almost as "wet" as statement 8 ("Since prohibition is a major cause of corruption in public life, lawlessness, immoral acts, and juvenile delinquency, the sale and use of alcohol should be legalized"). Yet, most of us would probably agree that statement 8 is considerably more "wet" than item 6.

The investigators also found (not surprisingly) that those with extreme positions on the issue did not change their opinions after hearing the message. On the other hand, individuals who had more moderate attitudes toward prohibition did show some evidence of attitude change.

Based on these findings, and other work in the area of social judgment theory, Sherif, Sherif, and Nebergall (1965) developed a number of hypotheses about the impact of ego-involvement on attitude change. They argued that the more ego-involved individuals are in their positions, the less "open" they are to different positions on the issue. Specifically, Sherif et al. contended that individuals who are highly (ego) involved in an issue should have large latitudes of rejection relative to their latitudes of acceptance; by contrast, individuals who are low in involvement should have relatively small latitudes of acceptance and rejection and relatively large latitudes of noncommitment. In addition, social judgment scholars argued that highly involved persons assimilate messages over a smaller range of discrepancies than low-involved individuals; they also maintained that highly involved subjects are more likely to exhibit a contrast effect when evaluating a communication. The upshot of all this, according to social judgment theory, is that highly involved persons are relatively unlikely to change their attitudes in response to a persuasive message, whereas low-involved individuals are likely to exhibit greater attitude change.

Sherif et al. (1965) concluded that these hypotheses had been strongly supported by the research conducted during the 1950s and 1960s. However, contemporary scholars have noted that there are several methodological problems with the early research on involvement. The next section discusses these problems, and presents a contemporary perspective on involvement that integrates the early social judgment theory research with studies conducted by more cognitively oriented researchers.

INVOLVEMENT: A CRITICAL PERSPECTIVE

One of the major problems with the social judgment theory research on involvement is that research has confounded involvement with other variables. For example, Hovland, Harvey, and Sherif (1957) implicitly considered members of the Women's Christian Temperance Union (WCTU) and the Salvation Army to be high in ego-involvement, and they regarded Oklahoma university students to be low in involvement. The problem is that WCTU and Salvation Army members may have differed from university students in a variety of ways, only one of which was their level of involvement. For example, WCTU and Salvation Army members had more extreme positions on the drinking issue than did university students. Thus, extremity of initial position (rather than involvement in the cause) may have led the WCTU and Salvation Army participants to contrast the message position from their own and may also have exerted a strong impact on their evaluations of the message.

Although it is theoretically possible to separate out ego-involvement from issue extremity (Sherif et al., 1965; cf. O'Keefe, 1990), it has been empirically difficult to accomplish this task. Most of the early studies of ego-involvement confounded involvement with extremity of initial position, making it impossible to determine whether it was the individual's personal concerns about the issue or his or her extreme stand on the issue that accounted for his or her resistance to persuasion. To come up with a cleaner, less confounded measure of involvement, a number of researchers opted to manipulate involvement experimentally. These scholars deliberately chose issues that did not touch on individuals' values or self-concepts (e.g., a tuition increase or a senior comprehensive exam in one's major field of study). These experiments, as noted in chapter 5, found (in sharp contrast to social judgment theory) that messages could change attitudes under high-involvement conditions. For example, Petty, Cacioppo, and Goldman (1981) found that when individuals believed that a senior comprehensive exam policy would be instituted during their tenure at the university, they carefully scrutinized message arguments and actually changed their attitudes in the direction of advocacy.

This is clearly a confusing state of affairs. On the one hand, social judgment theorists have found that there is greater resistance to persuasion with increased involvement, whereas ELM scholars have reported just the opposite finding—increased persuasion with increased involvement. It may seem that the social judgment theory findings are inconsistent with the ELM research, until one recognizes that there are actually several different types of involvement, and that these different types of involvement have different effects on evaluations of persuasive messages.

This notion was suggested recently by Johnson and Eagly (1989). They carefully reviewed the research on involvement and persuasion and concluded that researchers have employed three very different definitions of involvement. The first, value-relevant involvement, is similar to the social judgment theory concept of ego-involvement, except it places a greater emphasis on values and assigns less importance to latitudes of rejection, acceptance, and noncommitment. Value-relevant involvement is defined as "the psychological state that is created by the activation of attitudes that are linked to important values" (Johnson & Eagly, 1989, p. 290).

The second type of involvement, outcome-relevant involvement, is the construct that ELM researchers have examined. It refers to the extent to which the attitudinal issue is relevant to message recipients' currently important goals or outcomes. Individuals may be said to be high in outcome-relevant involvement when they perceive that the outcome described in the message is relevant to their own lives. A proposed tuition increase, a recommendation that parking fees be increased, and a proposal to institute a senior comprehensive exam within a year are outcomes that (for many people) are highly involving.

Third, impression-relevant involvement concerns "the individual's concern with the consequences of his *response* or with the instrumental meaning of his opinion" (Zimbardo, 1960, p. 87). Individuals high in impression-relevant involvement anticipate that the opinion that they hold about a message will be made known to an evaluative audience. Thus, they are concerned about "holding an opinion that is socially acceptable to potential evaluators" (Johnson & Eagly, 1989, p. 292). Individuals who listen to a speech about affirmative action and expect to have to present their view on this issue to an audience composed of attorneys would be classified as high in impression-relevant involvement.

Johnson and Eagly (1989) conducted a meta-analysis of the research on involvement and persuasion. They found that persuasive messages exerted different effects, depending on the involvement level of the receiver. The researchers summarized their findings by noting that:

> We found that (a) with value-relevant involvement, high-involvement subjects were less persuaded than low-involvement subjects; (b) with outcome-relevant involvement, high-involvement subjects were more persuaded than low-involvement subjects by strong arguments and less persuaded by weak arguments; and (c) with impression-relevant involvement, high-involvement subjects were slightly less persuaded than low-involvement subjects. (p. 305)

Thus (as social judgment theory would predict), under conditions of high-value-relevant involvement, persuasive communications exert little or no impact on attitudes. This, of course, is our common experience. Messages that try to change people's attitudes toward religion, capital punishment, and abortion often fail because they tap into core values and key components of individuals' self-concepts.

By contrast, when the message concerns *outcomes* that are relevant to the individual, highly involved subjects are more likely to change their attitudes than low-involved subjects, provided the message arguments are strong and compelling. This is the finding that was obtained by ELM researchers and that we discussed in considerable detail in chapter 5. Notice that individuals can perceive that a particular outcome has important effects on their day-to-day routines without believing that this outcome is relevant to their basic values. Subjects may perceive that a proposal for a senior comprehensive exam will have an important effect on their academic routines, but they may not believe that the proposal is relevant to their fundamental values.[3]

EXHIBIT 9–1   215

Finally, when individuals anticipate that they will have to discuss the message with an evaluative audience (high-impression-relevant involvement), they are also apt to resist the persuasive appeal. Individuals who are concerned about presenting a socially acceptable position may fear that if they adopt a strong position on the issue, they will turn off their audience. Interestingly, under high-impression-relevant involvement, subjects may attend to the message to acquire arguments that will enable them to make a maximally positive impression on their audience (Leippe & Elkin, 1987). However, highly involved subjects typically will be reluctant to change their attitude in the direction of advocacy for fear of adopting a position that might turn off their audience.

Johnson and Eagly's findings have interesting implications for persuasion. They suggest that it is not enough to know whether the audience is high or low in involvement; one must know the particular type of involvement that is operating in a given situation. Communicators will want to choose different strategies, depending on whether audience members are high (or low) in value-relevant, outcome-relevant, or impression-relevant involvement.

CONCLUSIONS

Like the other theories we have discussed, social judgment theory has both weaknesses and strengths. Its main weakness is that it does not spell out how factors such as assimilation and contrast and latitudes of acceptance and rejection relate to attitude change. As Granberg (1982) noted: "Beyond pointing out that the communication fell deep within the person's latitude of rejection, no psychodynamic explanation is offered by social judgment theory as to why the observed response occurred" (p. 325).

On the other hand, social judgment theory contains a number of distinctive concepts that are not included in other theories of attitude change (notably, assimilation and contrast and the latitudes). In addition, social judgment theory has called attention to the ways in which own attitude and ego-involvement shape and color interpretations of persuasive messages. The results of studies conducted by social judgment theorists have served to remind researchers that there are clear limits to the impact of persuasive messages on attitudes.

* * *

EXHIBIT 9–1
BIASED PERCEPTIONS OF CAPITAL PUNISHMENT

Social judgment theorists emphasize that people's attitudes, preconceived notions, and unquestioned assumptions guide their interpretations of social communications. This point was made forcefully by Lord, Ross, and Lepper (1979) in a study of biased assimilation of social science evidence. Lord et al. (1979) began their article by observing that:

> Often, more often than we care to admit, our attitudes on important social issues reflect only our preconceptions, vague impressions, and untested assumptions. We respond to social policies concerning compensatory education, water fluoridation, or energy conservation in terms of the symbols or metaphors they evoke . . . or in conformity with views expressed by opinion leaders we like or respect. (p. 2098)

Lord and his colleagues argued that when people hold strong attitudes about a social issue, they process information that bears on this issue in a highly biased manner. The researchers tested their hypothesis by presenting supporters and opponents of capital punishment with the findings, methodologies, and critiques of two empirical investigations of the death penalty's effectiveness.

Subjects read brief descriptions of two purported investigations of the death penalty's deterrent effects. One study always reported evidence that the death penalty was effective, as this example indicates:

> Kroner and Phillips (1977) compared murder rates for the year before and the year after adoption of capital punishment in 14 states. In 11 of the 14 states, murder rates were lower after adoption of the death penalty. This research supports the deterrent effect of the death penalty.

Another study used similar statistics to make the opposite point—that the death penalty was an ineffective deterrent against crime:

> Palmer and Crandall (1977) compared murder rates in 10 pairs of neighboring states with different capital punishment laws. In 8 of the 10 pairs, murder rates were higher in the state with capital punishment. This research opposes the deterrent effect of the death penalty.

After reading a description of one of the studies, subjects indicated whether they had changed their attitudes toward capital punishment. Next, they read a detailed description of the study's methodology, along with criticisms of the study and the authors' rebuttals. Subjects then evaluated the quality of the study, and wrote down "why they thought the study they had just read did or did not support the argument that capital punishment is a deterrent to murder." Following completion of this task, subjects went through the same procedure for the second study.

Thus, subjects read one study that supported, and one study that opposed, their position on the death penalty. The evidence in support of the death penalty's deterrent effect was virtually the same as the evidence that purported to question the death penalty's effectiveness. Nevertheless, proponents of capital punishment managed to find the prodeath penalty study more convincing than the antideath penalty investigation. Opponents of capital punishment perceived that the anti-death penalty study was more persuasive than the prodeath penalty investigation. Subjects also were more critical of the evidence that "disconfirmed" their position, although it was no weaker than the evidence that "confirmed" their point of view.

EXHIBIT 9-2   217

For example, here is how two subjects (one who favored the death penalty and one who opposed it) reacted to the same evidence.

> The proponent of capital punishment reacted to the procapital-punishment study in this way: "It does support capital punishment in that it presents facts showing that there is a deterrence effect and seems to have gathered data properly." The proponent reacted to the anticapital-punishment study in this way: "The evidence given is relatively meaningless without data about how the overall crime rate went up in those years." The opponent of capital punishment reacted to the procapital-punishment study in this way: "The study was taken only 1 year before and 1 year after capital punishment was reinstated. To be a more effective study they should have taken data from at least 10 years before and as many years as possible after." The opponent reacted to the anticapital punishment study in this way: "The states were chosen at random, so the results show the average effect capital punishment has across the nation. The fact that 8 out of 10 states show a rise in murders stands as good evidence." (Information from Lord et al., 1979, p. 2103)

The effect of this biased processing was to increase subjects' support for their initial position on the issue. Thus, after reading the description of the purported investigations, proponents of capital punishment indicated that they were more in favor of the death penalty than they had been at the outset of the study, and opponents reported that they were more opposed to capital punishment than they had been at the beginning of the study.

Clearly, then, when persons have strong attitudes on a topic, they process the relevant facts and figures in a highly biased manner. They assimilate ambiguous evidence to their position and reject facts that "disconfirm" their opinion on the issue. Lord et al. (1979) wryly noted that the tendency to selectively process evidence is not a recent phenomenon. They observed that philosopher Frances Bacon had reached a similar conclusion about the workings of the human mind in 1620. Bacon observed that:

> The human understanding when it has once adopted an opinion draws all things else to support and agree with it. And though there be a greater number and weight of instances to be found on the other side, yet these it either neglects and despises, or else by some distinction sets aside and rejects, in order that by this great and pernicious predetermination the authority of its former conclusion may remain inviolate. (Bacon, 1960)

* * *

EXHIBIT 9-2
PRO-ISRAELI AND PRO-PALESTINIAN PARTISANS REACT TO NEWS COVERAGE OF THE MIDDLE EAST

During the summer of 1982, Israel invaded Lebanon to eliminate Syrian and Palestine Liberation Organization forces. The war received substantial coverage on American television networks, and the media coverage stimulated considerable controversy. Both Arab and Jewish groups monitored the media coverage carefully to determine whether it portrayed their side in a negative light. After a time, the TV coverage (its emphases, biases, and effects) became the story.

I remember the controversy well. As a persuasion scholar, I was intrigued by the fact that mass media coverage could itself become the focus of interest and concern. Several years later, I decided to study the issue systematically (Perloff, 1989).

The first step was to construct a fairly objective rendition of the media coverage of the war. I spent several days at the Vanderbilt University Television News Archives, watching coverage of the war. It was a sobering experience. One was exposed to battle scenes, tragic stories of human losses, and (perhaps worst of all) the almost daily stream of statements and hope-filled promises that this negotiator or that diplomat would bring an end to the conflict in the Middle East. Of course, no such peaceful ending came then (and no such peace has come to the region as of this writing).

Eventually, I assembled a 13-minute news videotape that began with the story that the Israeli ambassador to Great Britain had been critically wounded, proceeded to show the Israeli invasion in great and sometimes gory detail, cut to footage from an attack on a Jewish synagogue in Rome that sources blamed on the Palestine Liberation Organization (PLO), and ended with Dan Rather noting that a temporary settlement to the conflict was "imminent."

I then showed this videotape to ardent supporters of both Israel and the Palestine Liberation Organization (PLO). My pro-Israeli supporters were, for the most part, Orthodox Jews with a strong commitment to the state of Israel. My pro-Palestinian supporters were generally Muslims—young people who, for the most part, had grown up in the land they called Palestine, but who now lived in one or another city in Ohio. These young adults strongly supported the PLO. Supporters of both sides were students. I traveled, videotape in hand, to six universities in the state of Ohio; I showed the videotape to participants from one or the other side and then asked them a series of questions about their responses to the tape. I also showed the videotape to undergraduates who attended a state university in Ohio. This group of students functioned as a control. These students did not have strong attitudes toward either Israel or the PLO, and they did not perceive that the Middle East was personally relevant.

The findings revealed strong and striking differences among the three groups. Pro-Israeli partisans perceived that the news coverage was biased against Israel and in favor of the PLO. Pro-Palestinian partisans saw things differently. They perceived that the news was biased against the PLO and in favor of Israel. By contrast, control group subjects did not believe that the news placed either side in a particularly negative light.

In addition, pro-Israeli partisans, who believed the tape was biased against their side, indicated that 61% of the incidents contained in the videotape were negative to Israel. By contrast, they believed that only 29% of the news coverage placed the PLO in a negative light. The fascinating thing was that the Palestinian partisans reacted in exactly the opposite way. They perceived that 20% of the incidents placed Israel in a negative light, whereas (in their view) 74% of the references were negative to the PLO cause. Although both groups had watched the same videotape, their responses suggested to me that they really had seen quite different things—their ego-involvement in the cause had colored their perceptions such that they had psychologically "seen" different incidents on the same physical videotape.

As if this were not enough, partisans also differed in their beliefs about the effects that the news coverage would have on neutral viewers. Pro-Israel partisans

EXHIBIT 9–2   **219**

perceived that the news would cause a neutral audience to become more negative to Israel and more positive to the PLO. Pro-Palestinian partisans believed that the news would lead neutral viewers to feel more positively about Israel and more negatively about the PLO. Control group subjects perceived that the news would have approximately the same impact on attitudes toward Israel and the PLO.

To assess the accuracy of respondents' perceptions, I conducted a second study, in which I showed the videotape to a separate group of university students. If pro-Palestinian partisans were correct, these students should have become more favorable to Israel after watching the videotape. If pro-Israeli activists were correct, the students should have become more sympathetic with the PLO after viewing the tape. Yet, as it turned out, the videotape had no significant impact on these students' attitudes. The news coverage did not change students' opinions about who was right and who was wrong in the Middle East. In general, the findings show that when people are ego-involved in an issue that the mass media are covering, they tend to have distorted and exaggerated perceptions of the impact that news reports will exert on a neutral audience.[4]

On a broader level, the study's findings help explain why it is so difficult for pro-Palestinian and pro-Israeli groups to sit down and talk with each other. They see culture, history, and politics through very different lenses; and their perceptions powerfully influence their attitudes, actions, and interactions with members of the opposing camp.

10

Cognitive Dissonance Theory

Sam: Why is it what you just said strikes me as a mass of rationalizations?
Michael: Do not knock rationalizations. Where would we be without it?
   I do not know anyone who could get through the day without two or
   three juicy rationalizations. They're more important than sex.
Sam: Ah, come on. Nothin's more important than sex.
Michael: Oh Yeah? You ever gone a week without a rationalization? (*The
   Big Chill,* 1982.) (From Steele, 1988)

R ationalizations play an important part in the theory of cognitive
   dissonance. Indeed, one might say that dissonance theory is a
   theory that assigns central importance to the human need to
rationalize the performance of behaviors that cause psychological discomfort. In this chapter, I discuss cognitive dissonance theory, one of the
oldest, most original, and most controversial theories of attitude change.

   The theory was developed by Leon Festinger in 1957. Since the publication of Festinger's book, *A Theory of Cognitive Dissonance,* over 1,000
studies of cognitive dissonance have been published. These studies have
tested different aspects of Festinger's theory, challenged hypotheses
derived from the theory, and applied it to contexts ranging from marketing
to religion. (See Exhibit 10–1: The End of the World Is at Hand, p. 250.)[1]

   In this chapter, I review the major tenets of dissonance theory and
discuss the findings that have emerged from tests of the theory's hypotheses. The chapter is divided into four sections. The first section defines
dissonance and presents an overview of the theory. The second section
summarizes the early research on dissonance theory. The third section
reviews the major criticisms of dissonance theory, discusses alternative
explanations of dissonance phenomena, and describes the resolutions of
these disputes. The fourth section focuses on contemporary perspectives
on cognitive dissonance phenomena.

OUTLINE OF THE THEORY

Definition

Dissonance theory is essentially concerned with the relationship between cognitions (beliefs or opinions). The theory stipulates that two cognitions can be in an irrelevant, consonant, or dissonant relationship. When two cognitions have nothing to do with each other, the relationship between them is one of irrelevance. For example, the belief that "Exercise is good for your health" is irrelevant to the cognition that "There is going to be a lunar eclipse in March." Two cognitions are consonant when one cognitive element follows from the other. For example, the statement that "I eat lots of meat and potatoes" is consonant with the belief that "Meat and potatoes build strong bones." Two cognitions are in a dissonant relationship when the opposite of one cognitive element follows from the other. For example, the cognition that "I eat lots of meat and potatoes" is dissonant (inconsistent) with the belief that "A meat and potatoes diet is bad for the heart."

Festinger (1957) argued that when an individual simultaneously holds two inconsistent cognitions, he or she experiences discomfort, even distress. More formally, the theory states that an inconsistency between cognitions (such that one cognitive element implies the opposite of the other) gives rise to an uncomfortable psychological state called cognitive dissonance. Festinger (1957) contended that: "The existence of dissonance, being psychologically uncomfortable, will motivate the person to try to reduce the dissonance and achieve consonance" (p. 3).

Elaborating on this notion, Aronson (1968) stated that a dissonance is: "a negative drive state which occurs whenever an individual simultaneously holds two cognitions (ideas, beliefs, opinions) which are psychologically inconsistent" (p. 6).

Notice that Aronson said "psychologically inconsistent." Two cognitions can be logically inconsistent, yet not arouse cognitive dissonance. For example, the cognition that "I eat lots of meat and potatoes" is not logically inconsistent with the belief that "A meat and potatoes diet is bad for the heart." To paraphrase Aronson (1968), having the information that a meat and potatoes diet increases the risk of heart disease does not make it illogical to regularly eat meat and potatoes. However, the two cognitions arouse dissonance because, psychologically, it does not make sense to engage in a behavior (eating potatoes and meat) that can increase the risk of suffering a heart attack.

Magnitude of Dissonance. Cognitions vary in the amount of dissonance they arouse. Certain pairs of cognitions arouse a great deal of dissonance; others arouse very little. The magnitude of dissonance between two cognitions depends on (a) the importance of the cognitive elements, and (b) the proportion of elements that are dissonant (Brehm & Cohen, 1962).

If two cognitions are not very important to a person, then they will arouse very little dissonance. As Festinger (1957) suggested, the individual who gives a dime to a panhandler and then finds out that the panhandler did not need the money is not likely to experience much dissonance; the two cognitions are not likely to be very important to the person. However, the individual who continues to regularly eat meat and potatoes after having been warned that the consumption of these products is bad for his heart is likely to experience a great deal of dissonance. These cognitive elements are likely to be considerably more important to the person than the cognitions associated with giving a dime to a panhandler.

The magnitude of dissonance is also a function of the proportion of relevant cognitions that are dissonant. For example, the more facts that a person acquires about the relationship between a high-cholesterol diet and heart disease, the greater the dissonance produced by continued heavy consumption of meat and potatoes.

Ways to Reduce Dissonance. Dissonance can be reduced in three ways. First, individuals can change one of the elements so as to make the relationship between the two elements a consonant one. When one of the dissonant elements is a behavior, the individual can change or eliminate the behavior. However, this mode of dissonance reduction frequently presents problems for people, as it is often difficult for people to change well-learned behavioral responses.

A second (cognitive) method of reducing dissonance is to add consonant cognitions. For example, our hypothetical consumer might think up all the reasons why he likes meat and potatoes; he might also note that if he did not keep to this diet, he would start smoking again, which would have even more negative consequences for his health.

A third way to reduce dissonance is to alter the importance of the cognitions. Our friend could convince himself that it is better to "live for today" than to "save for tomorrow." In other words, he could tell himself that a short life filled with culinary and sensual pleasures is better than a long life devoid of such joys. In this way, he would be decreasing the importance of the dissonant cognition ("A meat and potatoes diet can be bad for one's heart").

Notice that dissonance theory does not state that these modes of dissonance reduction will actually work, only that individuals who are in a state of cognitive dissonance will take steps to reduce the extent of their dissonance. One of the points that dissonance theorists are fond of making is that people will go to all sorts of lengths to reduce dissonance. Aronson (1968) commented that dissonance theory does not assume that man is a rational animal, but rather a "rationalizing animal — (one who) attempts to appear rational, both to others and himself" (p. 6).

Now that you know something about the theory of cognitive dissonance, let us move on to the research that has tested the major theoretical hypotheses.

EARLY RESEARCH

Dissonance and Decision Making

Life is filled with decisions, and decisions (as a general rule) arouse dissonance. For example, suppose you had to decide whether to accept a job in an absolutely beautiful area of the country, or turn down the job so you could be near your friends and family. Either way, you would experience dissonance. If you took the job you would miss your loved ones; if you turned the job down, you would pine for the beautiful streams, mountains, and valleys. Both alternatives have their good points and bad points. The rub is that making a decision cuts off the possibility that you can enjoy the advantages of the unchosen alternative, yet it assures you that you must accept the disadvantages of the chosen alternative.

People have several ways to reduce dissonance that is aroused by making a decision (Festinger, 1964). One thing they can do is to change the behavior. As noted earlier, this is often very difficult, so people frequently employ a variety of mental maneuvers. A common way to reduce dissonance is to increase the attractiveness of the chosen alternative and to decrease the attractiveness of the rejected alternative. This is referred to as "spreading apart the alternatives."

Brehm (1956) was the first to demonstrate that people spread apart the alternatives after making a decision. Female subjects were informed they would be helping out in a study funded by several manufacturers. Subjects also were told that they would receive one of the products at the end of the experiment to compensate for their time and effort. The women then rated the desirability of eight household products that ranged in price from $15 to $30. The products included an automatic coffee maker, an electric sandwich grill, an automatic toaster, and a portable radio.

Subjects in the control group were simply given one of the products. Because these subjects did not make a decision, they did not have any dissonance to reduce. Individuals in the low-dissonance group chose between a desirable product and one rated 3 points lower on an 8-point scale. Subjects in the high-dissonance condition chose between a highly desirable product and one rated just 1 point lower on the 8-point scale.

After reading reports about the various products, individuals rated the products again.

Subjects in the high-dissonance condition spread apart the alternatives significantly more than did subjects in the other two conditions. In other words, they were more likely than subjects in the other two conditions to increase the attractiveness of the chosen alternative and to decrease the attractiveness of the unchosen alternative.

There is no objective reason that subjects should have revised their evaluations of the products over the course of the experiment. After all, they had not received any information that indicated that the product they had chosen was superior to the one they had rejected. Quite clearly, they experienced dissonance as a consequence of making the decision. The dissonance was particularly bothersome for high-dissonance subjects inasmuch as it involved a decision involving two desirable items. To reduce the dissonance, subjects (particularly those in the high-dissonance group) increased the attractiveness of the chosen alternative and reduced the attractiveness of the unchosen alternative.

Generally speaking, there are two factors that determine the degree of dissonance following a decision (Kiesler, Collins, & Miller, 1969). The first factor is the importance of the decision. An important decision arouses stronger decision than an unimportant decision. Thus, a decision to buy one house rather than another will result in more dissonance than a decision to purchase one brand of toothpaste rather than another. Secondly, the greater the "cognitive overlap" (i.e., similarity) between two objects, the less the dissonance. Assuming both objects are of equal attractiveness, a decision to buy one stereo system rather than another will arouse less dissonance than the decision to buy a stereo system rather than a personal computer. This is because there is greater cognitive overlap between the two stereo systems than between the stereo system and the computer.

Although dissonance theorists originally assumed that dissonance reduction was set in motion as soon as a decision was made, the results of subsequent research forced them to modify this statement. In a monograph published in 1964, 7 years after the publication of the theory, Festinger acknowledged that a period of "regret" ensued shortly after the decision was made. During this period, individuals are believed to focus in great detail on the positive attributes of the rejected alternative and on the negative attributes of the chosen alternative. This intense concentration on the dissonant elements causes individuals to (temporarily) evaluate the unchosen alternative more positively (Walster, 1964). As time passes, these feelings of regret are replaced by a need to rationalize the decision. Thus, individuals come to evaluate the chosen alternative more favorably with the passage of time.

Another variable that was not discussed by Festinger (1964), but that turned out to exert an important impact on dissonance reduction following a decision, is the irrevocability of the decision. Wicklund and Brehm (1976) noted that: "Dissonance reduction does not seem to be set in motion until the decision is definite, nor until the person knows with certainty what he is accepting and rejecting by making his decision" (p. 123).

This principle was demonstrated nicely in a study that applied dissonance theory to (of all things) gambling. Knox and Inkster (1968) arranged for an experimenter to approach individuals 30 seconds before they placed a $2 bet at a British Columbia race track. The experimenter asked bettors to indicate how confident they were that their horse would win. A second experimenter approached bettors 30 seconds after they had placed their bets and asked them the same question.

Once the individual has placed a bet, dissonance is aroused. The decision to bet on one horse is dissonant with the knowledge that the horse has shortcomings that may prevent it from winning the race. An easy way to reduce the dissonance is to increase the attractiveness of the chosen alternative. This can be accomplished by convincing oneself that the horse one has selected has an excellent chance of winning the race. Consistent with this prediction, Knox and Inkster found that bettors were more confident that their horse would win after placing the bet than before.[2] One bettor's comment illustrates how far people will go to reduce dissonance aroused by a decision:

> Are you working with that other fellow there (indicating the prebet experimenter who was by then engaged in another interview)? Well, I just told him that my horse had a fair chance of winning. Will you have him change that to a good chance? No, by God, make that an excellent chance. (p. 322)

Dissonance and the Expenditure of Effort

Have you ever wondered why fraternity pledges come to like a fraternity more after they have undergone a severe initiation procedure? Ever been curious why law students who have gone through the torturous experience of being called on in front of a large class come to think highly of their law school professors? Or why it is that army recruits who have suffered physical and verbal abuse during boot camp have fond memories of army training? An explanation of these phenomena can be found in the application of dissonance theory to the expenditure of effort.

The core notion here is quite simple. Aronson and Mills (1959) stated that:

> No matter how attractive a group is to a person it is rarely completely positive; i.e., usually there are some aspects of the group that the

individual does not like. If he has undergone an unpleasant initiation to gain admission to the group, his cognition that he has gone through an unpleasant experience for the sake of membership is dissonant with the cognition that there are things about the group that he does not like. (p. 177)

One way to reduce the dissonance is to convince oneself that the group has many positive characteristics that justified the expenditure of effort.

Aronson and Mills (1959) were the first to test this hypothesis. Female college students were told that they would be participating in several group discussions concerned with the psychology of sex. The women were informed that the group had been meeting for several weeks and that they would be replacing a woman who dropped out because of scheduling conflicts. The experimenter told experimental group subjects that he had decided to screen new people before granting them formal admission into the group.

The screening procedure was an embarrassment test that consisted of reading some sexually oriented words out loud in the presence of a male experimenter. Subjects in the severe initiation condition read aloud 12 obscene words and 2 graphic descriptions of sexual activity from contemporary novels. Women in the mild initiation condition read five sex-related words that were not obscene. Subjects in both conditions were then informed that they had done a satisfactory job and had therefore been admitted into the group. Control subjects also were informed that they had been accepted into the group. There was no requirement that they recite any sexually oriented words in front of the experimenter.

All subjects then listened to a tape-recorded discussion from a group meeting. The discussion was made to seem dull and banal: "Participants spoke dryly and haltingly . . . contradicted themselves and one another, mumbled several non sequiturs . . . and in general conducted one of the most worthless and uninteresting discussions imaginable" (Aronson & Mills, 1959, p. 179). The discussion had been made to seem as uninteresting as possible to provide severe initiation subjects with the greatest possible amount of dissonance. Subjects then evaluated the group discussion on a number of semantic differential scales.

As dissonance theory predicted, subjects in the severe-initiation condition evaluated the group discussion significantly more positively than did mild-initiation or control-group subjects. This is an intriguing finding. You might think that subjects who had gone through a stressful initiation procedure to join a group would intensely dislike the group. On the contrary, however, severe-initiation subjects exhibited the most positive evaluations of the discussion group. Aronson and Mills suggested that these subjects had the greatest need to justify (i.e., rationalize) the fact that they had undergone a painful initiation procedure to join a boring group.

To reduce the dissonance, they convinced themselves that the group had a number of positive characteristics that justified the expenditure of effort.

Criticisms.   Aronson and Mills' study sparked the first of a number of controversies in the dissonance area. Several researchers argued that the results could be explained by processes other than dissonance reduction (Chapanis & Chapanis, 1964; Gerard & Mathewson, 1966; Schopler & Bateson, 1962). For example, Chapanis and Chapanis (1964) argued that the severe initiation procedure did not embarrass the women, but, instead, aroused them sexually. According to this view, subjects in the severe-initiation condition, having been aroused by the task of reading obscene words to a male experimenter, were excited about the prospect of joining a group that, it stood to reason, might regularly discuss sexual issues. Thus, their greater liking for the group was due to their excitement and arousal rather than to their need to reduce dissonance.

Chapanis and Chapanis also suggested an "afterglow" hypothesis to explain Aronson and Mills' findings. Chapanis and Chapanis noted that subjects who had undergone both the severe initiation and the mild initiation had been appraised that they had passed the embarrassment test. Presumably, the knowledge that one had passed the embarrassment test might have produced a greater sense of accomplishment (an afterglow) among subjects who had undergone the severe initiation. This afterglow might have been transferred over to other aspects of the task, including the evaluation of the group.

To rule out these alternative explanations of the effort justification paradigm, Gerard and Mathewson (1966) used a different set of procedures than that employed by Aronson and Mills (1959). Subjects in Gerard and Mathewson's experiment were informed that to gain admission into a group, they would have to undergo a series of physiological tests (which involved electric shocks). Half of the subjects received severe electric shocks and half received mild shocks. To rule out the afterglow interpretation, Gerard and Mathewson told half of the subjects they had passed the screening test. However, they did not provide this feedback to the other half of the subjects. If the afterglow interpretation was correct, then only subjects who believed they had passed the test would evaluate the group positively. After receiving the electric shocks and being given feedback (or no feedback), subjects listened to and evaluated a boring group discussion concerning cheating in college. The results indicated that, regardless of whether they were told they had passed the screening test, subjects who received strong electric shocks evaluated the group more positively than those who received mild electric shocks.

These findings provided strong support for dissonance theory. Contrary to Chapanis and Chapanis (1964), the results could not be explained by sexual arousal or the induction of positive feelings. Clearly, the electric shock initiation procedure did not induce a pleasant mood state. Also, contrary to the afterglow hypothesis, subjects who believed they had passed the screening test were not more likely to evaluate the group positively than those who were not given this information.[3]

As suggested at the beginning of this section, the research on effort justification has a number of practical implications. It helps explain why fraternity pledges, law school students, and military recruits often come to evaluate fraternities, law school, and boot camp more favorably after having participated in stressful initiation procedures. It also provides a somewhat novel explanation for why clients who expend considerable amounts of time (and money) in counseling and therapy may sometimes evaluate their therapeutic experiences quite positively (Cooper & Axsom, 1982).

Induced Compliance

What happens if a person is induced to publicly argue for a position he or she privately does not accept? Further, what if the individual is paid a paltry sum to take this position? Suppose you gave a speech that defended the university's decision to raise tuition, although you privately opposed the tuition hike. Suppose someone paid you a quarter to argue in favor of the tuition hike proposal. Dissonance theory makes the unusual prediction that, under these circumstances, you would actually come to evaluate the tuition increase more favorably.

This prediction, and a set of related hypotheses, are part of a phenomenon known as *induced compliance*. Induced compliance occurs when an individual performs an action that is inconsistent with his or her beliefs. Typically, the individual receives a small or a large reward (or punishment) for performing the behavior. The classic study of induced compliance was conducted over 30 years ago by Festinger and Carlsmith (1959). I discuss the study's procedures, relying as much as possible on the experimenters' own words.

Subjects were students at Stanford University. Subjects were instructed to perform two tasks that were phenomenally boring. The first task involved putting 12 spools onto a tray, emptying the tray, refilling it with spools, and so on. Subjects did this for a half hour. The experimenter then removed the tray and spools and placed in front of the subject a board containing 48 square pegs. His task was to turn each peg a quarter turn clockwise, then another quarter turn, and so on. This also took a half hour.

Following the completion of the tasks, the experimenter asked experimental group subjects if they would do him a favor. He explained that he normally had a helper around to describe the study to some of the subjects. Today, he said, there was a glitch.

The fellow who normally does this for us couldn't do it today—he just phoned in, and something or other came up for him—so we've been looking around for someone that we could hire to do it for us. . . . Now Professor _____ , who is in charge of this experiment, suggested that perhaps we could take a chance on your doing it for us.

The experimenter explained that he needed the subject to describe the study to another student who was also participating in the experiment. Specifically, he requested that the subject tell the other student that the experiment was a lot of fun. These were the words the subject was asked to use to describe the spool-removing task: "It was very enjoyable, I had a lot of fun, I enjoyed myself, it was very interesting, it was intriguing, it was exciting." Of course, this was a bald-faced lie. The study had been nothing if not monotonous. The experimenter hoped that telling the lie would arouse cognitive dissonance.

Some subjects were paid $20 for telling the lie, whereas other subjects were paid $1. Subjects in a control condition did not tell the lie. Instead, they waited in an adjoining room for several minutes. Subsequently, subjects were asked to rate the enjoyableness of the task and to indicate how willing they would be to participate in a similar experiment again. You would think that someone who was paid $20 for performing a activity (lying about the enjoyableness of a boring task) would evaluate the task more favorably than someone paid $1. But precisely the opposite finding was obtained.

Subjects paid $1 to lie about the task evaluated the task more favorably than did subjects in the other two conditions. As Table 10.1 shows, $1 subjects actually indicated that they enjoyed the task more, regarded it as more scientifically important, and exhibited a greater willingness to participate in similar experiments in the future than did subjects in the other conditions.

How can we explain these findings? According to dissonance theory, the

TABLE 10.1
Average Ratings on Interview Questions for Each Condition

Question on Interview	Experimental Condition		
$1	Control	$20	
How enjoyable tasks were (rated from −5 to +5)	1.45	+1.35	−.05
Scientific importance (rated from 0 to 10)	5.60	6.45	5.18
Participate in similar experiments (rated from −5 to +5)	−.62	+1.20	−.25

From Festinger and Carlsmith (1959)

cognition that "The spool-removing task was really boring" was dissonant with the cognition that "I just told someone that it was lots of fun." The $20 provided subjects with a strong external justification for telling the lie. It allowed them to add a consonant cognition to their cognitive systems ("Telling that lie netted me $20."). This in turn helped to reduce the magnitude of the dissonance. A $20 subject might have thought:

> The money I got for this experiment makes it all seem worthwhile. Yeah, I know I said the task was fun when it really wasn't. But, look at the reward I got. This is great—getting that kind of money for unpacking some spools and then saying something about the whole study to somebody else. This is just terrific.

By contrast, the $1 subjects could not justify their behavior by pointing to the money that they had received. Lacking a sufficient external justification, they had to turn inward to get one. They desperately needed to bring their private attitude toward the task in line with their public behavior. One way to do this (i.e., to rationalize the fact that they had publicly contradicted their private attitude) was to change their attitude toward the task. A $1 subject might have thought:

> Gee, I told that student this job was interesting. Now that's not what I really believe. It kind of bothers me, I mean, that I said something I don't believe. I'd like to feel better about this whole thing, you know. Let me think about this, backtrack a little bit. I did this thing with the spools, put them on the tray, refilled the tray, then turned these pegs a little bit. You know, now that I think of it, that wasn't so bad. It was kind of challenging, took a little dexterity. Yeah, it wasn't so bad, not at all.

The findings are exactly the opposite of what you would expect on the basis of common sense. Therefore, they attracted a great deal of interest and stimulated a considerable amount of research. Subsequent studies extended Festinger and Carlsmith's (1959) experiment by demonstrating that the *negative incentive effect* (greater attitude change under conditions of low-reward) could be obtained for other tasks as well. For example, following a riot at Yale University, which produced charges of police brutality, Cohen (1962) asked students to write a counterattitudinal essay entitled "Why the New Haven Police Actions were Justified." He paid subjects $10, $5, $1, or 50¢ for writing the essay. Once again, the negative incentive effect emerged. Students paid $10 changed their attitudes the least, and students paid 50¢ changed their attitudes the most.

Cohen's findings have interesting implications for real-world persuasion. For example, they help explain the strange events that took place in China following the 1949 revolution. As discussed in chapter 1, the Chinese government designed an elaborate program to resocialize the public in the

Marxist–Leninist image. Intellectuals, students, and religious leaders were brought to isolated places and were subjected to a battery of psychological techniques designed to change their attitudes toward Communism. At the end of the program, some intellectuals renounced their materialistic "bourgeois" upbringing and pledged to commit themselves to Communism. Western observers called this brainwashing and concluded that the Chinese had concocted a strange blend of mind-manipulation techniques.

Dissonance theory suggests an alternative explanation. Rather than viewing Chinese thought reform as brainwashing or coercion, dissonance theory would regard it as a sophisticated form of persuasion. For example, the government typically encouraged students and intellectuals to write a final essay that praised Communism and condemned capitalism. Here is an excerpt from the essay one ex-philosophy professor wrote:

> I now consider the fundamental ideological source for my personal crust of selfishness to be the extremely depraved, epicurean, liberalist, and bourgeois ideology of striving after individual freedom. . . . In actual life at school, this ideology was manifested in my attempt to maintain my life of ease and comfort and to build up a crust of special privileges. . . . I am now close to sixty, and I am a criminal for having sinned against the people. From now on, however, I shall strive to become a new man and a teacher of the people in substance as well as in name. (Lifton, 1961, pp. 483–484)

According to dissonance theory, this essay constitutes a counterattitudinal advocacy that was written under conditions of low-external justification. That is, the position the professor took in the essay was inconsistent with his private point of view, and he was given little external reward or incentive to write the essay. One way to rationalize this inconsistency was to adopt a more positive attitude toward the new Communist state.

Cohen's (1962) findings also help explain why many young people who joined the Unification Church (as well as other religious cults) came to adopt a favorable attitude toward the cult. Many Moonies spent considerable amounts of time trying to recruit new members to the Church (Lofland, 1977). Thus, they frequently defended the Church and its practices. Given that these young people had typically grown up in middle-class environments, which stood for a different set of values than did the Unification Church, the act of defending the Moonies in all likelihood aroused dissonance. One way to reduce this dissonance was to strengthen one's belief in the Church and its theology.

Summary of the Early Research

Dissonance theory captured the imagination of the social psychological community during the 1960s. Not only did dissonance theory have a number of practical implications for persuasion in everyday life, it also made predictions that diverged significantly from those made by the dominant learning theories of the day. For a generation of social psychologists who found themselves frustrated with the mechanistic orientation of reinforcement approaches, dissonance theory represented an exciting development. In an interview with Aron and Aron (1989), dissonance researcher Aronson described the impact that the early dissonance studies (notably Festinger and Carlsmith) had on attitude researchers working during the 1960s:

> As a community we have yet to recover from the impact of this research — fortunately! You see, for many working social psychologists, these results generated a great deal of enthusiasm and excitement, but for others, skepticism and anger. Because the finding departed from the general orientation accepted either tacitly or explicitly by most social psychologists in the 1950s: (that) high reward—never *low* reward—is accompanied by greater learning, greater conformity, greater performance, greater satisfaction, greater persuasion. . . . (But in Festinger and Carlsmith,) either reward theory made no prediction at all or the opposite prediction. These results represented a striking and convincing act of liberation from the dominance of a general reward-reinforcement theory. (Aron & Aron, 1989, p. 116)

CHALLENGES AND RECONCILIATIONS

During the 1960s, dissonance theory was in its prime. It was the dominant theory of attitude change, and it had stimulated a number of studies, some of which had obtained some rather unusual and provocative findings. (See Exhibit 10–2: Persuading People to Eat (and like) Grasshoppers, p. 252.) By the mid-1960s, however, questions began to surface. Researchers argued that there were methodological problems with the early studies, and they suggested that there were alternative interpretations of the results. At the same time, new theories were advanced that provided a different perspective on dissonance phenomena. Three challenges to dissonance theory were mounted during the 1960s and 1970s. They were: (a) the early criticisms of the induced compliance paradigm, (b) Bem's self-perception theory, and (c) the impression management approach.

Criticisms of Induced Compliance

Prior to the formulation of dissonance theory, Janis and his colleagues articulated an alternative theory of counterattitudinal advocacy. According to Janis and Gilmore (1965):

When a person accepts the task of improvising arguments in favor of a point of view at variance with his own personal convictions, he becomes temporarily motivated to think up all the good positive arguments he can, and at the same time suppresses thoughts about the negative arguments. . . . This "biased scanning" increases the salience of the positive arguments and therefore increases the chances of acceptance of the new attitude position. (pp. 17–18)

Presumably, a large reward should enhance the motivation to engage in a "biased scanning process"; thus, according to Janis, a large reward should increase attitude change. You may recall that Festinger and Carlsmith found exactly the opposite finding (less attitude change for high-reward). However, Janis and Gilmore argued that the high-reward ($20) aroused suspicion and guilt, and that these negative affects prevented subjects from devoting their full cognitive energies to the counterattitudinal advocacy. Presumably, however, when the reward generates positive feelings, there should be a positive relationship between reward and attitude change (more attitude change for high-reward). Elms and Janis (1965) obtained strong support for this prediction.

Rosenberg (1965) also advanced an alternative explanation of the dissonance results. In articulating his view, Rosenberg drew on the concept of evaluation apprehension. According to this view, "The typical subject will be likely to experience *evaluation apprehension;* that is, an active, anxiety-toned concern that he win a positive evaluation from the experimenter, or at least that he provide no grounds for a negative one" (p. 29).

Rosenberg contended that the typical subject in the dissonance studies suspected that the experimenter was testing his or her ability to resist a bribe. In particular, Rosenberg argued that the individual who was given a large reward ($20 subject in Festinger and Carlsmith) probably came to reason that "they probably want to see whether getting paid so much will affect my own attitude, whether I am the kind of person whose views can be changed by buying him off" (p. 29). To prove to the experimenter that he or she most definitely was not the type of person who could be bought off, the typical subject in the high-reward condition refused to change his or her attitude toward the task. By contrast, the typical subject in the low-reward condition ($1 subject in Festinger and Carlsmith) experienced less evaluation apprehension and, consequently, had less reason to maintain his or her original attitude toward the boring task. Rosenberg (1965) devised an ingenious experiment in which he went to elaborate lengths to eliminate these methodological problems. Rosenberg found, contrary to dissonance theory, that subjects who were given a large reward to argue for a counterattitudinal position displayed more attitude change than those who were given a small reward to defend this position.

Needless to say, these results aroused a great deal of dissonance among researchers committed to the cognitive dissonance perspective. A debate between supporters and opponents of dissonance theory ensued, with each side arguing that there were methodological or conceptual problems with the other's research (Carlsmith, Collins, & Helmreich, 1966; Elms, 1967; Hoyt, Henley, & Collins, 1972; Linder, Cooper, & Jones, 1967). The dialogue between dissonancers and their opponents led to some important revisions in dissonance theory. Specifically, researchers concluded that there would be greater attitude change under conditions of low-reward only when: (a) the behavior produced strong aversive consequences for the individual or his or her audience, and (b) the individual accepted responsibility for having caused or contributed to these consequences (Calder, Ross, & Insko, 1973; Hoyt, Henley, & Collins, 1972). Both conditions are necessary for the counterattitudinal act to lead to attitude change. Thus, as Hoyt, Henley, and Collins (1972) noted:

> Mere knowledge of aversive consequences, without a concomitant sense of personal responsibility, is a common occurrence and one not likely to produce intrapsychic conflict. If responsibility is not self-attributed, subjects in high aversive consequences conditions should not experience dissonance or need to make "adjustments" to maintain cognitive consistency. (p. 206)

By the same token, mere responsibility (or choice) is not a sufficient condition for counterattitudinal advocacy to lead to attitude change. If the individual accepts responsibility for having caused an action, but does not perceive that the act did anyone any harm, he or she will experience little cognitive dissonance.

An example, based on one suggested by Cooper and Worchel (1970), should help to clarify these points. Suppose a young woman graduated from college with a bachelor of arts degree in journalism and was offered a job as a reporter on a suburban daily. Suppose she took the job and was told that, if she wanted, she could make some extra money by writing editorials on current social and political issues. Let us say her editor asked her to write an editorial for the Saturday morning newspaper, which argued that styrofoam containers posed few environmental dangers and therefore they should be used by all fast-food restaurants. Let us further assume that the young woman was very committed to preserving the environment and, as a result, opposed the use of styrofoam containers in fast-food restaurants.

According to the revised view of induced compliance, the young woman would experience dissonance only if she believed that her editorial would be effective in changing readers' attitudes toward styrofoam containers (aversive consequences) and she made an internal attribution of responsibility (responsibility or choice). Thus, if the woman knew that no one read the Saturday morning editorial page, she would not experience dissonance. As Cooper and Worchel (1970) noted, "in the absence of undesired consequences," no dissonance should be produced.

The second condition necessary for dissonance arousal is the assumption of personal responsibility. This entails the perception of choice—the belief that one could (if one wished) turn down the request.[4] If the reporter perceived that she had no choice but to write the editorial, she would not experience much dissonance. If her editor had walked into the newsroom and said "You write that editorial or you're fired," the woman might have written the editorial, but she probably would not have felt a need to change her attitude or to employ other dissonance-reducing tactics.

The emphasis on responsibility (and choice) underscores a point made in chapter 1: All persuasion is fundamentally self-persuasion. If a individual perceives that he or she has no choice but to accept a communicator's recommendations, then the individual may publicly comply with the communicator's request, but will not privately change his or her attitude about the issue. However, if an individual freely chooses to perform an action, and the action arouses cognitive dissonance, then the individual will feel highly motivated to reduce the dissonance. Notice that the communicator is not the only one who is putting pressure on the individual; the person is also applying pressure. The individual is devising rationalizations, increasing the attractiveness of the chosen alternative, and perhaps even changing his or her attitude to reduce dissonance. Ultimately, the individual is attempting to persuade him- or herself that the action performed was justified and correct.

Bem's Self-Perception Theory

Although Janis role-playing approach and Festinger's dissonance theory made different predictions about incentive effects, they both assumed that cognitions play an important part in the persuasion process. In 1965, Bem proposed a theoretical account of dissonance phenomena that took a distinctly noncognitive tack. Bem was profoundly influenced by the behaviorist perspective of B. F. Skinner, and he derived an interesting hypothesis from Skinner's (1957) work. Bem argued that when you or I want to understand our own internal states, we rely on the same external cues that others use when they want to know what we're feeling or what our attitude is about an issue. Bem (1970) noted that: "When we want to know how a person feels, we look to see how he acts. Accordingly, my theory about the origins of an individual's self-knowledge predicts that he might also infer his own internal states by observing his own overt behavior" (p. 57).

Bem argued that when internal cues are weak (i.e., when people are not sure what they are feeling about a person or issue), they are particularly likely to turn their attention outward and infer their attitude from their behavior. Actually, people make these inferences every day. Consider these examples:

- Your mother asks if you like oat bran muffins. "I guess I do," you reply. "I'm always eating them."
- A classmate finds out that you're a word processing whiz, confides that she is having trouble mastering WordPerfect, and asks if you would mind spending some time helping her get her term paper in shape. It's finals week and you have a number of deadlines of your own, but you agree. Later, you think to yourself, "Why did I help that person? I was besieged by deadlines." "Well," you say to yourself, "I must be a very nice, cooperative person. Why else would I have done her a favor when I'm so busy myself?"
- You've just taken a new job and you find you're spending a lot of time working late at the office. It's a "no-sweat" job, and the employer has put no pressure on you to complete the assignments. "I must really be dedicated," you think to yourself. "I must really be a hard-working, ambitious person. Why else would I be here till midnight every night?"

In each of these cases, the individual comes to understand his or her feelings and attitudes by inferring them from observations of his or her behavior. In such cases, Bem (1972) said, "an individual is functionally in the same position as an outside observer who must necessarily rely upon these same external cues to infer the individual's inner states" (p. 2). This is the essence of Bem's self-perception theory. Although dissonance theory assumes that people are motivated to reduce internal discomfort, self-perception theory assumes that internal discomfort is of relatively little consequence. Although dissonance theory assumes that people need to justify their behavior, self-perception theory assumes that people are concerned primarily with explaining their behavior. In an interview with Aron and Aron (1989), Bem provided a personal anecdote that nicely illustrated his theoretical approach:

> My wife (Sandra Bem, an influential social psychologist in the area of sex roles) could not possibly have made up self-perception theory because at the end of the day she'll say something like, "I'm feeling kind of depressed, I wonder why," and then she'll review the day's events to find out why. I'm much more likely to say, "Gee, I wonder how I feel? Well, today this happened and that happened. I guess I'm a little depressed." (p. 124)

Self-Perception Versus Dissonance. Bem (1967) argued that his self-perception theory provided an alternative explanation of induced compliance. Bem naturally had a much different explanation for why subjects (in Festinger and Carlsmith's, 1959, experiment) who were paid $1 to engage in a boring task evaluated the task more favorably than subjects who were paid $20.

Bem argued that subjects in Festinger and Carlsmith's study employed the same external cues to explain their own behavior as outside observers would have employed if they had been asked to interpret subjects' actions. According to self-perception theory, $20 subjects noted that they had just been paid a large sum of money to tell a student that a boring task was interesting; "Now, why would I do that?" subjects asked themselves. Bem argued that subjects quickly concluded that they had "done it for the money." Thus, they attributed their behavior to an external, situational factor (the money). Having arrived at a plausible explanation for their behavior, they had no need to probe their inner thoughts and attitudes to understand why they had acted as they had. Thus, when asked to say what their attitudes toward the task were, $20 subjects reported the same attitudes as control subjects who had not been asked to lie to a fellow student.

On the other hand, subjects who were paid $1 to lie about the task had a different orientation. Like $20 subjects, they looked dispassionately at their behavior and asked themselves why they had decided to lie to a fellow student. But, unlike $20 subjects, they could not attribute their behavior to an external cause. "I sure didn't do it for the money," they must have thought to themselves. Having ruled out a situational explanation for their behavior, they looked to see whether an "internal" explanation could be found. According to Bem, $1 subjects introspected a bit and concluded that they must have really believed that the task was interesting. Thus, Bem reasoned that subjects in the $1 condition observed that "I just told a student that the task was interesting; I guess I found the task kind of fun."

Notice that Bem's explanation for why Festinger and Carlsmith's subjects changed their attitudes differs dramatically from the interpretation advanced by Festinger. Festinger assumed that subjects were bothered by the fact that they had lied to a student and, to reduce their dissonance, they changed their attitude toward the task. In contrast, Bem argued that subjects merely wanted to understand why they had performed the task for so little money, and inferred that they must have liked the task (otherwise, why would they have done it for such a little reward?). Dissonance theory "contains the idea that people are willing to delude themselves and to twist the facts" (Cohen, 1977, p. 139). Bemian theory assumes that people are cool cats who behave first and think later, and who only introspect when they need to understand why they behaved in a particular way.

Bem conducted a series of "interpersonal simulation" studies to test his interpretation of the induced compliance findings. The procedure in these studies was very simple. Bem provided subjects with a description of the induced compliance experiments; then he asked them to predict what the attitudes of subjects in the various conditions of the experiments were likely to be. For example, in his simulation of Festinger and Carlsmith's (1959) study, Bem described the $1 condition of the experiment to one group of subjects, presented a description of the $20 condition to a second group, and provided an account of the control procedures to a third group. Bem then asked each group of subjects to predict the attitude of a participant in the original study. Bem's subjects did a good job of predicting Festinger and Carlsmith's findings. Subjects predicted that the most favorable attitude toward the task would be held by a participant who had been paid $1 to lie, and that a less favorable attitude would be harbored by a participant paid $20 and by a student in the control condition.

Bem (1970) argued that these findings supported his hypothesis. The fact that subjects in a completely different experiment came up with exactly the same answers to the attitude questions as did the participants in the original study seemed to suggest (at least to Bem and his followers) that the self-perception hypothesis was correct. Bem argued that the findings lent some support to his notion that "in identifying his own internal states, an individual partially relies on the same external cues that others use when they infer his internal states" (p. 50).

Bem's reinterpretation of cognitive dissonance effects stimulated a great deal of debate. Dissonance scholars argued that Bem had not created an authentic replication of the induced compliance experiments. The dissonance researchers subsequently conducted studies that used simulation procedures that more closely resembled the methodology employed in the original experiments. Contrary to Bem's prediction, these studies found that outside observers could not accurately predict the attitudes held by the original subjects (Piliavin, Piliavin, Loewenton, McCauley, & Hammond, 1969; see also Jones, Linder, Kiesler, Zanna, & Brehm, 1968). Bem then criticized the simulation methodology that the dissonance researchers had employed, and another debate (this one focusing on the salience of subjects' initial attitudes) filled the academic journals (Bem & McConnell, 1970; Snyder & Ebbesen, 1972). The debate failed to resolve the problem as the studies yielded conflicting results.

A reconciliation between the dissonance and self-perception camps came in 1977 with the publication of an experiment by Fazio, Zanna, and Cooper. Fazio et al. (1977) argued that both theories were right, but that they applied to different domains. The investigators predicted (and found) that when individuals were asked to argue for a position that was slightly discrepant from their own point of view, but well within the latitude of acceptance, self-perception processes accounted for attitude change. However, when subjects were induced to advocate a discrepant position that fell within the latitude of rejection, dissonance processes accounted for attitude change.

Thus, when we advocate a position that is slightly discrepant from our own position, we behave like self-perception theorists: We look dispassionately at our own behavior, and we examine whether the situation "coerced" us into behaving in the way that we did. If we decide that situational forces were not operative, we are likely to conclude that the behavior reflects our true attitudes ("I must believe it; why else would I have said it?"). On the other hand, when we make a statement that falls into the latitude of rejection, we are more apt to behave like dissonance theorists. In this case, we experience a great deal of discomfort, and feel impelled to change our attitude to reduce the internal distress.

The Impression Management Approach

A third view of dissonance phenomena, articulated by Tedeschi, Schlenker, and Bonoma (1971) and Schlenker (1982), emphasizes the role of "self-presentational" or "impression management needs." The central thesis of this approach is this: "Attitude change following counterattitudinal advocacy is conceived of as nothing more than an attempt to manipulate one's impression in the eyes of a high status experimenter and to absolve oneself from the embarrassment of appearing inconsistent" (Cooper & Croyle, 1984, p. 406).

According to this view, subjects in the $1 condition of the Festinger and Carlsmith (1959) study feared that the experimenter would look down on them for selling their souls for a paltry sum of money (Cooper & Fazio, 1984). The $1 subjects figured that if they indicated on the questionnaire that the task was really enjoyable, the experimenter would believe that they liked the task. This would foster the impression that they had behaved consistently, and it would improve their status in the experimenter's eyes.

To test this notion, impression management researchers have induced subjects to argue for positions with which they disagree, and then have asked one group to indicate their attitudes toward the issue on a paper and pencil questionnaire, and another group to indicate their attitudes on a lie detector-type device (the bogus pipeline) that subjects believe has the power to discover falsehood (Riess, Kalle, & Tedeschi, 1981). According to impression management theory, subjects should be reluctant to misrepresent their attitudes on the lie detector apparatus because the experimenter could easily catch them. By contrast, subjects should feign their attitudes (e.g., they should indicate that they liked a boring task) when attitudes are measured on a paper and pencil questionnaire. Several studies have tested this hypothesis and have found evidence consistent with the impression management interpretation (Gaes, Kalle, & Tedeschi, 1978; Malkis, Kalle, & Tedeschi, 1982; see also, Baumeister & Tice, 1984).

The impression management view has made a useful contribution to the dissonance literature. Impression management researchers have called attention to the fact that subjects in dissonance experiments were concerned with making a positive impression on the experimenter. These researchers have made salient the possibility that a self-presentational motive may have influenced subjects' evaluations of the experimental tasks.[5] However, there are two problems with the research generated by impression management. First, there are methodological problems with the bogus pipeline that cast doubt on the validity of some of the findings. For example, it is possible to explain the bogus pipeline results obtained by impression management researchers without invoking impression management needs (Arkin, 1981; Scheier & Carver, 1980; Tetlock & Manstead, 1985).[6] Second, on a more general level, it is difficult to see how the impression management view can account for the totality of findings on induced compliance. There is little doubt that people are concerned about how they come across to others, and there is little question that people try to manage the impressions they present to others. But, as Cooper and Croyle (1984) asked, "Is the management of impressions the *only* or even major concern that people have when they are faced with inconsistency?" (p. 407). It is difficult to believe that, in the many dissonance studies, all subjects were concerned with was making a positive impression.

Summary

Festinger and Carlsmith (1959) found that subjects induced to advocate a counterattitudinal position for a small reward changed their attitudes to conform with their behavior. These findings stimulated a great deal of controversy and generated a number of empirical investigations. We now know that the negative incentive effect (greater attitude change for low-reward) will not emerge unless certain conditions are met. Specifically, the individual must perceive that the counterattitudinal act led to aversive consequences and that he or she was responsible for having brought about these consequences.

Critics of dissonance theory have argued that the induced compliance findings can be more parsimoniously explained by self-perceptions (Bem) or by impression management needs (Tedeschi and Schlenker). As we have suggested, these theories have difficulty accounting for the totality of findings on induced compliance. The evidence that counterattitudinal advocacy involves physiological arousal (see next section) is difficult to explain on the basis of Bem's self-perception approach; his theory, after all, contends that the act of advocating a counterattitudinal position does not involve any internal discomfort. In addition, the findings from the impression management studies can be interpreted in a variety of ways, not all of which are compatible with the notion that people are motivated to present their attitudes in the best possible light.

Can one say, then, that dissonance theory is right and the other theories are wrong? Unfortunately, there is no simple answer to this question. Although dissonance theory probably provides the best interpretation of the findings on induced compliance, there are (as we noted in our discussion of self-perception theory) some situations in which the processes emphasized by one theory are operative and other situations in which the processes emphasized by another theory are operative. In other words, there are probably some induced compliance contexts in which people behave like anguished rationalizers, others in which they act like cool Bemian observers, and still others in which they behave like shrewd manipulators of their public self-image. It is also likely that all three processes—consistency motives, self-perceptions, and impression management needs—operate in a single individual at a particular time. Unfortunately, it has been difficult to separate out these processes—a necessary condition for conducting "crucial experiments" that determine the conditions under which the variables emphasized by one theory are operative (Greenwald, 1975; Tetlock & Manstead, 1985).

CONTEMPORARY PERSPECTIVES

In this section, I discuss contemporary approaches to cognitive dissonance. Two streams of research dominate the field today. The first focuses on the physiological effects of dissonance, whereas the second examines the interaction between dissonance and the self-concept. (See also Exhibit 10–3: Selective Exposure.)

The Physiology of Dissonance

One of the most provocative aspects of dissonance theory is the notion that cognitive dissonance is a drive state that has measurable physiological effects. None of the other persuasion theories that we have discussed claims that a core variable has drive-like energizing properties. The claim that dissonance is a drive state was first made by Festinger (1957). In recent years, a number of studies have examined whether Festinger was correct. These investigations have focused specifically on the arousal properties of dissonance.

There is now abundant evidence to support the contention that dissonance is an arousal state. The evidence comes from two different lines of research.[7] First, manipulations of cognitive dissonance produce measurable changes in physiological arousal. Elkin and Leippe (1986) provided convincing evidence that dissonance involves arousal. Subjects wrote a counterattitudinal essay advocating that students pay a parking fee of $15 each semester. Half of the subjects wrote the essay under high-choice conditions, whereas the other half wrote the essay under low-choice conditions. Elkin and Leippe reasoned that if dissonance involves physiological arousal, subjects who experienced the greatest amount of dissonance (those who wrote a counterattitudinal essay under a high-choice condition) would exhibit the greatest amount of arousal. The results supported Elkin and Leippe's hypothesis: Relative to low-choice subjects, subjects who wrote the counterattitudinal essay under high-choice conditions showed greater increases in physiological arousal (and more attitude change).

The second body of research that concerns the arousal properties of dissonance is the work of scholars who have studied the cognitive interpretation of physiological arousal states. Studies in this area (Cooper & Fazio, 1984) indicate that "like the arousal involved in emotions, the state of dissonance requires appropriate interpretation and labeling for attitude change to occur" (p. 244). This second body of research is an outgrowth of psychological research on emotions, which has found that emotions are a combination of arousal and cognitive interpretations (Schachter & Singer, 1962). An example may help you appreciate the findings from this complex area of research.

Suppose you are going to meet a friend whom you have not seen in 10 years. As you drive over to see your friend, you feel butterflies in your stomach. You dismiss the feelings at first, but they come back, so you think about what it is you're feeling. At first you decide it's fear ("Will she look better than me?"). But then as you muse about the matter, you decide that perhaps you were too hasty in making the assessment. You're not scared about what your friend will think about you; you're eager—excited even— about the prospect of seeing someone whom you haven't seen for over 10 years. Thus, the label the individual applies to the arousal (fear vs. excitement) determines the nature of the emotional experience.

In the same fashion, researchers have found that the label that an individual uses to interpret arousal produced by advocating a counterattitudinal message can influence the extent of attitude change. Zanna and Cooper (1974) provided strong evidence that cognitive labeling mediates the impact of dissonance-produced arousal on attitude change. Subjects in Zanna and Cooper's experiment wrote counterattitudinal essays concerning banning inflammatory speakers from campus under high- and low-choice conditions. Subjects also ingested a pill that they believed contained perfectly harmless chemical elements. In fact, the pill only contained powdered milk. One third of the subjects were told that the pill would make them feel tense, another third expected the pill to relax them, whereas the final third were informed that the pill had no side effects.

Zanna and Cooper predicted that the standard dissonance effect would emerge for the no side effects subjects: greater attitude change under high-choice conditions. The investigators also hypothesized that subjects in the high-choice condition who were led to believe the pill would make them feel tense would "misattribute" (i.e., mistakenly attribute) their arousal to the pill. It was expected that these subjects would feel tense because they had written an essay that violated their beliefs. However, given that they had been told that their tension was due to the pill, it was predicted that these subjects would have a satisfactory (although false) explanation for their arousal. Consequently, the investigators predicted that high-choice subjects who believed the pill would make them feel tense would exhibit relatively little attitude change.

Finally, the researchers predicted that subjects who believed the pill would relax them would have a strong need to reduce dissonance through attitude change. Zanna and Cooper noted that subjects in the relaxation condition expected to feel relaxed after taking the pill. However, as a result of having advocated a position that was contrary to their beliefs, these subjects felt jittery and aroused. Yet, unlike the subjects in the tension condition, these subjects could not infer that their arousal was due to the pill they had just ingested, because (in their case) the pill was supposed to make them feel relaxed. Thus, the investigators predicted that subjects in the relaxation condition would feel a strong need to reduce the resultant dissonance by changing their attitudes in the direction of the position they had just defended.

As Fig. 10.1 indicates, the results supported the hypotheses. Subjects in the no side effects condition exhibited the standard dissonance effect: greater attitude change under high-choice conditions. High-choice subjects who expected that the pill would make them feel tense showed considerably less evidence of attitude change. By contrast, high-choice subjects who expected the pill would relax them were significantly more likely to change their attitudes to reduce dissonance. Thus, the results indicated that advocating a counterattitudinal position will not lead to attitude change if the individual can be persuaded to misattribute his or her arousal to a different source. For a counterattitudinal advocacy to lead to attitude change, the individual must attribute arousal to the appropriate source (i.e., he or she must infer that his or her arousal has resulted from the decision to endorse a counterattitudinal position).

The contemporary approach to dissonance arousal has extended Festinger's early theorizing on this topic. Festinger's approach to dissonance arousal had a mechanistic quality to it. He drew an analogy between dissonance and biological drives such as hunger. He emphasized that inconsistent cognitions propelled or drove people to do something to reduce the painful arousal state. By contrast, contemporary theorists have a more dynamic view of the process by which dissonance leads to attitude change.

For example, a model proposed by Cooper and Fazio (1984) stipulates

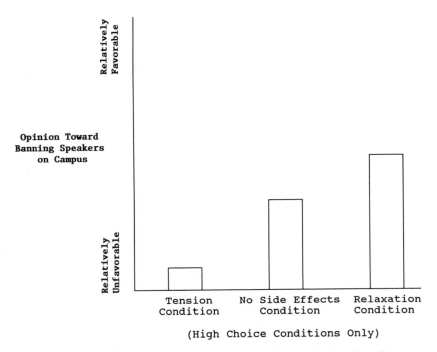

FIG. 10.1 Opinions as a function of attributions of arousal (data from Zanna & Cooper, 1974).

that the perception that one has brought about an unwanted event arouses dissonance. The model makes an important distinction between *dissonance arousal* and *dissonance motivation*. Dissonance arousal is a general and undifferentiated state that follows the attribution of responsibility for an unwanted event. Thus, when an individual accepts responsibility for having brought about a negative outcome, he or she feels jittery and aroused. This arousal will not motivate an individual to change his or her attitude.[8] Instead, as Cooper and Fazio (1984) noted, "like the arousal involved in emotions, the state of dissonance requires appropriate interpretation and labeling for attitude change to occur" (p. 244). This brings us to the concept of dissonance motivation, an internal pressure to change one's attitude or to restore consonance.

Given that an individual feels aroused as a result of having freely brought about a particular outcome, he or she should seek to interpret or understand this arousal. If the individual labels the arousal positively ("This is a pleasant sensation") and attributes the arousal to an external source ("I'm feeling good because I just had a lot to drink"), he or she should not experience dissonance motivation. In addition, if he or she labels the arousal negatively ("This is an unpleasant sensation") and attributes the arousal to an external source ("I'm feeling bad because I just took a pill"), he or she should not experience dissonance motivation. It is only when the individual labels the arousal negatively and attributes the state of arousal to having freely brought about a negative outcome ("I'm feeling an unpleasant sensation because I just told someone a lie they may believe") that dissonance motivation will occur. Under these latter circumstances, the individual will feel a need to reduce dissonance—he or she can be expected to select from a number of strategies, including denial, distortion, attitude change, and behavior change.

Thus, for counterattitudinal advocacy to lead to attitude change, a number of things must happen on both a physiological and psychological level. Furthermore, Cooper and Fazio's (1984) model assumes that processes emphasized by both Festinger (dissonance reduction) and Bemian theorists (attribution for one's arousal) must be considered.

Dissonance and the Self

Contemporary research also has focused on the intersection between dissonance reduction and the self-concept. According to self-esteem theorists, dissonance can usefully be viewed in the larger context of the need to preserve a positive self-concept. Aronson (1968) was the first to argue that self-esteem needs play an important part in the induced compliance paradigm:

> [A]lthough we may not have been fully aware of it at the time, in the clearest experiments performed to test dissonance theory, the dissonance involved was between a self concept and cognitions about a behavior that violated this self concept. In the experiments on counterattitudinal advocacy, for example, I would suggest that it is incorrect to say that dissonance existed between the cognition "I believe the task is dull" and "I told someone that the task was interesting." This is not dissonant for a psychopathic liar—indeed, it is perfectly consonant. What is dissonant is the cognition "I am a decent, truthful human being" and the cognition "I have misled a person; I have conned him into believing something which just isn't true; he thinks that I really believe it and I cannot set him straight because I probably won't see him again." (p. 24)

Nel, Helmreich, and Aronson (1969) conducted a study to test this hypothesis. Students at the University of Texas were paid 50¢ (small incentive) or $5 (large incentive) to make a video recording of a counterattitudinal message arguing that marijuana had few serious side effects and therefore should be legalized. (In the late-1960s, students on the Texas campus tended to oppose the legalization of marijuana.) Some subjects were led to believe that the recording would be shown to a group of students who had no prior opinion about marijuana, whereas other subjects were told that the tape would be played before students who favored or opposed the legalization of marijuana.

The investigators assumed that, for subjects in the first group, the cognition that they were good and decent people would be dissonant with the cognition that they had just conned a group of naive individuals into believing something that was not true and that might have serious behavioral consequences. Further, the investigators predicted that the negative incentive effect (greater attitude change for low-reward) would only emerge among subjects in this condition. The results confirmed this hypothesis: Subjects who were paid 50¢ to make a videotape that (they thought) would be played before an audience of students who had no prior opinion about marijuana use were more likely than subjects in any other group to exhibit dissonance-reducing attitude change (i.e., they were most favorable to the proposition that marijuana should be legalized).

A second variant on the dissonance-reduction-as-self-concept-preservation approach has been proposed by Steele (1988). Although Nel et al. (1969) have argued that people are motivated to maintain consistency in their self-concepts, Steele has contended that dissonance reduction has less to do with a need to maintain a consistent self-image than with the need to affirm a healthy and positive image of the self. Steele and Liu (1983) argued that: "If dissonance stems from the threat to the self (ego) inherent in a given inconsistency, then after dissonance has been aroused, thoughts and actions that affirm an important aspect of the self-concept should reduce dissonance by casting the self in a positive light" (p. 6).

In one study, Steele and Liu (1981) asked subjects to complete an attitude scale that included the item "I am in favor of high funding priority for research into treatment and facilities for chronic illness and handicaps." Some subjects were led to believe that they would later be given the opportunity to record exams onto audio cassettes for use by blind students. Other students were not given this expectation. Students then wrote forceful essays opposing increased state funding for facilities that serve the handicapped. Attitudes toward increased government funding for handicap facilities were then assessed.

Only subjects who wrote counterattitudinal essays and who were not given the expectation that they could help blind students exhibited dissonance-reducing attitude change. In other words, subjects who wrote essays opposing increased government funding for the handicapped changed their attitudes in the direction of advocacy, presumably to reduce the dissonance aroused by advocating such a counterattitudinal position. By contrast, students who expected they would have the opportunity to help blind students after the experiment did not exhibit dissonance-reducing attitude change. Presumably, these students also experienced dissonance after writing the essays opposing increased state funding for handicap facilities. However, they knew that they could salvage their conception of themselves as good and decent people by providing assistance to blind students after the experiment. This eliminated the need to change their attitudes in the direction of advocacy.

Steele and Liu (1983) provided stronger evidence for the self-affirmation hypothesis. They argued that affirmation of an important component of the self-concept should reduce dissonance, even when the self-affirming thoughts have nothing to do with the dissonant act. During the pretesting phase of the study, students filled out a value activities questionnaire that measured six general value orientations. Only subjects who scored very high or very low on the economic–political dimension of the scale were considered eligible for the study. In other words, only individuals who attached considerable value to economic and political activities, and those who attached relatively little value to these pursuits, were asked to participate in the actual study.

During the first phase of the experiment, subjects listed the strongest arguments they could think of in favor of a tuition increase at the university. Subjects wrote down their thoughts under high- or low-choice conditions. Students subsequently completed a values scale that tapped their economic and political value orientations. (This scale was slightly different from the questionnaire they had filled out earlier.) Attitudes toward the tuition increase were measured either before or after the completion of the values inventory.

The authors reasoned that writing a counterattitudinal essay advocating a tuition increase would arouse cognitive dissonance. Steele and Liu hypothesized that for subjects who scored low on the economic and political values scale, completing the second values questionnaire would do little to alleviate this dissonance. Consequently, the investigators predicted that these subjects would change their attitudes to reduce dissonance (i.e., they would adopt a more favorable position toward the tuition increase). On the other hand, Steele and Liu argued that completing the economic–political values inventory would provide subjects who scored high on this value dimension with an opportunity to affirm their core values, and thereby reduce the dissonance that had been aroused by writing the counterattitudinal essay. Thus, a subject who scored high on the economic–political values inventory might try to reduce dissonance by going through the following cognitive sequence:

> What kind of person agrees to write an essay that contradicts his beliefs? Not a very smart one, that's for sure. But I've just expressed my true beliefs (on the values scale). I've reaffirmed my commitments, my values, and my deepest aspirations. I've gotten in touch with my true self and I feel pretty good about the kind of person I am.

Steele and Liu hypothesized that subjects who scored high on the value inventory and who could affirm their economic and political values prior to indicating their attitude toward the tuition increase would exhibit relatively little dissonance-reducing attitude change. The results strongly supported the investigators' hypothesis.

Steele's research has interesting implications for how people reduce cognitive dissonance in everyday situations. Consider the plight of the cigarette smoker who knows all too well that "I smoke a pack a day" and that "Smoking causes lung cancer." In addition to the multitude of strategies to reduce dissonance that we have discussed throughout this chapter, Steele (1988) suggested another approach—one that is distinctive in its emphasis on the global integrity of the self.

> To reduce the disturbing impact of his dilemma, the smoker need not—in contrast to Festinger's view—resolve the provoking inconsistency. He need only engage in some affirmation of general self-integrity, even when that affirmation bears no relationship to smoking or to the inconsistency that smoking produces. He might, for example, join a valued cause, spend more time with his children, or try to accomplish more at the office, and in these ways affirm a larger sense of being an adequate person. The inconsistency would remain, of course, yet in the context of other valued self-concepts, it should pose less threat to global self-integrity and thus be more tolerable. (p. 262)

Dissonance: Past and Present

Dissonance theory has been revised substantially over the years. Festinger originally proposed that dissonance is aroused by psychological inconsistency. However, the results of studies conducted over the past 35 years make it clear that variables other than inconsistency must be present for dissonance to be aroused. Research conducted in the wake of the controversy over induced compliance indicated that an individual's counterattitudinal advocacy would arouse dissonance only if the advocacy had the effect of bringing about aversive outcomes, and only if the individual perceived that he or she was responsible for causing or contributing to these outcomes. Contemporary studies have taken this line of thinking one step further.

Scher and Cooper (1989) argued that if dissonance is aroused by the perception that one has brought about a negative state of affairs, then it should not matter whether the dissonant behavior is proattitudinal or counterattitudinal. In other words, they contended that a person could write a proattitudinal essay (one that confirmed a preexisting position) and still feel dissonance—provided he or she perceived that the essay would bring about negative consequences. This hypothesis, of course, is not compatible with Festinger's approach, because he argued that dissonance is driven by consistency needs. Thus, the original theory would predict that dissonance should be aroused only among subjects who wrote counterattitudinal essays. Yet Scher and Cooper found that, regardless of whether they wrote a proattitudinal essay or a counterattitudinal essay, subjects experienced dissonance, provided that they perceived that their essays might lead to a negative outcome (increasing student fees). Scher and Cooper (1989) noted that:

> Most obviously, this study would seem to lay to rest the notion that dissonance is driven by a "master motive" for consistency. Our results provide strong evidence that even when there are no inconsistent behaviors, dissonance can be aroused. Rather, dissonance is a theory about the consequences of being responsible for negative events. (p. 903)

In a similar vein, self-esteem theorists (Greenwald, Steele, and Schlenker) also have downplayed the role of consistency motives. They have argued that dissonance effects have their root in a need to preserve a positive self-image.

These arguments and findings have interesting implications for the student of attitude change. They suggest that people may not be as bothered by cognitive inconsistency—by imbalance among cognitive elements—as theorists of the 1960s assumed. People may be able to tolerate a great deal of inconsistency. What may bother them is the belief that they are responsible for having caused negative events. Or as self-concept theorists have noted, people are not bothered by the mere inconsistency between cognitions, but by the fact that the inconsistency makes them feel incompetent or malevolent, or both.

CONCLUSIONS

When Edward Jones, a distinguished social psychologist, was asked to indicate the number one achievement of social psychology, he pointed to cognitive dissonance theory (Aron & Aron, 1989). Jones argued that, by challenging the conventional wisdom that reinforcement determines attitude change, dissonance theory changed the way researchers thought about attitudes and behavior. Festinger's work opened up new arenas of inquiry and led to new ways of thinking about attitudes and persuasion.

Over the years, a number of modifications have been made in dissonance theory. The concepts of regret and irreversibility were not part of the original theoretical account of decision making, yet they were added to incorporate the results of a number of experiments. Similarly, the interpretation of induced compliance has changed dramatically over the years. The current version places little emphasis on cognitive consistency needs. Thus, one might say that dissonance theory has been highly resilient over the years: It has been revised in a number of ways, with each revision resulting in the addition of new concepts (e.g., aversive consequences, responsibility). On the other hand, critics have argued that this flexibility represents the theory's greatest weakness (Aronson, 1968). The theory has (in the course of being revised) increased in breadth to the point that it is difficult to separate out dissonance from related concepts (such as guilt, ego-defense, etc.; see Greenwald & Ronis, 1978). Yet, for all of its vagueness, dissonance has remained a powerful concept. Dissonance theory has generated a voluminous amount of research, much of which has supported the theory. Moreover, these studies have helped to explain a variety of important, yet previously inexplicable, social phenomena.

* * *

EXHIBIT 10–1
THE END OF THE WORLD IS AT HAND

Suppose an individual believes something with his whole heart; suppose further that he has a commitment to this belief, that he has taken irrevocable actions because of it; finally, suppose that he is presented with evidence, unequivocal and undeniable evidence, that his belief is wrong: what will happen? The individual will frequently emerge, not only unshaken, but even more convinced of the truth of his beliefs than ever before. Indeed, he may even show a new fervor about convincing and converting other people to his view. (Festinger, Riecken, & Schachter, 1956, p. 3)

So began one of the most interesting studies of cognitive dissonance ever conducted. The study, undertaken by Festinger, Rieken, and Schachter (1956), focused on how a group of believers who prophesized that a flood would destroy their hometown maintained their beliefs even after the prophesy had been unconfirmed. Festinger et al. launched their investigation when they came across the following headline and article in a local newspaper:

PROPHECY FROM PLANET. CLARION CALL TO CITY: FLEE THAT FLOOD. IT'LL SWAMP US ON DEC. 21, OUTER SPACE TELLS SUBURBANITE.

Lake City will be destroyed by a flood from Great Lake just before dawn, Dec. 21, according to a suburban housewife. Mrs. Marian Keech, of 847 West School street, says the prophecy is not her own. It is the purport of many messages she has received by automatic writing, she says. . . . The messages, according to Mrs. Keech, are sent to her by superior beings from a planet called "Clarion." These beings have been visiting the earth, she says, in what we call flying saucers. During their visits, she says, they have observed fault lines in the earth's crust that have foretoken the deluge. Mrs. Keech reports she was told the flood will spread to form an inland sea stretching from the Arctic Circle to the Gulf of Mexico. At the same time, she says, a cataclysm will submerge the West Coat from Seattle, Wash. to Chile in South America. (Festinger, Riecken, & Schachter, 1956, pp. 30–31)

Realizing that this was a once-in-a-lifetime opportunity to test some of their ideas about cognitive consistency, the researchers contacted Mrs. Keech to see if she

EXHIBIT 10-1   251

knew of other individuals who also believed that a flood would destroy Lake City on December 21. The investigators discovered that there were indeed others who believed in the prediction, and they learned that these individuals belonged to a group called the Seekers. Festinger and his colleagues discovered that the Seekers believed that they (the faithful few) would be rescued by a flying saucer at midnight on December 20. The researchers arranged to join the group to observe their reactions to the disconfirmation of their prophecy. As Batson and Ventis (1982), two experts in the psychology of religion, noted in their description of the study by Festinger et al., field investigations of this kind run into some practical problems:

> The social psychologists wished to keep accurate, verbatim records of what group members said and did, but they did not wish to "blow their cover." Further, although they wanted to be accepted as members of the group, they did not want to influence the beliefs of other group members. In order to get as accurate a record as possible, they frequently resorted to hiding in the bathroom or on the porch, where they frantically scribbled notes. The efforts to avoid too direct participation reached a droll climax when one of the social psychologists was asked to act as a medium and receive messages from outer space. He kept a long silence. Finally, Mrs. Keech said with some irritation, "What do you see?" "Nothing," he replied. "That's not nothing," he was told, "that's the Void." (Festinger et al., 1956, p. 243) (excerpted from Batson & Ventis, 1982, p. 187)

As it happened, on the fateful day, many of the student members of the group were at home, on Christmas break. However, 10 members who lived in Lake City gathered at Mrs. Keech's house and got ready to be picked up by the flying saucer. Mrs. Keech informed them that "precisely at midnight a spaceman would come to the door and escort them to the place where the saucer (tola) was parked" (Festinger et al., 1956, p. 160). The members thoroughly rehearsed the passwords that they believed they would have to use in boarding the flying saucer. They also removed all traces of metal from their clothing, for (according to Mrs. Keech) metallic objects were dangerous on flying saucers.

The atmosphere grew tense as the midnight hour approached. Then when the clock struck 12, the members "sat motionless . . . their faces seemingly frozen and expressionless." No one said a word, but it was clear that they were deeply disturbed by the fact that the saucer had not arrived and that a rescue effort was clearly not underway.

For a time, the members searched for an explanation. They reexamined the original communication that indicated that at midnight on the 20th, the group would be taken to the saucer. They tried to reinterpret the message in light of the previous events, but to no avail. Suddenly, at 4:45 a.m., Mrs. Keech summoned the group into the living room and ecstatically read an announcement that she had received:

> For this day it is established that there is but one God of Earth, and He is in thy midst, and from his hand thou has written these words. And mighty is the word of God—and by his word have ye been saved—for from the mouth of death have ye been delivered and at no time has there been such a force loosed upon the Earth. (Festinger et al., 1956, p. 169).

The announcement changed everything. The atmosphere changed from despair to elation. The message that Mrs. Keech had received provided an explanation of the disconfirmation. The group, "sitting all night long, had spread so much light that God had saved the world from destruction" (Festinger et al., 1956, p. 169).

The members, who previously had shunned the publicity they had received in the newspapers, now actively sought it out. They called up reporters to give their explanation for why the saucers had not rescued them and why the flood had failed to destroy Lake City. Why did the Seekers engage in such behaviors? Festinger et al. suggested that by prosletyzing their message, believers hoped to reduce the dissonance that had been aroused by the disconfirmation of their prophecy. As Festinger et al. wrote:

> *If more and more people can be persuaded that the system of belief is correct, then clearly it must, after all, be correct.* Consider the extreme case: if everyone in the whole world believed something there would be no question at all as to the validity of this belief. It is for this reason that we observe the increase in proselyting following disconfir- mation. If the proselyting proves successful, then by gathering more adherents and effectively surrounding himself with supporters, the believer reduces dissonance to the point where he can live with it. (p. 28)

* * *

EXHIBIT 10-2
PERSUADING PEOPLE TO EAT (AND LIKE) GRASSHOPPERS

One way to rationalize the performance of counterattitudinal behavior is to convince oneself that the behavior was not so bad (i.e., the person can change his or her attitude so that it conforms with his or her behavior). As we have noted, researchers have conducted a variety of studies to test this hypothesis. One of the most imaginative of these experiments involved convincing army reservists to eat (and like) fried grasshoppers.

Now what does eating fried grasshoppers have to do with dissonance theory? According to Zimbardo, Ebbesen, and Maslach (1977):

> Since most people in our culture would initially have the cognition, "I do not like fried grasshoppers, they're ucky," the knowledge that they were biting off the head of the grasshopper and chewing on the eyes would create dissonance under the right circumstances. Specifically, dissonance would arise if the justification for eating the grasshopper were minimal. There is probably more justification to comply to discrepant requests made by attractive, well-liked people than requests made by disliked, unappealing people. Therefore, greater dissonance should be experienced when the unpleasant behavior of eating the grasshopper is requested by a *negative* communicator than by a *positive* one. (p. 105)

In other words, a pleasant communicator provides a strong external justification for eating the grasshopper. The individual can rationalize the decision to eat grasshoppers by thinking "I'm doing it to please this suave and attractive speaker." On the other hand, there is less incentive to go along with an unattractive communicator. If the individual does accede to the request (i.e., if he or she eats

EXHIBIT 10–2   **253**

grasshoppers) he or she will experience dissonance between the behavior (eating a grasshopper) and his or her attitude (I hate fried grasshoppers). One way of reducing the dissonance is to change the attitude so that it is consistent with the behavior.

Subjects in Zimbardo, Weisenberg, Firestone, and Levy's (1965) study were college students and army reservists. There were two experimental groups (positive and negative communicator) and a series of notreatment controls.

Experimental group subjects first indicated their attitudes toward a variety of food items, including (of course) fried grasshoppers. The positive communicator "interacted with his 'assistant' . . . gave politely phrased requests to the assistant, called him by his first name, responded to a 'mistake' by the assistant with equanimity, and in general was considerate and pleasant" (Zimbardo et al., 1965, p. 239). By contrast, the negative communicator called the assistant by his last name and ordered him about. In addition:

> When the assistant mistakenly brought in the "wrong" experimental food, a tray of eels, the E (experimenter), who was in the process of talking to the Ss (subjects) in his most pleasant manner, suddenly blew up and said, "Oh, dammit, can't you remember the schedule? That food is for the next group. . . . Let us get with it and hurry up about it." (p. 239)

An assistant then brought in a plate with five fried grasshoppers and placed it before the subjects. The communicator remarked that:

> Before asking you to eat the experimental food, I want to make it clear that this part of the experiment is *voluntary*, and no one has to eat these fried grasshoppers if they do not want to. However, for the purposes of the study, I would like you to try at least one and preferably to eat all on the plate. (p. 240)

Subjects then indicated their attitudes toward the food items once again and completed several other scales.

Approximately 50% of the subjects ate at least one grasshopper. The negative communicator was significantly more effective in changing attitudes toward grasshoppers than was the positive communicator. Among those who ate a grasshopper, the negative communicator induced more attitude change (55%) than did the positive communicator (5%). Moreover, subjects in the negative communicator condition also were more likely to endorse statements like "I've tried (the food) personally, found it to be very tasty, and would certainly recommend it."

These findings provide one explanation for the so-called "Stockholm Syndrome"—the tendency of individuals who have been held captive to like (or even love) those who have held them captive. In such intensive indoctrination situations, the captives frequently must perform actions that are (to say the least) inconsistent with their beliefs and attitudes. In many cases, the requests for compliance come from individuals who are (to say the least) unsavory, highly negative communicators. When the directive comes in the form of an order, dissonance theory clearly does not apply. However, in some instances, persons who are held captive may perceive that they are free to turn down the request. In such cases, the findings of Zimbardo et al. (1965) apply, for they help us understand how people might come to enhance their liking for the communicator to justify their decision to perform a disliked behavior.

Consider, for example, the case of Cambodian Prince Norodom Sihanouk. Sihanouk, the former leader of Cambodia, was taken prisoner by the vicious Khmer Rouge. During the years of his captivity, Sihanouk contemplated suicide and was on hand when his son was killed by the Khmer Rouge. Yet, after he was released, Sihanouk arranged for his prison guard to be his private butler and body guard. Clearly, the findings of Zimbardo et al. provide one explanation for this strange, difficult-to-fathom behavior.

* * *

EXHIBIT 10-3
SELECTIVE EXPOSURE

Consider this scenario: It's June, you've just graduated from college, and you're starting a job in an advertising agency downtown. Plus, you just got your first pay check, and it's a whopper. After years of borrowing and renting cars, you decide that it's time you bought your own car. You drop over to local dealerships and test drive some cars. You read through *Consumer Reports* and talk to friends. Finally, you narrow the choice down to the Pontiac Sunbird and the Ford Escort. After test driving the cars a little more and sizing up the good and bad points of each car, you decide to buy the Sunbird. A few days after you buy the car, you have some regrets. You wonder if you should have bought the Escort, because it had a better repair record than the Sunbird.

According to Festinger (1957), you might seek to reduce this postdecisional dissonance by seeking out information that confirms the wisdom of your choice (i.e., by rereading the various materials you received about the Sunbird—materials that described the Sunbird's sporty features, handling ability, and gas mileage). You also might consciously avoid information that questions the wisdom of your decision (e.g., by refusing to look over any of the materials the Ford dealer gave you). The tendency to seek out information that supports one's decision is called *selective exposure,* and the tendency to avoid information that calls one's choice into question is called *selective avoidance.*

The conventional wisdom in the 1950s was that people engaged in selective exposure and selective avoidance to reduce dissonance following a decision. In those days, audience members were viewed as stubborn, obstinate creatures who were driven to maintain consistency between their thoughts and actions (Klapper, 1960). People were believed to be relatively intolerant when it came to accepting information that contradicted their point of view. This view changed in the 1960s. Several studies reported that subjects exhibited a preference for information that was dissonant (rather than consonant) with their decisions (Feather, 1963; Freedman & Sears, 1965; Rosen, 1961).[9]

Today, the prevailing view is that selective exposure occurs some of the time. The consensus is that, under some conditions, people will seek out supportive information following a decision, whereas under other conditions, they will not exhibit a preference for supportive information and may even seek out dissonant information (Frey, 1986; Wicklund & Brehm, 1976). Thus, sometimes people are

EXHIBIT 10–3   255

closeminded decision confirmers who are doggedly determined to convince themselves that their decision was right. On other occasions, people are openminded information seekers who are determined to get all the facts, no matter whether they contradict the person's decision. The research question (as you may have surmised) is determining when people seek out supportive information and when they are open to nonsupportive information.

An individual is likely to seek out supportive information following a decision when (a) the person makes the decision freely and of his or her own volition, (b) the decision is irreversible, and (c) the person is highly committed to one of the choice alternatives (Frey, 1986). On the other hand, an individual is likely to seek out nonsupportive information (i.e., facts that are inconsistent with his or her decision) when (a) the information will be useful to the individual, (b) the person is curious about the information, (c) the individual feels an obligation to be fair to both sides, and (d) the person believes that the dissonant information is easy to refute. Frey concluded that:

> People are relatively open to new information (supporting and opposing their belief or decision or hypotheses) as long as they see a possibility for revision. When, for varying reasons (e.g., external constraints, internal resistance to change), this possibility is not seen to exist, subjects tend to ignore nonsupportive information and increase their preferences for information that lends them support. (pp. 73–74)

Although there is evidence that selective exposure occurs (at least under some conditions), there is considerably less evidence that people selectively avoid information that is dissonant with their choices. Frey (1986) suggested that people may realize that some dissonant information may in fact be useful for future decisions.

PART III
COMMUNICATION
APPROACHES

The thrust of the discussions up to this point have been psychological in nature. The focus has been on the psychology of persuasive communication, in particular social psychological theories of message effects. In this final section, the focus is on communication approaches to persuasion. Chapter 11 explores theory and research in interpersonal persuasion, and chapter 12 examines the processes and effects of mass media information campaigns.

11
Interpersonal Persuasion

You have been dating the same person for the past 6 months, and you've begun to develop a more intense attachment to your partner. One morning you get a call from an old acquaintance whom you haven't seen in 2 years. The two of you had been romantically involved some time ago, and your acquaintance mentions that he or she is just in town for the day and would love to get together tonight, even for a short time. The problem is that you have a standing date with your new friend, and you know that he or she needs very much to talk to you tonight. How would you try to convince your friend to let you see your acquaintance? (adapted from Miller, Boster, Roloff, & Seibold, 1977)

You're living in an apartment not far from campus. Every night for the past week you have been kept awake at night by the sound of the neighbor's barking dog. The trouble is once his dog starts barking it causes other dogs around the neighborhood to begin howling. How would you approach your neighbor to convince him to curb his dog's nighttime antics? (adapted from Cody, McLaughlin, & Jordan, 1980)

It's lunch time, and you've decided to eat your bag lunch in the foyer of a building on campus. You're enjoying your meal and daydreaming a bit. You look up and notice that someone has sat down near you and has lit up a cigarette. You're angry and upset. The smoke is getting in your eyes and in your food, so you decide to do something about the situation. Which of these techniques do you think you would use?

"Grab the cigarette from the person's mouth and crush it." Tell him "to put out that cigarette before I get upset." Tell him if you'll "quit smoking right now, I'll buy you a drink."

Ask him, "How can you keep on smoking, knowing that it causes cancer? You should put it out."

Ask them to "do me a favor by putting out the cigarette; I have an allergic reaction to them." (Schenck-Hamlin, Georgacarakos, & Wiseman, 1982, p. 173)

These examples are a testament to the fact that a great deal of persuasion occurs in ordinary situations in our everyday lives. Indeed, when asked "who tries to persuade you?" and "who do you try to persuade?", college students named people they knew well—members of their immediate family, extended family members, and close friends (Rule, Bisanz, & Kohn, 1985). Yet we ordinarily think of persuasion as something dramatic or unusual, as exemplified by cults or presidential debates. We do not think of it as an everyday phenomenon, and we rarely see ourselves as cast in the role of the persuader.

This chapter focuses on persuasion in ordinary, everyday interpersonal settings. It draws heavily on research in interpersonal communication. Interpersonal communication scholars have offered a unique and valuable perspective on persuasion—one that differs sharply from the programs of research we have discussed in previous sections of this book. Miller and Burgoon (1978) noted that most research on persuasion can be characterized by four assumptions. In a classic article, Miller and Burgoon (1978) identified these assumptions and then discussed how they had produced a distorted view of the persuasion process. We will briefly describe each assumption below, along with Miller and Burgoon's critique.

Assumption 1. Persuasion is a "One-to-Many" Process in Which a Communicator Delivers a Message to a Large Number of Individuals. This is the classic image of persuasion (e.g., the charismatic speaker addresses throngs of supporters at a rally, two candidates square off in a televised presidential debate, a commercial for a soft drink attracts a large national audience. Miller (1972) questioned the accuracy of this view of persuasion:

> When one reflects on the communicative transactions of most persons, it becomes clear that only a small percentage of them consist of lengthy periods of uninterrupted discourse directed at sizable target audiences. In the give-and-take of dyadic dialogue, the communication flow of the small group . . . one finds most of the communication action. . . . (p. 397)

Assumption 2. Persuasion is a One-Way Unidirectional Process. According to this view, which probably dates back to the earliest studies of persuasion, persuasion is something that a communicator does "to" an audience. Interpersonal communication researchers reject this notion, arguing that "persuasion is not something one person does *to* another but something he or she does *with* another" (Reardon, 1981, p. 25). Smith (1982) viewed persuasion as the "symbolic exchange of messages," and other scholars use words like "transaction" and "interaction" to describe interpersonal persuasion. Reardon (1987) pointed out that a persuader's selection of influence strategies is determined by "what each person has said and done during the course of the interaction. Each communicator's contributions shape the course of interpersonal persuasion" (p. 148).

To appreciate this perspective, consider the smoking scenario described earlier. You're eating lunch and you ask a smoker to put out his cigarette. Suppose the smoker refuses, adamantly saying that he has as much right to do what he wants as you do. You might respond angrily that he is polluting your air and has no right do this. But what if the smoker politely demurs that he has an exam in a half hour and is very nervous. You probably would soft-pedal your request, trying to show empathy for his needs, while at the same time asserting your rights. Notice that the smoker's response to your request influences the nature of your response. In many interpersonal settings, persuasion is bidirectional, with both source and receiver sending out messages and then adapting their messages to fit their interpretations of the responses of the other party.

Assumption 3. Persuasion is "Issue-Centered." Persuasion researchers have traditionally examined the impact of a message on an individual's attitude toward a particular issue. Issues have been diverse, ranging from a tuition increase to political reform to capital punishment. Interpersonally oriented researchers argue that, by focusing on issues, researchers have neglected other aspects of the persuasion process. A great deal of persuasion takes place in the context of relationships, and, as a consequence, communicators are frequently concerned with achieving interpersonal objectives (convincing a close friend to reevaluate his or her commitment to a relationship) and with accomplishing self-presentational goals (trying to alter a friend's impression of their lifestyle). Miller and Burgoon (1978) noted that "most people devote the preponderance of their persuasive energies to selling themselves and to a lesser extent, other persons" (p. 33).

Assumption 4. Persuasion Focuses Primarily on Strategies for Changing Social Attitudes. Interpersonally oriented researchers have argued that there has been an overabundance of research concerned with devising messages to change attitudes. These scholars have emphasized that it is also important to understand the techniques people employ to change and influence behaviors, particularly their strategies for obtaining behavioral compliance.

This chapter focuses on three major areas of interpersonal persuasion research: compliance-gaining, constructivism, and sequential influence strategies. Of the three areas, compliance-gaining has captured the lion's share of research attention, so the research in this area is reviewed first.

COMPLIANCE-GAINING

This section is divided into three parts: (a) a description of the strategies for measuring compliance-gaining, (b) a discussion of the impact of situational and individual difference factors on message selection, and (c) an analysis of contemporary perspectives on compliance-gaining behavior.

Marwell and Schmitt (1967) introduced the concept of compliance-gaining. They observed that:

> It is clear that people spend a good deal of time trying to get others to act in ways they desire. It is equally clear that people vary in the ways they go about attempting such interpersonal control. Yet, students of social control have only recently begun to explore these variations. Most research has concentrated on why people comply rather than on how they go about gaining compliance. (p. 350)

There are several rather precise definitions of compliance-gaining. Schenck-Hamlin, Wiseman, and Georgacarakos (1982) defined it as "the attempt of some actor—the source of communication—to effect a particular, preconceived response from some target—the receiver of the persuasive effort" (p. 92). Wheeless, Barraclough, and Stewart (1983) defined compliance-gaining as a "communicative behavior in which an agent engages so as to elicit from a target some agent-selected behavior" (p. 111).

It is important to differentiate between compliance-gaining strategies and tactics. Strategies are "plans for achieving broad overall objectives"; they are "abstract and provide general guidelines for action" (Berger, 1985, pp. 484–485). Tactics are specific and concrete; they are "specific deployments and maneuvers in the field designed to achieve limited objectives" (Berger, 1985, p. 484). Strategies subsume or encompass tactics.

Assessing compliance-gaining in the real world is no simple matter. People use many different strategies and tactics to get their way. Situations differ, and people differ. Are we to sit down and observe what people do each and every time they want to gain compliance from others? Clearly, this would be an impossible task. Should we then study compliance-gaining in the laboratory, in which case we would manipulate a strategy and see if it leads to more compliance? The problem with this approach is that it fails to answer the compelling question that Marwell and Schmitt originally posed: namely, how do people go about trying to gain compliance in everyday life?

To measure compliance-gaining, researchers have taken a different tack. They have asked their subjects to indicate what techniques they use to gain compliance from others. In a sense, this parallels the receiver-oriented approach that source credibility researchers used to study credibility in the 1960s. Like the source credibility research, compliance-gaining studies have been roundly criticized on methodological grounds. But, unlike credibility studies, compliance-gaining research has produced a number of useful findings and conclusions.

The goal of the early research on compliance-gaining was to discover the general strategies that people use to gain compliance from others. Realizing that an infinite number of tactics were probably used in everyday situations, researchers wanted to boil down these tactics. They wanted to discover the commonalities and locate the overall strategies people use to gain compliance. Using factor analysis, cluster analysis, and other data-reducing techniques, they constructed typologies or classification schemes. A number of different compliance-gaining typologies have been proposed (Clark, 1979; Cody, McLaughlin, & Jordan, 1980; Falbo, 1977; Marwell & Schmitt, 1967; Schenck-Hamlin, Wiseman, & Georgacarakos, 1982). Three representative typologies are discussed in the next section.

Marwell and Schmitt: A Deductive Approach

Marwell and Schmitt (1967) derived their approach to compliance-gaining from theories of social power (French & Raven, 1960; Parsons, 1963). The investigators used these theories to help generate compliance-gaining tactics. Thus, concepts such as "reward power" and "expert power" were translated into techniques that persuaders could use to gain compliance. Marwell and Schmitt came up with 16 different tactics, including promise, liking altruism, and debt. During the course of the study, subjects read over descriptions of four situations in which one person was trying to gain compliance from another. One of the scenarios presented this problem to subjects: "Your teenage son, Dick, who is a high school student, has been getting poor grades. You want him to increase the amount of time he spends studying from 6 to 12 hours a week." Respondents then indicated the likelihood that they would use each of the 16 compliance-gaining tactics to induce Dick to comply with their request. (See Exhibits 11-1 and 11-2, pp. 293-296.) However, Marwell and Schmitt were not simply interested in determining which techniques individuals employed in the four situations. Instead, they wanted to boil down the techniques even further to see if there were any commonalities across techniques. Therefore, they performed a factor analysis on their data and found that five factors underlied the techniques that subjects reported they would use in the four hypothetical situations. The factors (or strategies) were: (a) rewarding activity, (b) punishing activity, (c) expertise, (d) activation of impersonal commitments, and (e) activation of personal commitments.

In a subsequent study, communication researchers Miller and Parks (1982) argued that the Marwell and Schmitt tactics could be ordered along two dimensions. One dimension was reward-punishment (did the persuader try to use rewarding or punishing techniques to gain compliance?). The other dimension was communicator-recipient onus—did the persuader attempt to manipulate rewards and punishments directly (communicator onus) or did he or she try to stimulate positive and negative self-persuasion techniques (recipient onus) (see Fig. 11.1).

```
                              REWARD
                             ORIENTED
                                |
Promise                         |          Positive Moral Appeal
Positive Expertise              |          Positive Self-feeling
Pre-giving                      |          Altruism
Positive Esteem                 |          Positive Altercasting
                                |
COMMUNICATOR ───────────────────┼─────────────── RECIPIENT
    ONUS                        |                   ONUS
                                |
Threat                          |          Negative Moral Appeal
Negative Expertise              |          Negative Self-feeling
Aversive Stimulation            |          Debt
Negative Esteem                 |          Negative Altercasting
                                |
                            PUNISHMENT
                             ORIENTED
```

FIG. 11.1 Four-category typology of compliance-gaining message strategies (*Note:* Miller and Parks made several modifications in Marwell and Schmitt's scheme; they deleted the liking category, and they divided moral appeal into two categories: positive and negative moral appeal. From Miller, 1987).

Although Marwell and Schmitt's scheme is credited with having stimulated a multitude of studies on compliance-gaining, it has several weaknesses (Miller, Boster, Roloff, & Seibold, 1987; Seibold, Cantrill, & Meyers, 1985). Its main shortcoming is that it may not reflect the strategies people actually use in everyday situations. Wiseman and Schenck-Hamlin (1981) questioned whether Marwell and Schmitt's techniques are "representative or exhaustive of the strategies encountered in persuasive situations" (p. 253). Cody, McLaughlin, and Jordan (1980) reported that when subjects were asked to write down the strategies they would use in three persuasion situations, between 44% and 72% of the strategies listed were not included in Marwell and Schmitt's checklist.

To resolve these problems, researchers have used a different procedure to assess compliance-gaining. Rather than asking subjects to choose from a list of preformulated strategies, they have asked subjects to write down the strategies they would use to gain compliance (Falbo, 1977; Wiseman & Schenck-Hamlin, 1981). These approaches are inductive in that compliance-gaining tactics are generated by subjects themselves rather than from checklists deduced from communication theories. One exemplar of the inductive approach is the typology developed by Falbo (1977).

Falbo: "How I Get My Way"

Falbo (1977) assessed compliance-gaining in a very straightforward way. She handed subjects a sheet of paper. The following instructions appeared at the top of the page: "On this page, write a paragraph about 'How I Get My Way.' Please be frank and honest."

Three coders then classified subjects' responses into different categories. Sixteen different tactics emerged, ranging from compromise to hinting to deceit. (See Exhibit 11-3, p. 296.) Falbo then wanted to know if certain strategies subsumed these tactics. She discovered that two different dimensions of compliance-gaining strategies emerged: direct–indirect and rational–nonrational. Thus, students indicated that "they got their way" by being direct (making assertions and simple statements) or by being indirect (hinting and bargaining), by adopting a rational approach (reason and compromise) or by employing a nonrational approach (evasion and threat). In addition, the categories overlapped so that a tactic could be both direct and rational (persistence), direct and nonrational (threat), indirect and rational (bargaining), and indirect and nonrational (deceit).

Wiseman and Schenck-Hamlin: Another Inductive Approach

Wiseman and Schenck-Hamlin (1981) noted that Falbo (1977) had asked a subject to indicate "how I get my way" in general, across situations. The investigators pointed out that persuasion is context-bound, and that different influence strategies are likely to be employed in different situations (see also, Schenck-Hamlin et al., 1982). The researchers employed a three-step procedure to develop a compliance-gaining typology that was sensitive to situational factors. First, they asked subjects to evaluate each of 10 persuasion situations in terms of the believability, importance, and reasonableness of the request. Subjects then chose the three compliance-gaining situations with which they could most easily empathize and developed a message for each of the situations. Finally, subjects wrote an essay on the subject of "how I get others to do what I want them to do." After examining the essays, the researchers derived a typology of persuasion strategies that reflected the strategies subjects discussed in their essays. (See Exhibit 11-4, p. 297.)

The investigators subsequently found that the strategies that had emerged in subjects' essays had four significant properties: (a) explicitness of the persuader's intent (is the speaker roundabout or straightforward?), (b) manipulation of rewards and punishments (is the message positive or negative toward the listeners?), (c) locus of control of reinforcements (does the persuader treat the target as an equal or does the communicator totally dominate the listener?), and (d) explicitness of a rationale for compliance (is the message reasonable or unreasonable?).

Critique

The first generation of research on compliance-gaining focused on the development of typologies; the aim was to categorize individuals' tactics into broader categories. You may wonder, then, what are the major strategies individuals use to get others to go along with their requests? There is no simple answer to this question. The compliance-gaining studies have uncovered a variety of different strategies. Moreover, different researchers have found different clusters of strategies. Much depends on the methodology that is used to measure compliance-gaining.

Researchers have used one of two procedures. The *checklist,* or *strategy selection procedure,* provides subjects with a list of preformulated strategies (e.g., liking, threat, and altruism). Subjects then indicate the likelihood that they would use each of the strategies to gain compliance in a particular situation. Marwell and Schmitt (1967) employed the strategy selection procedure.

The construction procedure is a more openended approach. Subjects write out (or construct) the messages that they would use to get another to go along with their request. Falbo (1977) and Schenck-Hamlin et al. (1982) have employed the construction approach (see also, Clark, 1979).

It turns out that different strategies emerge, depending on whether the researcher uses the strategy selection or the construction procedure (Burleson et al., 1988). Each approach has its adherents. Proponents of the construction procedure have argued that the selection method gives an artificial assessment of compliance-gaining behavior. The argument is that the selection procedure forces subjects to choose from a list of preformulated tactics that have been provided by the researcher. The problem is that, left to his or her own devices, the individual might not choose any of these tactics, but (given that he or she must choose from the list) may make a choice that does not reflect his or her own true preferences.

In an exhaustive critique of the selection procedure, Burleson et al. (1988) showed that subjects give "socially desirable" responses to strategy selection checklists. In one study, they asked subjects to indicate how likely they would be to use each of the 16 Marwell and Schmitt tactics to gain compliance. Then they asked students to evaluate the social appropriateness of each of the various tactics. They found that there was a significant correlation between the likelihood that a particular tactic would be used and its social appropriateness. For example, positive expertise, altruism, and liking were all regarded as the most socially acceptable ways to gain compliance. Subjects also indicated they would be extremely likely to use these strategies.

Burleson and his colleagues argued that this was precisely the point: People report that they would use these strategies only because they seem to be the "right" or "socially correct" techniques to use. Consequently, the selection procedure may not assess people's actual strategies for gaining compliance, but only their perceptions of what the socially appropriate strategy happens to be. Burleson et al. contended that the construction procedure provides a more valid assessment of compliance-gaining, particularly the preference for socially inappropriate techniques. "When left to their own devices," they argued, "people may well employ less polite (i.e., less appropriate) forms of behavior in the effort to get their way" (p. 476).

Proponents of the selection procedure have responded in several ways to these criticisms. Boster (1988) questioned whether the existence of a correlation between social appropriateness of strategy and its likelihood of use proves that people choose strategies because they are socially desirable. In addition, Boster noted that, under some conditions, some individuals do indicate that they would employ negative antisocial strategies and that the selection procedure is capable of accurately reflecting these behavioral preferences. Seibold et al. (1985) have noted that, for all of its vaunted advantages, there is little evidence that the construction procedure does a better job than the checklist of assessing compliance-gaining behavior in the real world.

For now, the uncomfortable truth is that there is no one answer to the question Marwell and Schmitt posed in 1967: What strategies do people use to gain compliance? There are a variety of typologies; although the tactics sometimes overlap, the typologies obtain different clusters of compliance-gaining strategies. Furthermore, there are other factors that determine when a particular strategy will be employed. I now turn to the impact that situational and personality factors exert on compliance-gaining behavior—the focus of the second generation of research in this area.

Situational Influences

What techniques do you use to try to get your way? Are you direct or indirect? Do you use rewards or threats? Are you up-front or manipulative? Well, you may reply, it depends on the situation. "Exactly," a compliance-gaining researcher would respond, but "what do you mean by the situation?"

This may seem like a simple question. We all have first-hand knowledge of situations, and if someone asked you to define the term *situation*, you might begin by ticking off a variety of different of situations (e.g., work, leisure time, time spent with friends, time spent with family, etc.). Researchers have provided a more precise definition of *situation*. Pervin (1978) stated that a situation "is defined by who is involved, what is going on, and where the action is taking place" (pp. 79–80). Scholars have noted that situations have different psychological characteristics. Thus, Pervin (1978) found that people experience situations as friendly or unfriendly, tense or calm, interesting or dull, and constrained or free.

Cody and McLaughlin (1980) found six different perceptual dimensions of persuasion situations. The dimensions are:

1. *Intimacy.* A situation high in intimacy involves trying to convince a boy- or girlfriend to let you see an old flame. A low-intimacy situation involves trying to persuade a classmate to lend you his or her notes.

2. *Dominance.* These situations concern the distribution of power in a relationship. You may attempt to persuade a superior (as when you try to convince a professor to let you take his or her class although you have not fulfilled the prerequisites). An attempt to persuade a subordinate is illustrated by the dorm adviser who tries to persuade a freshman to spend more time studying for a calculus course.

3. *Personal benefits.* A situation high in self-benefits might involve persuading a teaching assistant to change your grade. A situation low in self-benefits might involve convincing a family member to let you watch a particular television show.

4. *Consequences.* A persuasion attempt can have long-term consequences for the relationship, or only short-term consequences. A long-term consequences situation is persuading your parents to accept your decision to marry someone of a different race, whereas a short-term consequences situation is persuading a friend to take you to the doctor on his or her day off.

5. *Rights.* A situation high in rights involves convincing a person who is smoking in a nonsmoking section to put out his or her cigarette. A typical low-rights situation would be convincing an art dealer to lower the price of an oil painting.

6. *Resistance.* In many persuasion situations, the persuadee resists the attempt at persuasion. A typical high-resistance situation would be persuading a smoker to put out his or her cigarette after she has refused your initial requests. An example of a low-resistance situation is persuading a friend who wants to play tennis with you to meet you on the courts on Saturday morning.

Now that we have identified the psychological dimensions of situations, we can see if people use different message strategies in different situations. You should keep in mind that our knowledge of situational effects on message strategies is limited in three respects. First, there have been only a handful of studies that have explored situational effects. Second, several studies have found that certain situations exert a small impact on compliance-gaining behavior (e.g., Dillard & Burgoon, 1985). Third, because researchers have frequently used only one type of situation to tap a complex situational factor, the generalizability of the research is limited (Jackson & Backus, 1982). Nonetheless, there is enough evidence that people use different message strategies in different situations to convince researchers that situational factors are an important variable in the compliance-gaining mix. I now discuss situational effects using Cody and McLaughlin's (1980) classification scheme. I focus on three key situational factors: intimacy, dominance, and resistance.[1]

Intimacy. Situations vary along an intimacy continuum. *Noninterpersonal situations* are the least intimate. In these situations, communicators are likely to use cultural and sociological data to make predictions about the effects of social influence attempts (Miller & Steinberg, 1975). *Interpersonal situations* involve attempts to persuade acquaintances, colleagues, and friends. Miller and Steinberg argued that in these situations, people use psychological information about the other person to help them decide whether an influence attempt will succeed. On the other hand, *intimate situations* involve attempts to influence close friends, lovers, and family members. In these situations, individuals bring a rich storehouse of knowledge to bear on their message strategy choices.

Miller et al. (1977) found that subjects indicated they would use different strategies, depending on whether the situation was interpersonal or noninterpersonal, or involved short- or long-term consequences. The only strategy that exhibited a high likelihood of use across situations was liking. Miller et al. (1977) noted that "respondents apparently had a general preference for a strategy that places the intended persuadee in a positive frame of mind" (p. 48).

Dillard and Burgoon (1985) found that increases in intimacy were (modestly) associated with the use of more prosocial strategies. On the other hand, one investigation (Fitzpatrick & Winke, 1979) obtained somewhat different results. Fitzpatrick and Winke's study examined a dilemma we all can relate to—the attempt to reduce conflict in an interpersonal relationship.

Specifically, Fitzpatrick and Winke (1979) examined the strategies that individuals use to reduce conflict in same-sex and opposite-sex relationships. (I focus on the findings on opposite-sex relationships in this section.) Opposite-sex relationships ranged from low intimacy (casual involvement with the individual) to moderate intimacy (serious involvement with the other person) to high intimacy (married partners). Fitzpatrick and Winke discovered that the level of intimacy predicted use of conflict-reducing strategies. Married persons indicated that they were most likely to employ emotional appeals ("appeal to this person's love and affection for me") and personal rejections ("withhold affection and act cold until he or she gives in") to resolve their differences. Those who exhibited the least commitment to the relationship (those casually involved with one another) reported that they were least likely to employ emotional appeals to get their way. Instead, these individuals indicated that they were most inclined to employ manipulation ("be especially sweet before bringing up the subject of disagreement"). Fitzpatrick and Winke noted that:

Individuals in a more committed relationship generally have less concern about the strength of the relational bonds. Consequently, they employ more spontaneous and emotionally toned strategies in their relational conflicts. As commitment increases, these strategies are probably perceived as less risky since the cohesiveness of the relationship precludes easy termination. In the less committed relationships, the cohesiveness of the partners is still being negotiated. . . . Undoubtedly, it would be too risky for them to employ the more open conflict strategies of the firmly committed. (p. 10)

Remember, however, that other studies found that intimacy is associated with the use of more prosocial message strategies. These findings may appear to conflict with those obtained by Fitzpatrick and Winke until one considers the possibility that intimates may be more likely than nonintimates to use aggressive strategies when they are angered, but less likely when they are in an "even frame of mind" (Dillard & Burgoon, 1985).

We also should point out that intimacy in all likelihood interacts with other variables to determine compliance-gaining strategy selections. Length of the relationship, satisfaction with the relationship (Fitzpatrick & Winke, 1979), the individual's attributions about the other's communication behavior, and the individual's mood state when the conflict erupts undoubtedly influence the choice of verbal message strategies. It should be noted that only a few studies have explored the effects of intimacy on verbal message strategies, hence our knowledge of the influences of intimacy on compliance-gaining behavior is rather limited.

Dominance. People use different compliance-gaining strategies, depending on whether they are trying to persuade a superior, a subordinate, or a peer.

Putnam and Wilson (1982) asked graduate teaching assistants (TA) to indicate how they would deal with course-related conflicts. When interacting with the course supervisor, TAs opted for such nonconfrontational strategies as sidestepping disagreements when they came up or easing conflict by claiming the disagreement was trivial. When they were asked to indicate how they would behave when they were in the role of superior, TAs opted for a different strategy. When interacting with a disgruntled undergraduate student, TAs indicated that they would be most likely to "argue insistently for my stance," "dominate arguments until the other person understands my position," and to use other controlling strategies.

Similarly, Kipnis, Schmidt, and Wilkinson (1980) found that professional managers used assertive tactics ("demanded that he or she do what I requested") and sanctions ("threatened him or her with loss of promotion") more often to influence subordinates than co-workers or superiors. They were more likely to use rationality tactics ("explained the reasons for my request," "used logic to convince him or her") on superiors than on peer workers or subordinates. When individuals lack power, they are more likely to employ rational and indirect tactics "because no other power base is available to them" (Cody & McLaughlin, 1985).

Resistance. It is unusual for persuaders to gain compliance on the first try. In many situations, speakers encounter resistance from members of their target audience. What impact does resistance exert on message strategy selections?

Kipnis and Cohen (1980) found that agents increased the use of personal negative sanctions when targets refused to comply with their first request. deTurck (1985) extended these findings by examining the impact of resistance in interpersonal and noninterpersonal situations. deTurck contended that persuaders employ different strategies to overcome resistance, depending on whether the influence attempt takes place in an interpersonal or a noninterpersonal context. In an interpersonal situation, deTurck (1985) argued, "the desire to continue an attractive interpersonal relationship is likely to override persuasive agents' tendency to punish a relationally intimate but noncompliant persuasive target" (p. 57). Therefore, persuaders should increase their use of reward-oriented strategies to try to overcome the target's resistance. In a noninterpersonal situation, deTurck argued, persuasive agents are less constrained by the need to maintain relational harmony. Therefore, they should increase their preference for punishment-oriented strategies and decrease their preference for reward-type strategies.

To test the hypotheses, deTurck presented subjects with a variety of hypothetical compliance-gaining scenarios. Resistance was manipulated by twice informing subjects that their influencing attempt had failed. Here is one of the vignettes that subjects received.

Interpersonal Short-Term Consequences

Initial Attempt. You have promised your best same-sex friend (opposite sex) that you will go to the movies with him or her on Saturday night. It is your best friend's favorite movie and he or she has been looking forward to the evening for some time. Unfortunately, an old friend of yours unexpectedly passes through town on Saturday afternoon and asks you if you would like to get together for a visit. You want to visit with your old friend, but you have already promised to go to the movies with your best friend.

Second Attempt. Your best friend refuses to give up your planned night out at the movies so you can visit with your (old) friend. You still want very much to visit with your old friend, but your best friend has made it very clear that he (she) expects you to go to the movies.

Third Attempt.   Even after your second attempt to get your best friend to let you visit with your old friend, he (she) insists that you forego visiting with your old friend and go to the movies. You still want very much to visit with your old friend (p. 62).

After reading the scenarios, subjects indicated the likelihood that they would select each of the 16 compliance-gaining tactics based on Marwell and Schmitt (1967). Consistent with the hypotheses, when persuaders encountered resistance in an interpersonal context, they increased their use of reward-oriented strategies (promise, positive expertise, positive self-feeling), whereas persuaders dealt with resistance in a noninterpersonal context by relying to a greater extent on punishment (threat, negative moral appeals, negative altercasting).

As interesting as these findings are, they should be accepted with caution because they were obtained by just one researcher who employed only one constellation of compliance-gaining scenarios. The effects of resistance on message selection strategy depends, in important ways, on the type of situation in which the influence attempt occurs and (as is discussed in the next section) on the type of person who initiates the attempt.

Individual Differences

Individuals differ profoundly in their use of persuasive message strategies. Certain people consistently employ manipulation and deceit, whereas others eschew these tactics. Some people use emotional appeals, whereas others resort to threat. Research has examined individual differences in compliance-gaining attempts to determine the impact that personality and demographic factors exert on message strategy selection. The focus here is on two key individual difference factors: gender and Machiavellianism.[2]

Gender Differences.   Women employ more polite compliance-gaining tactics than men. Baxter (1984) reported that women were more likely than men to employ positive politeness techniques, including trying "to be friendly toward the other person to get him/her in the right frame of mind before mentioning the request" and trying "to get on 'common ground' with the other person by showing how alike you are on things before mentioning the request" (p. 444). Women also were less likely to employ "face-threatening" message strategies, such as threatening to get the other person in trouble for refusing to comply with a request. It is likely that these gender differences have their roots in the differential socialization of males and females. Females are taught from an early age that it is important to be sensitive to others' feelings. Males, on the other hand, do not get as much training in empathy or in interpersonal skills development.

Men and women also use different techniques to resolve conflicts in intimate relationships. Fitzpatrick and Winke (1979) found that, to resolve a problem with their best friend, males were more likely to use a nonnegotiation strategy ("keep repeating my point of view until he or she gives in"). In contrast, females preferred to use a variety of socioemotional techniques, such as personal rejection, empathic understanding, and emotional appeals (e.g., withholding affection and acting cold until he or she gives in).

Burgoon and his colleagues have argued that people have stereotyped views about how men and women should try to gain compliance and that these expectations influence message evaluations. Burgoon, Dillard, and Doran (1983) contended that males are stereotypically expected to employ verbally aggressive compliance-gaining strategies, whereas females are expected to adopt a prosocial approach. Burgoon et al. (1983) found that when men do not employ aggressive strategies, they "negatively violate expectations," and are therefore less persuasive. On the other hand, when women do not use prosocial compliance-gaining strategies, they are less effective.

Burgoon, Birk, and Hall (1991) extended this research by examining the effects of gender differences on compliance in a health context. Burgoon et al. (1991) found that when male physicians violated patients' expectations, by employing either more instrumentally aggressive techniques or more affiliative tactics, compliance increased. On the other hand, when female physicians employed instrumentally aggressive strategies, compliance decreased. Apparently, male persuaders have greater freedom to choose an effective compliance-gaining strategy than do female persuaders.

Machiavellianism. Named after the Italian writer who, four centuries ago, advocated that rulers should be strategic and exploitive, the Machiavellian personality scale taps a personality type who has little respect for ethical standards and is eminently capable of lying to achieve his or her goals.

There is evidence that individuals high in Machiavellianism (high machs) employ a different constellation of compliance-gaining strategies than persons who are low in Machiavellianism (low machs). High machs are more likely to use psychological force and punishing techniques to gain compliance in interpersonal situations (Roloff & Barnicott, 1978). High machs also report that they use tactics "that directly involve manipulating their own facial expressions or the affect of the target in order to get their way" (Falbo, 1977, p. 546).

Recent research has found that Machiavellianism does not consist of just one dimension, but four: immorality, cynicism, flattery, and deceit (Hunter, Gerbing, & Boster, 1982). Immorality is the rejection of the belief that others adhere to ethical standards. Cynicism is the belief that other people are ruthless and untrustworthy. Deceit involves the belief that it is acceptable to lie to other people. Flattery is the perception that it is wise to flatter influential others.

O'Hair and Cody (1987) argued that these components of Machiavellianism should predict compliance-gaining strategy selection. They reasoned that individuals who scored high in immorality should use relatively few exchange tactics ("I'll help you with your statistics if you'll go to the movies with me"). To employ an exchange tactic, you have to trust that the other person will return the favor. Individuals who score high in immorality lack this basic trust in humanity. O'Hair and Cody (1987) found that individuals who were high in immorality were less likely to select exchange tactics than persons low in immorality. The investigators also argued that individuals who were highly cynical would select tactics that reflected their belief that people are self-interested and vicious. The researchers hypothesized and found that subjects who were high in cynicism were more likely than their less cynical counterparts to use indirect tactics. O'Hair and Cody (1987) noted that cynics believe that "one should keep one's true reasons for wanting something hidden from others" (p. 283).

The investigators also found that the effects of Machiavellianism depended on the situation. For example, actors high in cynicism were more likely to use indirect tactics than were their less cynical counterparts. However, this was only true when individuals were trying to obtain personal benefits from the other party. When the motives were altruistic, even cynical actors shied away from using indirect techniques. One important implication of these findings is that personality and situational factors interact to influence message strategy selections.

Limits of the Compliance-Gaining Research

Although these studies have advanced our knowledge of the impact of situational and individual difference factors on compliance-gaining, they have several limitations.

First, participants in the various studies are probably more mindful and self-conscious about their message strategy selections than are communicators in the real world. By asking respondents to respond to a series of hypothetical scenarios or to construct a persuasive message, researchers are requiring respondents to reflect and deliberate on their persuasion behavior. In actual interactions, people often act "mindlessly"—without thinking, and by employing culturally acquired "scripts" (Langer, 1978; Roloff, 1980).

Second, the laboratory studies do not adequately reflect the complexity of real-world communication situations. Miller et al. (1987) noted that "participants in most studies are presented with fixed, static situations rather than dynamic, fluid ones" (p. 103). In everyday situations, people have to operate on a number of psychological fronts, balancing their choice of a strategy with the interpersonal requirements of the situation and their desire to present a positive self-image. The laboratory studies typically do not present subjects with such demanding choices.

Third, the overwhelming majority of compliance-gaining studies do not measure actual behavior, but, rather, a choice of a particular message strategy (Boster & Stiff, 1984; Dillard & Burgoon, 1985). We do not know if an individual would actually translate his or her choice into action. Certainly, Fishbein and Ajzen's (1975) research makes us cautious about glibly assuming that people would behave in accordance with their preferences. Finally, the research fails to tell us whether a particular compliance-gaining strategy actually produces compliance. The findings tell us which strategies people think would be effective or which strategies they think would be appropriate, but they do not tell us if these strategies actually succeed in gaining compliance.

Current Perspectives on Compliance-Gaining Research

In response to these criticisms, researchers are asking new questions about compliance-gaining. A number of theories have been advanced to explain message strategy selection (Hunter & Boster, 1987; Meyer, 1990; Reardon, 1987; Rule et al., 1985). A dominant trend in theory construction has been cognitive. Berger (1985) defined compliance gaining strategies in cognitive terms; he defined strategies as "cognitive schemata that are abstract and provide general guidelines for action." Smith (1984) argued that individuals have developed expectations about the nature of persuasive situations, and that these expectations influence their actions. Individuals' expectations take the form of "If expected consequence X, in context Z, (occurs), then persuasive behavior Y" should be undertaken" (p. 491).

In a similar vein, several social psychologists have argued that people have developed mental "persuade packages" that contain their ideas about how to gain compliance (Rule et al., 1985; Schank & Abelson, 1977). Research has only begun to examine the impact that these persuasion schema exert on the compliance-gaining process. Presumably, individuals' beliefs about how people go about the business of persuasion will influence their compliance-gaining behavior.

As suggested earlier, one shortcoming in compliance-gaining research is that the studies typically do not relate message strategy selections to other aspects of interpersonal communication. Burgoon and her colleagues have conducted several studies that take a broader look at compliance-gaining strategy selection. Burgoon et al. (1987) examined the relationship between compliance-gaining and communication between doctors and patients. The researchers conducted telephone interviews with adults who had seen a physician at least once during the past 6 months. Individuals then indicated how certain they were that the doctor had employed each of 17 compliance-gaining tactics based on Marwell and Schmitt's (1967) taxonomy. Respondents also evaluated the doctor's relational communication behavior, including his or her composure ("relaxed, calm, and poised"), immediacy ("intensely involved"), formality ("made the interaction very formal"), and receptivity ("open to patient concerns").

Physicians who conveyed composure and receptivity employed an altruism strategy ("a doctor might tell you what a big help it would be if you did what he or she recommended"), positive moral appeals ("a doctor might indicate that the only ethical thing to do would be to comply with his or her recommendations"), and positive self-feeling ("a doctor might tell you that you will feel good about yourself if you comply with his or her recommendations"). By contrast, the use of debt (the doctor might tell you that he or she "has helped you out in the past and now it is your turn to return the favor and comply with his or her recommendations") conveyed less composure and receptivity. Burgoon et al. (1987) noted that:

> To convey the most favorable relational message and thus achieve the most satisfaction, health care providers are best advised to minimize the use of debt or implied debt ("you owe me") and positive expertise ("if you comply, I know from experience you will get better") and to rely most on positive and negative moral appeals ("you have an ethical or moral obligation to comply"), promise, negative expertise, liking, and positive self-feeling. (p. 321)

CONSTRUCTIVISM

"We shall assume that what each man does is based not on direct and certain knowledge, but on pictures made by himself or given to him" (Lippmann, 1941, p. 25). "Man looks at his world through transparent patterns or templets which he creates and then attempts to fit over the realities of which the world is composed" (Kelly, 1955, pp. 8–9).

These two comments, written by very different observers of the persuasion process, capture the essence of constructivism. Constructivism is an interpersonal approach to communication that assumes that individuals "never directly apprehend another's intentions, inner qualities, or attitudes" (Delia & O'Keefe, 1979, p. 161). Instead, constructivists argue that individuals "see" the world through a set of acquired meanings or cognitive constructs.

Constructivism is not a theory that contains specific hypotheses. Instead, it is a perspective, or an overall approach, that brings under one heading ideas from developmental psychology, social cognition, symbolic interactionism, and interpersonal communication. Thus, constructivism combines the developmental psychology of Werner (1957), the social psychological theories of Kelly (1955) and Crockett (1965), and contemporary perspectives on interpersonal communication.

The centerpiece of the constructivist approach is the term *construct*. A construct is a cognitive structure that directs and organizes thinking about social objects. Constructs are the lenses people wear to read other people and to view social reality; they constrain and control people's vision of the external world. Constructivists have examined three different aspects of interpersonal persuasion. They have focused on the development of persuasive communication skills, individual differences in the construction of persuasive arguments, and the application of constructs to everyday interpersonal persuasion situations. Let us begin with the developmental issues.

Cognitive Development

In his theory of cognitive development, Werner (1957) noted that development "proceeds from a state of relative globality and lack of differentiation to a state of increasing differentiation and hierarchic integration" (p. 127). Applying this theory to social and cognitive development, researchers have found that with age children develop an increasingly rich and differentiated system of interpersonal constructs. These advances in children's cognitive maturity have important implications for the development of persuasive communication skills. As Clark and Delia (1977) noted:

> If a child employs a very limited number of constructs (dimensions) in forming impressions of other individuals, he is less likely to be able to distinguish among communication recipients along dimensions functionally relevant to effective adaptation of messages. For instance, very young children frequently categorize others along global dimensions (e.g., "mean versus nice"). Such gross differentiations provide little basis for specific adaptation of messages. But as children become older, they typically acquire considerably larger and more functional sets of constructs for understanding others. For example, construals along a construct such as "generous versus selfish" may provide the communicator with essential information if he is attempting to select between an altruistic and selfish appeal in constructing a persuasive message. (p. 128)

Thus, as children grow older, they develop more complex cognitive systems and an increased ability to take others' perspective (i.e., to put themselves in others' shoes). Cognitive developmentalists have noted that individuals cannot design effective persuasive messages until they have developed the ability to take the perspective of the message recipient. Only when a person can take the perspective of another can he or she adapt the message to the target's needs.

Delia, Kline, and Burleson (1979) convincingly demonstrated that as children grow older they become more adept at constructing "listener-adapted messages." For example, in one study Delia et al. examined the relationship between age and the development of communications that took the listener's point of view into account. Subjects were 211 children and adolescents (kindergarten through 12th grade). Subjects were asked to role-play convincing their mother to permit them to have an overnight birthday party, and to role-play persuading a female stranger to keep a puppy that they had found. Children were asked to imagine that the interviewer was the target. They were instructed to verbalize whatever they would say to convince the target to go along with their request.

The investigators coded children's persuasive arguments into nine categories. The major categories, with an example for each role-playing task, are listed here:

I. No Discernible Recognition of and Adaptation to the Target's Perspective ("Mommy, can I have someone over to sleep on my bed?"; "Could you keep this dog?")
II. Implicit Recognition of and Adaptation to the Target's Perspective
   A. Elaboration of the necessity, desirability, or usefulness of the persuasive request ("My friends like me a lot. They would like to have a party and want you to let them come over. They'll be really disappointed if they can't 'cause they've been wanting to come over for a long time"; "This dog is really skinny and he doesn't have any place to go.").
   B. Elaborated acknowledgment of and dealing with multiple anticipated counterarguments ("Mother, can I have six kids over. We'll make up our sleeping bags and we'll fix our own popcorn"; "It's big enough to stay outside and you only have to feed him and water him and that doesn't take all day.").
III. Explicit Recognition of and Adaptation to the Target's Perspective ("You've been saying you wanted to get to know my friends better. If you let me have a party, you can get to know them"; "You need a watchdog around here because like there have been some break-ins around here. This dog might be able to help you."). (Delia et al., 1979, pp. 248–249)

There was a significant relationship between age and level of strategy. The older the child, the more likely he or she was to accommodate the message to the perceived needs of the target.

These findings are interesting on several levels. They provide us with some of our only knowledge of how persuasion skills develop over the course of childhood. They also demonstrate that cognitive development is an important precondition for communication effectiveness. If children are to successfully adapt a message to fit the needs of a target, they must have acquired a set of constructs for understanding others; and they need to have developed a rudimentary ability to take another's point of view. At a young age, children are egocentric persuaders: They do not consider the needs of the target, and they do not explain why a particular person should go along with the recommendations advanced by the speaker. Instead, they make their arguments known through the sheer force of their voices, or through "pester power." Although these tactics may work—a parent may break down and buy the child a toy, a sibling may give the youngster a puppet—they do not persuade the other person to change his or her attitude on the issue. Instead, they produce only a temporary change in behavior. As children mature, they develop the ability to persuade other people, by learning how to accommodate their strategies to fit the needs of the target (Haslett, 1983).

Individual Differences

Delia et al. (1979) found that even among kindergarten and 1st grade children there were individual differences in the ability to construct persuasive messages. Why is it that some speakers adapt their messages to fit the perspectives of their listeners, whereas others fail to take into account the needs of a target audience? Constructivists argue that differences in cognitive complexity and construct abstractness underlie these individual differences.

Cognitive complexity is the extent of differentiation in a cognitive system. Complexity is measured by counting the number of different constructs that a person uses to describe a social object. The more constructs the person employs, the greater his or her cognitive complexity.[3] Typically, researchers ask a subject to describe two people he or she knows well, one liked and the other disliked. A cognitively simple person would employ relatively few terms to describe the other (e.g., nice and helpful for a liked other; nasty and boorish for a disliked other). A cognitively complex individual would use a variety of terms to describe the other (e.g., kind, empathic, cooperative, and intelligent for a liked other; insensitive, unpleasant, ambitious, and unfriendly for a disliked other).

Constructivists have argued that cognitively complex persons will formulate a greater number of persuasive strategies than less complex individuals. The idea is that if you are cognitively complex and have a rich, differentiated view of people, you are capable of employing a variety of different strategies to influence behavior. In addition, theorists have contended that complexity should predict the degree to which persuasive strategies are adapted to a target's needs.

On the other hand, construct abstractness refers to the extent to which an individual employs abstract, psychological terms to describe other people. An individual who scores low in abstractness might describe others by their physical characteristics and their overt behavior ("he is tall" or "she uses foul language"). Those who score high in abstractness might be more likely to invoke psychological traits and motivations ("she is introverted" or "he is obsessed with getting ahead"). Researchers have argued that construct abstractness should facilitate the development of listener-adapted persuasive strategies. An individual who has an abstract system of interpersonal constructs analyzes people in more holistic, psychologically centered ways. This enables him or her to devise arguments that are sensitively adapted to the listener's needs.

Consistent with these hypotheses, O'Keefe and Delia (1979) found that cognitive complexity was significantly associated with number of arguments and level of appeal justification. Applegate (1982) also found effects for construct abstractness, using an interesting dyadic communication measurement procedure.[4] Applegate first measured construct abstractness and then assigned subjects into different dyads based on their abstractness scores. One dyad was composed of two persons who were high in construct abstractness, whereas the other dyad consisted of two individuals who had low abstractness scores. The students were shown a $5 bill and were told that for the next 10 minutes "each was to try to persuade the other to let him/her have the five dollars using the best arguments each could muster." The students were asked to come up with arguments explaining why he or she should get the $5 rather than the partner. Applegate videotaped the interactions. He then counted the number of persuasive strategies subjects employed and classified them according to the extent to which they took the listener's needs into account. There was a highly significant relationship between construct abstractness and both the number of persuasive strategies and the level of listener-adapted strategy.

Conversational Strategies

One limitation in constructivism research is that researchers have asked subjects to role-play their reactions to hypothetical situations. This greatly limits the generalizability of the research. To remedy this problem, O'Keefe, Delia, and their colleagues have examined the persuasive strategies people use in ordinary conversations.

A persuader typically has multiple goals in such situations. For example, he or she may want to change the other person's mind about an issue, avoid relational damage, and maintain a positive self-image. Sometimes these goals are in conflict. When conflict develops, individuals can employ several different strategies to deal with the situation. O'Keefe and Delia (1982) proposed that persuaders can choose one of three strategies to pursue their goals: *selection*, *separation*, and *integration*. Let us illustrate these strategies with a practical example. Suppose you and a friend disagree about whether condoms should be sold in college dormitories.

Although you both believe that people should be encouraged to use condoms to prevent the spread of AIDS, you believe that extreme steps have to be taken now. Your friend believes that some people would find it distasteful to have condoms for sale in college dorms, and one must respect others' position on this issue. Let us say you decide to openly discuss the issue with your friend. O'Keefe and her colleagues' work suggests that there are three different ways you might approach the issue:

1. *Selection:* "Resolves conflict between competing aims or between aims and obstacles by selecting (giving priority and expression to) one outcome or situation feature and ignoring the other" (O'Keefe & Shepherd, 1987, p. 400).
   Example: Your politics are way behind the times. Who cares if other people object? It's people like you who are so concerned about what other people think who are partly responsible for this country's slow response to AIDS. We have to do something now.

2. *Separation:* "Resolves conflicts by dealing with competing situation features in temporally or behaviorally separated aspects of a message display . . . (incorporates) statements or phrases designed to account for, mitigate against, or minimize the negative implications of the posture" (O'Keefe & Shepherd, 1987, pp. 400–401).
   Example: Your politics are way behind the times. Now, I can see your point about people being embarrassed about the sale of condoms in public, but we have to do something about AIDS now. If selling condoms saves one life, I'm for it. I do not want to come down too hard on what you're saying, but I think that we have to do certain things to help prevent the spread of AIDS.

3. *Integration:* "Involves true reconciliation of competing aims, through message designs which simultaneously accomplish multiple aims or advance aims and remove obstacles . . . (and) by redefining the social situation . . . in such a way that the contradiction is genuinely resolved . . ." (O'Keefe & Shepherd, 1987, p. 401).
   Example: Look, we both agree that AIDS is the nation's number one problem and we both agree that the university has to educate people about the importance of using condoms. I think we'd both agree that a university is a place in which reforms and new ideas should be tested. By allowing vendors to sell condoms in dormitories, we get the opportunity to see if this idea is a useful and effective one. Let us give it a try.

In their discussion of these three strategies, O'Keefe and Shepherd (1987) noted that:

Construct differentiation and abstractness influence message production primarily through influencing the kind and number of goals a communicator construes as relevant in a situation; people who represent social situations in a more multidimensional fashion design messages addressing more goals simultaneously. (p. 396)

O'Keefe and Shepherd (1987) examined the impact of construct differentiation on goal management strategy in a conversational setting. Subjects appeared in pairs at a communication laboratory at the University of Illinois. Subjects completed a survey that assessed attitudes toward 15 contemporary issues. Then they completed a standard questionnaire to assess construct differentiation. While subjects filled out the construct differentiation questionnaires, their attitude surveys were surreptitiously examined. The experimenters compared the answers that the two students gave to the opinion questions, and selected the issue on which there was the greatest disagreement. After selecting the issue that had sparked the greatest disagreement, the experimenter told subjects they had 15 minutes to discuss this issue. The discussions were videotaped, and arguments were classified according to strategy type (selection, separation, integration).

Individuals who had highly differentiated constructs used a greater number of separation and integration strategies than did persons low in construct differentiation. Subjects who had highly differentiated constructs were especially likely to use the integrative strategy. Interestingly, integrative strategy use was associated with interpersonal success. Increased use of integrative strategies predicted higher ratings on general communication competence and on partner's reporting liking of the subject.

SEQUENTIAL INFLUENCE TECHNIQUES

Professional persuaders have long recognized that one-shot influence techniques are rarely sufficient to get a person to behave in a particular way. Instead, they have concluded that they have to "soften up" a client over time by using a variety of techniques. For example, Alcoholics Anonymous has developed a 12-step program to help alcoholics break the habit, the Moonies recognized that there were a number of steps that recruits had to take before they would join the Church, and those quintessential practitioners of persuasion—car salesmen—have long employed a succession of influence tactics to convince people to buy a car.

Scholars refer to these techniques as "sequential influence strategies" (Seibold, Cantrill, & Meyers, 1985). Seibold et al. (1985) noted that: "Interpersonal influence often proceeds in stages, each of which establishes the foundation for further changes in beliefs or behavior. Individuals slowly come to embrace new opinions, and actors often seduce others to gradually comply with target requests" (pp. 583–584).

This section discusses the role that sequential influence strategies play in the persuasion process. Underlying our discussion is the notion that persuasion is frequently a slow process that occurs in stages (Miller & Burgoon, 1978). There is an important difference between the research on sequential influence strategies and the studies of interpersonal persuasion that we discussed earlier in this chapter. For the most part, the studies of compliance-gaining and constructivism were concerned with describing the strategies people use to gain compliance; they did not explore whether the strategies were successful (i.e., whether they worked). Research on sequential influence techniques focuses on these latter questions.

Foot-in-the-Door Effect

The foot-in-the-door technique stipulates that an individual is more likely to comply with a second, larger request when he or she has agreed to perform a small initial request. The technique gets its name from the old expression of the same name – the notion that if a persuader can get his or her "foot in the door," or get past the first stage of the persuasion process, he or she will have increased the chances of obtaining compliance.

Freedman and Fraser (1966) were the first to demonstrate a foot-in-the-door effect. The researchers arranged for an experimental accomplice to knock on doors in the Palo Alto, California area to ask residents if they would mind going along with a small request. The experimenter told residents that he was from the Community Committee for Traffic Safety and that he was "visiting a number of homes in an attempt to make the citizens more aware of the need to drive carefully all the time." Then the experimenter made the pitch. Would the respondent mind taking a small 3-inch sign that said "Be a safe driver" and put it in a window or in the car "so that it would serve as a reminder of the need to drive carefully?"

Two weeks later, a different experimenter contacted households in which a resident had agreed to put up the 3-inch driving sign. This time residents were shown a picture of a large, unattractive sign that said "Drive Carefully." "Our men will come out and install it," the experimenter explained. "It makes just a small hole in your lawn, but if this is unacceptable to you we have a special mount which will make no hole." As a control, a separate group of households was contacted during this same period. Importantly, control group residents were approached only once and were asked if they would be willing to put the large "Drive Carefully" sign in their front lawns.

There were dramatic differences between the two groups. Seventeen percent of the control-group households indicated a willingness to have the "Drive Carefully" sign placed on their lawns. Yet 76% of the respondents who had agreed to display the "Be a safe driver" sign complied with the second request.[5]

A number of other studies, conducted after Freedman and Fraser's (1966) article was published, also have found evidence for a foot-in-the-door effect. For example, Pliner, Hart, Kohl, and Saari (1974) found that subjects who agreed to wear a Cancer Society pin in their lapels were more likely to donate money to the Cancer Society than individuals who did not accede to the initial request. Cann, Sherman, and Elkes (1975) reported that subjects were more likely to agree to pass out pamphlets on traffic safety if they had previously agreed to answer three background questions on the telephone than if they had not complied with the initial request. Dillard (1990) found that participants were more likely to indicate that they would help construct a hiking trail if they had previously agreed to address envelopes for an environmental group than if they had not acceded to the earlier request.

One of the most impressive things about the foot-in-the-door effect is its generality. Agreement with a first request facilitates compliance with a larger demand, even when the second request concerns a different topic than the first, the requests are put forth by different people, the individual agrees with but does not perform the initial request, and the time between the requests is varied. Two meta-analytic studies reviewed the research on the foot-in-the-door effect, examining the strength of the empirical findings. Although the investigators found that the effect was not as robust or as large as commonly assumed, they concluded that the effects were reliable, provided certain conditions had been met, and were statistically significant (Beaman, Cole, Preston, Klentz, & Steblay, 1983; Dillard, Hunter, & Burgoon, 1984).

What mechanisms underlie the foot-in-the-door effect? Why is it that people are more likely to comply with a second, larger request when they have done someone a small favor? One explanation emphasizes social judgment processes. According to this view, the initial request serves as the reference point or anchor against which subsequent demands are compared (Cantrill & Seibold, 1986; see also, Helson, 1964). Control group subjects who are asked only to comply with the larger request perceive the request to be quite large and unreasonable. However, subjects in the experimental group compare the second request to the first one and find it to be "not so bad" or "kind of like the first one in most respects." In social judgment terms, they assimilate the second request to the first one, and this causes the second request to appear less unreasonable and more agreeable to them. Unfortunately, there is little evidence to support this interpretation. Cantrill and Seibold (1986) put the social judgment explanation to the test and found that assimilation processes did not mediate the foot-in-the-door effect.

A second interpretation emphasizes self-perceptions. Based on Bem's self-perception theory, researchers argue that individuals infer from their own compliance that they are helpful, active, and cooperative people who are willing to do a little extra to help an individual or group. This attribution then influences their subsequent behavior. Freedman and Fraser (1966) noted that:

> What may occur is a change in the person's feelings about getting involved or about taking action. Once he has agreed to a request his attitude may change. He may become, in his own eyes, the kind of person who does this sort of thing, who agrees to requests made by strangers, who takes action on things he believes in, who cooperates with good causes. (p. 201)

Although self-perception theory cannot account for all the findings on the foot-in-the-door effect (Dillard et al., 1984), it offers the most parsimonious interpretation of this phenomenon.[6]

The foot-in-the-door technique is particularly effective under certain conditions. These include the following:

Prosocial Request. A foot-in-the-door technique is obtained only when the request concerns a prosocial issue (Dillard et al., 1984). When the persuader stands to gain from a request, the foot-in-the-door technique is less successful.

Moderate Initial Request. If the initial request is too large, people will refuse to comply. On the other hand, if the initial request is too small—such as asking a person to tell you what time it is—it may not trigger appropriate self-perceptions (Seligman, Bush, & Kirsch, 1976). "For the foot-in-the-door effect to succeed," noted Seligman et al. (1976), "the first request must be of sufficient size to commit the individual to further compliance" (p. 517).

Few External Rewards and Justifications. According to self-perception theory, if people are given a substantial reward to perform a task, they may infer that they are doing the job to obtain the reward. This perception may reduce their motivation to comply with a second task. This is called an overjustification effect—the external reward provides so much "external justification" that it actually undermines a person's internal, "heart-felt" motivation to comply (Uranowitz, 1975). As DeJong (1979) noted:

> If people comply with an initial request under conditions of strong external justification, they may come to infer that they are extrinsically motivated and that they are the kind of people who agree to such requests only when external pressures are present. As a result of this kind of changed self-perception, people may actually come to be less likely to comply with future requests when those kinds of pressures are absent. (p. 2231)

The overjustification effect has interesting implications for everyday persuasion activities. Imagine you have to complete a 20-page paper for an upper level course, and you anticipate that you are going to need some help with word processing. You have found that when you have done your own word processing the paper looks unprofessional: The margins are off and the pagination never works out correctly. You decide to approach an acquaintance who lives down the hall. This person, you know from previous conversations, is a whiz at word processing. You are afraid that if you ask the acquaintance for assistance straight out, she will turn you down. So you decide to soften her up by soliciting her assistance on a smaller task, which, you decide, will involve proofreading two pages of your paper.

Here is where the overjustification effect applies. If you offer to pay the acquaintance $2 for helping you proofread, your acquaintance might go along with your request, but she might infer that she was the type of person who only helped people out when the price was right. Then when you approached the acquaintance for the larger favor—helping you word process the 20-page paper—she might turn you down when she discovered that she was not going to get paid for her assistance this time. On the other hand, if you could convince your word-processing friend to help you proofread for free, you would be inducing her to think of herself as a generous person—the kind of person who is more than happy to help other people. Having encouraged her to think of herself in this way, you would have set the stage for the self-perception to influence action at the time of the second request.

Door-in-the-Face Effect

> In the popular comic strip *Blondie* one episode has recurred many times over the years. In the scene, Blondie enters the living room wearing a new hat, new shoes, and a new dress. She cheerfully calls her husband's attention to the wonderful bargains she has found. Her husband, Dag-wood, glares reproachfully at her from the couch and demands to know how much it all cost. After Blondie reveals the price, Dagwood becomes hysterical and orders Blondie to return the goods because he can't afford them. Blondie, in turn, begins to cry and bargains with Dagwood to keep only the hat. Observing her distress, Dagwood relents. Later the reader discovers that all Blondie wanted in the first place was the hat. The scene ends happily with Blondie congratulating herself for the success of her ploy and with Dagwood satisfied that the dress and shoes are to be returned. (Miller, Seligman, Clark, & Bush, 1976, p. 401)

This example illustrates what has come to be known as the door-in-the-face effect (Cialdini et al., 1975). In this case, a persuader begins by making a request that is so large that it is almost certain to be denied. After being turned down the first time, the persuader returns with a smaller request. This, of course, was the request that he or she had in mind from the beginning. Remember that in the case of the foot-in-the-door effect, the requester begins with a small request and then ups the ante. The door-in-the-face technique is exactly the opposite: The persuader starts large and then scales down the request size. Let us take a look at how the technique was used successfully in a study conducted by Cialdini and Ascani (1976).

Subjects were approached while they were moving along university walkways. The experimenter identified herself as a representative of the local blood services organization. In the door-in-the-face (or rejection-then-retreat condition), the experimenter gave this spiel:

> We're currently asking students to become involved in our Long-Term Donor Program. Long-term donors are those who pledge to give a unit of blood once every 2 months for a period of at least 3 years. This way we can be sure of a continual supply of blood. Would you be willing to enroll in our Long-Term Donor Program? (Cialdini & Ascani, 1976, p. 297)

Obviously, the request was outlandish. Imagine agreeing to give a unit of blood once every 2 months for at least 3 years. As the researchers expected, all of the subjects declined the request. At this point, the experimenter returned with the request for the smaller favor:

> Oh. Well, maybe you'd be interested in another program we're asking students to participate in, then. We have our annual university blood drive right here on campus tomorrow. We're asking students to come to our center here on campus and donate just 1 unit of blood sometime between 8:00 a.m. and 3:30 p.m. tomorrow? Would you be willing to volunteer just 1 unit of blood to our drive? (p. 297)

For students in the control group, the persuader did not make the extreme request. Instead, she simply said:

> We have our annual university blood drive right here on campus tomorrow. We're asking students to come to our center here on campus and donate just 1 unit of blood sometime between 8:00 a.m. and 3:30 p.m. tomorrow. Would you be willing to volunteer just 1 unit of blood to our drive? (p. 297)

The results showed a strong door-in-the-face effect. Forty-nine percent of the subjects in the "rejection-then-retreat" condition made a verbal commitment to donate one unit of blood the next day, compared with only 31.7% in the control group. Moreover, of the subjects who agreed to give blood, almost twice as many individuals in the experimental group than in the control indicated they would donate blood again.[7]

Researchers have found that the door-in-the-face technique can be used in a variety of prosocial persuasion situations, such as performing as a chaperone for a group of low-income children on a trip to the zoo and soliciting organ donations via telephone (Cantrill & Seibold, 1986; Cialdini et al., 1975). Like the foot-in-the-door, the door-in-the-face exerts a small, but reliable, effect on persuasion (Dillard et al., 1984).

Why does the door-in-the-face effect work? It certainly seems to fly in the face (so to speak) of what we would intuitively expect. After all, you would not think someone would go along with a second request when they have just slammed the door in your face the first time around. Yet (provided certain conditions are met) people are more willing to comply with a moderate request after having turned down an extreme request then they are to comply with the same moderate request under ordinary circumstances. Two interpretations of the door-in-the-face technique have been advanced. Cialdini argued that as a persuader moves from an extreme request (giving blood once every 2 months for 3 years) to a more moderate request (asking for a unit of blood the next day), he is seen by the target person as having made a concession. The target person now feels obligated to reciprocate this concession. Having learned the social rule that "You should make concessions to those who make concessions to you" or "You should meet the other fellow halfway," they agree to comply with the second request (Cialdini et al., 1975). This explanation suggests that a norm of reciprocity underlies the door-in-the-face effect.

A second interpretation emphasizes social judgment processes. According to this view, the extreme request functions as an anchor against which the second request is compared. After having heard the first request ("Would you mind donating a unit of blood once every 2 months for the next 3 years"), the second request ("Would you donate a unit of blood sometime tomorrow") seems less costly and less severe (Cantrill & Seibold, 1986). Control group subjects who are asked to comply only with the smaller request do not have this anchor available to them. Consequently, the request seems large and unreasonable. Of the two interpretations, the reciprocity norm view has received somewhat stronger empirical support.

For the door-in-the-face technique to work, certain conditions must be met. First, both requests ideally should be made by the same person. Cialdini et al. (1975) argued that a persuadee will not feel an obligation to reciprocate the concession if the requests are made by different people.

A second conditional factor is the size of the initial request. The first request must be sufficiently extreme so that it will be rejected by the target individual. If a consumer complies with the first request—he or she opens the door instead of slamming it shut—the stage is set for the operation of a foot-in-the-door effect.

A third factor is the time between requests. For the door-in-the-face technique to work, there can only be a short delay between the first and second requests (Dillard et al., 1984). If too long a time passes between requests, the target will forget that he or she has an obligation to reciprocate the concession. Also, the more time that passes between requests, the less salient is the contrast between the extreme first request and the smaller "more reasonable" alternative.

A fourth condition is the context in which the request is made. Most studies find that the door-in-the-face technique works best in prosocial contexts. The door-in-the-face technique may be more difficult to use in business contexts, because people are naturally wary of the persuader's motives. Given people's cynicism, it is more difficult to convince the target that the persuader has made a legitimate concession that is worthy of reciprocating. However, one study found that the door-in-the-face technique did increase compliance in a marketing situation (Mowen & Cialdini, 1980). Indeed, Mowen and Cialdini (1980) suggested that bill collectors might try "to increase the repayment rate by first demanding payment of the entire bill and then asking for a smaller portion of the debt" (p. 257).

Low-Balling

Low-balling is a common technique that sales agents, particularly car salespersons, employ to secure final commitment and behavioral compliance. Cialdini, Cacioppo, Bassett, and Miller (1978), who have investigated the technique, noted that:

> The critical component of the procedure is for the salesperson to induce the customer to make an *active decision* to buy one of the dealership's cars by offering an extremely good price, perhaps as much as $300 below competitors' prices. Once the customer has made the decision for a specific car (and has even begun completing the appropriate forms), the salesperson removes the price advantage in one of a variety of ways. For example, the customer may be told that the originally cited price did not include an expensive option that the customer had assumed was part of the offer. More frequently, however, the initial price offer is rescinded when the salesperson "checks with the boss," who does not allow the deal because "we'd be losing money." . . . In each instance, the result is the same: The reason that the customer made a favorable purchase decision is removed, and the performance of the target behavior (i.e., buying that specific automobile) is rendered more costly. The increased cost is such that the final price is equivalent to, or sometimes slightly above, that of the dealer's competitors. Yet, car dealership lore has it that more customers will remain with their decision to purchase the automobile, even at the adjusted figure, than would have bought it had the full price been revealed before a purchase decision had been obtained. (p. 464)

The low-balling technique gets its name from the observation that persuaders try to induce compliance by "throwing the customer a low ball." In low-balling, the persuader gets the individual to comply with a particular request and then "ups the ante" by increasing the cost of the decision. Having made the initial decision to comply, individuals feel impelled to comply with the second request. Low-balling is similar to the foot-in-the-door technique in that the persuader begins with a small request and follows it up with a more costly alternative. The difference is that in low-balling, the action requested initially is in fact the target behavior; in the case of the foot-in-the-door, the behavior that the persuader initially asks the individual to perform may be related to the larger request, but it is not the target behavior (Cialdini et al., 1978).

Cialdini et al. have shown that the low-ball procedure can induce compliance. In one study, an experimenter told subjects that he was working with the United Way, and that he was asking students to display posters for the charity. Control-group subjects were then told that "there are packets at the dorm desk downstairs which contain a window poster and a door poster. They'll only be there for the next hour; then they'll be taken to another area." Subjects were then asked if they would be willing to pick up the posters within an hour and display one on their window and the other on the door of their room.

By contrast, low-ball subjects were first asked to display the posters. Those who complied with the request then received the low ball—they were informed that they would have to procure the poster packet from the dorm desk within an hour.

The investigators then looked to see how many rooms displayed the posters the next day. Subjects in the low-ball group were more likely to have the posters displayed on the windows and doors of their rooms than were subjects in the control group.

Why does low-balling increase compliance? One view is that the act of making a decision powerfully commits an individual to the chosen course of action; the ensuing commitment then "freezes" the individual's decisional cognitions and makes it difficult for the person to undo what he or she has already decided (Kiesler, 1971). Thus, once an individual has cognitively committed himself to a decision, he is loathe to change his mind, even when the cost associated with the decision is raised significantly (Cialdini et al., 1978).[8]

The Ethics of Persuasion

I close this chapter on an ethical note. You have read about how people employ all sorts of techniques to gain compliance. The techniques are varied; they range from direct up-front reasoning to manipulation to deceit. One lesson from the studies of sequential influence strategies is that it is a good idea to first ask people to comply with a favor, and then hit them up later with your real request. The implication is that if you have to invent the initial request, so much the better; just make sure it is credible (i.e., not too small for foot-in-the-door and just large enough for door-in-the-face).

Varela, who has successfully used sequential influence techniques, argued that a persuader should:

> Size up your client, decide what is best for him, make a survey of his needs and possibilities and then design a persuasion to sell him those requirements. If he buys the amount and finds that he can sell it, then he will feel grateful, because at all times he will have the correct sensation that it was he himself who made the decision to buy. (quoted in Argyris, 1975, p. 478)

Isn't there something wrong with this approach? Argyris (1975), a persistent critic of persuasion techniques, noted that the entire approach can be questioned on ethical grounds. Argyris contended that this type of advice tends to convince the client that:

> He is making decisions when, in reality, it has all been managed by the persuader armed with results from experimental social psychology. . . . So we have a world in which the client is to feel genuinely better about himself as a human being because he has had an encounter with a canvasser who was schooled in winning and in controlling others. (p. 478)

Argyris has proposed an alternative approach to persuasion that emphasizes "valid information, free and informed choice, and internal commitment" (p. 482). Argyris seems to suggest that there is never any justification for manipulating individuals or for telling a lie. His approach is similar to that of Immanuel Kant who, two centuries ago, exhorted that an individual should never be treated as a means, only as an end. On the other hand, other philosophers adopt a situational perspective, arguing that different ethical standards are appropriate in different situations (Fletcher, 1966). You might criticize a salesperson who used the door-in-the-face technique to get you to buy a product, but would you be so quick to criticize the charity that used the same technique to raise $100,000 for homeless children? There are no simple answers to these questions. These issues have been long debated by philosophers, and there are many different philosophical approaches to ethics. The task for scholars and ethicists is to clarify the role that ethical issues play in everyday persuasion situations and to help people become more humane and sensitive interpersonal persuaders.

CONCLUSIONS

Research on interpersonal persuasion has focused on three general areas: compliance-gaining, constructivism, and sequential influence techniques.

Studies of compliance-gaining have begun to shed light on the strategies individuals use to gain compliance from others. A number of typologies have been developed; unfortunately, different typologies have uncovered different constellations of strategies. Much depends on whether a researcher provides subjects with preformulated strategies or asks subjects to construct messages themselves. Situational factors (such as intimacy, dominance, and resistance) and individual difference variables (such as gender and dogmatism) exert an impact on compliance-gaining, although the extent of their impact is a matter of some debate.

If compliance-gaining studies are to continue to advance our knowledge of the interpersonal persuasion process, they must link up with the broader field of persuasion (Burgoon & Miller, 1990). Compliance-gaining researchers should consider the ways in which individuals process persuasion situations—for example, How do persuaders' beliefs about the audience, the message, and the receiver influence their choice of message selection strategies? How do their interpretations of the situation shape their strategy selections? How do they cognitively process the receiver's acceptance of or resistance to their verbal strategy selections?).

The second line of interpersonal persuasion research (constructivism) has shed light on the role that cognitive constructs play in the interpersonal persuasion process. Studies have documented that as children mature, they develop increasingly complex and differentiated cognitive systems. These cognitive developments in turn help children develop messages that are adapted and geared to the listener's needs. Research has also shown that individuals who have highly differentiated and abstract constructs are more likely to construct messages that are geared to the perspective of the listener.

Contemporary researchers, noting that message production fundamentally involves the reconciliation of multiple objectives and goals, have argued that cognitive complexity and abstractness "influence message production primarily through influencing the kind and number of goals a communicator construes as relevant in a situation" (O'Keefe & Shepherd, 1987). Consistent with this view, there is evidence that individuals who have highly differentiated constructs are especially likely to attempt to persuade a partner by adopting an "integrative" strategy that involves the reconciliation of competing aims and perspectives.

Interpersonal persuasion research also has examined the effects of sequential influence techniques, such as foot-in-the-door, door-in-the-face, and low-balling. In particular, the foot-in-the-door and the door-in-the-face techniques have been shown to exert a significant impact on compliance. These techniques capitalize on the fact that attitudes are frequently resistant to change by "one shot influence attempts" or "cold calls." Researchers have

EXHIBIT 11-1   293

shown that these techniques are particularly likely to work in certain contexts, provided certain conditions are met.

A number of theories have been proposed to explain the impact of sequential influence techniques on compliance. However, there is still a debate as to which theory does the best job of explaining the effects of these tactics on compliance. Once again, we need to know how individuals cognitively process sequential influence attempts, and (ultimately) how they persuade themselves to go along with the communicator's request.

* * *

EXHIBIT 11-1
MARWELL AND SCHMITT'S COMPLIANCE-GAINING TYPOLOGY

1. Promise	(If you comply, I will reward you) "You offer to increase Dick's allowance if he increases his studying."
2. Threat	(If you do not comply I will punish you) "You threaten to forbid Dick the use of the car if he does not increase his studying."
3. Expertise (positive)	(If you comply you will be rewarded because of "the nature of things") "You point out to Dick that if he gets good grades he will be able to get into a good college and get a good job."
4. Expertise (negative)	(If you do not comply you will be punished because of "the nature of things") "You point out to Dick that if he does not get good grades he will not be able to get into a good college or get a good job."
5. Liking	(Actor is friendly and helpful to get target in "good frame of mind" so that he will comply with request) "You try to be as friendly and pleasant as possible to get Dick in the 'right frame of mind' before asking him to study."
6. Pregiving	(Actor rewards target before requesting compliance) "You raise Dick's allowance and tell him you now expect him to study."
7. Aversive stimulation	(Actor continuously punishes target making cessation contingent upon compliance) "You forbid Dick the use of the car and tell him he will not be allowed to drive until he studies more."
8. Debt	(You owe me compliance because of past favors) "You point out that you have sacrificed and saved to pay for Dick's education and that he owes it to you to get good enough grades to get into a good college."
9. Moral appeal	(You are immoral if you do not comply) "You tell Dick that it is morally wrong for anyone not

to get as good grades as he can and that he should study more."

10. Self-feeling (positive) — (You will feel better about yourself if you comply) "You tell Dick he will feel proud if he gets himself to study more."

11. Self-feeling (negative) — (You will feel worse about yourself if you do not comply) "You tell Dick he will feel ashamed of himself if he gets bad grades."

12. Altercasting (positive) — (A person with "good" qualities would comply) "You tell Dick that since he is a mature and intelligent boy he naturally will want to study more and get good grades."

13. Altercasting (negative) — (Only a person with "bad" qualities would not comply) "You tell Dick that only someone very childish does not study as he should."

14. Altruism — (I need your compliance very badly, so do it for me) "You tell Dick that you really want very badly for him to get into a good college and that you wish he would study more as a personal favor to you."

15. Esteem (positive) — (People you value will think better of you if you comply) "You tell Dick that the whole family will be very proud of him if he gets good grades."

16. Esteem (negative) — (People you value will think worse of you if you do not comply) "You tell Dick that the whole family will be very disappointed in him if he gets poor grades." (from Marwell & Schmitt, 1967)

* * *

EXHIBIT 11–2
COMPLIANCE-GAINING AT THE SCANDINAVIAN

What techniques do salespersons at the Scandinavian Health Spa use to induce customers to join? One of my students, Karen Karp, visited a local spa and talked to salespeople in search of an answer to this question. Karp pretended she was interested in joining the spa and then listened as the salesperson made his spiel. She then categorized his responses using the Marwell and Schmitt (1967) scheme. However, the salesman did not use all of the Marwell and Schmitt tactics. To illustrate how the Marwell and Schmitt scheme might be applied to the Scandinavian context, Karp went back to Marwell and Schmitt's taxonomy. Based on what the salesman had said, or her extrapolations from the interview, she and I provided an example of each of the 16 Marwell and Schmitt tactics. Keep in mind that this was not a scientific study of the techniques that Scandinavian salespeople use to gain compliance. Had it been such a study, Karp probably would have used a variety of compliance-gaining schemes, and she would have factor analyzed the

EXHIBIT 11-2   295

results to see what common factors emerged. However, Karp's analysis provides a useful illustration of how the compliance-gaining research can shed light on real-life influence attempts.

Tactics

1. Promise	(If you comply, I will reward you) "If you begin your membership today, you'll receive a bonus of three free months."
2. Threat	(If you do not comply I will punish you) "If you do not join today, you may find that people are kind of mean to you when you do join."
3. Expertise (positive)	(If you comply you will be rewarded because of "the nature of things") "Joining the spa will guarantee that you'll maintain your health and that you'll get all the benefits of a healthy, totally-in-shape body."
4. Expertise (negative)	(If you do not comply you will be punished because of "the nature of things") "If you do not join you'll end up looking fat."
5. Liking	(Actor is friendly and helpful to get target in "good frame of mind" so that he will comply with request) "I think it's great that you've decided to begin an exercise program. The staff is here to help you reach your fitness goals."
6. Pregiving	(Actor rewards target before requesting compliance) "I'll give you a $50 bonus for coming in today; now, let us talk about how I can help you slim out."
7. Aversive stimulation	(Actor continuously punishes target making cessation contingent upon compliance) "I won't let you leave this little room until you agree to join."
8. Debt	(You owe me compliance because of past favors) "I've spent an hour showing you the club and demonstrating the machines, now I'm sure that you are ready to join.
9. Moral appeal	(You are immoral if you do not comply) "Fitness is so important. I think it's almost immoral not to take good care of your health."
10. Self-feeling (positive)	(You will feel better about yourself if you comply) "Why don't you sign up right now? You'll feel so good about yourself once you begin a workout program."
11. Self-feeling (negative)	(You will feel worse about yourself if you do not comply) "You know how important regular exercise is. You'll feel bad about yourself if you do not take out a membership today."

12. Altercasting   (A person with "good" qualities would comply)
    (positive)   "I can tell that you're committed to looking and
                        feeling healthy and fit. You're the kind of person who
                        would really benefit from this club."

13. Altercasting   (Only a person with "bad" qualities would not com-
    (negative)   ply)
                        "It's only laziness that keeps people from joining, but
                        that's not you, is it?"

14. Altruism   (I need your compliance very badly, so do it for me)
                        (whispering) "I need to sign one more member this
                        week."

15. Esteem   (People you value will think better of you if you
    (positive)   comply)
                        "Begin a membership. Your family is going to be so
                        proud of you when you start a fitness program."

16. Esteem   (People you value will think worse of you if you do
    (negative)   not comply)
                        "Do not disappoint your family. Didn't you promise
                        them that you would start taking better care of
                        yourself?"

* * *

EXHIBIT 11-3
FALBO'S COMPLIANCE-GAINING TYPOLOGY

Strategy	Definition	Example
Assertion	Forcefully asserting one's way.	I voice my wishes loudly.
Bargaining	Explicit statement about reciprocating favors and making other two-way exchanges.	I tell her that I'll do something for her if she'll do something for me.
Compromise	Both agent and target give up part of their desired goals in order to obtain some of them.	More often than not we come to some sort of compromise, if there is a disagreement.
Deceit	Attempts to fool the target into agreeing by the use of flattery or lies.	I get my way by doing a good amount of fast talking and sometimes by some white lies.
Emotion-agent	Agent alters own facial expression.	I put on a sweet face. I try to look sincere.
Emotion-target	Agent attempts to alter emotions of target.	I try to put him in a good mood.
Evasion	Doing what one wants by avoiding the person who would disapprove.	I got to read novels at work as long as the boss never saw me doing it.
Expertise	Claiming to have superior knowledge or skill.	I tell them I have a lot of experience with such matters.
Fait accompli	Openly doing what one wants without avoiding the target.	I do what I want anyway.

EXHIBIT 11-4 **297**

Strategy	Definition	Example
Hinting	Not openly stating what one wants; indirect attempts at influencing others.	I drop hints. I subtly bring up a point.
Persistence	Continuing in one's influence attempts or repeating one's point.	I reiterate my point. I keep going despite all obstacles.
Persuasion	Simple statements about using persuasion, convincing, or coaxing.	I get my way by convincing others that my way is best.
Reason	Any statement about using reason or rational argument to influence others.	I argue logically. I tell all the reasons why my plan is best.
Simple statement	Without supporting evidence or threats, a matter-of-fact statement of one's desires.	I simply tell him what I want.
Thought manipulation	Making the target think that the agent's way is the target's own idea.	I usually try to get my way by making the other person feel that it is his idea.
Threat	Stating that negative consequences will occur if the agent's plan is not accepted.	I'll tell him I will never speak to him again if he doesn't do what I want. (from Falbo, 1977)

* * *

EXHIBIT 11-4
SCHENCK-HAMLIN, WISEMAN, AND GEORGACARAKOS'
COMPLIANCE-GAINING TAXONOMY

1. **Ingratiation:** Actor's proffered goods, sentiments, or services precede the request for compliance ("apple polishing," "brown-nosing," and favor-doing).
2. **Promise:** Actor's proffered goods, sentiments, or services are promised the target in exchange for compliance (trading-off, log-rolling, or finding a "middle of the road" solution).
3. **Debt:** Actor recalls obligations owed him or her as a way of inducing the target to comply ("After all I've done for you . . .").
4. **Esteem:** Target's compliance will result in automatic increase of self-worth ("Just think how good you will feel if you would do this").
5. **Allurement:** Target's reward arises from persons other than the actor or target ("You'll always have their respect").
6. **Aversive stimulation:** Actor continuously punishes target, making cessation contingent on compliance (pouting, sulking, crying, and acting angry).
7. **Threat:** Actor's proposed actions will have negative consequences for the target if he or she does not comply (black-mailing or the suggestion of firing, or breaking off a friendship).

8. **Guilt:** Target's failure to comply will result in automatic decreases of self-worth. (Areas of inadequacy might include professional ineptness, social irresponsibility, or ethical/moral transgressions.)

9. **Warning:** Target's punishment arises from persons other than the actor or target ("You'll make the boss unhappy" and "What will the neighbors say").

10. **Altruism:** Actor requests the target to engage in behavior designed to benefit the actor rather than the target ("It would help me if you would do this" and "Do a favor for me").

11. **Direct request:** The actor simply asks the target to comply ("If I were you, I would . . ." and "Why don't you think about . . .").

12. **Explanation:** One of several reasons are advanced for believing or doing something ("I know from experience," "Everything points to the logic of this step").

13. **Hinting:** Actor represents the situational context in such a way that the target is led to conclude the desired action or response ("It sure is hot in here").

14. **Deceit:** Actor gains target's compliance by intentionally misrepresenting the characteristics or consequences of the desired response ("By doing this, you'll be handsomely rewarded," but the actor does not have the ability to give that reward). (from Schenck-Hamlin, Wiseman, & Georgacarakos, 1982)

Copy chapt 11

Pg 259-
298

nd 3-2⁴

12
Information Campaigns

Man #1: So how's your cousin's new car? Man #2: Oh yeah. My cousin's new car. Man #1: Yeah. Man #2: He picked it up last week. Man #1: All right. Man #2: Big celebration. Man #1: Yeah. Man #2: And I felt like a jerk telling him that he should take a taxi home because he had one too many. Man #1: But you did. Man #2: No, I didn't. Man #1: What happened? Man #2: Totalled. Man #1: What? Man #2: Yeah. And him with it. Man #1: Oh no. Man #2: Oh yeah. Announcer: Take the keys. Call a cab. Take a stand. Friends don't let friends drive drunk. (Public Service Announcement sponsored by the U.S. Department of Transportation)

Announcer: Ladies and Gentlemen, the late Yul Brynner (The words, "Yul Brynner, 1920–1985" appear on the TV screen). Brynner voiceover: I really wanted to make a commercial when I discovered that I was that sick and my time was so limited. I wanted to make a commercial that says simply: Now that I'm gone, I tell you, do not smoke. Whatever you do, just do not smoke. . . . (Message sponsored by the American Cancer Society)

Krista: "I bet I know what you think about HIV. You think only certain people get it. Like people who mess around a lot . . . or drug users. You think it happens mostly in big cities . . . certainly not in little towns. You think it's no big deal because you do not know anyone who has it. And you think it won't happen to you. Sound familiar? Now think about this. My name is Krista Blake. I'm 19. I'm an honors student. I live in a town with a population of 5,000. I've never touched drugs. And guess what? My old boyfriend has HIV, and now so do I. Do you know why? I used to think like you. Announcer: Find out how you can prevent HIV. Call 1-800-342-AIDS. (A message from the Centers for Disease Control)

These three television public service announcements (PSAs) are examples of modern persuasion campaigns that are waged through the mass media. This chapter discusses the impact that such informational campaigns have on beliefs, attitudes, and behavior. It raises questions that probably have occurred to you as you watched television advertisements such as those just described. Do people actually pay any attention to these messages? Do they have any effect? Do they help ameliorate health problems that face American society? We discover that the questions that face communication specialists today are more complicated than ever before; and we find that the answers to these questions are constantly changing and full of implications for public policy. It is fitting that this book ends with a chapter on this topic, for research on information campaigns cuts across the diverse persuasion perspectives we have reviewed thus far. It also allows us to ponder the ways that persuasion research can contribute to the public good. (See Exhibit 12–1: History of Information Campaigns, p. 332.)

The first section of this chapter presents an overview of information campaigns, emphasizing the differences between research on campaigns and laboratory studies of persuasive communication. The second section summarizes the major theories of campaigns. The third section reviews the modern history of campaigns, culminating in a discussion of the conditions under which campaigns fail and succeed. In the fourth section, the implications of persuasion theory for communication campaigns are examined. The final portion of the chapter discusses ethical issues that bear on information campaigns.

DEFINING INFORMATION CAMPAIGNS

You may recall that chapter 1 noted that social influence techniques could be ordered along a continuum of coercion and choice. Information campaigns are probably the least coercive of all the social influence strategies, and they afford individuals a relatively high degree of freedom of choice. However, there are limits to this freedom.

For example, consider a cardiovascular campaign that tries to convince people to adopt a low-fat, low-cholesterol diet. Message recipients may be free—or perceive that they are free—to accept or reject the campaign's recommendations. However, their behavioral choices are limited by several factors, including the market (they can only buy those low-cholesterol foods that manufacturers place on the market) and their income levels (if they have a low income and low-cholesterol foods cost more than lunch at McDonald's, their behavioral options are restricted).

A word also needs to be said about the use of the word "information" in the term *information campaign*. Compared with "propaganda" or "manipulation," information has relatively positive connotations (Dervin, 1981; Rakow, 1989). A public relations practitioner would prefer that others view his or her task as "informing" or "imparting information" than as "trying to manipulate public opinion." One can readily understand this preference. Today, information is a go "word" (Dervin, 1976), an "in" concept.

Consequently, it is easy to reify the term and to forget the important role that judgments and perceptions play in the evaluation of information. To many people, information means facts that are true (i.e., free of bias and, in some sense, neutral and objective). However, as communication scholars are fond of pointing out, there is no such thing as an objective fact. The definition of a fact depends on judgments, perceptions, and points of view. Indeed, as anyone who has witnessed a traffic accident knows, different parties often have very different versions of the "facts" (Romano, 1987). In the campaign arena, facts are as slippery and as much a function of one's perspective as they are anywhere else. Salmon (1989) noted that:

> Many recent "straight facts" campaigns in support of mandatory seatbelt laws, for example, have been sponsored by insurance companies and automobile manufacturers. The stated concern justifying these campaigns may be public health and safety, but the vested interest is financial: If mandatory seatbelt laws are passed in a sufficient number of states, automobile manufacturers will not be required to install passive restraint systems, and insurance companies will not have to pay as much in benefits. Should not these facts, which might be of interest to citizens contemplating a referendum, be as prominently mentioned in corporate-sponsored campaigns? (pp. 35–36)

Given the ambiguity and complexity of the term *information campaign*, it is important to define the concept clearly. Scholars have offered several definitions of an information campaign. McGuire (1984) noted that a health information campaign:

> Involves convincing individuals to exercise personal responsibility for their health by altering their lifestyles in more healthful directions (through the use of) mass media and other communication channels to inform the public about dangers, motivate them to reduce risks, or train them in skills that enable them to adopt more healthful lifestyles. (p. 299)

Atkin (1981) noted that: "Information campaigns usually involve a series of promotional messages in the public interest disseminated through the mass media channels to target audiences" (p. 265).

More recently, Rogers and Storey (1987) pointed out that: "(1) A campaign intends to generate specific outcomes or effects (2) in a relatively large number of individuals, (3) usually within a specified period of time and (4) through an organized set of communication activities" (p. 821).

In essence, information campaigns are exemplars of persuasion in action. They involve the application of persuasion theory to real-world situations. However, whenever we apply basic research to a real-world setting, we must recognize that the contexts in which the findings were originally obtained are very different from the dynamic and fluid situations that are characteristic of real life. Civil engineers are well aware of this issue when they apply principles obtained from experimental physics to the problem of building a bridge. Physical chemists recognize that special issues and problems come up when they bring experimentally derived findings about macromolecules to bear on the practical problem of constructing a contact lens. In a similar vein, refinements must be made when theory and research on persuasion are applied to real-world communication campaigns. There are three differences between how persuasion has been studied in laboratory and other settings and how it is studied in campaign contexts:

1. The overwhelming majority of persuasion studies have been conducted in the laboratory, but information campaigns are by definition planned and evaluated in the real world. Many factors that the laboratory researcher can control remain elusive in the real world (Hovland, 1959). For example, experimental researchers can ensure that their subjects pay attention to the persuasive message (which, let us say, concerns the dangers of cigarette smoking). The investigators may find that the persuasive message fails to change attitudes in the desired direction, but, at the very least, they can be sure that their subjects attended to the communication. By contrast, campaign specialists have no guarantee that the anti-smoking PSAs they so carefully arranged to be shown during certain times of the day actually were seen or heard by the target audience.

2. Campaigns operate at several levels of analysis. Psychologically oriented persuasion researchers typically examine the effects of messages on individual-level variables (cognitions, affects, and behaviors). Compliance-gaining scholars explore persuasion in one-to-one situational contexts. By contrast, research on campaigns examines effects on both the individual and the dyadic level, and on the broader institutional or systems level as well. In addition to examining whether a drunk driving campaign changes individuals' attitudes toward driving while intoxicated, planners may also want to know whether it influenced the formation of active protest groups (e.g., Mothers Against Drunk Drivers [MADD]) and led to the implementation of new state laws on drunk driving. This broader emphasis requires that information campaign scholars draw on micro- and macrolevel theories.

3. Political considerations exert a much stronger influence on the design of information campaigns than on laboratory studies of persuasive communication. There are relatively few factors that constrain or restrict experimentally oriented researchers' choice of stimulus materials. If the investigators want to use racy materials, they probably can use them. If they want to employ an unconventional measure of compliance, they probably can do so, provided the human subjects committee does not object. By contrast, real-world political variables often constrain the design

choices available to campaign specialists. For example, the planners of an AIDS campaign may be told that a message on the topic of AIDS and homosexuality is too controversial for a prime-time audience. Or they may learn at the last minute that the city council will not allow them to hand out condoms to launch an AIDS communication campaign.

THEORETICAL APPROACHES

Communication campaigns operate at both the microlevel (individual) and the macrolevel (social system). Messages seek to influence psychological variables (knowledge, attitudes, and behaviors). However, these same messages are received in the context of the larger social environment in which the individual lives and works. Thus, theories of campaigns have focused on the individual and on the larger social system. In this section, two representative theories of campaign effects are reviewed: McGuire's (1985) communication/persuasion model concentrates on individual-level processes and effects, whereas the social marketing perspective (Kotler & Zaltman, 1971) focuses on the larger social system.

The Input/Output Model of Persuasive Communication

McGuire (1985) has proposed an input/output matrix model of persuasive communication effect that builds on Hovland, Janis, and Kelley's (1953) classic work in this area. As Fig. 12.1 indicates, the input column labels consist of the the "variables out of which a communication can be constructed"; the output row headings constitute "the successive response steps that the receivers must be induced to take if the communication is to have its intended persuasive impact" (McGuire, 1985, p. 258). Communication can be constructed by manipulating the input variables (source, message, channel, receiver, and destination). The input headings incorporate the many theories of communication effects that we have discussed throughout this book (e.g., attributional approaches to source credibility, the ELM, the protection motivation approach, etc.).

The output side of the model depicts persuasion as a long and complex process. As Fig. 12.1 indicates, a message must clear many hurdles if it is to succeed in changing attitudes and behavior. The message recipient must tune into the message, attend to its content, like what he or she hears, comprehend the arguments, learn how to perform the recommended behaviors, yield to the advocated position, store the message arguments or one's own cognitive elaborations in long-term memory, retrieve these cognitions at the time of decision, utilize this information in decision making, behave in accord with the decision, rehearse and reinforce the

INPUT: Independent (Communication) Variables / OUTPUT: Dependent Variables (Response Steps Mediating Persuasion)	SOURCE				MESSAGE					CHANNEL			RECEIVER				DEST-INATION		
	number	unanimity	demographics	attractiveness	credibility ••	type appeal	type information	inclusion/omission	organization	repetitiveness ••	modality	directness	context ••	demographics	ability	personality	life style ••	immediacy/delay	prevention/cessation	direct/immunization ••
1. Exposure to the communication																				
2. Attending to it																				
3. Liking, becoming interested in it																				
4. Comprehending it (learning what)																				
5. Skill acquisition (learning how)																				
6. Yielding to it (attitude change)																				
7. Memory storage of content and /or agreement																				
8. Information search and retrieval																				
9. Deciding on basis of retrieval																				
10. Behaving in accord with decision																				
11. Reinforcement of desired acts																				
12. Post-behavioral consolidating																				

FIG. 12.1 The communication/persuasion model as an input/output matrix (from McGuire, 1989).

desired actions, and consolidate or integrate the behavioral act within one's overall belief system.

According to McGuire (1989), "the probability that the communication will evoke each of the 12 output steps is conditional upon the occurrence of all preceding steps" (p. 49). In fact, many messages do not even make it to Step 1. For example, individuals low in socioeconomic status (SES) often do not receive the latest facts about health and safety matters. As Freimuth (1990) observed, low SES persons "are often locked into an information ghetto. . . . Their information system is a closed one" (p. 176). Moreover, even if the campaign message evokes Steps 1 through 9, it may not elicit behavioral imitation (Step 10), which is a necessary condition for long-term behavioral change. McGuire also emphasized that campaign messages can have a positive effect on one mediator (as when a humorous message captures individuals' attention), but have a negative influence on another output step (as when the same message gets people laughing so much that they do not pay attention to the message arguments).

There has been mixed support for McGuire's (1989) model. In particular, the input/output matrix assumes that persuasion occurs in the sequence posited earlier. However, other researchers have postulated different causal sequences. For instance, Ray (1973) argued that, under low-involvement conditions, messages influence knowledge, behavior, and attitudes, in that order.[1] Yet McGuire argued that attitude change precedes behavior change. Nonetheless, McGuire's model has made an important contribution, because it provides a useful framework for viewing a wide array of campaign effects and for designing campaign messages.

Social Marketing

Social marketing involves the application of marketing principles to the promotion of ideas, issues, and practices. One of its chief architects, Kotler (1975), defined it as:

> The design, implementation, and control of programs seeking to increase the acceptability of a social idea or practice in a target group(s). It utilizes concepts of market segmentation, consumer research, idea configuration, communication, facilitation, incentives, and exchange theory to maximize target group response. (p. 283)

Now wait a minute, you may think: Aren't there some differences between promoting brotherhood and selling soap? There are indeed. Social marketing differs from business marketing in several respects (Kotler & Zaltman, 1971; Lefebvre & Flora, 1988; Wiebe, 1952). In the first place, the criteria for success are somewhat different. The success of a commercial advertising campaign is measured in terms of dollars and cents (Do more people buy the product after the campaign than before it started?). Social marketing specialists evaluate their efforts by examining whether there have been significant changes in attitudes and social behaviors (Has the target population changed its attitude toward cocaine? Are fewer people using cocaine?).

Second, social marketers have greater difficulty determining whether a campaign has achieved its goals than do their commercial counterparts. Unlike businesses, which can monitor sales or market shares, social marketers may have only a vague statement of the program's goals or program objectives (Bloom & Novelli, 1981). Bloom and Novelli noted, in their discussion of the challenges facing social marketing, that:

Even after lengthy discussions with management, social marketers often have difficulty deciding whether a program is designed to create awareness of an issue, change people's behavior, save lives, or do something else. . . . Should one examine, for example, smoking quitting rates or cigarette sales to evaluate the success of a smoking cessation program? Should one examine measures that indicate something about the secondary or unintended effects of such a program, such as data on the consumption of junk food and alcohol by people who are persuaded to quit smoking. (p. 87)

Third, a commercial advertising campaign seeks to induce people to do something (invariably, to buy the product). By contrast, social marketing projects often try to get consumers *not* to engage in a certain activity (e.g., do not smoke, do not litter, do not share intravenous needles).

Notice that social marketing is not a theory of campaign effects, but rather a "perspective" or "approach." This means that social marketing does not tell us how a campaign can change attitudes or behaviors. What social marketing can do is provide general guidelines for campaign design based on the four major "Ps" of marketing: product, place, price, and promotion.

Product. Most of us do not conceive of information campaigns as involving products. However, social marketers point out that campaigns are selling things; it is just that their products are less tangible than those pedaled by business marketers (Lefebvre & Flora, 1988). The products promoted by social marketers come in different forms. Some are physical (a birth control pill, a Neighborhood Watch poster), whereas others are social ideas (do not drink when you drive; keep America beautiful).

Place. Place is the distribution channel (usually an organization) that transports the product so it is available to the target group. Solomon (1989) lamented that:

Many social campaigns have failed because they did not have an adequate distribution system for their messages and products. No commercial company would consider promoting a product that is not available on the shelves of the local store, yet many social campaigns have simply said, "Contact your local (agency) office," without giving specific telephone numbers or addresses, without having adequate staff on hand to answer requests, and without supplying adequate printed materials. (p. 93)

Studies of persuasive communication reinforce this point. In an early study of fear appeals, Leventhal, Singer, and Jones (1965) found that subjects were more likely to get a tetanus shot when the message aroused fear and contained specific information about where to go and what to do to get a tetanus shot than when the message contained only a high-fear recommendation.

Price. We ordinarily think of price in strictly monetary terms. Social marketers remind us that there is a price tag for adopting a new idea or practice, and it can take forms other than money. These include time costs (the time it takes to stick around a party to sober up before driving home), social costs (the embarrassment a person may experience after asking a sex partner if he has a condom), and emotional costs (the stresses and strains associated with quitting smoking). Just as commercial advertisers consider the cost of the product before devising an advertising campaign, social marketers are advised to consider the costs associated with new social practices.

Price is a tricky factor. In some countries, change agents find that it is easier to charge a small fee for contraceptives than to give them away for free. One psychological theory—Brock's (1968) commodity theory—provides an explanation: Products are perceived to have more value when there is a cost associated with them.[2] Furthermore, dissonance theory suggests that once individuals commit themselves to paying a higher-than-desired price, they will convince themselves that the product was worth the investment (Doob, Carlsmith, Freedman, Landauer, & Tom, 1969).

Promotion. Promotion involves all the strategies that are employed to make people aware of the product, to change their attitudes, and to influence their behaviors. Although commercial marketers have long recognized that promotion plays a critical role in marketing products, social marketers have, until recently, tended to neglect promotional activities. For example, Martin (1968) pointed out that the Indian government failed to view family planning as a marketing problem:

> Selling birth control is as much a marketing job as selling any other consumer product. And where no manufacturer would contemplate developing and introducing a new product without a thorough understanding of the variables of the market, planners in the highest circles of Indian government have blithely gone ahead without understanding that marketing principles must determine the character of any campaign of voluntary control. The Indians have done only the poorest research. They have mismanaged distribution of contraceptive devices. They have ignored the importance of "customer service." They have proceeded with grossly inadequate undertrained staffs; they have been blind to the importance of promotion and advertising.

Contemporary researchers recognize that such standard promotional strategies as advertising, publicity, and personal selling must be employed to promote social ideas and practices. Campaign specialists place particular emphasis on market segmentation, or dividing a market (target audience) into smaller homogeneous groups or segments. Markets can be segmented into demographic groups (e.g., the elderly), psychographic categories (Yuppies), values and lifestyles (consumers concerned with looking athletic and thin), and geographical regions (e.g., the South).

CAMPAIGN EFFECTS

Can campaigns reduce the incidence of smoking, get people to wear seat belts, and change attitudes toward AIDS? In this section, we try to answer these questions as we review the many studies of the effects of information campaigns. Rogers and Storey (1987) argued that there have been three generations of research on campaigns. The first generation (The Era of Minimal Effects) was dominated by the view that campaigns have limited effects on attitudes and behavior. The second generation of researchers benefited from the mistakes of their predecessors and designed campaigns that succeeded in influencing behavior (The Era of Campaign Success). The third generation of researchers took a longer perspective: They recognized that both the weak effects and the strong effects views had merit. They concluded that, under some conditions, campaigns were likely to succeed, whereas under other conditions they were likely to fail (The Era of Moderate Effects).

The Minimal Effects Era

In 1947, the city of Cincinnati launched an ambitious, 6-month campaign to change attitudes toward the United Nations. The campaign was designed to make the city "United Nations conscious." As the organizing committee put it, the campaign hoped to demonstrate "how a community may become so intelligently informed on world affairs as to be a dynamic force in the creation of an ordered and eventually a peaceful world" (Star & Hughes, 1950, p. 389). Numerous events and activities were planned. For example:

> 12,868 people were reached through the Parent-Teachers Associations which devoted programs to the topic of world understanding. Every school child was given literature on the United Nations to take home; the schoolteachers kept the subject constantly before their pupils and were themselves supplied with instruction and materials at teachers' mass meetings. . . . The radio stations broadcast facts about the United Nations, one of them scheduling spot programs 150 times a week. The newspapers played up United Nations news and information throughout

the six months. In the last three months 225 meetings were served with literature and special speakers. In all, 59,588 pieces of literature were distributed and 2,800 clubs were reached by speakers supplied by a speakers' bureau and by circular. . . . (Star & Hughes, 1950, p. 390)

Two researchers (Star & Hughes, 1950) conducted a systematic evaluation of the campaign. They measured knowledge of and attitudes toward the United Nations before the campaign began and after it had been underway for 6 months. Their conclusion: The campaign failed to achieve its major objectives. For example, prior to the campaign, 30% of the respondents could not identify the primary purpose of the United Nations; 6 months later, the percentage of respondents who could not identify the United Nation's primary purpose had dropped, but only by 2 percentage points.

The campaign also failed to change beliefs about the strengths and weaknesses of the United Nations. The only glimmer of hope was the finding that those respondents with the greatest exposure to campaign materials were more likely than those with little exposure to informational messages to agree that the United Nations should play an active role in world affairs. But even this conclusion was tempered by the strong possibility that those who took the time to read over campaign materials were already favorably disposed to the United Nations, which meant that the campaign had not changed their attitudes, but had merely reinforced an existing point of view.

Other studies of campaign effects reached an equally pessimistic conclusion (e.g., Hyman & Sheatsley, 1947). By 1960, the notion that campaigns had minimal effects had become part of the prevailing wisdom. In a review of the research on mass communication effects, Klapper (1960) stated that:

Communications research strongly indicates that persuasive mass communication is in general more likely to reinforce the existing opinions of its audience than it is to change such opinions. Minor attitude change appears to be a more likely effect than conversion and a less likely effect than reinforcement. . . . Mass communication *ordinarily* does not serve as a necessary and sufficient cause of audience effects, but rather functions among and through a nexus of mediating factors and influences. (pp. 49–50; p. 8).

The New Look. This pessimistic assessment began to change in the 1960s. As television advertising budgets grew and candidates for political office began to tailor their campaigns to the mass media, it seemed preposterous to argue that persuasive mass communications exerted minimal effects. After all, the same year that Klapper (1960) published his pessimistic assessment, political commentators everywhere were proclaiming that the televised presidential debates between Kennedy and Nixon had turned the

This is the way many people deal with HIV.

A lot of people don't think they have to worry about HIV. But the truth is, anyone can get HIV infection by sharing drug needles and syringes or having sex with an infected person. Call your State or local AIDS hotline, or the National AIDS Hotline at 1-800-342-AIDS. Call 1-800-243-7889 (TTY) for deaf access.

HIV is the virus that causes AIDS.

AMERICA RESPONDS TO AIDS

CDC U.S. DEPARTMENT OF HEALTH AND HUMAN SERVICES
Public Health Service
Centers for Disease Control

These two posters were used in a national AIDS information campaign sponsored by the Centers for Disease Control.

If You're Dabbling In Drugs... You Could Be Dabbling With Your Life.

Skin popping, on occasion, seems a lot safer than mainlining. Right? You ask yourself: What can happen? Well, a lot can happen. That's because there's a new game in town. It's called AIDS. So far there are no winners. If you share needles, you're at risk. All it takes is one exposure to the AIDS virus and you've just dabbled your life away.

For more information about AIDS, call 1-800-342-AIDS.

This is a message from the U.S. Centers for Disease Control.

tide in Kennedy's favor and had brought about Kennedy's election as president (see Kraus, 1962).

In the 1960s and early 1970s, a new scholarly consensus emerged (Chaffee, 1988; Wartella & Middlestadt, 1991). The revised view of campaign effects was reflected aptly by the title of a paper that Mendelsohn published in 1973: "Some Reasons Why Information Campaigns Can Succeed." (Some 25 years earlier, Hyman and Sheatsley had published a paper in the same journal entitled "Some Reasons Why Information Campaigns Fail.") Mendelsohn, along with other communication scholars of the 1960s, noted that there were serious problems with the minimal effects perspective.

In the first place, these scholars noted, the early researchers had unrealistically high expectations of success. Emboldened by the U.S. victory in World War II and by the optimism that swept the country during the early 1950s, researchers believed that information campaigns could achieve massive effects. When the campaigns failed to meet these expectations, the researchers drew the conclusion that the campaigns had failed. Had the researchers possessed a more reasonable set of expectations, they might have viewed campaign effects somewhat differently (see Becker, McCombs, & McLeod, 1975). For example, Salmon (1989) noted that Star and Hughes reported that 51% of their sample failed to remember the slogan, "Peace Begins with the United Nations—the United Nations Begins with You." Yet, Salmon (1989) pointed out that: "A different interpretation of the same data is that 49 percent of the citizens *did* recall the slogan after the six-month effort, a result that would be hailed by contemporary social and commercial marketers" (p. 41).

A second shortcoming in the minimal effects position is the tendency to blame the audience for the lack of campaign effects. According to one view, the reason why the United Nations campaign failed was because the audience consisted of a "hard core of chronic know-nothings" who were impervious to influence. However, Atkin (1981) argued that it is more likely that the campaign failed because the messages were dry, dull, and unpersuasive. A related view is that the message failed to "make sense" to receivers; that is, it did not contain any arguments with which receivers could make a personal connection (Dervin, 1981). Mendelsohn (1973) suggested that: "Most evidence on the failures of information campaigns actually tells us more about flaws in the communicator—the originator of messages—than it does about shortcomings either in the content or in the audience" (p. 51).

A third problem with the early research was methodological: The measurement technologies available to researchers of this era were not sophisticated enough to locate the subtle effects that campaigns exerted on attitudes and behavior. It is possible that researchers "failed to measure the right thing, in the right way, at the right time, in the right place, with the right people" (Wallack, 1981, p. 240).

Fourth, the campaigns were conducted in the pretelevision era. Television is particularly effective in conveying emotion and in presenting simple pieces of information. Thus, one reason why the early campaigns failed to change attitudes is that they employed media (print and radio) that lacked the power (and reach) of television.

The Era of Campaign Success

Mendelsohn's (1973) article ("Some Reasons Why Information Campaigns Can Succeed") set the tone for the second generation of campaign research. A review of campaigns conducted from the late-1960s through the early 1980s indicates that campaigns did achieve a great deal of success (see Douglas, Westley, & Chaffee, 1970; Warner, 1977). Two prominent examples of campaign success are the Stanford Heart Disease Prevention Campaign and the Take a Bite Out of Crime Program.

The Stanford Campaign. Concerned about the mounting death rates resulting from cardiovascular disease, a group of investigators at Stanford University launched a three-community information campaign to effect changes in smoking, diet, and exercise. The researchers chose three California cities that were comparable in characteristics. The cities were Watsonville (population 14,500), Gilroy (population 12,700), and Tracy (14,700). Two of the cities (Watsonville and Gilroy) received a multimedia campaign; and in one city (Watsonville), individuals who were at high risk for heart disease received both media programs and intensive face-to-face instruction.[3] The third community (Tracy) served as the control town. Baseline measurements of knowledge about cardiovascular disease risk factors were obtained from a random sample of residents of each city before the campaign started and again at the end of the first, second, and third years. Physiological measurements of amount of dietary cholesterol and of cigarette consumption were also obtained.

The media campaign consisted of about 40 television spots, numerous radio PSAs, newspaper "dietary columns," and billboards. Health and lifestyle education packets were sent to residents of Gilroy and Watsonville. The intensive interpersonal instruction (Watsonville only) employed behavior modification techniques, such as skills training and psychological incentives to help high-risk subjects make changes in diet, exercise, and consumption of cigarettes. For example:

> In diet, guided practice of new behavior was achieved by each subject's planning and reporting on the food he or she ate on a weekly menu plan

over a period of four weeks. Each person's progress was recorded in terms of weight loss and a progress report feedback system. . . . Smokers were encouraged to substitute sugar-free lozenges, to walk, to breathe deeply, and to try other substitutes in the presence of cues for smoking. The instructor also suggested breaking up habitual patterns associated with smoking by doing such things as changing brands weekly or buying only one pack of cigarettes at a time. (Maccoby & Farquhar, 1975, p. 121)

The campaign had a strong impact on knowledge and behavior (see Fig. 12.2). The group that received both media and interpersonal instruction (Watsonville) showed the greatest improvements. However, the media-

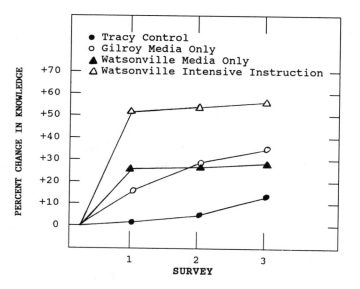

Percentage of change from baseline (0) in knowledge of cardiovascular disease risk factors after the three annual follow-up surveys.

Note: The Watsonville intensive instruction group experienced the greatest improvements in knowledge over the course of the campaign. Interestingly, a second group of Watsonville subjects, those who received only the media campaign, also exhibited significant increases in knowledge. Indeed, individuals in this group exhibited greater changes than those in the control (Tracy)-- in part because of the extensive interpersonal communication that the campaign stimulated in Watsonville. Most importantly, all three groups (Watsonville intensive instruction, Watsonville media only, and Gilroy) experienced greater increases in knowledge than the control (Tracy).

FIG. 12.2 Effects of Stanford cardiovascular health information campaign on knowledge of heart disease risk factors (from Meyer et al., 1980).

only treatment had significant effects as well. Residents of the city that received only media materials (Gilroy) experienced greater changes in health-related knowledge and behavior than did participants in the control town (Tracy).

The findings were particularly striking in the case of knowledge gain. For example, in Watsonville, the percentage of people who said that eating eggs can be harmful to your heart rose from 64.6% (at the initial survey) to 86.3% (at the end of Year 1); in Gilroy, the percentage jumped from 67.2% to 77.4%; however, in Tracy, there was no change from Time 1 (75.6%) to Time 2.

The campaign was enormously successful in influencing dietary cholesterol intake. The group that received intensive instruction plus media (Watsonville) and the town that was subjected to media programming only (Gilroy) displayed significantly greater reductions in dietary cholesterol intake than did the control community (Tracy).[4] In addition, the Watsonville group achieved significantly greater reductions in the number of cigarettes smoked per day and in the overall percentage of cigarette smokers than did the other groups (Meyer, Nash, McAlister, Maccoby, & Farquhar, 1980). The changes were dramatic. As Meyer et al. (1980) noted: "The Watsonville intensive instruction group experienced a 50% cessation rate and a 51% reduction in cigarettes smoked per day. Thus, there were 20 fewer smokers in this group at the final survey than at baseline" (p. 139).

The McGruff Campaign. In response to citizens' concern about rising crime rates, a coalition of government and private sector groups developed a campaign to increase public participation in crime prevention programs. The program became known as the "Take a Bite Out of Crime" campaign. It featured an animated trench-coated dog named McGruff who urged individuals to take a variety of steps "to take a bite out of crime." The McGruff campaign called on individuals to take safety precautions when they were outside, to make certain the doors and windows in their homes were securely locked, and to participate in neighborhood crime watch programs.

The messages were widely disseminated. Public service announcements appeared on television stations across the country. At the same time, radio, newspapers, magazines, and billboards carried the McGruff campaign message. Across the country, community groups, businesses, and local police forces supplemented the campaign with a wide range of activities.

Communication researcher O'Keefe conducted a series of studies to determine if, bottom-line, all the publicity had made a dent in people's crime-related attitudes and behaviors (O'Keefe, 1985; O'Keefe & Reid, 1989). O'Keefe mounted a two-pronged attack to see if the campaign had achieved its objectives. He interviewed a national sample of 1,200 adults

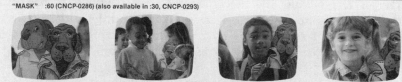

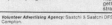

A number of information campaigns have been launched in recent years. The storyboard above was used in the McGruff anti-crime campaign; the storyboard on p. 317 was employed in a campaign to recruit teachers.

RECURITING NEW TEACHERS

TV PUBLIC SERVICE SPOTS

Available in :60, :30 and :15 lengths.
Please discontinue use: December 1, 1991.

"OLMOS"   60 SECONDS

(MUSIC UP) | SINGERS: WAKE UP ALL THE TEACHERS | TIME TO TEACH | A NEW WAY:

MAYBE THEN THEY'LL LISTEN | TO WHAT YOU HAVE TO SAY. (VO): The power of teaching... | SINGERS: THEY'RE THE ONES WHO'S COMING UP AND THE WORLD IS IN THEIR HANDS: | WHEN YOU TEACH THE CHILDREN, TEACH 'EM THE VERY BEST YOU CAN...

THE WORLD WON'T GET NO BETTER, | IF WE JUST LET IT BE...OH, OHH... | (VO): The power to wake up young minds. | The power to wake up the world.

Teachers have that power. Reach for it. Teach. | SINGERS: WAKE UP ALL THE TEACHERS, TIME TO TEACH A NEW WAY... MAYBE THEN THEY'LL LISTEN... | (VO): Reach for the power. Teach. I'm Edward James Olmos, | and we're Recruiting New Teachers. For information call 1-800-45-TEACH.

Recruiting New Teachers, Inc.
6 Standish Street
Cambridge, Mass. 02138

A Public Service Campaign of the Advertising Council

Campaign Director: Bruce S. Mowery, Apple Computer, Inc.   CNYT-9160/9130/9115   191

approximately two years into the campaign. In addition, he conducted interviews with 426 individuals in three representative U.S. cities shortly before the campaign had begun, and again two years later.

Over 50% of the national sample reported that they had heard or seen at least one of the McGruff public service announcements. More than half of the respondents who recalled the ads claimed that the ads had made them more concerned about crime. Over half of these adults also indicated that the public service announcements had increased their belief in the effectiveness of citizen crime prevention efforts. Clearly, then, the campaign succeeded in reaching large numbers of citizens and in raising their consciousness about crime prevention efforts. However, from a crime prevention perspective, it is not enough to raise awareness levels; it is also important to influence crime prevention behaviors. To determine the effects of the campaign on behavior, O'Keefe (1985) examined the responses of the 426 adults who were interviewed before and after the campaign had begun.

The data from this second study provided strong and compelling evidence that the McGruff campaign had influenced crime prevention behaviors. Exposure to the campaign led to significant increases in a number of crime prevention behaviors (e.g., asking neighbors to watch the house, keeping a watch on the neighborhood, leaving the outdoor lights on, reporting suspicious activities to the police, and joining with others to prevent crime).[5]

The Contemporary Era of Moderate Effects

The pendulum switched again in the 1980s. There was no denying that campaigns could influence attitudes and behavior, but neither could it be denied that modern campaigns sometimes failed to achieve their objectives. Several campaigns that were launched in the 1970s turned out to be colossal failures (Atkin, 1981; see Exhibit 12–2: Seat Belt Use: A Campaign Failure, p. 333). Contemporary scholars argued that communication effects are ultimately contingent on a variety of contextual variables. Thus, campaigns can fail or succeed, depending on factors external to the campaign. During the current generation of campaign research, scholars have identified the impediments to campaign success, as well as the factors that make it more likely that a campaign will succeed.

Impediments to Success

Messages Do Not Always Reach Their Target Audience.   There is abundant evidence that low-income and less-educated individuals are more likely to smoke, have poor nutritional habits, and be exposed to health hazards at the workplace than their more affluent and better educated counterparts. Health communication scholar Freimuth (1990) noted that:

> Health communicators often are confronted with the challenge of reaching target groups of low-income and poorly educated individuals because these low socioeconomic (SES) groups are frequently at higher risk for many health problems. Yet when these same campaigns are evaluated, these groups usually emerge as less exposed, less knowledgeable, and less likely to change their behaviors. (p. 171)

For these reasons, health information campaigns frequently direct their messages at economically and educationally disadvantaged adults. Yet, for a variety of reasons, these health messages never reach their target audience. As noted earlier, disadvantaged adults are locked into a closed information system. Information from the outside frequently fails to penetrate the closed walls of the community; if it does make it inside the system, it is subjected to great scrutiny and criticism precisely because it is perceived as different and foreign (Freimuth, 1990). In addition, many poor people have developed a fatalistic orientation: They perceive that their lives are governed by fate or forces beyond their control. Believing that they are helpless to effect change in their lives or in their environments, low-income individuals frequently do not seek out information about how to improve their health, and they often do not systematically process health information that they encounter in the course of their everyday lives. Furthermore, poor and disadvantaged adults frequently lack basic communication skills such as reading and listening; these cognitive deficits also hamper their efforts to acquire new information about health and safety. Thus, before the health information campaign begins, disadvantaged adults are likely to lag behind their more advantaged counterparts in knowledge about the target issue.

To make matters worse, there is evidence that media campaigns widen, rather than close, gaps between the information-rich and the information-poor. According to the knowledge gap hypothesis, increasing the flow of media publicity about a topic leads to greater acquisition of knowledge among the better educated and more affluent members of the population (Tichenor, Donohue, & Olien, 1970). The knowledge gap hypothesis suggests that a health information campaign may actually increase existing knowledge gaps between the advantaged and disadvantaged members of the population (see Fig. 12.3).

It should be noted that the knowledge gap hypothesis was developed to account for the disappointing results of campaigns designed to increase knowledge of public affairs and science. Thus, there is somewhat more evidence that public affairs campaigns increase knowledge gaps than that health campaigns widen existing differences in knowledge levels. Never-

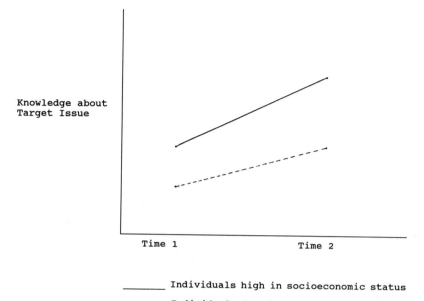

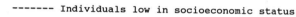

FIG. 12.3 Schematic diagram of the knowledge gap hypothesis.

theless, it is reasonable to conclude from the theory and research in this area that an important impediment to success in the area of health information campaigns is the tendency for campaigns to fail to reach and influence the individuals who are in the greatest need of receiving the information.[6]

Campaigns Are Unlikely to Change Strongly Held Attitudes. Social judgment theory suggests that receivers will cognitively distort campaign messages that focus on strong values or opinions. Thus, "hot issue" campaigns that focus on such issues as abortion or gun control are likely to meet with considerable resistance (Grunig, 1989). In addition, campaigns that touch on cultural values or societal norms are likely to face opposition.

A number of years ago, a Peruvian health official mounted a campaign to change attitudes toward boiling water among residents of Los Molinos, a small Peruvian village. Rogers (1983) noted that "water boiling is an important health practice for villagers and urban poor in Peru. Unless they boil their drinking water, patients who are cured of infectious diseases in village medical clinics often return within a month to be treated again for the same disease" (p. 2). Unfortunately, water boiling is associated with illness among residents of Los Molinos. Custom has it that boiled water is suitable only for the sick. Thus, as Rogers (1983) noted, "if a person is not ill, he is prohibited by village norms from drinking boiled water" (p. 4). A 2-year campaign to change villagers' attitudes toward water boiling failed, partly because it challenged cultural beliefs and social values.

It Is Difficult to Produce Long-Term Behavioral Change. According to McGuire's (1985) model of persuasive communication, a message must clear many hurdles to achieve persuasive success. Changing behavior is particularly difficult because behavior patterns have been reinforced by powerful environmental contingencies over the course of the individual's life. Integration of the behavior into the person's value system (the last step in McGuire's model of the persuasion process) is even more difficult. Thus, an AIDS campaign may induce an IV drug user to enter treatment, but the effect may be short-lived; faced with external pressures and tempting offers from his or her friends on the street, the addict may return to the fold shortly after the campaign ends.

Ingredients for Success

Certain factors maximize the likelihood that a campaign will succeed. Research suggests that five factors are critical (Lazarsfeld & Merton, 1949; Wallack, 1981).

Monopolization. Campaigns are more likely to succeed when there are few alternative voices or countercommunications that question the thrust of the campaign. The concept of monopolization helps explain why some AIDS campaigns that were launched in the early 1980s probably failed to influence attitudes toward AIDS. During this period, few, if any, of the dominant institutions in American society had committed themselves to fighting the AIDS epidemic. AIDS was largely viewed as a weird disease that affected only a bunch of "deviants." This perspective, of course, no longer characterizes the America of the 1990s. The surgeon general has declared AIDS to be a critical public health issue; physicians, medical associations, and insurance providers have published papers on the subject; presidents and presidential candidates have made statements regarding the plight of persons with AIDS; and a basketball star with an international reputation (Magic Johnson) announced (in 1991) that he had the HIV virus and that he would dedicate himself to working to help the plight of persons with AIDS.

Thus, AIDS campaigns that are launched during the 1990s are likely to benefit from the support of major public institutions and should be able to "ride on the wave of public opinion and concern" (O'Keefe & Reid, 1990). For this reason, AIDS campaigns that are launched in the 1990s may be more likely to change attitudes and behavioral intentions than those which were sponsored in the 1980s.

The concept of monopolization also helps to explain why the McGruff anticrime PSAs were so successful in influencing beliefs and attitudes about crime. As O'Keefe and Reid (1990) pointed out:

> While the McGruff PSAs had impact prior to the development of adequate supplemental support systems, they also had the advantage of being disseminated during the highly "crime conscious" early 1980s. They were therefore supplemented by extensive news media coverage about crime in general, as well as a number of more localized prevention campaign efforts. Part of the campaign's impact may have resulted from its "fitting in" with the social environment of the times, and perhaps in its own way accelerating public awareness that citizens could responsibly contribute to crime reduction. (p. 84)

Canalization. This second condition stipulates that campaigns will succeed "if what is called for is not the creation of new attitudes or behavior patterns in some degree of conflict with old patterns but simply the channeling of existing attitudes or behavior in a different but similar direction" (Wallack, 1981, p. 233). Thus, canalization occurs when existing attitudes or behavior patterns are channeled in a new direction. Advertising frequently employs canalization when it tries to convince consumers to switch from one toothpaste to another. In a similar fashion, canalization helps explain why the McGruff campaign was so effective. People already were convinced that steps had to be taken to curb the spread of crime; McGruff helped them to channel their behavioral energies in a useful and socially constructive direction.

Supplementation. Supplementation occurs when a media message is reinforced by similar messages that are delivered through other communication modalities. A number of studies have found that supplementation enhances campaign effects. For example, evaluations of the Stanford heart disease prevention campaign found that the combination of media and interpersonal instruction led to the greatest reductions in smoking behavior. Similar results were obtained in the North Karelia, Finland antismoking campaign (Puska et al., 1979). In addition, a drunk driving campaign that supplemented media messages with spot-check police enforcement reported that it had achieved some degree of success in influencing drinking and driving behavior (see Wallack, 1981).

Social learning theory helps explain why campaign effects are more likely when media messages are reinforced by similar messages that are delivered through interpersonal communication channels. Mediated messages are effective in teaching people behavioral information. However, people do not always perform what they have learned. Interpersonal agents can help individuals to develop the requisite skills, and they can increase respondents' motivation by providing positive feedback for their accomplishments (Green & McAlister, 1984).

Campaigns also are more likely to be successful when the mediated messages are supplemented and reinforced by similar messages that are delivered by local organizations and institutions. Brown and Einsiedel (1990) have pointed out that health campaigns "will not have long-term effects unless they are conducted in environments that encourage and support healthy behavior" (p. 158). Similarly, Green and McAlister (1984) have observed that:

> The mass media alone will not be effective unless organizational, economic and environmental changes enable, and interpersonal communications reinforce, the behavioral change objectives. Systematic plans for organizing the community to support behavioral objectives need to be developed in coordination with the planned use of mass communication. The mass media can be powerful influences in society. But in the complex process of social change for health promotion, the mass media represent only one of the numerous sectors that must be activated. (p. 336)

Creation of New Opinions. It is probably easier to introduce a new belief than to change a well-developed one. There is abundant evidence that the mass media can create new opinions on issues (Klapper, 1960), but there is much less evidence that the media can change strongly held attitudes. Researchers at the University of North Carolina were apparently cognizant of these findings when they designed an antismoking campaign in 1986. They decided that it made more sense to persuade young people not to start smoking than to convince smokers to give up the habit (Bauman et al., 1988).

Making a Personal Connection. A campaign is likely to succeed to the extent that it can induce receivers to make a personal connection with the message (Dervin, 1981). A message must "make sense" to a receiver; that is, it must link up with the receiver's own needs and values. The notion of personal connectiveness helps explain the popularity of a PSA that used a fried egg as a metaphor for the damage that drugs can do to the human brain. Most people, after all, know what it is like to fry an egg. Therefore, they could easily relate to the PSA that used the fried egg as a symbol for frying your brain on cocaine.

Although contemporary researchers have "a more balanced view" of campaign effects (Rogers & Storey, 1987), there is still considerable debate about what constitutes a successful campaign. Given the difficulty of reaching at-risk groups, is it sufficient for a campaign to increase awareness of the problem? Or should success be defined in more behavioral terms? How does one balance out positive effects on one part of the social system with negative effects on another sector of society? These are difficult questions; the answers ultimately depend on the focus of the campaign, the available resources, and the value priorities of the campaign planners.

APPLYING PERSUASION THEORY
TO COMMUNICATION CAMPAIGNS

The strength of the research on campaigns is that it examines message effects in the real world. Its weakness is that studies are not often derived from theory, but instead are one-shot attempts to evaluate a particular campaign. Persuasion theories can enrich our understanding of campaign effects. They can identify the processes by which campaign messages influence attitudes and behavior. This section outlines the implications that major persuasion theories have for information campaigns. In the case of each theoretical approach, a specific, highly practical suggestion for campaign practitioners is derived.

Use a Trustworthy Communicator. During World War II, the U.S. government enlisted singer Kate Smith to help persuade Americans to buy war bonds. Smith was a phenomenal success. "At the zenith of her career," Klapper (1960) noted, "Kate Smith succeeded in obtaining 'thirty-nine million dollars of (war) bond pledges in the course' of an 18-hour radio marathon" (p. 102). Smith's success was due in no small measure to the widespread perception that she was a trustworthy source. Her message seemed all the more persuasive because it could not easily be attributed to knowledge or reporting biases. Some individuals bought war bonds simply on the advice of Kate Smith. Asked what they thought of Smith, these persons said that: "She talk how the mother talk to the children." "You know what she says is true. Next to God she comes when she tells it to you" (Merton, 1946, p. 150).

Needless to say, campaign specialists cannot assume that a source who they regard as trustworthy (or as credible) will be viewed in this light by members of the target audience. A campaign planner may believe that the U.S. surgeon general is a credible source for conveying AIDS information, but members of the target audience (IV drug users) may distrust established sources, especially government leaders. A peer or a convert communicator may be more effective with IV drug users (Perloff & Pettey, 1991). Thus, it behooves campaign architects to pretest campaign materials on members of their target audience before beginning the actual campaign.[7]

Target Salient Beliefs. Fishbein and Ajzen (1975) argued that messages are most likely to change attitudes when the arguments target salient beliefs. Following Fishbein and Ajzen's procedure, Bauman et al. (1988) asked ninth graders to indicate the likelihood that they would experience various negative consequences if they smoked. The researchers then performed statistical analyses to determine the consequences that best predicted whether nonsmokers continued to abstain from cigarettes a year later. The consequences that best predicted continued nonsmoking were bad breath, difficulty concentrating, loss of friends, and trouble with adults; these were salient negative consequences of smoking cigarettes. Notice that none of the teenagers listed "dying of cancer" as a negative consequence of smoking. To a teenager, death is far off and foreboding— it is not something that occurs to an adolescent when he or she thinks about smoking cigarettes. The researchers took this information into account when they devised their ads. Their PSAs focused on beliefs (such as those listed above) that were salient and of central importance to teenagers. A sample PSA is given here.

Teenage actor:	I don't think any of my friends would be glad if I started smoking cigarettes. Some people put up with smoking, you know, but . . . but, they really don't like it. And some of my friends think smoking is really pretty stupid. That about wraps it up. There's no way I'm going to start smoking.
Teenage announcer:	Not smoking. The right choice.
	(from Bauman et al., 1988, p. 519)

Promote Self-Efficacy. To produce permanent changes in behavior, persuasive messages must convince individuals that they are personally capable of modifying their behavior. Communicators must persuade audience members that they "have got it within themselves" to change the maladaptive behavior. The belief that one is personally capable of performing a recommended behavior is called a self-efficacy perception (see chapter 7). Thus, if you want to get people to quit smoking, adopt a low-cholesterol diet, or practice safe sex, you have to convince them that they have the psychological ability to make these behavioral changes.

Stanford University researchers put self-efficacy theory into practice by devising a series of messages that were designed to promote self-efficacy on the topics of diet and exercise (Maibach, Flora, & Nass, 1991). The promotional materials consisted of media public service announcements, eight-page newsletters, self-help behavior change kits, and contests (including a contest in which smokers who had successfully kicked the habit could win a trip to Hawaii).

Maibach et al. (1991) found that the information campaign increased perceptions of self-efficacy. That is, campaign exposure increased participants' confidence that they could avoid eating fatty foods, that they could reduce their intake of eggs and red meat, and that they could exercise regularly. These increments in self-efficacy in turn contributed to changes in dietary and exercise behavior.

Get People Thinking. The cognitive response approach contends that a message will change attitudes to the extent that it stimulates the development of positive thoughts (see chapter 5). One way to stimulate proarguments is to provide the individual with the opportunity to cognitively elaborate on a campaign message. A recent AIDS advertisement adopted this approach. The spot showed a couple dancing at a party. Subsequently, the man and woman verbalized their thoughts about the situation.

> Boy (thinking to self): I wonder if she'd go out to the car with me. I meant to buy a rubber, but it's not easy and it can be embarrassing. Maybe she's on the pill. Girl (thinking to self): I want to be closer to him but I don't want to get pregnant, and I suppose I should worry about AIDS. Boy (talking aloud): Let's go back to the car. Voice over: Think before you go back to the car. Girl (talking aloud): Are you protected? Voice over: Learn to talk to each other. Deciding to have sex is a serious matter. (from Freimuth, Hammond, Edgar, & Monahan, 1990, p. 787)

Inoculate the Receiver. Inoculation theory argues that one can increase resistance to persuasion by exposing people to a weakened dose of the message you want them to resist and then providing them with counterarguments to refute this information.

McAlister, Perry, and Maccoby (1979) employed inoculation theory techniques in an educational curriculum developed for junior high school students. Students created skits in which they were first called "chicken" for not accepting a cigarette (inoculation). Resistance was then instilled by having the child respond by saying "I would be a chicken if I smoked just to impress you." The investigators compared cigarette intake among children exposed to the program with those in a control school that did not receive the treatment. The results indicated that the program led to a significant reduction in cigarette consumption; indeed, the students told the investigators that "hardly anybody smokes now."

Use Involvement Strategically. Flora and Maibach (1990) argued, based on the ELM, that different AIDS messages should be directed at individuals high and low in involvement. The investigators measured involvement by asking their college student subjects to indicate the degree to which seven Likert-type items described their own cognitive activity with respect to AIDS (e.g., I think about sexually transmitted diseases and AIDS a great deal; I consider myself at risk of developing a sexually transmitted disease or AIDS). Then they showed subjects three rational and three emotionally oriented PSAs. In one rational spot, Carlos Imperado, "a young Latino actor from the show Fame, (discusses) how AIDS can and cannot be contracted." In an emotional spot, "a white nurse in her late-30s with a former intravenous drug habit (explains) how she contracted AIDS and what she would change about her life if she could" (Flora & Maibach, 1990, p. 765).

Low-involved subjects remembered the emotional PSAs better than the rational spots. However, there were no differences for highly involved subjects. The results suggest that the target audience's level of involvement must be taken into account in planning an AIDS information campaign. If the audience consists predominately of individuals who do not care much about AIDS and do not see it as "their problem," the messages should make sure they use vivid emotional images and capture viewers' attention.

Strategically Promote Inconsistencies.   According to contemporary dissonance theorists, dissonance is aroused when an individual performs a behavior that is discrepant with an important aspect of his or her self-concept. A similar approach, one with interesting implications for information campaigns, has been developed by Rokeach (1971). Rokeach and his colleagues deliberately provoked an inconsistency by giving individuals information that suggests their cognitions are inconsistent with their self-concepts. This was designed to motivate individuals to change the dissonant cognitions. Ball-Rokeach, Rokeach, and Grube (1984) employed this technique in a unique communication campaign called The Great American Values Test. The Great American Values Test was broadcast over three television stations in eastern Washington state. The program was co-hosted by actor Ed Asner and Sandy Hill, a former anchorperson of ABC's "Good Morning America." The co-hosts first discussed what values are and how they are measured. Then they introduced viewers to the self-confrontation treatment that was "intended gently to prod viewers to examine their own values and attitudes for internal consistency and, more important, for consistency with idealized self-conceptions" (Ball-Rokeach et al., 1984, p. 73). One treatment tried to get viewers to reflect on their commitment to the value of a world of beauty. Hill observed that:

> Young people start out with a natural appreciation of beauty. But in the process of growing up we somehow knock this appreciation out of them. Eleven year olds rank *a world of beauty* seventh in importance. Fifteen year olds rank it fourteenth. And by the time they reach adulthood, *a world of beauty* has plummeted to seventeenth down the list of importance . . . and there it remains for most adult Americans (a full-screen graphic of these statistics was shown). Maybe that explains why so many Americans are willing to live with pollution and ugliness. (p. 76)

Hill then noted individuals who have little regard for environmental beauty rank "a *comfortable life* higher than they rank *a world of beauty.*" But

she added, "it is the other way around when you survey environmental-
ists. They rank *a world of beauty* sixth on the average and a *comfortable life*
seventeenth" (p. 76). Hill was trying to prod viewers into considering the
possibility that they had lost touch with the value they had once placed on
a world of beauty. The treatment worked. Viewers who lived in the city in
which the program had been shown donated nearly twice as much money
to an environmental cause as did individuals who lived in a control city.

Get People to Resist a Bad Message. In the 1980s, a popular media
campaign urged adolescents to "just say no to drugs." The goal of the
campaign, from an interpersonal persuasion perspective, was to provide
teenagers with a new compliance-resisting strategy. But do adolescents
actually employ this technique in everyday interactions?

To explore this question, Reardon, Sussman, and Flay (1989) asked a
sample of seventh graders to indicate how they would resist smoking in
different situations. Situations varied in terms of the type of the relationship (acquaintance vs. friend), amount of pressure placed on the subject to
smoke (one request or two requests), and the number of others present
(dyad vs. group). For example, one pair of questions asked:

1. Imagine that you and your best friend are somewhere alone. Your
best friend is smoking a cigarette and is pressuring you to smoke too. You
do not want to smoke. What would you say to your best friend?
2. What if he/she really wanted you to smoke, and kept pressuring you?
What would you say then? (p. 313)

The researchers found that adolescents used 18 strategies to resist peer
pressure. The most popular strategies were:

1. Simple rejection, or Just say no (e.g., "No, No Thank you").
2. Statements about the usual behavior of the person being offered the
cigarette ("I do not smoke, and never will," "You know I do not smoke").
3. Statements which describe negative beliefs about smoking or expressions of want, need, or desire ("I do not think you should smoke"; "I do
not feel like it").
4. Excuses ("I have a headache," "My mother is calling me").
5. Repeating the strategy used previously ("I'd say the same thing," "I'd
tell him again"). (p. 316)

The results offered mixed support for the usefulness of the popular "just
say no" strategy. On the one hand, it was one of the most preferred
strategies. However, its usefulness differed, depending on the situation.
Adolescents chose to "just say no" when they were dealing with pressure
from less intimate others (acquaintances rather than friends) and when

they were with groups rather than in two-person situations. In two-person situations, adolescents preferred to express their own beliefs, attitudes, and feelings about smoking ("I do not think you should smoke," "I do not feel like it"). Adolescents indicated that they would use more intense compliance-resisting techniques when they were pressured to smoke a second time and when the pressure was coming from more than one person.

These findings have intriguing implications for information campaigns. They suggest that campaign ads that relied exclusively on the simple "just say no" strategy may have missed the mark with many teenagers. Ads should employ the "just say no" appeal only when they depict a situation in which nonintimate others (acquaintances) are putting pressure on a teenager to light up a cigarette. Many situations do not involve acquaintances, however. Friends often try to get friends to smoke—and sometimes these friendly persuaders continue to apply pressure even when the target refuses to comply with their requests. Reardon and her colleagues' research suggests that PSAs that depict these situations should use appeals other than the familiar "just say no." For example, they might have the nonsmoker take a strong stand on the issue, emphatically explaining why cigarettes are bad for people's health and noting that only people with a death wish smoke cigarettes anyway. Or the ads might depict the smoker walking away from the situation.

Summary

If there is one theme that runs through all these theories it is this: Understand the psychology of the audience. The theories differ as to how they address this issue. Some focus on audience members' beliefs, others stress the emotions, and still others examine how individuals select interpersonal persuasion strategies. Despite these differences, there is general agreement that campaign success hinges on an adequate understanding of how the audience member "makes sense of" the campaign situation (Dervin, 1981). Put somewhat differently, there is consensus that researchers must appreciate the Yin and Yang of processes and effects. One cannot achieve campaign effects without understanding how audience members process campaign information.

VALUE AND ETHICAL IMPLICATIONS

Most discussions of campaigns (and of persuasion, too) end with the latest developments in research. This is unfortunate because an exclusive focus on research prevents one from seeing the larger political and social context in which campaigns take place. Campaigns do not take place in a vacuum.

They take place in a particular society at a particular time. They are also profoundly shaped by the political and economic structure of a society. Consider campaigns against smoking and drug-taking. As Beauchamp (1979) noted, smoking and drug-taking have two important defining features:

> First, they occur to a relative minority of our population (even though that minority might number millions of people). Second, they result in significant part from arrangements that are providing substantial benefits or advantages to a majority or powerful minority of citizens. Thus, solving or minimizing these problems requires painful losses, the restructuring of society and the acceptance of new burdens by the most powerful and the most numerous on behalf of the least powerful or the least numerous. (p. 443)

Salmon (1989) noted that most communication campaigns are sponsored and conducted by groups that have substantial power and economic resources. He argued that campaigns conducted by socially disadvantageous groups are unlikely to succeed, because such groups possess relatively few political and economic resources.

The recognition that values play a role in campaigns requires that we take a longer view of campaign effects. Campaigns may have effects on a number of levels, and the effects may cancel out each other. A campaign can be functional at one level (benefit one sector of society) and be dysfunctional at another (harm another institution or group). Pollay (1989) suggested that:

> Nutritional and health programs encouraging weight control may actually exacerbate problems of anorexia or bulimia. Fund-raising pleas, persistently tugging at people's heart strings, may create a numbed indifference to the plight of others, no matter how terrible or pathetic those plights might be. . . . Campaigns about drug use, whether against street drugs or drunk driving, can backfire by role modeling the undesirable behavior and communicating the commonness of the "crime," implying its minor nature. (pp. 189–190)

Scholars like Pollay remind us that values and ethics cannot be separated from the construction of campaigns. Given the large amounts of money spent on campaigns, and their potential to promote social change, it is important to consider these questions and issues. Pollay (1989) sensitively articulated the problem that confronts modern persuasion practitioners:

> There is clearly a substantial social responsibility that accompanies the possession of the power to persuade. . . . The ecological pollution of manufacturing smokestack industries may have a parallel in cultural and

sociological pollution of persuasion industries. Like early ecological pollution, the alleged negative impacts of persuasion may at first be inadvertent and unintended. As more is learned, however, the new knowledge changes moral and political responsibilities and views. What is tolerated or excusable in naivete can become reprehensible with awareness. There is a need to study the cultural effects of the large and still growing persuasion industry, of which information campaigns are a major part. (p. 195)

CONCLUSIONS

Information campaigns are not new—they have been around for at least 200 years. However, campaigns are more plentiful than ever before, and they are capitalizing on the newest techniques in electronic media wizardry. Do campaigns work? Once again, it depends on the circumstance. Happily, modern communication research has provided us with some specific information regarding the conditions under which campaigns are particularly likely to succeed and fail.

Campaigns are particularly successful in creating new opinions and in influencing moderately or weakly held attitudes. They are likely to succeed when the dominant forces of society are behind them, when they try to activate existing beliefs and attitudes, and when they are supplemented by interpersonal influence agents.

Information campaigns often face an uphill fight, however. Unlike business marketers, social marketers frequently "face target markets having the strongest negative dispositions toward their offerings" (Bloom & Novelli, 1981, p. 82). These target markets include drivers who do not use their seat belts, heavy smokers, and adolescents who are experimenting with drugs. An additional obstacle to campaign success is that campaigns frequently fail to reach those in greatest need of information. The knowledge gap research suggests that campaigns may widen existing knowledge gaps between individuals high and low in socioeconomic status. Once again, however, the picture is not entirely bleak. Research suggests that campaigners can close gaps if they adapt the campaign to the cultural beliefs held by members of the target audience, use simple messages, and encourage audience members to attend to the campaign.

It is important to remember that campaigns take place in a larger social and economic context. Campaigns that support the status quo have a built-in advantage. They are likely to receive the lion's share of financial and cultural resources. In addition, it is worth remembering that campaigns can have a positive effect on one sector of society, and a negative impact on another. Yet, when all is said and done, campaigns are a positive force. They represent attempts to use persuasion theory for pro-social purposes, and they represent efforts to channel persuasion concepts in a socially constructive direction. Paisley (1981) put it very well: "To paraphrase Winston Churchill, public communication campaigns seem like a noisy and inefficient way to achieve social change—until you consider the alternatives" (p. 40).

* * *

EXHIBIT 12-1
HISTORY OF INFORMATION CAMPAIGNS

Communication campaigns are profoundly American institutions. Campaigns reflect a basic faith (rooted in the American experience) that people will change their minds in response to sound, fair-minded arguments. Paisley (1981) noted that:

> A society that relies on coercion to implement its plans will refine the arts of coercion. Conversely, a society that relies on persuasion will refine the arts of persuasion. Despite regressions into mob rule and official violence, and despite buy-offs of leaders and constituencies, three centuries of recognizably "American" experience testify that we never refined the arts of coercion and bribery. However, persuasion is another story. Largely through persuasion, one of the most ungovernable societies in the world also became one of the most progressive. The path that winds through three centuries from colonial town meetings to today's national multimedia campaigns shows how the arts of persuasion were cultivated in America. (p. 17)

Radical activists like Ben Franklin, John Adams, and Thomas Paine disseminated leaflets, brochures, and even books (including Paine's *Common Sense*, the intellectual best seller of the late-18th century). Yet even as they agitated for political reform, American activists sowed the seeds for later social and health campaigns by making a public case for the rights of Blacks and women, and by arguing for abstinence from alcohol (Paisley, 1981).

One of the most celebrated campaigns of the 19th century was the fight to ban alcoholic substances, launched by the Women's Christian Temperance Union (WCTU). The WCTU used media publicity, contests, and exhibits to convince Americans to "just say no to alcohol." One study of the WCTU noted that:

> No effort in our era at mass communications about alcohol comes close to matching the outpouring of materials for the mass audience by the temperance movement in the nineteenth century. For decades the American public was flooded with temperance pamphlets, temperance novels, temperance newspapers, temperance sermons, and temperance lectures—the longest sustained and perhaps the largest organized effort at mass communication about a social issue that the country has ever seen. (Room, 1977, p. 22)

While the WCTU was pressing for the prohibition of alcoholic substances, other social reformers, including abolitionists, women's suffragists, and the urban muckrakers, were waging public campaigns to effect social change.

EXHIBIT 12-2   **333**

The beginning of the 20th century brought a qualitative change in the nature of information campaigns. Campaigns of the early 20th century capitalized on the new media technologies (film and radio) and were spearheaded by governments that wanted to mobilize public support for the war effort during World War I (Jowett & O'Donnell, 1986).

The enormous success of the U.S. information campaign during World War I suggested to many observers that a new era of mass media communication was at hand. Edward Bernays, the nephew of Sigmund Freud, adapted his uncle's theories to the new field of public relations. Bernays, working for the tobacco industry, came up with the idea that cigarette companies could make millions by appealing to an entirely new market—women. Based on Freud's theory, Bernays argued that women were looking for a "torch of freedom"; cigarettes, he suggested, could give women this freedom. Bernays arranged to have a parade take place in midtown Manhattan, and he made sure that women were photographed lighting a cigarette—the new "torch of freedom." The idea caught on, and the cigarette companies were on their way to making millions of dollars from the new "liberated female market."

At the same time, journalist Walter Lippmann was writing about the important role that a new force exerted in the field of mass persuasion. Lippmann called this force public opinion; he argued that mass media had the power to steer and mold public opinion in a variety of directions. During the 1930s and 1940s, governments expended enormous time and effort to manipulate public opinion. The Nazis used documentary films and media psychology as practiced by Joseph Goebbels (as well as a heavy dose of barbarism and terror), to induce the German people to support the Nazi movement. The United States waged a full-fledged information campaign to mobilize public opinion behind the war effort; Hollywood directors (Frank Capra) and show business personalities (Kate Smith) were employed to boost morale for the Allied side.

The next major development in campaigns came in the 1960s, with the movement to persuade Americans to quit smoking. Groups like the American Cancer Society developed numerous antismoking PSAs and mounted large-scale campaigns to educate Americans about the dangers of cigarette smoking. Partly as a result of these efforts, tobacco ads were banned from radio and television; the ban took effect in 1971.

Over the past two decades, numerous groups have waged grass-roots information campaigns. Campaigns have focused on such issues as drinking and driving, seat-belt use, teenage pregnancy, drugs, and, of course, AIDS. Two centuries after the first American political campaign was waged by Franklin, Paine, and their colleagues, campaigns remain an integral part of the American landscape.

* * *

EXHIBIT 12-2
SEAT BELT USE: A CAMPAIGN FAILURE

Federal authorities estimate that thousands of fatalities and injuries from car crashes would be prevented if seat belts were used; yet 75% of adults fail to use a seat belt (Geller, 1989). Over the past 20 years, numerous campaigns have tried to convince individuals that they should buckle up their safety belts. One of the most famous of these campaigns was conducted in the early 1970s by Robertson. Robertson et al. (1974) used fear appeals to convince the public to buckle up its seat belts. An example of one of their PSAs appears here:

> A teenaged girl is shown sitting in a rocking chair looking out a window. She says "I'm not sick or anything. I could go out more but since the car crash, I just do not. . . . The crash wasn't Dad's fault. I go for walks with my father after dark . . . that way, I don't get, you know, stared at." She turns enough to reveal a large scar on what was the hidden side of her face. She continues, "It doesn't hurt anymore." An announcer says off-camera, "Car crashes kill two ways: right away and little by little. Wear your safety belts and live!" (p. 1073)

The messages were shown for 9 months on one cable of a dual cable TV system. Households that subscribed to this cable constituted the experimental group, whereas homes that had the other cable or did not have cable TV at all served as the control.

Robertson had observers monitor seat belt use prior to the campaign and a month after the campaign had ended. Observers noted whether the driver was wearing a seat belt; they also wrote down the vehicle license plate number. With the help of city authorities, Robertson et al. were able to match license plate numbers with names and addresses; subsequently, they were able to match names and addresses with the cable that was assigned to particular households.

The campaign had no impact on seat belt use. Robertson and his colleagues found that drivers who subscribed to the experimental cable channel and those who subscribed to the control channel did not differ in their use of seat belts. Robertson (1976) aptly titled an article describing the campaign, "The Great Seat Belt Campaign Flop."

What happened? Why did the campaign fail? In the first place, seat-belt use is a well-learned habit, and habits are hard to change. Attitudes are less likely to predict behavior in cases where strong habits have been formed. In such cases, individuals have less volitional control over their behavior, and they are less capable of translating attitudes into action.

Second, the seat belt message ran into cognitive and emotional barriers. The message that serious consequences befall those who do not wear their seat belts is inconsistent with everyday experience. Most people are well aware that on a number of occasions they failed to put on their seat belts, yet did not get into an accident of any kind. Statistics showing that people are more likely to survive an accident if they are wearing a seat belt run up against individuals' knowledge, obtained from direct experience, that this has not happened to them.

The campaign also ran up against individuals' perceptions that they are invulnerable to bad events. People harbor an "illusion of invulnerability," a belief that they are somehow shielded from life's misfortunes (Perloff & Fetzer, 1986; Weinstein, 1980). Thus, a viewer might acknowledge that failure to wear safety belts increases the chances of getting hurt or killed in a car crash; but he or she undoubtedly would perceive that "this kind of thing happens to other people. . . . I drive safely; this won't happen to me."[8]

More recent seat belt campaigns have employed a different strategy. Soames Job

EXHIBIT 12-2   **335**

(1988) argued that most people do not believe that death is a likely outcome of not wearing a seat belt. People are more likely to fear that they will be stopped by a police officer and given a ticket. Soames Job (1988) reported that a message emphasizing the latter consequence significantly influenced seat belt usage. Geller (1989) argued that modeling approaches are more effective than fear appeals in the area of safety communications. He contended that if popular television characters were shown putting on a safety belt whenever they drove a car, this would increase the use of seat belts among the viewing public.

Endnotes

Chapter 1

1. The quoted comments are excerpted from Jones (1984, pp. 259–266).
2. Naftulin, Ware, and Donnelly (1973, p. 630).
3. Naftulin, Ware, and Donnelly (1973, pp. 631–632); see, also, Padgett and Brock (1988).
4. See *Time*, March 26, 1984.
5. Puska et al. (1979, p. 27).
6. The various comments attributed to Shelley Liebert are excerpted from Enroth (1977, pp. 97–121). Enroth did not use the actual names of the individuals he interviewed; he changed the names to protect the anonymity of the participants.
7. Lofland (1977).
8. On the other hand, one army psychiatrist who studied the Korean War indoctrination concluded that one third of all American soldiers captured in Korea sympathized with the Communists or collaborated with them (see *U.S. News and World Report*, 1956). However, temporary changes in attitude or confessions under physical and psychological duress are not synonymous with giving up one's cherished values and accepting communist ideals.

Chapter 2

1. Pratkanis (1989) has suggested that, in addition to being supported by bipolar and unipolar knowledge structures, attitudes also are supported by technical knowledge structures, scripts (organized sets of expectations about events), and other types of knowledge schemas.
2. At present, there is little research that can guide practitioners who seek to tailor their persuasive strategies to the type and structure of the attitudes that are held by audience members. For example, Zanna and Rempel (1988) suggest that emotional appeals are most effective in influencing attitudes based on affect, whereas Millar and Tesser (1986) might suggest that asking people to think about the reasons why they hold an affectively based attitude (a cognitive strategy) would

be most effective.

3. For purposes of simplicity, we have referred to only two of the products that Shavitt used in her 1990 study. It should be noted that Shavitt (1990) presented subjects with two products that serve a utilitarian function (coffee and air conditioners) and two products that serve a social identity function (perfume and greeting cards). She found that for coffee and air conditioners, the utilitarian appeal was more effective, whereas for perfume and greeting cards, the social identity ad exerted a stronger impact on attitudes.

4. I have borrowed from, and substantially adapted, the form Zimbardo, Ebbesen, and Maslach (1977) used to present attitude scales.

5. A number of studies have also probed the ways in which question wording, order of questions, and context can influence responses to questions tapping social and political attitudes. A detailed review of this literature is beyond the scope of this chapter; however, the interested reader may wish to consult Robinson and Meadow (1982), Schuman and Kalton (1985), and Tourangeau, Rasinski, Bradburn, and D'Andrade (1989).

Chapter 3

1. Some writers (e.g., Merikle, 1982) have distinguished between "objective" and "subjective" criteria for stimulus awareness. Specifically, these researchers distinguish "objective" awareness criteria, wherein individuals cannot recognize stimuli presented at subliminal exposure durations at better-than-chance levels in any situation from "subjective" criteria, wherein subjects claim that they cannot recognize a stimulus, but are, in fact, able to perform at levels that exceed chance in subsequent recognition tasks. Some researchers have argued that early studies employed subjective awareness criteria when they should have used objective criteria.

2. Psychophysiological studies have provided strong evidence that stimuli perceived without awareness can influence judgments (Bevan, 1964; Dixon, 1971). Silverman and Spiro (1967) tested the hypothesis, derived from Freudian theory, that subliminal stimuli can activate unconscious wishes, and thereby influence behavior. Silverman and Spiro found support for this hypothesis (see Balay & Shevrin, 1988, for a critique). Most recently, experimental social psychologists have shown that subliminal stimuli can, through a process of psychological priming, influence perceptions of unfamiliar others (Bargh & Pietromonaco, 1982; Kitayama, 1990; Niedenthal, 1990).

3. The tendency to assume that subliminal advertising messages seduce people into buying products should be viewed in the larger context of people's predisposition to overestimate media effects on others (Davison, 1983; Gunther, 1991) and the popular assumption that new communications technologies will exert a strong negative impact on attitudes (Wartella & Reeves, 1985).

4. My own suspicion is that the student dressed up in a black bag to protest the depersonalized, overly bureaucratic, and deindividuated atmosphere of the big university. Remember, this was the 1960s.

5. In contrast to these findings, Fink, Monahan, and Kaplowitz (1989) found that repeated exposure to simple stimuli exerted a stronger impact on affective prefer-

ences than did exposure to complex stimuli. In fact, the role that stimulus complexity plays in moderating the mere exposure effect continues to be an issue that stimulates debate.

6. Some researchers take a cognitive view of mere exposure, arguing that for mere exposure to work subjects must subjectively recognize the stimulus (Birnbaum & Mellers, 1979). Others argue that mere exposure is more affective; they assert that individuals can come to like stimuli to which they have been repeatedly exposed in the absence of any conscious awareness of the stimuli (Bornstein, Leone, & Galley, 1987; Moreland & Zajonc, 1979). There is more evidence on the side of the affective theorists, which led Zajonc (1980) to conclude that "preferences need no inferences."

7. Thus, there is strong evidence that repeated exposure to products—in this case, political products—leads to increased liking. However, we need to be careful about making simple generalizations about advertising effects based on findings from mere exposure research. Most of the studies that we have discussed have examined repeated exposure to nonsense syllables or other unfamiliar stimuli. However, television advertisements present stimuli (product images and product information) that are both more familiar and more complex than the stimuli used in these experiments (Sawyer, 1981). Thus, the effects of repetition of consumer products on liking depend on a host of other factors, including the nature of the product, the consumer's involvement with the ad, and the emotional level of the ad (Ray, 1973; Thorson, 1989).

8. One might also expect, based on the results of a recent study conducted by Cacioppo and his colleagues, that classical conditioning effects would be stronger when individuals have little knowledge about the ethnic group (CS) than when they have a great deal of knowledge about the racial or ethnic group (Cacioppo, Marshall-Goodell, Tassinary, & Petty, 1992).

Chapter 4

1. It is important to emphasize that if instead of encouraging the individual to focus attention on the self, the situation encourages the person to analyze the reasons why he or she holds a particular attitude, the correlation between attitude and behavior is likely to be relatively low. In such a situation, a person may obsessively think about why he or she feels the way that he or she does, and this may put the person out of touch with the feelings and affective evaluations that play such an important role in guiding and influencing the behavior (see Millar & Tesser, 1986; Wilson, Dunn, Kraft, & Lisle, 1989).

More precisely, Wilson et al. (1989) argued that thinking about reasons "causes people to recast their attitudes in cognitive terms, and that these attitudes then conflict with behavior that is affectively based" (p. 319). (See Millar & Tesser, 1986, for a somewhat different explanation of the effects of thinking about reasons on attitude–behavior correspondence.) To make matters more complicated, there is also evidence that self-focus and self-reflection can have different effects on A–B consistency, depending on whether the action is affectively or cognitively driven (Millar & Tesser, 1986).

2. Not only do individuals differ in the extent to which they exhibit attitude–be-

havior consistency, but the same individual typically exhibits A–B consistency for some behaviors, and some attitudes, but not for others (see Norman, 1976). This point has been discussed in some detail by Zanna and Rempel (1988). Zanna and Rempel argued that an attitude is best conceptualized as a global evaluation that is based on three different classes of information: cognitive information (factual beliefs), affective information (feelings), and behavioral information (information concerning previous behaviors).

According to this view, attitudes should predict behavior when the attitude is based on consistent sources of information; however, attitudes should be unlikely to predict behavior when the sources of information contradict each other. As an example, consider an individual whose attitude toward sex roles is based on consistent sources of information, but whose attitude toward religion is based on inconsistent sources of information. In the first case, the individual may strongly believe in affirmative action for women (cognitive information), and may also evaluate the Women's Liberation Movement very favorably (affective information). In addition, the individual may in the past have shared child-care responsibilities with his wife (behavioral information). According to Zanna and Rempel (1988), the individual's attitude toward sex roles should predict his behavior.

On the other hand, the same individual may be more ambivalent about religion. Although he may have good feelings about his religion as a result of a strong religious upbringing (affective information), he may have negative beliefs about religion as a result of having subjected his religious philosophy to serious questions during his undergraduate years (cognitive information). At the same time, he may have attended religious services occasionally over the past couple of years (behavioral information). Zanna and Rempel's (1988) model suggested that, in the case of religion, this individual should exhibit relatively little attitude–behavior correspondence. More generally, Zanna and Rempel have noted that "attitudes (and behavior) of individuals with ambivalent attitudes will be highly variable or volatile, and seemingly inconsistent" (p. 326).

3. There is currently a debate about whether more than two factors underlie the self-monitoring scale. For example, Briggs, Cheek, and Buss (1980) conducted a factor analysis of the self-monitoring scale and found that there were three underlying factors: acting ability, extraversion, and other directedness. However, Snyder (1987) has questioned these results, based on the results of his own factor analytic studies of self-monitoring (Gangestad & Snyder, 1985). Snyder (1987) contended that self-monitoring is a "latent causal entity that is discretely distributed into two types: high and low self-monitoring" (p. 159). For a discussion of these and other issues relating to the structural properties of self-monitoring, see Briggs et al. (1980), Gangestad and Snyder (1985), and Lennox and Wolfe (1984).

4. Manstead et al. (1983), Sherman et al. (1982), and Songer-Nocks (1976) found that direct experience with the attitude object enhances the weight of the attitudinal component in forecasting behavioral intentions. Schlegel and DiTecco (1982) have found that in the case of attitudes toward marijuana, A–B consistency increases with more experience, but only if a comprehensive multidimensional measure of attitude is used.

5. Ajzen and his colleagues have acknowledged that these problems plague the theory of reasoned action (Ajzen & Madden, 1985; Schifter & Ajzen, 1985). In an effort to come to grips with these problems, Ajzen (1985) proposed a theory of planned behavior. According to Ajzen, there are a number of situations in which

individuals only have limited control over their behavior. For example, an individual may intend to quit smoking, but, for a variety of psychological reasons, he or she may be unable to do so; in this situation, intention to quit smoking will not predict actual behavior. This represents an important shortcoming in the theory of reasoned action.

Ajzen's (1985, 1989) theory of planned behavior extends the theory of reasoned action by postulating that behavioral intention is a function of three antecedent factors: attitude, subjective norm, and perceived behavioral control, "the person's belief as to how easy or difficult performance of the behavior is likely to be" (Ajzen & Madden, 1986, p. 457). Two studies have provided strong support for the theory (Ajzen & Madden, 1986; Schifter & Ajzen, 1985). Ajzen and Madden found that the planned behavior theory allowed more accurate prediction of intentions and behavior than did the theory of reasoned action. In addition, in a study of prediction of weight loss behavior, Schifter and Ajzen (1985) found that intention to lose weight predicted weight loss behavior only for subjects who perceived that they could control attainment of the weight loss goal.

6. The accessibility notion helps us understand how attitudes influence behavior. One can take the "how" question further, however, by trying to determine just how accessible attitudes guide action. Fazio (1986) developed a model of attitude–behavior relations that spells out the processes by which attitude activation leads to behavior. Fazio (1986) argued that for an attitude to influence behavior, it must first be activated (i.e., come spontaneously to mind) when the individual encounters the attitude object. Second, the attitude must influence perceptions of the object. Thus, if a person has a positive attitude toward the object (e.g., a product), the individual is expected to dwell on the positive aspects of the object, whereas if the individual has a negative attitude toward the object, he or she is expected to focus primarily on the negative aspects of the object. Third, these perceptions should influence the person's definition or interpretation of the event (the behavior or context in which the behavior occurs). These interpretations should in turn influence behavior.

7. For evidence that chronic attitude accessibility can be validly assessed by response latency measures, see Fazio, Sanbonmatsu, Powell, and Kardes (1986).

8. See Wu and Shaffer (1987) and the discussion of low-involvement processing in chapter 5.

9. Fazio's model and the theory of reasoned action make different assumptions about the processes by which attitudes guide behavior. Fazio's model stipulates that attitudes guide behavior through spontaneous, automatic processes, whereas Ajzen and Fishbein assume that attitudes influence action through more "effortful reasoning" (Fazio, 1990). However, the models should be viewed as complementary. In fact, Fazio (1990) has argued that his model provides a more useful explanation of attitude–behavior correspondence in the case of everyday decisions that are made with little conscious reflection (such as everyday consumer purchases), whereas the theory of reasoned action is ideally suited for explaining decisions that involve more conscious deliberation (such as the decision to accept a job in a different city).

Chapter 5

1. Distraction has the opposite effect in the case of a proattitudinal message. In this situation, distraction blocks the formulation of proarguments, which reduces

yielding to the message. Petty, Wells, and Brock (1976) have proposed a thought disruption interpretation of distraction effects. According to this view, distraction blocks the dominant cognitive response to a message. To simplify issues, we have focused only on the counterattitudinal side – the notion that distraction facilitates persuasion by blocking arguments with a counterattitudinal message.

2. It should be noted that one analysis of the distraction research (Buller, 1986) found little support for the cognitive response view. However, other reviews (e.g., Perloff & Brock, 1980; Petty, & Brock, 1981) have argued that the cognitive response approach offers the best interpretation of the available data. Moreover, by no means all of the studies Buller examined in his meta-analysis permitted an estimate of the effect of distraction on counterarguing. Thus, as Buller acknowledged, his study may not have been able to put the cognitive response explanation to a fair test.

3. Although Osterhouse and Brock's (1970) study resolved some of the methodological problems that plagued early distraction research, it did not rule out an interpretation based on cognitive dissonance theory (see chapter 10). According to this view, it requires a great deal of effort to listen to a counterattitudinal message under conditions of distraction. Dissonance theory contends that when people have to expend effort on an unpleasant activity, they experience cognitive dissonance. Dissonance is an unpleasant state, hence people are motivated to reduce it. One way that subjects can reduce dissonance is to change their attitude in the direction advocated by the message (i.e., to rationalize to themselves that the effort they expended in listening to the message was worth it because the speaker had a lot of good things to say).

Petty, Wells, and Brock (1976) pitted the effort justification hypothesis against the cognitive response view. They constructed two messages: one that was easy to counterargue (it contained weak arguments), and one that was difficult to counterargue (it had solid, cogent arguments that were hard to contest). Subjects listened to the messages under conditions of high, moderate, low, and no distraction. The effort justification interpretation predicts that with increasing distraction, there should be increasing effort expended; therefore there should be increasing agreement with both messages. On the other hand, the cognitive response view emphasizes that the two messages should disrupt different types of thoughts, and therefore should have very different effects.

The logic is that under normal (nondistracting) conditions, the easy-to-counterargue message will evoke counterarguments. After all, if the message is easy to argue with, then subjects should have no trouble coming up with counterarguments. To the extent that the distraction inhibits the production of counterarguments, increased persuasion should result. By contrast, under normal conditions, a difficult-to-argue message should primarily evoke positive thoughts or proarguments. To the extent that subjects are distracted from generating these favorable thoughts, they should be less likely to accept the position advocated in the message. The results provided strong support for the cognitive response view.

4. Recently, scholars have argued that reception processes may play a greater role in attitude change than has been previously assumed. Chaiken and Stangor (1987) argued that simple measures of message recall are, by their very nature, insensitive indices of message reception processes. Several recent studies, using more sensitive measurement procedures, have reported strong associations between mea-

sures of argument retention and attitudes (e.g., Chattopadhyay & Alba, 1988). In addition, Tesser and Shaffer (1990) have noted that there may be some conditions (perhaps when two-sided messages are employed) in which recall is a particularly important mediator of message effects.

5. On the other hand, Bretl and Dillard (1991) found that externally generated thoughts predicted attitude change better than internally generated cognitions. Thus, although there is strong evidence that individuals remember their own cognitions better than those of others, the impact of own thoughts on persuasion appears to be more complicated than Perloff and Brock (1980) originally assumed. Clearly, own thoughts influence the attitude change process; however, the extent of their influence and the conditions that facilitate their impact have yet to be determined by empirical research.

6. The ELM also provides a framework for viewing and understanding the different theories of persuasion. Thus, the central route refers to a family of persuasion theories that emphasizes that attitude change results from the diligent processing of issue-relevant information. These theories include the Yale Theories of Attitude Change (Hovland, Janis, & Kelley, 1953; McGuire, 1969), the cognitive response approach, information integration theory (Anderson, 1971), and the theory of reasoned action (Fishbein & Ajzen, 1975). The peripheral route refers to a group of persuasion theories that emphasizes that attitude change can occur in the absence of message-relevant thinking. These theories include classical conditioning, script theory, and other theories that suggest that people go along with messages to comply with a powerful source or to obtain social approval from others.

7. See, for example, Petty, Cacioppo, and Heesacker (1985); Cacioppo, Petty, Kao, and Rodriguez (1986); and Wu and Shaffer (1987).

8. There is a debate about whether involvement leads to biased or objective processing (Johnson & Eagly, 1989; Petty & Cacioppo, 1990). We have sidestepped this issue by focusing on extremity of initial attitude. The debate about involvement is discussed in chapter 9.

9. Just as attractiveness can serve as a peripheral cue in some situations and a central argument in others, so too can attractiveness operate as a peripheral factor for some people and as a central issue for others. Consider the case of self-monitors. DeBono and Harnish (1988) argued that high self-monitors should be more attentive to a source's attractiveness, given their concern with appearances. Low self-monitors, being more concerned with the expression of underlying values, should regard attractiveness as peripheral to the arguments in the message and should focus instead on source expertise. DeBono and Harnish (1988) found that high self-monitors were sensitive to the quality of message arguments when they were delivered by a highly attractive source, but were less responsive when the same arguments were presented by an expert communicator. By contrast, low self-monitors processed the arguments more superficially when the attractive source delivered the message, but were more mindful when the expert gave the speech.

10. Stiff and Boster (1987) argued that the ELM is unable to specify a priori (or at the beginning of the study) the contextual and individual difference factors that will determine whether a particular variable serves as a peripheral cue or a persuasive argument. Until the model does this, they argued, it will be possible for adherents to explain any outcome and conclude that any finding is consistent with the model.

Stiff and Boster's (1987) point is worth considering. However, it in no way represents a fatal flaw in the model. There are a variety of ways that the model can make a priori predictions as to whether a given variable will serve as a peripheral cue or a persuasive argument. For example, one would expect that, everything else being equal, message arguments are more likely to be processed centrally by individuals high than low in the need for cognition, and that stimuli that are processed centrally are more likely to exert an impact over time than those which are processed peripherally. These predictions can be made a priori, and therefore they are capable of being falsified. Other a priori predictions also can be generated, but they need to be made explicit if the ELM is to continue to make important contributions to the field of persuasion research.

11. Notice that the ELM views voters as either dutiful citizens or passive processors, depending on their level of involvement. This suggests that, under some conditions, voters are described by the "rational voter" model (Campbell, Converse, Miller, & Stokes, 1960), whereas under other conditions they are best described by affective theories of political decision making (Abelson, Kinder, Peters, & Fiske, 1982).

12. Space limitations prohibit a description of all of the various avenues of cognitive response research. One area of research deserves comment, however. This is Cacioppo and his colleagues' work on the interface between cognitive responses and physiological functioning. In an early study, Cacioppo and Petty (1979) found that when subjects were forewarned that the university was considering a plan to increase tuition and were led to believe that they would hear a message describing this proposal, they not only generated more counterarguments, they also showed increased activity in the heart and speech musculature. This suggested that cognitive responding could produce certain (highly specific) physiological effects. Cacioppo and his colleagues have integrated these findings into a general model of psychophysiology and cognitive responses. A more detailed description of this line of research can be found in Cacioppo and Sandman (1981) and Cacioppo and Petty (1987).

13. The ELM states that there are two routes to persuasion: a central route and a peripheral pathway. Although the evidence is consistent with this notion, it is difficult to say for sure whether two pathways exist. This type of inference would require pinpoint-accurate knowledge about the human mind, and this type of knowledge is difficult to obtain at the present time.

As a result, there has been a great deal of debate about how people process persuasive messages (Chaiken, Liberman, & Eagly, 1989; Stiff, 1986; Tesser & Shaffer, 1990). Kahle and Homer (1985) contended that there is just one route under which information is processed—they argued that "information is processed in fundamentally the same way for both high- and low-involvement; however, information processing ends more quickly for low involving products" (p. 955). Other scholars have agreed that there are two processing routes, but they have suggested that the routes are not mutually exclusive. Moore, Hausknecht, and Thamodaran (1986) pointed out that central and peripheral processing can co-occur (as when an individual focuses on both the message arguments and the attractiveness of the source).

14. Salzman and O'Reilly (1991, p. 46).

15. Salzman and O'Reilly (1991, p. 46).

16. Salzman and O'Reilly (1991, p. 47).
17. Salzman and O'Reilly (1991, p. 47).
18. Salzman and O'Reilly (1991, p. 31).
19. Salzman and O'Reilly (1991, p. 47).

Chapter 6

1. According to Eagly et al. (1978) the reporting bias corresponds more closely to the concept of communicator trustworthiness than does the knowledge bias. However, it could be argued that a speaker who has transcended a knowledge bias also would be regarded as a trustworthy source. Such a speaker should be perceived to have overcome the biases of his or her background; he or she should be seen as having decided freely and of his or her own volition to adopt the particular position on the issue. Thus, the communicator should be seen as less biased, more objective, and (in a word) more trustworthy than a counterpart who was believed to harbor a knowledge bias on the issue.

2. Chaiken (1986) has interpreted this evidence as consistent with the view that attractiveness functions as a heuristic cue.

3. The excerpts from Tommy's speech are taken from Robertson (1988, pp. 116–117).

Chapter 7

1. One other perspective on fear appeals, noted by Boster and Mongeau (1984) in their excellent review of the fear-appeals literature, is resistance theory. According to the resistance explanation, there should be a negative relationship between the amount of fear-arousing information in a persuasive message and attitude change (i.e., the greater the amount of fear-arousing material, the less the attitude change). However, as we noted earlier, the research strongly indicated that there is a positive relationship between perceived fear and attitudes.

2. One of the persistent issues involving protection motivation theory is the way in which the components combine or interact to influence persuasion. Originally, Rogers (1975) suggested that the components should combine in a multiplicative fashion. However, the results have not supported this prediction (e.g., Maddux & Rogers, 1983). Boster (personal communication) noted that, according to his reading of protection motivation theory, there should be the greatest conformity with message recommendations when noxiousness, probability of occurrence, efficacy of recommended action, and self-efficacy are high; yet he argued that the bulk of the data are not consistent with this claim. It now appears as if the protection motivation components interact in rather complex ways. For example, Maddux and Rogers (1983) found that if any two of the following three components (probability of occurrence, efficacy of recommended action, and self-efficacy) were at a high level, then "a threshold was reached beyond which additional information did not have a significant effect" (p. 476). Clearly, the question of how the protection motivation components combine to influence message acceptance is an important issue for future research.

3. In addition, the way in which the message is communicated *nonverbally*

influences message evaluations. A number of studies have examined the impact of such nonverbal behaviors as eye contact, facial activity, and illustrator gestures on credibility judgments. A detailed review of this literature is beyond the scope of this book. Interesting findings on the nonverbal correlates of perceived persuasiveness have been reported by Burgoon, Birk, and Pfau (1990); Mehrabian and Williams (1969); and London (1973).

4. More specifically, the ELM stipulates that (like other persuasion variables) speed of speech can operate as a peripheral cue or a persuasive argument (if relevant to a decision about the central aspects of the issue), or it can instigate issue-relevant thinking. Thus, for a low-involving decision, speed of speech functions as a peripheral cue; in those (relatively few) decisions in which speaking rate is relevant to a determination of the key aspects of the issue, speed of speech can function as a persuasive argument. Finally, when individuals are moderately knowledgeable about the issue or are trying to reduce uncertainty on the issue, they are likely to examine the persuasion situation to determine if the message is worth thinking about. The fact that the communicator speaks quickly may convince message recipients that the speaker is knowledgeable about the issue, and this may induce listeners to attend more closely to the message arguments.

5. Of course, the bottom line is whether speech style influences jurors' decisions, and here the case for language effects is less compelling. There is scant evidence that subjects in mock jury trials award greater damages to plaintiffs who use powerful (as opposed to powerless) speech (Bradac, Hemphill, & Tardy, 1981).

6. Originally, polite language (e.g., use of intensifiers, deferential speech) was believed to fall into the category of powerless speech. It was thought that being polite expressed deference to authorities. However, when used in the right way, polite language can be a useful weapon in the powerful speech arsenal. Cantor demonstrated this in a field experiment conducted in 1979. Cantor (1979) focused on one form of polite speech—the polite imperative (e.g., "Please contribute to our fund"). She argued that the polite imperative contains a coercive appeal whose very grammar forecloses a response. "Grammatically speaking," Cantor (1979) noted, "it does not anticipate a verbal reply at all; rather, it expects the requested action itself" (p. 298). Cantor (1979) found that volunteers raised more money for the American Cancer Society when they asked individuals to "please contribute to our fund" than when they used other one-line appeals (e.g., "Would you like to contribute to our fund?"; "We are asking you to contribute to our fund").

7. One of the most interesting aspects of the research on speech style is the debate about whether men and women use different forms of speech, and whether people evaluate male and female speech patterns differently. In a book entitled *Language and Woman's Place*, Lakoff (1975) argued that women have been socialized to speak in a powerless fashion; "women's speech," as Lakoff (1975) called it, reflects and reinforces sex role stereotypes and prejudice.

A number of studies have examined whether, in fact, women use language differently than men. Although the research has yielded mixed results (Zahn, 1989), there is general support for the hypothesis that there are gender-linked differences in language use. Thus, women are more likely than men to be polite (Hartman, 1976), more likely to ask tag questions (McMillan, Clifton, McGrath, & Gale, 1977), more inclined to use disclaimers or qualifying phrases (Hartman,

1976), and less likely to interrupt (Eakins & Eakins, 1976; Mulac, Wiemann, Widenmann, & Gibson, 1988).

8. It should be noted that Giles and Smith (1979) have argued that convergence will not lead to favorable evaluations if receivers attribute the speaker's communication behavior to an attempt to ingratiate him or herself with the audience. In addition, these authors have pointed out that there are some conditions under which divergence may enhance evaluations of a speaker (e.g., when listeners perceive that it is socially inappropriate for the speaker to speak in the same stylistic fashion as the audience). Giles and Smith's (1979) arguments have underscored the important role that listener attributions and perceptions play in the communication process.

9. Another language myth is that noncontent cues (such as speed of speech and vocal pitch) exist in isolation. In reality, these speech markers interact. Cappella and Street (1989) pointed out that "fast speech with negative facial affect and in a loud voice can signal anger or criticism whereas fast speech with positive facial affect and a moderately intense voice can signal enthusiasm and poise" (p. 44).

Chapter 8

1. Chaiken and Eagly (1976) derived their hypothesis, in part, from Hovland, Janis, and Kelley's (1953) notion that message comprehensibility enhances attitude change. Based on the theory of Hovland et al., they hypothesized that with difficult messages, comprehension (and, therefore, persuasion) should be greatest when the message is written; and that with easy messages, comprehension should be equivalent across modalities. The results supported their predictions.

2. Chaffee and Mutz (1988) noted that experimental research of this type focuses on the general question of which channel would be most effective if each channel carried identical content and if levels of exposure, attention, and comprehension remained constant across individuals. They suggested that in real life, channels carry different content, and that individuals have different levels of exposure and attention to, as well as comprehension of, this content. Therefore, they argued that research on channel effects in natural settings should focus on the question of "which channel, mass or interpersonal, has been more effective given the content typically carried by each channel and the degree of exposure, attention, and comprehension of these messages that typically occurs" (p. 40). Methodological problems have impeded research of this kind; however, Chaffee and Mutz (1988) provided some suggestions to overcome these problems.

3. Research has examined the impact of a number of individual difference variables on persuasion, including dogmatism (Adams & Beatty, 1977; Roloff & Barnicott, 1978), anxiety (Millman, 1968), and intelligence (Hovland, Lumsdaine, & Sheffield, 1949). We have focused our discussion on gender, self-esteem, and self-monitoring because they have generated a great deal of research and because they allow us to examine the major theoretical perspectives on personality and persuasibility.

4. Eagly (1978) argued, based on the socialization view, that studies published prior to 1970 should reveal greater evidence of female influenceability than those published during the 1970s. Prior to 1970, sex role norms were strictly in force and

women were given little freedom to explore alternatives to the traditional female role. However, in the early 1970s, the Women's Liberation Movement took hold, and it helped to change sex role attitudes and to expand the opportunities available to women. Eagly (1978) found that studies published prior to 1970 revealed greater evidence of female influenceability than those published during the 1970s.

5. Other explanations of the gender differences in influenceability have also been advanced. One view is that the researchers themselves harbored a bias in favor of seeing women as more influenceable than men. Eagly and Carli (1981) found that 79% of the authors of the studies were male; this in itself would not prove that the researchers harbored a bias in favor of seeing women as more influenceable than men. However, studies that were conducted by male investigators were significantly more likely than experiments conducted by female researchers to report women as more susceptible to influence. It is possible that the researchers' gender role stereotypes influenced them in subtle ways. For example, male researchers may have treated the female and male subjects differently; they may have accorded the male subjects more respect, which encouraged them to resist the influence attempt. On the other hand, these researchers may have assumed that the female subjects needed more tender, loving care, which in turn encouraged the women to behave in a more submissive, succorant way. However, Eagly and Carli (1981) dismissed this possibility, noting that there is little evidence that experimenter gender exerts a consistent impact on experimental outcomes.

Eagly and Carli noted that the relationship between gender of authors and gender differences in influenceability may have its roots in the tendency of male and female authors to report results somewhat differently. Noting that researchers may be more likely to report results in a subjective or biased manner when findings of no gender differences are obtained, Eagly and Carli speculated that female researchers may have been more likely to report nonsignificant sex differences in influenceability because they were happy to discover that, contrary to the stereotype, women were not more influenceable than men.

6. Recent studies have explored the processes by which individuals change their attitudes in response to functionally relevant or functionally irrelevant information. DeBono and Harnish (1988) argued that for persuasion to occur there must be "a match between the needs of a message recipient and the potential rewards offered by a message source" (p. 545). Consistent with their hypothesis, DeBono and Harnish (1988) found that high self-monitors processed a message more systematically when the message was delivered by a highly attractive source than by an expert communicator; however, the reverse was true for low self-monitoring individuals. It remains to be seen whether individuals who fall at different ends of the continuum of other personality variables would also systematically process messages that they perceive to be functionally relevant.

Chapter 9

1. There is abundant evidence that own position serves as an anchor for appraising mass mediated political messages, including advertisements and debates (Rouner & Perloff, 1988; Sears & Chaffee, 1979; see also, Kraus, 1962, 1988 for general discussions of debate perceptions and effects).

2. However, according to social judgment theory, unambiguous messages will not be subject to assimilation or contrast effects (Granberg & Brent, 1974). However, such messages probably are few and far between in most persuasive communication situations.

3. Petty and Cacioppo (1990) challenged Johnson and Eagly's (1989) reconceptualization of involvement. Petty and Cacioppo (1990) argued that the negative relationship between value-relevant involvement and persuasion is due to confounding factors—that involvement was confounded with other variables, such as knowledge and prior experience with the attitude object. In contrast to Johnson and Eagly (1989), Petty and Cacioppo (1990) contended that it is more useful to view involvement as one of several variables that determine the intensity of message processing, and to view the direction of message processing (pro or con) as determined by other factors (such as prior issue position). In support of their view, they have interpreted results reviewed by Johnson and Eagly (1989) as indicating that "when involvement is high (whether value relevant or outcome relevant), the quality of the arguments in a message accounts for more variance in attitudes than when involvement is low" (Petty & Cacioppo, 1990, p. 370). In part, the debate between Johnson and Eagly (1989) and Petty and Cacioppo (1990) boils down to whether involvement should be defined as a one-dimensional construct (Petty and Cacioppo's view) or as a multidimensional construct (Johnson and Eagly's position). The debate over whether variables should be defined as one- or multidimensional constructs has a long history in attitude research. Indeed, it harks back to the classic issue of whether attitude itself should be viewed as consisting of three components (cognition, affect, and behavior), or as essentially one component (affect).

4. In social judgment theory terms, the results might be regarded as a contrast effect. In all likelihood, pro-Israeli and pro-Palestinian partisans did not change their own attitudes toward Israel or the PLO after watching the news coverage. Quite the contrary, they probably cognitively rebutted the news reports and came away feeling even more convinced that their side was correct. Yet, as we have noted, they perceived that the same news reports would cause neutral viewers to become more critical of their side.

Chapter 10

1. Cognitive dissonance was one of a number of cognitive consistency theories that was developed in the 1950s and 1960s. These included Heider's (1958) balance theory, Osgood and Tannenbaum's (1955) congruity principle, Rokeach and Rothman's (1965) belief congruence theory, and Rosenberg's (1960) affective–cognitive consistency approach. The central assumption in these theories is that people have an overarching need to maintain cognitive harmony and to avoid inconsistencies between beliefs.

2. Regan and Kilduff (1988) made a similar prediction in a study of voters' decision making in the 1984 presidential election. They hypothesized and found that voters were more confident of their candidate's chances of winning the election after voting than before.

3. Gerard and Mathewson (1966) also sought to rule out a "relief" or "contrast"

interpretation. According to this view, "any experience following the 'severe' initiation . . . would by contrast seem more pleasant than it would following the 'mild' initiation" (p. 281). To rule out this interpretation, the investigators led half of the subjects to believe that they were volunteering for a discussion group and the other half to believe that they were signing up for a psychology experiment. If the "relief" hypothesis was correct, then subjects in both groups should evaluate the group discussion positively. However, according to dissonance theory, only subjects who believed they were volunteering for a discussion group should evaluate the group positively because only they were motivated to reduce the dissonance that had been aroused by agreeing to perform an unpleasant task to join a worthless discussion group. The results supported the dissonance interpretation.

4. Strictly speaking, there are two ingredients of personal responsibility: perceived freedom—"the perception that an action was undertaken freely without having been constrained by the environment" (Cooper & Fazio, 1984, p. 236), and perceived foreseeability—the perception that the consequences could have been foreseen.

5. In a modified account of impression management theory, Schlenker (1982) argued that subjects in dissonance studies are primarily concerned with preserving and protecting their identity. He argued that subjects employ a variety of accounts, explanations, and justifications to excuse potentially reprehensible actions and preserve a positive view of self.

6. For example, Scheier and Carver (1980) argued that the bogus pipeline calls subjects' attention to their initial (negative) attitudes toward the task. This has the effect of reducing the likelihood that individuals will change their attitudes on the posttest. Also, Arkin (1981) suggested that demand characteristics operate when subjects indicate their attitudes using the bogus pipeline procedure.

7. Cooper and Fazio (1984) noted that a third line of research also supports the contention that dissonance is a state of arousal. This line of investigation found that, like other arousal states, dissonance manipulations energize dominant responses (i.e., they facilitate performance on simple tasks, but disrupt performance on more complex tasks). A detailed discussion of this line of research is beyond the scope of this chapter. However, the interested reader can find discussions of this issue in Waterman and Katkin (1967), Pallak and Pittman (1972), and Kiesler and Pallak (1976).

8. There is currently some debate as to whether dissonance arousal is a general and undifferentiated state, as Cooper and Fazio (1984) argued, or whether it is intrinsically unpleasant, as Higgins, Rhodewalt, and Zanna (1979) have proposed. Cooper and Fazio argued that a state of heightened and undifferentiated arousal precedes dissonance motivation, whereas Higgins et al. (1979) suggested that arousal is not a necessary component of dissonance motivation; instead, "the unpleasantness of the dissonance state is sufficient" (p. 28).

9. In a classic article, Freedman and Sears (1965) observed that in the course of their everyday lives, people are more exposed to supportive information than to nonsupportive material. They called this "de facto selectivity." Freedman and Sears noted that the fact that people are exposed to a disproportionate amount of supportive information does not mean that they are psychologically predisposed to prefer supportive to nonsupportive information. Because this issue does not bear directly on dissonance theory, I have not discussed its ramifications in this chapter.

Chapter 11

1. For a discussion of the effects on compliance-gaining of other situational variables (e.g., perceived benefits to self and others, consequences, and rights), see Dillard and Burgoon (1985), Boster and Stiff (1984), and Cody and McLaughlin (1985).

2. There is also evidence that individuals from different cultures employ considerably different compliance-gaining strategies (Burgoon, Dillard, Doran, & Miller, 1982; Lustig & Myers, 1983; Neuliep & Hazleton, 1985). Burgoon et al. (1982) and Lustig and Myers (1983) found that Asians were more likely than Americans to employ positive strategies (e.g., self-feeling and positive expertise). On the other hand, Neuliep and Hazleton (1985) reported that American subjects were more likely to select promise and positive expertise, whereas Japanese subjects gravitated toward explanation, direct request, and deceit. One explanation for the differences between the studies is that Neuliep and Hazleton (1985) questioned Japanese subjects who were living in Japan at the time of the study, whereas the other two investigators queried non-American subjects who were living in the United States at the time of the investigation. It is possible that Asians living in the United States felt socially obligated to select more positively toned strategies than their counterparts who were living in Japan.

3. Researchers use a rather specific procedure to assess complexity (see, e.g., Delia, Clark, & Switzer, 1974, and Beatty & Payne, 1985, for a methodological critique).

4. Interestingly, Applegate has argued that among adolescents and adults, construct abstractness predicts strategy level better than does cognitive complexity (Applegate, 1982; Applegate & Delia, 1980).

5. Freedman and Fraser (1966) noted that both requests concerned the same issue (driving safely) and involved the same task (putting up a sign in your yard). On one level, these findings only tell us that once people make a commitment to a cause, they can be persuaded to increase their commitment to the same cause. This is an interesting finding; however, it would be more convincing if an investigator could show that once individuals comply with a small request, they are more likely to go along with a second larger request that involves a different task and issue. In an effort to explore the generality of the foot-in-the-door effect, Freedman and Fraser (1966) included three additional conditions in their experiment.

Freedman and Fraser (1966) manipulated similarity between the first and second requests along the task and issue dimensions. The task required the individual to display a sign or sign a petition. The issues concerned a driving safety campaign or a project to make California beautiful. There were four conditions. One group, which we have already described, was asked to display a small sign for driving safety and then to install a large sign on the same issue (same task–same issue). A second group was asked to install a small sign that said "Keep California Beautiful" and then to display the large unattractive "Drive Safely" sign (similar task–different issue). A third group was asked to sign a petition on driving safety and then was asked to comply with the more substantial request of displaying the ugly "Drive Safely" sign (different task–similar issue). For the fourth group, both the tasks and issues were different: Residents were asked to sign a petition to keep California beautiful and then to display the large driving safety sign.

Regardless of condition, residents who had agreed to a small initial request were more likely to display the large "Drive Safely" sign than control group subjects. Notably, 47% of the residents who signed a petition to keep California beautiful were willing to display the "Drive Safely" sign, compared to 17% of control-group subjects. Even when the second request differed from the first in terms of the task and the issue, a foot-in-the-door effect was obtained.

6. It should be noted that Dillard (1990) found that, contrary to self-perception theory, manipulation of request size and execution did not influence attitudes or compliance with a second request. Dillard suggested that self-presentational concerns may underly the foot-in-the-door effect.

7. Cialdini and Ascani (1976) also included a foot-in-the-door condition in their experiment. The investigators found that subjects were significantly more likely to comply with the critical request in the door-in-the-face than in the foot-in-the-door condition.

8. Burger and Petty (1981) provided evidence for another interpretation of low-balling. They argue that the low-balling technique is effective because agreement with the initial request produces an unfulfilled obligation to the requester.

Chapter 12

1. Perloff (1984) criticized the hierarchy of effects notion, pointing out that it makes assumptions that are inconsistent with our knowledge of human information processing (see also, Flay, 1981, for a discussion of other models of information campaign effects).

2. Commodity theory predicts that "any commodity will be valued to the extent that it is unavailable" (Brock, 1968, p. 246). Thus, a product that is given away for free should be more available—and hence, less valued—than one that costs something.

3. It should be noted that the Watsonville high-risk sample was divided into two subgroups. Two thirds of the respondents in the high-risk group were randomly assigned to intensive interpersonal instruction and skills training; the other third received the media campaign only (see Flora, Maccoby, & Farquhar, 1989; Meyer et al., 1980). For simplicity's sake, I have focused only on the intensive instruction group. Studies of the Stanford three-city campaign have generally found that the intensive instruction group exhibited the greatest improvements in health-related knowledge and behavior.

4. The three-cities campaign (which is described in this section) was followed by an expanded campaign to prevent cardiovascular disease: the Stanford Five City Project. The available evidence suggests that this campaign also has influenced knowledge of the ways in which a high-cholesterol diet contributes to heart disease risk (Chaffee, Roser, & Flora, 1989; Roser, Flora, Chaffee, & Farquhar, 1990), as well as perceived self-efficacy (Maibach, Flora, & Nass, 1991). We have not focused on the results of these studies in this section, because they were guided by more contemporary theoretical paradigms (i.e., they are not part of the second wave of campaigns research).

5. It might be argued that citizens changed their behaviors not as a result of the McGruff campaign, but because of "other factors." Perhaps other media programs

(including documentaries or news articles that had nothing to do with McGruff) convinced people to alter their behaviors. Maybe the change had nothing to do with the media at all: Perhaps it was instigated by individuals' personal experiences with crime. O'Keefe (1985) examined these possibilities; using statistical controls, he showed that the behavioral effects were not due to exposure to other media crime programs or to personal victimization experiences. These findings provided even stronger support for the conclusion that the McGruff campaign had influenced crime-related behaviors.

6. In fact, several recent communication campaigns have actually reduced, rather than widened, gaps in knowledge about health (see Ettema, Brown, & Luepker, 1983; Shingi & Mody, 1976). Contemporary scholars have argued that campaigns can close gaps, provided that communicators adapt the campaign to the cultural beliefs held by members of the target audience, use simple communications, and encourage audience members to attend to the campaign (Freimuth, 1990; Rogers & Storey, 1987).

7. For an excellent discussion of message pretesting and the larger issues involved in formative evaluation research, see Atkin and Freimuth (1989) and Brown and Einsiedel (1990).

8. Not only do individuals perceive that they are invulnerable to negative events, but they also "interpret risk information in mediated channels as relevant to society but not to themselves" (Dunwoody & Neuwirth, 1991, p. 29). This tendency complicates the job of campaign specialists who want to encourage individuals to personally interpret risk messages.

References

Abelson, R. P. (1982). Three modes of attitude–behavior consistency. In M. P. Zanna, E. T. Higgins, & C. P. Herman (Eds.), *Consistency in social behavior: The Ontario symposium* (Vol. 2, pp. 131–146). Hillsdale, NJ: Lawrence Erlbaum Associates.

Abelson, R. P., Kinder, D. R., Peters, M. D., & Fiske, S. T. (1982). Affective and semantic components in political person perception. *Journal of Personality and Social Psychology, 42,* 619–630.

Adams, W. C., & Beatty, M. J. (1977). Dogmatism, need for social approval, and the resistance to persuasion. *Communication Monographs, 44,* 321–325.

Ahlering, R. F. (1987). Need for cognition, attitudes, and the 1984 presidential election. *Journal of Research in Personality, 21,* 100–102.

Ajzen, I. (1985). From intentions to actions: A theory of planned behavior. In J. Kuhl & J. Beckman (Eds.), *Action-control: From cognition to behavior* (pp. 11–39). Heidelberg: Springer.

Ajzen, I. (1989). Attitude structure and behavior. In A. R. Pratkanis, S. J. Breckler, & A. G. Greenwald (Eds.), *Attitude structure and function* (pp. 241–274). Hillsdale, NJ: Lawrence Erlbaum Associates.

Ajzen, I., & Fishbein, M. (1977). Attitude–behavior relations: A theoretical analysis and review of empirical research. *Psychological Bulletin, 84,* 888–918.

Ajzen, I., & Fishbein, M. (1980). *Understanding attitudes and predicting social behavior.* Englewood Cliffs, NJ: Prentice-Hall.

Ajzen, I., & Madden, T. J. (1986). Prediction of goal-directed behavior: Attitudes, intentions, and perceived behavioral control. *Journal of Experimental Social Psychology, 22,* 453–474.

Ajzen, I., Timko, C., & White, J. B. (1981). Self-monitoring and the attitude–behavior relation. *Journal of Personality and Social Psychology, 42,* 426–435.

Allen, C. T., & Madden, T. J. (1985). A closer look at classical conditioning. *Journal of Consumer Research, 12,* 301–315.

Allport, G. W. (1935). Attitudes. In C. Murchison (Ed.), *A handbook of social psychology* (Vol. 2, pp. 798–844). Worcester, MA: Clark University Press.

Andersen, K. (1971). *Persuasion: Theory and practice.* Boston: Allyn & Bacon.

Anderson, N. H. (1971). Integration theory and attitude change. *Psychological Review, 78,* 171–206.

Apple, W., Streeter, L. A., & Krauss, R. M. (1979). Effects of pitch and speech rate on personal attributions. *Journal of Personality and Social Psychology, 37,* 715–727.

Applegate, J. L. (1982). The impact of construct system development on communication and impression formation in persuasive contexts. *Communication Monographs, 49,* 277–289.

Applegate, J. L., & Delia, J. G. (1980). Person-centered speech, psychological development, and the contexts of language usage. In R. St. Clair & H. Giles (Eds.), *The social and psychological contexts of language* (pp. 245–282). Hillsdale, NJ: Lawrence Erlbaum Associates.

Apsler, R., & Sears, D. O. (1968). Warning, personal involvement, and attitude change. *Journal of Personality and Social Psychology, 9,* 162–168.

Argyris, C. (1975). Dangers in applying results from experimental social psychology. *American Psychologist, 30,* 469–485.

Arkin, R. M. (1981). Self-presentational styles. In J. T. Tedeschi (Ed.), *Impression management theory and social psychological research* (pp. 311–333). New York: Academic Press.

Aron, A., & Aron, E. N. (1989). *The heart of social psychology: A backstage view of a passionate science* (2nd ed.). Lexington, MA: Lexington Books.

Aronovitch, C. D. (1976). The voice of personality: Stereotyped judgments and their relation to voice quality and sex of speaker. *Journal of Social Psychology, 99,* 207–220.

Aronson, E. (1968). Dissonance theory: Progress and problems. In R. P. Abelson, E. Aronson, W. J. McGuire, T. M. Newcomb, M. J. Rosenberg, & P. H. Tannenbaum (Eds.), *Theories of cognitive consistency: A sourcebook* (pp. 5–27). Chicago: Rand McNally.

Aronson, E., & Mills, J. (1959). The effect of severity of initiation on liking for a group. *Journal of Abnormal and Social Psychology, 59,* 177–181.

Aronson, E., Turner, J. A., & Carlsmith, J. M. (1963). Communicator credibility and communication discrepancy as determinants of opinion change. *Journal of Abnormal and Social Psychology, 67,* 31–36.

Atkin, C. K. (1981). Mass media information campaign effectiveness. In R. E. Rice & W. J. Paisley (Eds.), *Public communication campaigns* (pp. 265–280). Beverly Hills, CA: Sage.

Atkin, C. K., & Freimuth, V. (1989). Formative evaluation research in campaign design. In R. E. Rice & C. K. Atkin (Eds.), *Public communication campaigns* (2nd ed., pp. 131–150). Newbury Park, CA: Sage.

Atkins, A. L., Deaux, K. K., & Bieri, J. (1967). Latitude of acceptance and attitude change: Empirical evidence for a reformulation. *Journal of Personality and Social Psychology, 6,* 47–54.

Atwood, R. W., & Howell, R. J. (1971). Pupilometric and personality test score differences of female aggressing pedophiliacs and normals. *Psychonomic Science, 22,* 115–116.

Axsom, D., Yates, S., & Chaiken, S. (1987). Audience response as a heuristic cue in persuasion. *Journal of Personality and Social Psychology, 53,* 30–40.

Bacon, F. (1960). *The new organon and related writings.* New York: Liberal Arts Press. (Original work published 1620)

Balay, J., & Shevrin, H. (1988). The subliminal psychodynamic activation method: A critical review. *American Psychologist, 43,* 161–174.

Ball-Rokeach, S. J., Rokeach, M., & Grube, J. (1984). *The Great American Values Test: Influencing behavior and belief through television.* New York: Free Press.

Bandura, A. (1965). Influence of models' reinforcement contingencies on the acquisition of imitative responses. *Journal of Personality and Social Psychology, 1,* 589–595.

Bandura, A. (1971). Analysis of modeling processes. In A. Bandura (Ed.), *Psychological modeling: Conflicting theories* (pp. 1–62). Chicago: Aldine-Atherton.

Bandura, A., Grusec, J. E., & Menlove, F. L. (1966). Observational learning as a function of symbolization and incentive set. *Child Development, 37,* 499–506.

Bandura, A., Ross, D., & Ross, S. A. (1963). Imitation of film-mediated aggressive models. *Journal of Abnormal and Social Psychology, 66,* 3–11.

Bargh, J. A., & Pietromonaco, P. (1982). Automatic information processing and social perception: The influence of trait information presented outside of conscious awareness on impression formation. *Journal of Personality and Social Psychology, 43,* 437–449.

Barker, E. (1984). *The making of a Moonie: Choice or brainwashing?* Oxford: Basil Blackwell.

Batson, C. D., & Ventis, W. L. (1982). *The religious experience: A social-psychological view.* New York: Oxford Press.

Bauman, K. E., Brown, J. D., Bryan, E. S., Fisher, L. A., Padgett, C. A., & Sweeney, J. M. (1988). Three mass media campaigns to prevent adolescent cigarette smoking. *Preventive Medicine, 17,* 510–530.

Baumeister, R. F., & Tice, D. M. (1984). Role of self-presentation and choice in cognitive dissonance under forced compliance: Necessary or sufficient causes? *Journal of Personality and Social Psychology, 46,* 5–13.

Baxter, L. A. (1984). An investigation of compliance-gaining as politeness. *Human Communication Research, 10,* 427–456.

Beaman, A. L., Cole, C. M., Preston, M., Klentz, B., & Steblay, N. M. (1983). Fifteen years of foot-in-the-door research: A meta-analysis. *Personality and Social Psychology Bulletin, 9,* 181–196.

Beatty, M. J., & Payne, S. K. (1985). Is construct differentiation loquacity? A motivational perspective. *Human Communication Research, 11,* 605–612.

Beauchamp, D. E. (1979). Public health as social justice. In E. G. Jaco (Ed.), *Patients, physicians and illness.* New York: Free Press.

Beck, K. H., & Lund, A. L. (1981). The effects of health seriousness and personal efficacy upon intentions and behavior. *Journal of Applied Social Psychology, 11,* 401–415.

Becker, L. B., McCombs, M. E., & McLeod, J. M. (1975). The development of political cognitions. In S. H. Chaffee (Ed.), *Political communication: Issues and strategies for research* (pp. 21–63). Beverly Hills: Sage.

Bell, B. E., & Loftus, E. F. (1985). Vivid persuasion in the courtroom. *Journal of Personality Assessment, 49,* 659–664.

Beltramini, R. F., & Evans, K. R. (1985). Perceived believability of research results information in advertising. *Journal of Advertising, 14,* 18–24.

Bem, D. J. (1965). An experimental analysis of self-persuasion. *Journal of Experimental Social Psychology, 1,* 199–218.

Bem, D. J. (1967). Self-perception: An alternative interpretation of cognitive dissonance phenomena. *Psychological Review, 74,* 183–200.

Bem, D. J. (1970). *Beliefs, attitudes, and human affairs.* Belmont, CA: Brooks/Cole.

Bem, D. J. (1972). Self-perception theory. In L. Berkowitz (Ed.), *Advances in experimental social psychology* (Vol. 6, pp. 1–62). New York: Academic Press.

Bem, D. J., & McConnell, H. K. (1970). Testing the self-perception explanation of dissonance phenomena: On the salience of premanipulation attitudes. *Journal of Personality and Social Psychology, 14,* 23–31.

Benoit, W. L. (1991). A cognitive response analysis of source credibility. In B. Dervin & M. J. Voigt (Eds.), *Progress in communication sciences* (Vol. 10, pp. 1–19). Norwood, NJ: Ablex.

Bentler, P. M., & Speckhart, G. (1979). Models of attitude–behavior relations. *Psychological Review, 86,* 452–464.

Berger, C. R. (1985). Social power and interpersonal communication. In M. L. Knapp & G. R. Miller (Eds.), *Handbook of interpersonal communication* (pp. 439–499). Beverly Hills, CA: Sage.

Berger, S. M. (1962). Conditioning through vicarious instigation. *Psychological Review, 69,* 450–466.

Berlo, D. K., Lemert, J. B., & Mertz, R. J. (1969). Dimensions for evaluating the acceptability of message sources. *Public Opinion Quarterly, 33,* 563–576.

Berlyne, D. E. (1970). Novelty, complexity and hedonic value. *Perception and Psychophysics, 8,* 279–286.

Berscheid, E. (1966). Opinion change and communicator-communicatee similarity and dissimilarity. *Journal of Personality and Social Psychology, 4,* 670–680.

Bettinghaus, E. P., & Cody, M. J. (1987). *Persuasive communication* (4th ed.). New York: Holt, Rinehart & Winston.

Beuf, A. (1974). Doctor, lawyer, household drudge. *Journal of Communication, 24,* 142–145.

Bevan, W. (1964). Subliminal stimulation: A pervasive problem for psychology. *Psychological Bulletin, 61,* 81–99.

Birnbaum, M. H., & Mellers, B. A. (1979). Stimulus recognition may mediate exposure effects. *Journal of Personality and Social Psychology, 37,* 391–394.

Bloom, P. N., & Novelli, W. D. (1981). Problems and challenges in social marketing. *Journal of Marketing, 45,* 79–88.

Bochner, S., & Insko, C. A. (1966). Communicator discrepancy, source credibility, and opinion change. *Journal of Personality and Social Psychology, 4,* 614–621.

Bolton, G. M. (1974). The lost letter technique as a measure of community attitudes toward a major local issue. *Sociological Quarterly, 15,* 567–570.

Bornstein, R. F. (1989a). Subliminal techniques as propaganda tools: Review and critique. *Journal of Mind and Behavior, 10,* 231–262.

Bornstein, R. F. (1989b). Exposure and affect: Overview and meta-analysis of research, 1968–1987. *Psychological Bulletin, 106,* 265–289.

Bornstein, R. F., Leone, D. R., & Galley, D. J. (1987). The generalizability of subliminal mere exposure effects: Influence of stimuli perceived without awareness on social behavior. *Journal of Personality and Social Psychology, 53,* 1070–1079.

Boster, F. J. (1988). Comments on the utility of compliance-gaining message selection tasks. *Human Communication Research, 15,* 169–177.

Boster, F. J., & Mongeau, P. (1984). Fear-arousing persuasive messages. In R. N. Bostrom (Ed.), *Communication Yearbook 8* (pp. 330–375). Beverly Hills, CA: Sage.

Boster, F. J., & Stiff, J. B. (1984). Compliance-gaining message selection behavior. *Human Communication Research, 10,* 539–556.

Boston Phoenix. (1982, November 2), p. 7.

Bostrom, R. N. (1983). *Persuasion.* Englewood Cliffs, NJ: Prentice-Hall.

Bostrom, R. N., Baseheart, J. R., & Rossiter, C. M., Jr. (1973). The effects of three types of profane language in persuasive messages. *Journal of Communication, 23,* 461–475.

Bostrom, R. N., Vlandis, J. W., & Rosenbaum, M. E. (1961). Grades as reinforcing contingencies and attitude change. *Journal of Educational Psychology, 52,* 112–115.

Bowers, J. W. (1964). Some correlates of language intensity. *Quarterly Journal of Speech, 50,* 415–420.

Bradac, J. J., Bowers, J. W., & Courtright, J. A. (1979). Three language variables in communication research: Intensity, immediacy, and diversity. *Human Communication Research, 5,* 257–269.

Bradac, J. J., Hemphill, M. R., & Tardy, C. H. (1981). Language style on trial: Effects of "powerful" and "powerless" speech upon judgments of victims and villains. *Western Journal of Speech Communication, 45,* 327–341.

Bradac, J. J., & Mulac, A. (1984). A molecular view of powerful and powerless speech styles: Attributional consequences of specific language features and communicator intentions. *Communication Monographs, 51,* 307–319.

Bradley, P. H. (1981). The folk-linguistics of women's speech: An empirical examination. *Communication Monographs, 48,* 73–90.

Breckler, S. J. (1984). Empirical validation of affect, behavior, and cognition as distinct components of attitude. *Journal of Personality and Social Psychology, 47,* 1191–1205.

Brehm, J. W. (1956). Postdecision changes in the desirability of alternatives. *Journal of Abnormal and Social Psychology, 52,* 384–389.

Brehm, J. W., & Cohen, A. R. (1962). *Explorations in cognitive dissonance.* New York: Wiley.

Bretl, D. J., & Dillard, J. P. (1991). Persuasion and the internality dimension of cognitive responses. *Communication Studies, 42,* 103–113.

Brewer, W. F. (1974). There is no convincing evidence for operant or classical conditioning in adult humans. In W. B. Weimer & D. S. Palermo (Eds.), *Cognition and the symbolic processes* (pp. 1–42). Hillsdale, NJ: Lawrence Erlbaum Associates.

Briggs, S. R., Cheek, J. M., & Buss, A. H. (1980). An analysis of the self-monitoring scale. *Journal of Personality and Social Psychology, 38,* 679–686.

Brilhart, B. L. (1970). Relationships of speaker-message perception to perceptual field dependence. *Journal of Communication, 20,* 153–166.

Brinberg, D., & Durand, J. (1983). Eating at fast-food restaurants: An analysis using two behavioral intention models. *Journal of Applied Social Psychology, 13,* 459–472.

Brock, T. C. (1965). Communicator-recipient similarity and decision change. *Journal of Personality and Social Psychology, 1,* 650–654.

Brock, T. C. (1967). Communication discrepancy and intent to persuade as determinants of counterargument production. *Journal of Experimental Social Psychology, 3,* 296–309.

Brock, T. C. (1968). Implications of commodity theory for value change. In A. G. Greenwald, T. C. Brock, & T. M. Ostrom (Eds.), *Psychological foundations of attitudes* (pp. 243–275). New York: Academic Press.

Brock, T. C. (1981). Historical and methodological perspectives in the analysis of cognitive responses: An introduction. In R. E. Petty, T. M. Ostrom, & T. C. Brock (Eds.), *Cognitive responses in persuasion* (pp. 1–3). Hillsdale, NJ: Lawrence Erlbaum Associates.

Bromley, D. G., & Shupe, A. D., Jr. (1979). *"Moonies" in America: Cult, church, and crusade.* Beverly Hills, CA: Sage.

Brown, J. D., & Einsiedel, E. F. (1990). Public health campaigns: Mass media strategies. In E. Berlin Ray & L. Donohew (Eds.), *Communication and health: Systems and applications* (pp. 153–170). Hillsdale, NJ: Lawrence Erlbaum Associates.

Bryant, J., Brown, D., Silberberg, A. R., & Elliott, S. M. (1981). Effects of humorous illustrations in college textbooks. *Human Communication Research, 8,* 43–57.

Bryant, J., & Street, R. L., Jr. (1988). From reactivity to activity and action: An evolving concept and *weltanschauung* in mass and interpersonal communication. In R. P. Hawkins, J. M. Wiemann, & S. Pingree (Eds.), *Advancing communication science: Merging mass and interpersonal processes* (pp. 162–190). Newbury Park, CA: Sage.

Buller, D. B. (1986). Distraction during persuasive communication: A meta-analytic review. *Communication Monographs, 53,* 91–114.

Burger, J. M., & Petty, R. E. (1981). The low-ball compliance technique: Task or person commitment? *Journal of Personality and Social Psychology, 40,* 492–500.

Burgoon, J. K., Birk, T., & Pfau, M. (1990). Nonverbal behaviors, persuasion, and credibility. *Human Communication Research, 17,* 140–169.

Burgoon, J. K., Pfau, M., Parrott, R., Birk, T., Coker, R., & Burgoon, M. (1987). Relational communication, satisfaction, compliance-gaining strategies and compliance in communication between physicians and patients. *Communication Monographs, 54,* 307–324.

Burgoon, M. (1989). Messages and persuasive effects. In J. J. Bradac (Ed.), *Message effects in communication science* (pp. 129–164). Newbury Park, CA: Sage.

Burgoon, M., Birk, T., & Hall, J. R. (1991). Compliance and satisfaction with physician-patient communication: An expectancy theory interpretation of sender differences. *Human Communication Research, 18,* 177–208.

Burgoon, M., & Burgoon, J. K. (1975). Message strategies in influence attempts. In G. J. Hanneman & W. J. McEwen (Eds.), *Communication and behavior* (pp. 149–165). Reading, MA: Addison-Wesley.

Burgoon, M., Dillard, J. P., & Doran, N. E. (1983). Friendly or unfriendly persuasion: The effects of violations of expectations by males and females. *Human Communication Research, 10,* 283–294.

Burgoon, M., Dillard, J. P., Doran, N. E., & Miller, M. D. (1982). Cultural and situational influences on the process of persuasive strategy selection. *International Journal of Intercultural Relations, 6,* 85–100.

Burgoon, M., & Miller, G. R. (1990). Paths. *Communication Monographs, 57,* 152–160.

Burgoon, M., & Stewart, D. (1975). Empirical investigations of language intensity: I. The effects of sex of source, receiver, and language intensity on attitude change. *Human Communication Research, 1,* 224–228.

Burke, K. (1969). *A grammar of motives*. Berkeley, CA: University of California Press. (Original work published 1945)

Burleson, B. R., Wilson, S. R., Waltman, M. S., Goering, E. M., Ely, T. K., & Whaley, B. B. (1988). Item desirability effects in compliance-gaining research: Seven studies documenting artifacts in the strategy selection procedure. *Human Communication Research, 14,* 429–486.

Byrne, D. (1971). *The attraction paradigm*. New York: Academic Press.

Cacioppo, J. T., Harkins, S. G., & Petty, R. E. (1981). The nature of attitudes and cognitive responses and their relationships to behavior. In R. E. Petty, T. M. Ostrom, & T. C. Brock (Eds.), *Cognitive responses in persuasion* (pp. 31–54). Hillsdale, NJ: Lawrence Erlbaum Associates.

Cacioppo, J. T., Petty, R. E., Kao, C. F., & Rodriguez, R. (1986). Central and peripheral routes to persuasion: An individual differences perspective. *Journal of Personality and Social Psychology, 51,* 1032–1043.

Cacioppo, J. T., Marshall-Goodell, B. S., Tassinary, L. G., & Petty, R. E. (1992). Rudimentary determinants of attitudes: Classical conditioning is more effective when prior knowledge about the attitude stimulus is low than high. *Journal of Experimental Social Psychology, 28,* 207–233.

Cacioppo, J. T., & Petty, R. E. (1979). Attitudes and cognitive response: An electrophysiological approach. *Journal of Personality and Social Psychology, 37,* 2181–2199.

Cacioppo, J. T., & Petty, R. E. (1982). The need for cognition. *Journal of Personality and Social Psychology, 42,* 116–131.

Cacioppo, J. T., & Petty, R. E. (1987). Stalking rudimentary processes of social influence: A psychophysiological approach. In M. P. Zanna, J. M. Olson, & C. P. Herman (Eds.), *Social influence: the Ontario symposium* (Vol. 5, pp. 41–74). Hillsdale, NJ: Lawrence Erlbaum Associates.

Cacioppo, J. T., Petty, R. E., & Geen, T. R. (1989). Attitude structure and function: From the tripartite to the homeostasis model of attitudes. In A. R. Pratkanis, S. J. Breckler, & A. G. Greenwald (Eds.), *Attitude structure and function* (pp. 275–309). Hillsdale, NJ: Lawrence Erlbaum Associates.

Cacioppo, J. T., Petty, R. E., Losch, M. E., & Kim, H. S. (1986). Electromyographic activity over facial muscle regions can differentiate the valence and intensity of affective reactions. *Journal of Personality and Social Psychology, 50,* 260–268.

Cacioppo, J. T., Petty, R. E., & Morris, K. J. (1983). Effects of need for cognition on message evaluation, recall, and persuasion. *Journal of Personality and Social Psychology, 45,* 805–818.

Cacioppo, J. T., Petty, R. E., & Sidera, J. A. (1982). The effects of a salient self-schema on the evaluation of proattitudinal editorials: Top-down versus bottom-up message processing. *Journal of Experimental Social Psychology, 18,* 324–338.

Cacioppo, J. T., & Sandman, C. A. (1981). Psychophysiological functioning, cognitive responding and attitudes. In R. E. Petty, T. M. Ostrom, & T. C. Brock (Eds.), *Cognitive responses in persuasion* (pp. 81–103). Hillsdale, NJ: Lawrence Erlbaum Associates.

Calder, B. J., & Ross, M. (1973). *Attitudes and behavior*. Morristown, NJ: General Learning Press.

Calder, B. J., Ross, M., & Insko, C. A. (1973). Attitude change and attitude attribution: Effects of incentive, choice, and consequences. *Journal of Personality and Social Psychology, 25,* 84–99.

Campbell, A., Converse, P. E., Miller, W. E., & Stokes, D. E. (1960). *The American voter.* New York: Wiley.

Campbell, D. T. (1963). Social attitudes and other acquired behavioral dispositions. In S. Koch (Ed.), *Psychology: A study of a science* (Vol. 6, pp. 94–172). New York: McGraw-Hill.

Cann, A., Sherman, S. J., & Elkes, R. (1975). Effects of initial request size and timing of a second request on compliance: The foot in the door and the door in the face. *Journal of Personality and Social Psychology, 32,* 774–782.

Cantor, J. R. (1979). Grammatical variations in persuasion: Effectiveness of four forms of request in door-to-door solicitations for funds. *Communication Monographs, 46,* 296–305.

Cantor, J. R., Alfonso, H., & Zillmann, D. (1976). The persuasive effectiveness of the peer appeal and a communicator's first-hand experience. *Communication Research, 3,* 293–310.

Cantor, J. R., & Venus, P. (1983). The effect of humor on recall of a radio advertisement. *Journal of Broadcasting, 24,* 13–22.

Cantrill, J. G., & Seibold, D. R. (1986). The perceptual contrast explanation of sequential request strategy effectiveness. *Human Communication Research, 13,* 253–267.

Cappella, J. N., & Street, R. L., Jr. (1989). Message effects: Theory and research on mental models of messages. In J. J. Bradac (Ed.), *Message effects in communication science* (pp. 24–51). Newbury Park, CA: Sage.

Carli, L. L. (1990). Gender, language, and influence. *Journal of Personality and Social Psychology, 59,* 941–951.

Carlsmith, J. M., Collins, B. E., & Helmreich, R. L. (1966). Studies in forced compliance: I. The effect of pressure for compliance on attitude change produced by face-to-face role playing and anonymous essay writing. *Journal of Personality and Social Psychology, 4,* 1–13.

Carver, C. S. (1975). Physical aggression as a function of objective self-awareness and attitudes toward punishment. *Journal of Experimental Social Psychology, 11,* 510–519.

Chaffee, S. H. (1988). Differentiating the hypodermic model from empirical research: A comment on Bineham's commentaries. *Communication Monographs, 55,* 247–249.

Chaffee, S. H., & Mutz, D. C. (1988). Comparing mediated and interpersonal communication data. In R. P. Hawkins, J. M. Wiemann, & S. Pingree (Eds.), *Advancing communication science: Merging mass and interpersonal processes* (pp. 19–43). Newbury Park, CA: Sage.

Chaffee, S. H., Roser, C., & Flora, J. (1989). Estimating the magnitude of threats to validity of information campaign effects. In C. T. Salmon (Ed.), *Information campaigns: Balancing social values and social change* (pp. 285–301). Newbury Park, CA: Sage.

Chaiken, S. (1979). Communicator's physical attractiveness and persuasion. *Journal of Personality and Social Psychology, 37,* 1387–1397.

Chaiken, S. (1986). Physical appearance and social influence. In C. P. Herman, M. P. Zanna, & E. T. Higgins (Eds.), *Physical appearance, stigma, and social behavior:*

The Ontario symposium (Vol. 3, pp. 143–177). Hillsdale, NJ: Lawrence Erlbaum Associates.

Chaiken, S. (1987). The heuristic model of persuasion. In M. P. Zanna, J. M. Olson, & C. P. Herman (Eds.), *Social influence: The Ontario symposium* (Vol. 5, pp. 3–39). Hillsdale, NJ: Lawrence Erlbaum Associates.

Chaiken, S., & Eagly, A. H. (1976). Communication modality as a determinant of message persuasiveness and message comprehensibility. *Journal of Personality and Social Psychology, 34,* 605–614.

Chaiken, S., Liberman, A., & Eagly, A. H. (1989). Heuristic and systematic information processing within and beyond the persuasion context. In J. S. Uleman & J. A. Bargh (Eds.), *Unintended thought: Limits of awareness, intention, and control* (pp. 212–252). New York: Guilford.

Chaiken, S., & Stangor, C. (1987). Attitudes and attitude change. *Annual Review of Psychology, 38,* 575–630.

Chapanis, N. P., & Chapanis, A. C. (1964). Cognitive dissonance: Five years later. *Psychological Bulletin, 61,* 1–22.

Chattopadhyay, A., & Alba, J. W. (1988). The situational importance of recall and inference in consumer decision making. *Journal of Consumer Research, 15,* 1–12.

Childs, H. L. (1965). *Public opinion: Nature, formation, and role.* Princeton, NJ: Van Nostrand.

Cialdini, R. B. (1984). *Influence: The new psychology of modern persuasion.* New York: Quill.

Cialdini, R. B., & Ascani, K. (1976). Test of a concession procedure for inducing verbal, behavioral, and further compliance with a request to give blood. *Journal of Applied Psychology, 61,* 295–300.

Cialdini, R. B., Cacioppo, J. T., Bassett, R., & Miller, J. A. (1978). Low-ball procedure for producing compliance: Commitment then cost. *Journal of Personality and Social Psychology, 36,* 463–476.

Cialdini, R. B., & Insko, C. A. (1969). Attitudinal verbal reinforcement as a function of informational consistency: A further test of the two-factor theory. *Journal of Personality and Social Psychology, 12,* 342–350.

Cialdini, R. B., & Petty, R. E. (1981). Anticipatory opinion effects. In R. E. Petty, T. M. Ostrom, & T. C. Brock (Eds.), *Cognitive responses in persuasion* (pp. 217–235). Hillsdale, NJ: Lawrence Erlbaum Associates.

Cialdini, R. B., Vincent, J. E., Lewis, S. K., Catalan, J., Wheeler D., & Darby, B. L. (1975). Reciprocal concessions procedure for inducing compliance: The door-in-the-face technique. *Journal of Personality and Social Psychology, 31,* 206–215.

Clark, R. A. (1979). The impact of self interest and desire for liking on the selection of persuasive strategies. *Communication Monographs, 46,* 257–273.

Clark, R. A., & Delia, J. G. (1977). Cognitive complexity, social perspective-taking, and functional persuasive skills in second- to ninth-grade children. *Human Communication Research, 3,* 128–134.

Clavier, D. W., & Kalupa, F. B. (1983). Corporate rebuttals to "trial by television." *Public Relations Review, 9,* 24–36.

Cody, M. J., & McLaughlin, M. L. (1980). Perceptions of compliance-gaining situations: A dimensional analysis. *Communication Monographs, 47,* 132–148.

Cody, M. J., & McLaughlin, M. L. (1985). The situation as a construct in interpersonal communication research. In M. L. Knapp & G. R. Miller (Eds.),

Handbook of interpersonal communication (pp. 263–312). Newbury Park, CA: Sage.

Cody, M. J., McLaughlin, M. L., & Jordan, W. J. (1980). A multidimensional scaling of three sets of compliance-gaining strategies. *Communication Quarterly, 28,* 34–46.

Cohen, A. R. (1962). An experiment on small rewards for discrepant compliance and attitude change. In J. W. Brehm & A. R. Cohen (Eds.), *Explorations in cognitive dissonance* (pp. 73–78). New York: Wiley.

Cohen, A. R., Stotland, E., & Wolfe, D. M. (1955). An experimental investigation of need for cognition. *Journal of Abnormal and Social Psychology, 51,* 291–294.

Cohen, D. (1977). *Psychologists on psychology.* New York: Taplinger.

Comstock, G., Chaffee, S. H., Katzman, N., McCombs, M., & Roberts, D. (1978). *Television and human behavior.* New York: Columbia University Press.

Cook, S. W., & Selltiz, C. (1964). A multiple-indicator approach to attitude measurement. *Psychological Bulletin, 62,* 36–55.

Cook, T. D., Gruder, C. L., Hennigan, K. M., & Flay, B. R. (1979). History of the sleeper effect: Some logical pitfalls in accepting the null hypothesis. *Psychological Bulletin, 86,* 662–679.

Cooper, H. M. (1979). Statistically combining independent studies: A meta-analysis of sex differences in conformity research. *Journal of Personality and Social Psychology, 37,* 131–146.

Cooper, J., & Axsom, D. (1982). Effort justification in psychotherapy. In G. Weary & H. L. Mirels (Eds.), *Integrations of clinical and social psychology* (pp. 214–230). New York: Oxford Press.

Cooper, J., & Croyle, R. T. (1984). Attitudes and attitude change. *Annual Review of Psychology, 35,* 395–426.

Cooper, J., & Fazio, R. H. (1984). A new look at dissonance theory. In L. Berkowitz (Ed.), *Advances in experimental social psychology* (Vol. 17, pp. 229–266). Orlando, FL: Academic Press.

Cooper, J., & Worchel, S. (1970). Role of undesired consequences in arousing cognitive dissonance. *Journal of Personality and Social Psychology, 16,* 199–206.

Corey, S. M. (1937). Professed attitudes and actual behavior. *Journal of Educational Psychology, 28,* 271–280.

Craig, R. T. (1980). The message-attitude–behavior relationship from the point of view of the actor. In D. P. Cushman & R. D. McPhee (Eds.), *Message-attitude-behavior-relationship: Theory, methodology, and application* (pp. 273–287). New York: Academic Press.

Crandall, R. (1972). Field extension of the frequency-affect findings. *Psychological Reports, 31,* 371–374.

Crockett, W. H. (1965). Cognitive complexity and impression formation. In B. Maher (Ed.), *Progress in experimental personality research* (Vol. 2, pp. 47–90). New York: Academic Press.

Cronen, V. E., & Conville, R. L. (1973). Belief salience, summation theory, and the attitude construct. *Speech Monographs, 40,* 17–26.

Cronkhite, G., & Liska, J. (1976). A critique of factor analytic approaches to the study of credibility. *Communication Monographs, 43,* 91–107.

Cuperfain, R., & Clarke, T. K. (1985). A new perspective of subliminal perception. *Journal of Advertising, 14,* 36–41.

Davidson, A. R., & Jaccard, J. J. (1975). Population psychology: A new look at an old problem. *Journal of Personality and Social Psychology, 31,* 1073–1082.

Davis, D. K., & Kraus, S. (1982). Public communication and televised presidential debates. In M. Burgoon (Ed.), *Communication yearbook 6* (pp. 289–303). Beverly Hills, CA: Sage.

Davison, W. P. (1983). The third-person effect in communication. *Public Opinion Quarterly, 47,* 1–15.

Dawes, R. M., & Smith, T. L. (1985). Attitude and opinion measurement. In G. L. Lindzey & E. A. Aronson (Eds.), *Handbook of social psychology* (3rd ed., Vol. 1, pp. 509–566). New York: Random House.

DeBono, K. G. (1987). Investigating the social-adjustive and value-expressive functions of attitudes: Implications for persuasion processes. *Journal of Personality and Social Psychology, 52,* 279–287.

DeBono, K. G., & Harnish, R. J. (1988). Source expertise, source attractiveness, and the processing of persuasive information: A functional approach. *Journal of Personality and Social Psychology, 55,* 541–546.

DeFleur, M. L., & Petranoff, R. M. (1959). A televised test of subliminal persuasion. *Public Opinion Quarterly, 23,* 168–180.

DeJong, W. (1979). An examination of self-perception mediation of the foot-in-the-door effect. *Journal of Personality and Social Psychology, 37,* 2221–2239.

Delia, J. G., Clark, R. A., & Switzer, D. E. (1974). Cognitive complexity and impression formation in informal social interaction. *Speech Monographs, 41,* 299–308.

Delia, J. G., Kline, S. L., & Burleson, B. R. (1979). The development of persuasive communication strategies in kindergarteners through twelfth-graders. *Communication Monographs, 46,* 241–256.

Delia, J. G., & O'Keefe, B. J. (1979). Constructivism: The development of communication in children. In E. Wartella (Ed.), *Children communicating* (pp. 157–185). Beverly Hills, CA: Sage.

DePietro, R., & Clark, N. M. (1984). A sense-making approach to understanding adolescents' selection of health information sources. *Health Education Quarterly, 11,* 419–430.

Dervin, B. (1976). Strategies for dealing with human information needs: Information or communication? *Journal of Broadcasting, 20,* 324–333.

Dervin, B. (1981). Mass communicating: Changing conceptions of the audience. In R. E. Rice & W. J. Paisley (Eds.), *Public communication campaigns* (pp. 71–87). Beverly Hills, CA: Sage.

deTurck, M. A. (1985). A transactional analysis of compliance-gaining behavior: Effects of noncompliance, relational contexts, and actors' gender. *Human Communication Research, 12,* 54–78.

Diddling the subconscious: Subliminal advertising. (1957, October 5). *Nation, 185,* pp. 206–207.

Dillard, J. P. (1990). Self-inference and the foot-in-the-door technique: Quantity of behavior and attitudinal mediation. *Human Communication Research, 16,* 422–443.

Dillard, J. P., & Burgoon, M. (1982). An appraisal of two sequential request strategies for gaining compliance: Foot-in-the-door and door-in-the-face. *Communication, 11,* 40–57.

Dillard, J. P., & Burgoon, M. (1985). Situational influences on the selection of compliance-gaining messages: Two tests of the predictive utility of the Cody-McLaughlin typology. *Communication Monographs, 52,* 289–304.

Dillard, J. P., Hunter, J. E., & Burgoon, M. (1984). Sequential-request persuasive strategies: Meta-analysis of foot-in-the-door and door-in-the-face. *Human Communication Research, 10,* 461–488.

Dixon, N. F. (1971). *Subliminal perception: The nature of a controversy.* London: McGraw-Hill.

Doob, A. N., Carlsmith, J. M., Freedman, J. L., Landauer, T. K., & Tom, S., Jr. (1969). Effect of initial selling price on subsequent sales. *Journal of Personality and Social Psychology, 11,* 345–350.

Doob, L. (1947). The behavior of attitudes. *Psychological Review, 54,* 135–156.

Douglas, D. F., Westley, B. H., & Chaffee, S. H. (1970). An information campaign that changed community attitudes. *Journalism Quarterly, 47,* 479–487.

Duncan, C. P., & Nelson, J. E. (1985). Effects of humor in a radio advertising experiment. *Journal of Advertising, 14,* 33–40.

Dunwoody, S., & Neuwirth, K. (1991). Coming to terms with the impact of communication on scientific and technological risk judgments. In L. Wilkins & P. Patterson (Eds.), *Risky business: Communicating issues of science, risk, and public policy* (pp. 11–30). Westport, CT: Greenwood.

Dysinger, D. W. (1931). A comparative study of affective responses by means of the impressive and expressive methods. *Psychological Monographs, 41,* 14–31.

Eagly, A. H. (1978). Sex differences in influenceability. *Psychological Bulletin, 85,* 86–116.

Eagly, A. H. (1981). Recipient characteristics as determinants of responses to persuasion. In R. E. Petty, T. M. Ostrom, & T. C. Brock (Eds.), *Cognitive responses in persuasion* (pp. 173–195). Hillsdale, NJ: Lawrence Erlbaum Associates.

Eagly, A. H., & Carli, L. L. (1981). Sex of researchers and sex-typed communications as determinants of sex differences in influenceability: A meta-analysis of social influence studies. *Psychological Bulletin, 90,* 1–20.

Eagly, A. H., & Chaiken, S. (1984). Cognitive theories of persuasion. In L. Berkowitz (Ed.), *Advances in experimental social psychology* (Vol. 17, pp. 268–359). Hillsdale, NJ: Lawrence Erlbaum Associates.

Eagly, A. H., & Telaak, K. (1972). Width of the latitude of acceptance as a determinant of attitude change. *Journal of Personality and Social Psychology, 23,* 388–397.

Eagly, A. H., Wood, W., & Chaiken, S. (1978). Causal inferences about communicators and their effect on opinion change. *Journal of Personality and Social Psychology, 36,* 424–435.

Eakins, B., & Eakins, R. (1976). Verbal turn-taking and exchanges in faculty dialogue. In B. L. Dubois & I Crouch (Eds.), *The sociology of the languages of American women* (pp. 53–62). San Antonio, TX: Trinity University Press.

Ehrlich, D., Guttman, I., Schonbach, P., & Mills, J. (1957). Post-decision exposure to relevant information. *Journal of Abnormal and Social Psychology, 54,* 98–102.

Elkin, R. A., & Leippe, M. R. (1986). Physiological arousal, dissonance, and attitude change: Evidence for a dissonance-arousal link and a "don't remind me" effect. *Journal of Personality and Social Psychology, 51,* 55–65.

Elms, A. C. (1967). Role playing, incentive, and dissonance. *Psychological Bulletin, 68,* 132–148.

Elms, A. C., & Janis, I. L. (1965). Counter-norm attitudes induced by consonant versus dissonant conditions of role-playing. *Journal of Experimental Research in Personality, 1,* 50–60.

Enroth, R. (1977). *Youth, brainwashing, and the extremist cults.* Grand Rapids, MI: Zondervan.

Erickson, B., Lind, E. A., Johnson, B. C., & O'Barr, W. M. (1978). Speech style and impression formation in a court setting: The effects of "powerful" and "powerless" speech. *Journal of Experimental Social Psychology, 14,* 266–279.

Eshleman, J. G., & Neuendorf, K. A. (1989 August). *Perspectives on humor and their application to mass media comedy.* Paper presented to the annual convention of the Association for Education in Journalism and Mass Communication, Washington, DC.

Ettema, J. S., Brown, J. W., & Luepker, R. V. (1983). Knowledge gap effects in a health information campaign. *Public Opinion Quarterly, 47,* 516–527.

Falbo, T. (1977). Multidimensional scaling of power strategies. *Journal of Personality and Social Psychology, 35,* 537–547.

Fazio, R. H. (1986). How to attitudes guide behavior? In R. M. Sorrentino & E. T. Higgins (Eds.), *The handbook of motivation and cognition: Foundations of social behavior* (pp. 204–243). New York: Guilford.

Fazio, R. H. (1989). On the power and functionality of attitudes: The role of attitude accessibility. In A. R. Pratkanis, S. J. Breckler, & A. G. Greenwald (Eds.), *Attitude structure and function* (pp. 153–179). Hillsdale, NJ: Lawrence Erlbaum Associates.

Fazio, R. H. (1990). Multiple processes by which attitudes guide behavior: The MODE model as an integrative framework. In M. P. Zanna (Ed.), *Advances in experimental social psychology* (Vol. 23, pp. 75–109). San Diego: Academic Press.

Fazio, R. H., Powell, M. C., & Williams, C. J. (1989). The role of attitude accessibility in the attitude-to-behavior process. *Journal of Consumer Research, 16,* 280–288.

Fazio, R. H., Sanbonmatsu, D. M., Powell, M. C., & Kardes, F. R. (1986). On the automatic activation of attitudes. *Journal of Personality and Social Psychology, 50,* 229–238.

Fazio, R. H., & Williams, C. J. (1986). Attitude accessibility as a moderator of the attitude-perception and attitude–behavior relations: An investigation of the 1984 presidential election. *Journal of Personality and Social Psychology, 51,* 505–514.

Fazio, R. H., & Zanna, M. P. (1978). Attitudinal qualities relating to the strength of the attitude–behavior relationship. *Journal of Experimental Social Psychology, 14,* 398–408.

Fazio, R. H., & Zanna, M. P. (1981). Direct experience and attitude–behavior consistency. In L. Berkowitz (Ed.), *Advances in experimental social psychology* (Vol. 14, pp. 162–202). New York: Academic Press.

Fazio, R. H., Zanna, M. P., & Cooper, J. (1977). Dissonance and self-perception: An integrative view of each theory's proper domain of application. *Journal of Experimental Social Psychology, 13,* 464–479.

Feather, N. T. (1963). Cognitive dissonance, sensitivity, and evaluation. *Journal of Abnormal and Social Psychology, 66,* 157–163.

Festinger, L. (1954). A theory of social comparison processes. *Human Relations, 7,* 117–140.

Festinger, L. (1957). *A theory of cognitive dissonance*. Stanford, CA: Stanford University Press.

Festinger, L. (1964). *Conflict, decision, and dissonance*. Stanford, CA: Stanford University Press.

Festinger, L., & Carlsmith, J. M. (1959). Cognitive consequences of forced compliance. *Journal of Abnormal and Social Psychology, 58*, 203–210.

Festinger, L., & Maccoby, N. (1964). On resistance to persuasive communications. *Journal of Abnormal and Social Psychology, 68*, 359–366.

Festinger, L., Riecken, H. W., & Schachter, S. (1956). *When prophecy fails*. Minneapolis: University of Minnesota Press.

Finckenauer, J. O. (1982). *Scared straight and the panacea phenomenon*. Englewood Cliffs, NJ: Prentice-Hall.

Fine, B. J. (1957). Conclusion-drawing, communicator credibility, and anxiety as factors in opinion change. *Journal of Abnormal and Social Psychology, 54*, 369–374.

Fink, E. L., Monahan, J. L., & Kaplowitz, S. A. (1989). A spatial model of the mere exposure effect. *Communication Research, 16*, 746–769.

Fishbein, M. (1967). A consideration of beliefs, and their role in attitude measurement. In M. Fishbein (Ed.), *Readings in attitude theory and measurement* (pp. 257–266). New York: Wiley.

Fishbein, M., & Ajzen, I. (1975). *Belief, attitude, intention, and behavior: An introduction to theory and research*. Reading, MA: Addison-Wesley.

Fishbein, M., & Ajzen, I. (1980). Predicting and understanding consumer behavior: Attitude–behavior correspondence. In I. Ajzen & M. Fishbein (Eds.), *Understanding attitudes and predicting social behavior* (pp. 148–172). Englewood Cliffs, NJ: Prentice-Hall.

Fishbein, M., & Ajzen, I. (1981). Attitudes and voting behavior: An application of the theory of reasoned action. In G. M. Stephenson & J. M. Davis (Eds.), *Progress in applied social psychology* (Vol. 1, pp. 253–313). New York: Wiley.

Fishbein, M., Jaccard, J. J., Davidson, A., Ajzen, I., & Loken, B. (1980). Predicting and understanding family planning behaviors: Beliefs, attitudes, and intentions. In I. Ajzen & M. Fishbein (Eds.), *Understanding attitudes and predicting social behavior* (pp. 130–147). Englewood Cliffs, NJ: Prentice-Hall.

Fitzpatrick, M. A., & Winke, J. (1979). You always hurt the one you love: Strategies and tactics in interpersonal conflict. *Communication Quarterly, 27*, 1–11.

Flay, B. R. (1981). On improving the chances of mass media health promotion programs causing meaningful changes in behavior. In M. Meyer (Ed.), *Health education by television and radio* (pp. 56–91). Munich: Saur.

Fleming, D. (1967). Attitude: The history of a concept. *Perspectives in American History, 1*, 287–365.

Fletcher, J. (1966). *Situation ethics: The new morality*. Philadelphia: Westminster.

Flora, J. A., Maccoby, N., & Farquhar, J. W. (1989). Communication campaigns to prevent cardiovascular disease: The Stanford community studies. In R. E. Rice & C. K. Atkin (Eds.), *Public communication campaigns* (2nd ed., pp. 233–252). Newbury Park, CA: Sage.

Flora, J. A., & Maibach, E. W. (1990). Cognitive responses to AIDS information: The effects of issue involvement and message appeal. *Communication Research, 17*, 759–774.

Frandsen, K. D. (1963). Effects of threat appeals and media of transmission. *Speech Monographs, 30*, 101–104.

Frankena, W. K. (1973). *Ethics* (2nd ed.). Englewood Cliffs, NJ: Prentice-Hall.

Freedman, J., Carlsmith, M., & Sears, D. O. (1970). *Social psychology*. Englewood Cliffs, NJ: Prentice-Hall.

Freedman, J. L., & Fraser, S. C. (1966). Compliance without pressure: The foot-in-the-door technique. *Journal of Personality and Social Psychology, 4*, 195–202.

Freedman J. L., & Sears, D. O. (1965). Selective exposure. In L. Berkowitz (Ed.), *Advances in experimental social psychology* (Vol. 2, pp. 58–97). New York: Academic Press.

Freimuth, V. S. (1990). The chronically uninformed: Closing the knowledge gap in health. In E. B. Ray & L. Donohew (Eds.), *Communication and health: Systems and applications* (pp. 171–186). Hillsdale, NJ: Lawrence Erlbaum Associates.

Freimuth, V. S., Hammond, S. L., Edgar, T., & Monahan, J. L. (1990). Reaching those at risk: A content-analytic study of AIDS PSAs. *Communication Research, 17*, 775–791.

Freimuth, V. S., & Marron, T. (1978). The public's use of health information. *Health Education, 9*, 18–20.

French, J. R. P., Jr., & Raven, B. (1960). The bases of social power. In D. Cartwright & A. Zander (Eds.), *Group dynamics* (pp. 607–623). New York: Harper & Row.

Frey, D. (1986). Recent research on selective exposure to information. In L. Berkowitz (Ed.), *Advances in experimental social psychology* (Vol. 19, pp. 41–80). Orlando, FL: Academic Press.

Gaes, G. G., Kalle, R. J., & Tedeschi, J. T. (1978). Impression management in the forced compliance situation: Two studies using the bogus pipeline. *Journal of Experimental Social Psychology, 14*, 493–510.

Galanter, M. (1989). *Cults: Faith, healing, and coercion*. New York: Oxford.

Gangestad, S., & Snyder, M. (1985). "To carve nature at its joints": On the existence of discrete classes in personality. *Psychological Review, 92*, 317–349.

Gardner, H. (1982). *Developmental psychology* (2nd ed.). Boston: Little, Brown.

Gardner, M. (1966). The eerie mathematical art of Maurits C. Escher. *Scientific American, 214*, 110–121.

Geller, E. S. (1989). Using television to promote safety belt use. In R. E. Rice & C. K. Atkin (Eds.), *Public communication campaigns* (2nd ed., pp. 201–203). Newbury Park, CA: Sage.

Gelman, E. (1985, May 6). Coke tampers with success. *Newsweek*.

Gerard, H. B., & Mathewson, G. C. (1966). The effect of severity of initiation on liking for a group: A replication. *Journal of Experimental Social Psychology, 2*, 278–287.

Gerbner, G., Gross, L., Morgan, M., & Signorielli, N. (1980). The "mainstreaming" of America: Violence Profile No. 11. *Journal of Communication, 30*, 10–29.

Gergen, K. J. (1973). Social psychology as history. *Journal of Personality and Social Psychology, 26*, 309–320.

Giles, H., & Smith, P. M. (1979). Accommodation theory: Optimal levels of convergence. In H. Giles & R. N. St. Clair (Eds.), *Language and social psychology* (pp. 45–65). Baltimore, MD: University Park Press.

Giles, H., & Street, R. L., Jr. (1985). Communicator characteristics and behavior. In M. L. Knapp & G. R. Miller (Eds.), *Handbook of interpersonal communication* (pp. 205–261). Beverly Hills, CA: Sage.

Gilkinson, H., Paulson, S. F., & Sikkink, D. E. (1954). Effects of order and authority in an argumentative speech. *Quarterly Journal of Speech, 40,* 183–192.

Gillig, P. M., & Greenwald, A. G. (1974). Is it time to lay the sleeper effect to rest? *Journal of Personality and Social Psychology, 29,* 132–139.

Gleicher, F., & Petty, R. E. (1992). Expectations of reassurance influence the nature of fear-stimulated attitude change. *Journal of Experimental Social Psychology, 28,* 86–100.

Goethals, G. R., & Nelson, R. E. (1973). Similarity in the influence process: The belief-value distinction. *Journal of Personality and Social Psychology, 25,* 117–122.

Goldstein, M. J. (1959). The relationship between coping and avoiding behavior and response to fear-arousing propaganda. *Journal of Abnormal and Social Psychology, 58,* 247–257.

Gorn, G. J. (1982). The effects of music in advertising on choice behavior: A classical conditioning approach. *Journal of Marketing, 46,* 94–101.

Granberg, D. (1982). Social judgment theory. In M. Burgoon (Ed.), *Communication yearbook 6* (pp. 304–329). Beverly Hills, CA: Sage.

Granberg, D., & Brent, E. E. (1974). Dove-hawk placements in the 1968 election: Application of social judgment and balance theories. *Journal of Personality and Social Psychology, 29,* 687–695.

Granberg, D., & Jenks, R. (1977). Assimilation and contrast in the 1972 election. *Human Relations, 30,* 623–640.

Granberg, D., & Seidel, J. (1976). Social judgments of the urban and Vietnam issues in 1968 and 1972. *Social Forces, 55,* 1–15.

Green, L. W., & McAlister, A. (1984). Macro-intervention to support health behavior: Some theoretical perspectives and practical reflections. *Health Education Quarterly, 11,* 323–339.

Greenberg, B. S., & Miller, G. R. (1966). The effects of low-credible sources on message acceptance. *Speech Monographs, 33,* 127–136.

Greenspoon, J. (1955). The reinforcing effect of two spoken sounds on the frequency of two responses. *American Journal of Psychology, 68,* 409–416.

Greenwald, A. G. (1968). Cognitive learning, cognitive response to persuasion, and attitude change. In A. G. Greenwald, T. C. Brock, & T. M. Ostrom (Eds.), *Psychological foundations of attitudes* (pp. 147–170). New York: Academic Press.

Greenwald, A. G. (1975). On the inconclusiveness of "crucial" cognitive tests of dissonance versus self-perception theories. *Journal of Experimental Social Psychology, 11,* 490–499.

Greenwald, A. G., & Ronis, D. L. (1978). Twenty years of cognitive dissonance: Case study of the evolution of a theory. *Psychological Review, 85,* 53–57.

Greenwald, A. G., Spangenberg, E. R., Pratkanis, A. R., & Eskenazi, J. (1991). Double-blind tests of subliminal self-help audiotapes. *Psychological Science, 2,* 119–122.

Greenwald, J. (1985, July 22) Coca-Cola's big fizzle. *Time.*

Gruder, C. L., Cook, T. D., Hennigan, K. M., Flay, B. R., Alessis, C., & Halamaj, J. (1978). Empirical tests of the absolute sleeper effect predicted from the discounting cue hypothesis. *Journal of Personality and Social Psychology, 36,* 1061–1074.

Gruner, C. R. (1985). Advice to the beginning speaker on using humor—What the research tells us. *Communication Education, 34,* 142–147.

Grunig, J. E. (1989). Publics, audiences and market segments: Segmentation principles for campaigns. In C. T. Salmon (Ed.), *Information campaigns: Balancing social values and social change* (pp. 199–228). Newbury Park, CA: Sage.

Grush, J. E., McKeough, K. L., & Ahlering, R. F. (1978). Extrapolating laboratory exposure research to actual political elections. *Journal of Personality and Social Psychology, 36*, 257–270.

Gulley, H. E., & Berlo, D. K. (1956). Effect of intercellular and intracellular speech structure on attitude change and learning. *Speech Monographs, 23*, 288–297.

Gunther, A. C. (1991). What we think others think: Cause and consequence in the third-person effect. *Communication Research, 18*, 355–372.

Guttman, L. (1944). A basis for scaling qualitative data. *American Sociological Review, 9*, 139–150.

Hamlin, S. (1988). *How to talk so people listen: The real key to job success.* New York: Harper & Row.

Hannah, D. B., & Sternthal, B. (1984). Detecting and explaining the sleeper effect. *Journal of Consumer Research, 11*, 632–642.

Harmon, R. R., & Coney, K. A. (1982). The persuasive effects of source credibility in buy and lease situations. *Journal of Marketing Research, 19*, 255–260.

Harrison, A. A. (1977). Mere exposure. In L. Berkowitz (Ed.), *Advances in experimental social psychology* (Vol. 10, pp. 40–83). New York: Academic Press.

Hart, R. P. (1984). *Verbal style and the presidency: A computer-based analysis.* Orlando, FL: Academic Press.

Hartman, M. (1976). A descriptive study of the language of men and women born in Maine around 1900 as it reflects the Lakoff hypothesis in "Language and women's place." In B. L. Dubois & I. Crouch (Eds.), *The sociology of the languages of American women* (pp. 81–90). San Antonio, TX: Trinity University Press.

Haslett, B. (1983). Preschoolers' communicative strategies in gaining compliance from peers: A developmental study. *Quarterly Journal of Speech, 69*, 84–99.

Hass, R. G. (1981). Effects of source characteristics on cognitive responses and persuasion. In R. E. Petty, T. M. Ostrom, & T. C. Brock (Eds.), *Cognitive responses in persuasion* (pp. 141–172). Hillsdale, NJ: Lawrence Erlbaum Associates.

Hass, R. G., & Linder, D. E. (1972). Counterargument availability and the effects of message structure on persuasion. *Journal of Personality and Social Psychology, 23*, 219–233.

Hawkins, D. (1970). The effects of subliminal stimulation on drive level and brand preference. *Journal of Marketing Research, 8*, 322–326.

Heider, F. (1958). *The psychology of interpersonal relations.* New York: Wiley.

Heingartner, A., & Hall, J. V. (1974). Affective consequences in adults and children of repeated exposure to auditory stimuli. *Journal of Personality and Social Psychology, 29*, 719–723.

Helson, H. (1964). *Adaptation-level theory: An experimental and systematic approach to behavior.* New York: Harper & Row.

Herek, G. M. (1987). Can functions be measured? A new perspective on the functional approach to attitudes. *Social Psychology Quarterly, 50*, 285–303.

Hess, E. H. (1965). Attitude and pupil size. *Scientific American, 212*, 46–54.

Higbee, K. L. (1969). Fifteen years of fear arousal: Research on threat appeals: 1953–1968. *Psychological Bulletin, 72*, 426–444.

Higgins, E. T., Rhodewalt, F., & Zanna, M. P. (1979). Dissonance motivation: Its nature, persistence, and reinstatement. *Journal of Experimental Social Psychology,* *15,* 16–34.

Horai, J., Naccari, N., & Fatoullah, E. (1974). The effects of expertise and physical attractiveness upon opinion agreement and liking. *Sociometry, 37,* 601–606.

Hosman, L. A. (1989). The evaluative consequences of hedges, hesitations, and intensifiers: Powerful and powerless speech styles. *Human Communication Research, 15,* 383–406.

Hovland, C. I. (1959). Reconciling conflicting results derived from experimental and survey studies of attitude change. *American Psychologist, 14,* 8–17.

Hovland, C. I., Harvey, O. J., & Sherif, M. (1957). Assimilation and contrast effects in reactions to communication and attitude change. *Journal of Abnormal and Social Psychology, 55,* 244–252.

Hovland, C. I., Janis, I. L., & Kelley, H. H. (1953). *Communication and persuasion.* New Haven, CT: Yale University Press.

Hovland, C. I., Lumsdaine, A. A., & Sheffield, F. D. (1949). *Experiments on mass communication.* Princeton, NJ: Princeton University Press.

Hovland, C. I., & Mandell, W. (1952). An experimental comparison of conclusion-drawing by the communicator and by the audience. *Journal of Abnormal and Social Psychology, 47,* 581–588.

Hovland, C. I., Mandell, W., Campbell, E. H., Brock, T., Luchins, A. S., Cohen, A. R., McGuire, W. J., Janis, I. L., Feierabend, R. L., & Anderson, N. H. (Eds.). (1957). *The order of presentation in persuasion.* New Haven, CT: Yale University Press.

Hovland, C. I., & Sherif, M. (1952). Judgmental phenomena and scales of attitude measurement: Item displacement in Thurstone scales. *Journal of Abnormal and Social Psychology, 47,* 822–832.

Hovland, C. I., & Weiss, W. (1951). The influence of source credibility on communication effectiveness. *Public Opinion Quarterly, 15,* 635–650.

Hoyt, M. F., Henley, M. D., & Collins, B. E. (1972). Studies in forced compliance: Confluence of choice and consequence on attitude change. *Journal of Personality and Social Psychology, 23,* 205–210.

Huff, D. (1954). *How to lie with statistics.* New York: Norton.

Hunter, E. (1951). *Brain-washing in Red China.* New York: Vanguard.

Hunter, E. (1956). *Brainwashing: The story of men who defied it.* New York: Farar, Strauss & Cudahy.

Hunter, J. E., & Boster, F. J. (1987). A model of compliance-gaining message selection. *Communication Monographs, 54,* 63–84.

Hunter, J. E., Gerbing, D. W., & Boster, F. J. (1982). Machiavellian beliefs and personality: Construct invalidity of the Machiavellianism dimension. *Journal of Personality and Social Psychology, 43,* 1293–1305.

Hyman, H. H., & Sheatsley, P. B. (1947). Some reasons why information campaigns fail. *Public Opinion Quarterly, 11,* 412–423.

Insko, C. A. (1965). Verbal reinforcement of attitudes. *Journal of Personality and Social Psychology, 2,* 621–623.

Insko, C. A. (1967). *Theories of attitude change.* New York: Appleton-Century-Crofts.

Insko, C. A., & Cialdini, R. B. (1969). A test of three interpretations of attitudinal verbal reinforcement. *Journal of Personality and Social Psychology, 12,* 333–341.

Jaccard, J. J., & Davidson, A. R. (1972). Toward an understanding of family planning behaviors: An initial investigation. *Journal of Applied Social Psychology, 2,* 228–235.

Jackson, S., & Backus, D. (1982). Are compliance-gaining strategies dependent on situational variables? *Central States Speech Journal, 33,* 469–479.

Janis, I. L., & Gilmore, J. B. (1965). The influence of incentive conditions on the success of role-playing in modifying attitudes. *Journal of Personality and Social Psychology, 1,* 17–27.

Janis, I. L., Kaye, D., & Kirschner, P. (1965). Facilitating effects of "eating-while-reading" on responsiveness to persuasive communications. *Journal of Personality and Social Psychology, 1,* 181–186.

Janis, I. L., & King, B. T. (1954). The influence of role playing on opinion change. *Journal of Abnormal and Social Psychology, 49,* 211–218.

Janis, I. L., & Leventhal, H. (1968). Human reaction to stress. In E. F. Borgotta & W. W. Lambert (Eds.), *Handbook of personality theory and research* (pp. 1041–1085). Chicago: Rand McNally.

Janis, I. L., & Mann, L. (1965). Effectiveness of emotional role playing in modifying smoking habits and attitudes. *Journal of Experimental Research in Personality, 1,* 84–90.

Johnson, B. T., & Eagly, A. H. (1989). Effects of involvement on persuasion: A meta-analysis. *Psychological Bulletin, 106,* 290–314.

Johnson, H. H., & Scileppi, J. A. (1969). Effects of ego-involvement conditions on attitude change to high and low credibility communicators. *Journal of Personality and Social Psychology, 13,* 31–36.

Johnson, J. T., & Taylor, S. E. (1981). The effect of metaphor on political attitudes. *Basic and Applied Social Psychology, 2,* 305–316.

Jones, E. E., & Sigall, H. (1971). The bogus pipeline: A new paradigm for measuring affect and attitude. *Psychological Bulletin, 76,* 349–364.

Jones, R. (1984). The third wave. In A. Pines & C. Maslach (Eds.), *Experiencing social psychology: Readings and projects* (2nd ed., pp. 259–266). New York: Knopf.

Jones, R. A., Linder, D. E., Kiesler, C. A., Zanna, M. P., & Brehm, J. W. (1968). Internal states or external stimuli: Observers' attitude judgments and the dissonance theory-self-persuasion controversy. *Journal of Experimental Social Psychology, 4,* 247–269.

Jones, S. B., & Burgoon, M. (1975). Empirical investigations of language intensity: II. The effects of irrelevant fear and language intensity on attitude change. *Human Communication Research, 1,* 248–251.

Jowett, G. S., & O'Donnell, V. (1986). *Propaganda and persuasion.* Beverly Hills, CA: Sage.

Judd, C. M., Drake, R. A., Downing, J. W., & Krosnick, J. A. (1991). Some dynamic properties of attitude structures: Context-induced response facilitation and polarization. *Journal of Personality and Social Psychology, 60,* 193–202.

Judd, C. M., Kenny, D. A., & Krosnick, J. A. (1983). Judging the positions of political candidates: Models of assimilation and contrast. *Journal of Personality and Social Psychology, 44,* 952–963.

Kahle, L. R., & Homer, P. M. (1985). Physical attractiveness of the celebrity endorser: A social adaptation perspective. *Journal of Consumer Research, 11,* 954–961.

Karlins, M., & Abelson, H. I. (1970). *Persuasion: How opinions and attitudes are changed.* New York: Springer.

Katz, D. (1960). The functional approach to the study of attitudes. *Public Opinion Quarterly, 24,* 163–204.

Keen, J. (1990, July 16). Heavy metal on trial: Nevada judge will decide landmark suit. *USA Today,* 1A.

Kelly, G. A. (1955). *The psychology of personal constructs.* New York: W.W. Norton.

Kelly, J. S. (1979). Subliminal embeds in print advertising: A challenge to advertising ethics. *Journal of Advertising, 8,* 20–24.

Kelman, H. C. (1958). Compliance, identification, and internalization: Three processes of attitude change. *Journal of Conflict Resolution, 2,* 51–60.

Kelman, H. C., & Hovland, C. I. (1953). "Reinstatement" of the communicator in delayed measurement of opinion change. *Journal of Abnormal and Social Psychology, 48,* 327–335.

Key, W. B. (1974). *Subliminal seduction.* New York: Signet Books.

Kiesler, C. A. (1971). *The psychology of commitment.* New York: Academic Press.

Kiesler, C. A., Collins, B. E., & Miller, N. (1969). *Attitude change: A critical analysis of theoretical approaches.* New York: Wiley.

Kiesler, C. A., & Kiesler, S. B. (1964). Role of forewarning in persuasive communications. *Journal of Abnormal and Social Psychology, 68,* 547–549.

Kiesler, C. A., & Pallak, M. S. (1976). Arousal properties of dissonance manipulations. *Psychological Bulletin, 83,* 1014–1025.

Kihlstrom, J. F. (1987). The cognitive unconscious. *Science, 237,* 1445–1452.

Kilbourne, W. E., Painton, S., & Ridley, D. (1985). The effect of sexual embedding on responses to magazine advertisements. *Journal of Advertising, 14,* 48–56.

Kinder, D. R., & Sears, D. O. (1985). Public opinion and political action. In G. Lindzey & E. Aronson (Eds.), *Handbook of social psychology* (Vol. 2, pp. 659–741). New York: Random House.

King, C. S. (1969). *My life with Martin Luther King, Jr.* New York: Holt, Rinehart & Winston.

King, B. T., & Janis, I. L. (1956). Comparison of the effectiveness of improvised versus nonimprovised role-playing in producing opinion change. *Human Relations, 9,* 177–186.

King, M. (1977–1978). Assimilation and contrast of presidential candidates' issue positions, 1972. *Public Opinion Quarterly, 41,* 515–522.

King, S. W., Minami, Y., & Samovar, L. A. (1985). A comparison of Japanese and American perceptions of source credibility. *Communication Research Reports, 2,* 76–79.

Kipnis, D., & Cohen, E. S. (1980, April). *Power tactics and affection.* Paper presented at the annual meeting of the Eastern Psychological Association, Philadelphia.

Kipnis, D., Schmidt, S. M., & Wilkinson, I. (1980). Intraorganizational influence tactics: Explorations in getting one's way. *Journal of Applied Psychology, 65,* 440–452.

Kitayama, S. (1990). Interaction between affect and cognition in word perception. *Journal of Personality and Social Psychology, 58,* 209–217.

Klapper, J. T. (1960). *The effects of mass communication.* New York: Free Press.

Kluckhohn, C. (1951). Values and value orientations in the theory of action. In T. Parsons & E. A. Shils (Eds.), *Toward a general theory of action.* Cambridge, MA: Harvard University Press.

Knower, F. H. (1936). Experimental studies of changes in attitudes: I. A study of the effect of oral argument on changes of attitude. *Journal of Social Psychology, 6,* 315–347.

Knox, R. E., & Inkster, J. A. (1968). Postdecision dissonance at posttime. *Journal of Personality and Social Psychology, 8,* 310–323.

Korzybski, A. (1933). *Science and sanity: An introduction to non-Aristotelian systems and general semantics* (2nd ed.). Lancaster, PA: International Non-Aristotelian Library.

Kothandapani, V. (1971). Validation of feeling, belief, and intention to act as three components of attitude and their contribution to prediction of contraceptive behavior. *Journal of Personality and Social Psychology, 19,* 321–333.

Kotler, P. (1975). *Marketing for nonprofit organizations.* Englewood Cliffs, NJ: Prentice-Hall.

Kotler, P., & Zaltman, G. (1971). Social marketing: An approach to planned social change. *Journal of Marketing, 35,* 3–12.

Kraus, S. (Ed.). (1962). *The great debates: Background, perspective, effects.* Bloomington, IN: Indiana University Press.

Kraus, S. (1988). *Televised presidential debates and public policy.* Hillsdale, NJ: Lawrence Erlbaum Associates.

Kraus, S., & Davis, D. (1976). *The effects of mass communication on political behavior.* University Park: Pennsylvania State University Press.

Kutner, B., Wilkins, C., & Yarrow, P. R. (1952). Verbal attitudes and overt behavior involving racial prejudice. *Journal of Abnormal and Social Psychology, 47,* 649–652.

LaBarbera, P., & Maclachlan, J. (1979). Time compressed speech in radio advertising. *Journal of Marketing, 43,* 30–36.

Lakoff, R. T. (1975). *Language and woman's place.* New York: Harper & Row.

Lammers, H. B., Leibowitz, L., Seymour, G. E., & Hennessey, J. E. (1983). Humor and cognitive responses to advertising stimuli: A trace consolidation approach. *Journal of Business Research, 11,* 173–185.

Langer, E. J. (1978). Rethinking the role of thought in social interaction. In J. H. Harvey, W. J. Ickes, & R. F. Kidd (Eds.), *New directions in attribution research* (Vol. 2, pp. 35–58). Hillsdale, NJ: Lawrence Erlbaum Associates.

LaPiere, R. T. (1934). Attitudes vs. action. *Social Forces, 13,* 230–237.

Lazarsfeld, P. F., & Merton. R. K. (1949). Mass communication, popular taste and organized social action. In W. Schramm (Ed.), *Mass communications* (pp. 459–480). Urbana, IL: University of Illinois Press.

Lefebvre, R. C., & Flora, J. A. (1988). Social marketing and public health intervention. *Health Education Quarterly, 15,* 299–315.

Leippe, M. R., & Elkin, R. A. (1987). When motives clash: Issue involvement and response involvement as determinants of persuasion. *Journal of Personality and Social Psychology, 52,* 269–278.

Lennox, R. D., & Wolfe, R. N. (1984). Revision of the self-monitoring scale. *Journal of Personality and Social Psychology, 46,* 1349–1364.

Lerbinger, O. (1972). *Designs for persuasive communication.* Englewood Cliffs, NJ: Prentice-Hall.

Leventhal, H. (1970). Findings and theory in the study of fear communications. In L. Berkowitz (Ed.), *Advances in experimental social psychology* (Vol. 5, pp. 120–186). New York: Academic Press.

Leventhal, H., Singer, R., & Jones, S. (1965). Effects of fear and specificity of recommendation upon attitudes and behavior. *Journal of Personality and Social Psychology, 2*, 20–29.

Levine, J. M., & Valle, R. S. (1975). The convert as a credible communicator. *Social Behavior and Personality, 3*, 81–90.

Libby, W. L., Jr., Lacey, B. C., & Lacey, J. I. (1973). Pupillary and cardiac activity during visual attention. *Psychophysiology, 10*, 270–294.

Liebert, R. M., Sprafkin, J. N., & Davidson, E. S. (1982). *The early window: Effects of television on children and youth* (2nd ed.). Elmsford, NY: Pergamon.

Lifton, R. J. (1961). *Thought reform and the psychology of totalism: A study of "brainwashing" in China.* New York: W.W. Norton.

Likert, R. (1932). A technique for the measurement of attitudes. *Archives of Psychology, 140*, 1–55.

Linder, D. E., Cooper, J., & Jones, E. E. (1967). Decision freedom as a determinant of the role of incentive magnitude in attitude change. *Journal of Personality and Social Psychology, 6*, 245–254.

Linz, D. G., & Penrod, S. (1984). Increasing attorney persuasiveness in the courtroom. *Law and Psychology Review, 8*, 1–47.

Lippmann, W. (1941). *Public opinion.* New York: Macmillan.

Liska, J. (1978). Situational and topical variations in credibility criteria. *Communication Monographs, 45*, 85–92.

Lofland, J. (1977). "Becoming a world-saver" revisited. *American Behavioral Scientist, 20*, 805–818.

London, H. (1973). *Psychology of the persuader.* Morristown, NJ: General Learning Press.

Lord, C. G., Ross, L., & Lepper, M. R. (1979). Biased assimilation and attitude polarization: The effects of prior theories on subsequently considered evidence. *Journal of Personality and Social Psychology, 37*, 2098–2109.

Luchok, J. A., & McCroskey, J. C. (1978). The effect of quality of evidence on attitude change and source credibility. *Southern Speech Communication Journal, 43*, 371–383.

Lustig, M. W., & Myers, S. (1983, February). *Compliance-gaining strategy selection: A comparison of six countries.* Paper presented at the Western Speech Communication Association annual convention, Albuquerque, NM.

Maccoby, E. E., & Jacklin, C. N. (1974). *The psychology of sex differences.* Stanford, CA: Stanford University Press.

Maccoby, E. E., & Martin, J. (1983). Socialization in the context of the family: Parent–child interaction. In P. H. Mussen (Series Ed.) & E. M. Hetherington (Vol. Ed.), *Handbook of child psychology: Vol. 4. Socialization, personality, and social development* (4th ed., pp. 1–101). New York: Wiley.

Maccoby, N., & Farquhar, J. W. (1975). Communication for health: Unselling heart disease. *Journal of Communication, 25*, 114–126.

Madden, T. J., & Weinberger, M. G. (1984). Humor in advertising: A practitioner view. *Journal of Advertising Research, 24*, 23–29.

Maddux, J. E., & Rogers, R. W. (1983). Protection motivation and self-efficacy: A revised theory of fear appeals and attitude change. *Journal of Experimental Social Psychology, 19*, 469–479.

Maibach, E., Flora, J. A., & Nass, C. (1991). Changes in self-efficacy and health behavior in response to a minimal contact community health campaign. *Health Communication, 3*, 1–15.

Malkis, F. S., Kalle, R. J., & Tedeschi, J. T. (1982). Attitudinal politics in the forced compliance paradigm. *Journal of Social Psychology, 117,* 79–91.

Mann, L., & Janis, I. L. (1968). A follow-up study on the long-term effects of emotional role playing. *Journal of Personality and Social Psychology, 8,* 339–242.

Manstead, A. S. R., Proffitt, C., & Smart, J. L. (1983). Predicting and understanding mothers' infant-feeding intentions and behavior: Testing the theory of reasoned action. *Journal of Personality and Social Psychology, 44,* 657–671.

Markham, D. (1968). The dimensions of source credibility of television newscasters. *Journal of Communication, 18,* 57–64.

Markiewicz, D. (1974). Effects of humor on persuasion. *Sociometry, 37,* 407–422.

Martin, N. A. (1968). The outlandish idea: How a marketing man would save India. *Marketing/Communications, 297,* 54–60.

Marwell, G., & Schmitt, D. R. (1967). Dimensions of compliance-gaining behavior: An empirical analysis. *Sociometry, 30,* 350–364.

Mazursky, D., & Schul, Y. (1988). The effects of advertisement encoding on the failure to discount information: Implications for the sleeper effect. *Journal of Consumer Research, 15,* 24–36.

McAlister, A. L., Perry, C., & Maccoby, N. (1979). Adolescent smoking: Onset and prevention. *Pediatrics, 63,* 650–658.

McConnell, J. V., Cutler, R. L., & McNeil, E. B. (1958). Subliminal stimulation: An overview. *American Psychologist, 13,* 229–242.

McCroskey, J. C. (1966). Scales for the measurement of ethos. *Speech Monographs, 33,* 65–72.

McCroskey, J. C. (1969). A summary of experimental research on the effects of evidence in persuasive communication. *Quarterly Journal of Speech, 55,* 169–176.

McCroskey, J. C. (1972). *An introduction to rhetorical communication.* Englewood Cliffs, NJ: Prentice-Hall.

McCroskey, J. C., Holdridge, W. E., & Toomb, J. K. (1974). An instrument for measuring the source credibility of basic speech communication instructors. *Speech Teacher, 23,* 26–33.

McCroskey, J. C., Richmond, V. P., & Daly, J. A. (1975). The development of a measure of perceived homophily in interpersonal communication. *Human Communication Research, 1,* 325–332.

McGuire, W. J. (1962). Persistence of the resistance to persuasion induced by various types of prior belief defenses. *Journal of Abnormal and Social Psychology, 64,* 241–248.

McGuire, W. J. (1968). Personality and susceptibility to social influence. In E. F. Borgotta & W. W. Lambert (Eds.), *Handbook of personality theory and research* (pp. 1130–1187). Chicago: Rand McNally.

McGuire, W. J. (1969). The nature of attitudes and attitude change. In G. Lindzey & E. Aronson (Eds.), *Handbook of social psychology* (2nd ed., Vol. 3, pp. 136–314). Reading, MA: Addison-Wesley.

McGuire, W. J. (1970, February). A vaccine for brainwash. *Psychology Today, 3,* 36–39, 63–64.

McGuire, W. J. (1984). Public communication as a strategy for inducing health-promoting behavior change. *Preventive Medicine, 13,* 299–319.

McGuire, W. J. (1985). Attitudes and attitude change. In G. Lindzey & E. Aronson (Eds.), *Handbook of social psychology* (3rd ed., Vol. 2, pp. 233–346). New York: Random House.

McGuire, W. J. (1989). Theoretical foundations of campaigns. In R. E. Rice & C. K. Atkin (Eds.), *Public communication campaigns* (2nd ed., pp. 43–65). Newbury Park, CA: Sage.

McGuire, W. J., & Papageorgis, D. (1961). The relative efficacy of various types of prior belief-defense in producing immunity against persuasion. *Journal of Abnormal and Social Psychology, 62,* 327–337.

McLeod, J. M., Atkin, C. K., & Chaffee, S. H. (1972). Adolescents, parents, and television use: Adolescent self-report measures from Maryland and Wisconsin samples. In G. A. Comstock & E. A. Rubinstein (Eds.), *Television and social behavior* (Vol. 3, pp. 173–238). Washington, DC: U.S. Government Printing Office.

McMillan, J. R., Clifton, A. K., McGrath, D., & Gale, W. S. (1977). Women's language: Uncertainty or interpersonal sensitivity and emotionality. *Sex Roles, 3,* 545–559.

McMurran, K., Neill, M. (1990, July 30). One woman's brave battle with AIDS. *People,* 62–65.

McSweeney, F. K., & Bierley, C. (1984). Recent developments in classical conditioning. *Journal of Consumer Research, 11,* 619–631.

Meeker, B. F., & Weitzel-O'Neill, P. A. (1977). Sex roles and interpersonal behavior in task-oriented groups. *American Sociological Review, 42,* 91–105.

Mehrabian, A., & Williams, M. (1969). Nonverbal concomitants of perceived and intended persuasiveness. *Journal of Personality and Social Psychology, 13,* 37–58.

Mendelsohn, H. (1973). Some reasons why information campaigns can succeed. *Public Opinion Quarterly, 37,* 50–61.

Merikle, P. M. (1982). Unconscious perception revisited. *Perception and Psychophysics, 31,* 298–301.

Merton, R. K. (1946). *Mass persuasion.* New York: Harper & Brothers.

Meyer, A. J., Nash, J. D., McAlister, A. L., Maccoby, N., & Farquhar, J. W. (1980). Skills training in a cardiovascular health education campaign. *Journal of Consulting and Clinical Psychology, 48,* 129–142.

Meyer, J. R. (1990). Cognitive processes underlying the retrieval of compliance-gaining strategies: An implicit rules model. In J. P. Dillard (Ed.), *Seeking compliance: The production of interpersonal influence messages* (pp. 57–73). Scottsdale, AZ: Gorsuch Scarisbrick.

Middlebrook, P. N. (1974). *Social psychology and modern life.* New York: Knopf.

Milgram, S., Mann, L., & Harter, S. (1965). The lost-letter technique: A tool of social science research. *Public Opinion Quarterly, 29,* 437–443.

Millar, M. G., & Tesser, A. (1986). Effects of affective and cognitive focus on the attitude–behavior relationship. *Journal of Personality and Social Psychology, 51,* 270–276.

Miller, G. R. (1972). Speech: An approach to human communication. In R. W. Budd & B. D. Ruben (Eds.), *Approaches to human communication* (pp. 383–400). Rochelle Park, NJ: Spartan-Hayden.

Miller, G. R. (1987). Persuasion. In C. R. Berger & S. H. Chaffee (Eds.), *Handbook of communication science* (pp. 446–483). Newbury Park, CA: Sage.

Miller, G. R., Boster, F. J., Roloff, M. E., & Seibold, D. R. (1977). Compliance-gaining message strategies: A typology and some findings concerning effects of situational differences. *Communication Monographs, 44,* 37–51.

Miller, G. R., Boster, F. J., Roloff, M. E., & Seibold, D. R. (1987). MBRS rekindled:

Some thoughts on compliance gaining in interpersonal settings. In M. E. Roloff & G. R. Miller (Eds.), *Interpersonal processes: New directions in communication research* (pp. 89–116). Newbury Park, CA: Sage.

Miller, G. R., & Burgoon, M. (1978). Persuasion research: Review and commentary. In B. D. Ruben (Ed.), *Communication yearbook 2* (pp. 29–47). New Brunswick, NJ: Transaction Books.

Miller, G. R., & Parks, M. R. (1982). Communication in dissolving relationships. In S. Duck (Ed.), *Personal relationships 4: Dissolving relationships* (pp. 127–154). Orlando, FL: Academic Press.

Miller, G. R., & Steinberg, M. (1975). *Between people: A new analysis of interpersonal communication.* Chicago: Science Research Associates.

Miller, M. M., White, H. A., & Boone, J. (1990, August). *Need for cognition and self-report of persuasive message attributes.* Paper presented to the annual convention of the Association for Education in Journalism and Mass Communication, Minneapolis.

Miller, N., & Baron, R. S. (1973). On measuring counterarguing. *Journal for the Theory of Social Behavior, 3,* 101–118.

Miller, N., & Campbell, D. T. (1959). Recency and primacy in persuasion as a function of the timing of speeches and measurements. *Journal of Abnormal and Social Psychology, 59,* 1–9.

Miller, N., Maruyama, G., Beaber, R. J., & Valone, K. (1976). Speed of speech and persuasion. *Journal of Personality and Social Psychology, 34,* 615–624.

Miller, R. L., Seligman, C., Clark, N. T., & Bush, M. (1976). Perceptual contrast versus reciprocal concession as mediators of induced compliance. *Canadian Journal of Behavioral Science, 8,* 401–409.

Millman, S. (1968). Anxiety, comprehension and susceptibility to social influence. *Journal of Personality and Social Psychology, 9,* 251–256.

Mills, J., & Harvey, J. (1972). Opinion change as a function of when information about the communicator is received and whether he is attractive or expert. *Journal of Personality and Social Psychology, 21,* 52–55.

Mischel, W. (1966). A social-learning view of sex differences in behavior. In E. E. Maccoby (Ed.), *The development of sex differences* (pp. 56–81). Stanford, CA: Stanford University Press.

Moore, D. L., Hausknecht, D., & Thamodaran, K. (1986). Time compression, response opportunity, and persuasion. *Journal of Consumer Research, 13,* 85–99.

Moore, T. E. (1982). Subliminal advertising: What you see is what you get. *Journal of Marketing, 46,* 38–47.

Moreland, R. L., & Zajonc, R. B. (1979). Exposure effects may not depend upon stimulus recognition. *Journal of Personality and Social Psychology, 37,* 1085–1089.

Morgan, M. (1982). Television and adolescents' sex role stereotypes: A longitudinal study. *Journal of Personality and Social Psychology, 43,* 947–955.

Morley, D. D., & Walker, K. B. (1987). The role of importance, novelty, and plausibility in producing belief change. *Communication Monographs, 54,* 436–442.

Mowen, J. C., & Cialdini, R. B. (1980). On implementing the door-in-the-face compliance technique in a business context. *Journal of Marketing Research, 17,* 253–258.

Mulac, A. (1976). Effects of obscene language upon three dimensions of listener attitude. *Communication Monographs, 43,* 300–307.

Mulac, A., Wiemann, J. M., Widenmann, S. J., & Gibson, T. W. (1988). Male/ female language differences in same-sex and mixed-sex dyads: The gender-linked language effect. *Communication Monographs, 55*, 315–335.

Naftulin, D. H., Ware, J. E., & Donnelly, F. A. (1973). The Doctor Fox lecture: A paradigm of educational seduction. *Journal of Medical Education, 48*, 630–635.

Nel, E., Helmreich, R., & Aronson, E. (1969). Opinion change in the advocate as a function of the persuasibility of his audience: A clarification of the meaning of dissonance. *Journal of Personality and Social Psychology, 12*, 117–124.

Neuliep, J. W., & Hazleton, V., Jr. (1985). A cross-cultural comparison of Japanese and American persuasive strategy selection. *International Journal of Intercultural Relations, 9*, 389–404.

Newcombe, N., & Arnkoff, D. B. (1979). Effect of speech style and sex of speaker on person perception. *Journal of Personality and Social Psychology, 37*, 1293–1303.

Niedenthal, P. M. (1990). Implicit perception of affective information. *Journal of Experimental Social Psychology, 26*, 505–527.

Nilsen, T. R. (1974). *Ethics of speech communication* (2nd ed.). Indianapolis: Bobbs-Merrill.

Nisbett, R., & Ross, L. (1980). *Human inference: Strategies and shortcomings in social judgment.* Englewood Cliffs, NJ: Prentice-Hall.

Norman, R. (1975). Affective-cognitive consistency, attitudes, conformity, and behavior. *Journal of Personality and Social Psychology, 32*, 83–91.

Norman, R. (1976). When what is said is important: A comparison of expert and attractive sources. *Journal of Experimental Social Psychology, 12*, 294–300.

Notes and Comment. (1957, September 21). *New Yorker, 33*, p. 33.

Oetting, E. R., Spooner, S., Beauvais, F., & Banning, J. (1991). Prevention, peer clusters, and the paths to drug abuse. In L. Donohew, H. E. Sypher, & W. J. Bukoski (Eds.), *Persuasive communication and drug abuse prevention* (pp. 239–261). Hillsdale, NJ: Lawrence Erlbaum Associates.

Ogden, C. K., & Richards, I. A. (1926). *The meaning of meaning.* New York: Harcourt, Brace.

O'Hair, D., & Cody, M. J. (1987). Machiavellian beliefs and social influence. *Western Journal of Speech Communication, 51*, 279–303.

O'Keefe, B. J., & Delia, J. G. (1979). Construct comprehensiveness and cognitive complexity as predictors of the number and strategic adaptation of arguments and appeals in a persuasive message. *Communication Monographs, 46*, 231–240.

O'Keefe, B. J., & Delia, J. G. (1982). Impression formation and message production. In M. E. Roloff & C. R. Berger (Eds.), *Social cognition and communication* (pp. 33–72). Beverly Hills, CA: Sage.

O'Keefe, B. J., & Shepherd, G. J. (1987). The pursuit of multiple objectives in face-to-face persuasive interactions: Effects of construct differentiation on message organization. *Communication Monographs, 54*, 396–419.

O'Keefe, D. J. (1990). *Persuasion: Theory and research.* Newbury Park, CA: Sage.

O'Keefe, G. J. (1985). "Taking a bite out of crime": The impact of a public information campaign. *Communication Research, 12*, 147–178.

O'Keefe, G. J., & Reid, K. (1989). The McGruff crime prevention campaign. In R. E. Rice & C. K. Atkin (Eds.), *Public communication campaigns* (2nd ed., pp. 210–212). Newbury Park, CA: Sage.

O'Keefe, G. J., & Reid, K. (1990). The uses and effects of public service advertising.

In L. A. Grunig & J. E. Grunig (Eds.), *Public relations research annual* (Vol. 2, pp. 67–91). Hillsdale, NJ: Lawrence Erlbaum Associates.

O'Quin, K., & Aronoff, J. (1981). Humor as a technique of social influence. *Social Psychology Quarterly, 44*, 349–357.

Orne, M. T. (1962). On the social psychology of the psychological experiment: With particular reference to demand characteristics and their implications. *American Psychologist, 17*, 776–783.

Osgood, C. E. (1974). Probing subjective culture/Part I: Cross-linguistic tool-making. *Journal of Communication, 24*, 21–35.

Osgood, C. E., Suci, G. J., & Tannenbaum, P. H. (1957). *The measurement of meaning.* Urbana, IL: University of Illinois Press.

Osgood, C. E., & Tannenbaum, P. H. (1955). The principle of congruity in the prediction of attitude change. *Psychology Review, 62*, 42–55.

Oskamp, S. (1977). *Attitudes and opinions.* Englewood Cliffs, NJ: Prentice-Hall.

Osterhouse, R. A., & Brock, T. C. (1970). Distraction increases yielding to propaganda by inhibiting counterarguing. *Journal of Personality and Social Psychology, 15*, 344–358.

Ostrom, T. M. (1969). The relationship between the affective, behavioral, and cognitive components of attitudes. *Journal of Experimental Social Psychology, 5*, 12–30.

Ostrom, T. M. (1973). The bogus pipeline: A new ignis fatuus? *Psychological Bulletin, 79*, 252–259.

Padgett, V. R., & Brock, T. C. (1988). Do advertising messages require intelligible content? A cognitive response analysis of unintelligible persuasive messages. In S. Hecker & D. W. Stewart (Eds.), *Nonverbal communication in advertising* (pp. 185–203). Lexington, MA: D.C. Heath.

Page, B. I., & Brody, R. A. (1972). Policy voting and the electoral process: The Vietnam War issue. *American Political Science Review, 66*, 979–995.

Page, M. M. (1969). Social psychology of a classical conditioning of attitudes experiment. *Journal of Personality and Social Psychology, 11*, 177–186.

Paisley, W. J. (1981). Public communication campaigns: The American experience. In R. E. Rice & W. J. Paisley (Eds.), *Public communication campaigns* (pp. 15–40). Beverly Hills, CA: Sage.

Pallak, M. S., & Pittman, T. S. (1972). General motivational effects of dissonance arousal. *Journal of Personality and Social Psychology, 21*, 349–358.

Pallak, S. (1983). Salience of a communicator's physical attractiveness and persuasion: A heuristic versus systematic processing interpretation. *Social Cognition, 2*, 156–168.

Papageorgis, D. (1968). Warning and persuasion. *Psychological Bulletin, 70*, 271–282.

Papageorgis, D., & McGuire, W. J. (1961). The generality of immunity to persuasion produced by pre-exposure to weakened counterarguments. *Journal of Abnormal and Social Psychology, 62*, 475–481.

Parsons, T. (1963). On the concept of influence. *Public Opinion Quarterly, 27*, 35–62.

Patzer, G. L. (1983). Source credibility as a function of communicator physical attractiveness. *Journal of Business Research, 11*, 229–241.

Pearce, W. B., & Conklin, F. (1971). Nonverbal vocalic communication and perceptions of a speaker. *Speech Monographs, 38*, 235–241.

Perloff, L. S., & Fetzer, B. K. (1986). Self-other judgments and perceived vulnerability to victimization. *Journal of Personality and Social Psychology, 50,* 502–510.

Perloff, R. M. (1978). *An attributional and cognitive response approach to personality and persuasibility.* Unpublished doctoral dissertation, University of Wisconsin-Madison.

Perloff, R. M. (1984). Political involvement: A critique and a process-oriented reformulation. *Critical Studies in Mass Communication, 1,* 146–160.

Perloff, R. M. (1989). Ego-involvement and the third person effect of televised news coverage. *Communication Research, 16,* 236–262.

Perloff, R. M., & Brock, T. C. (1980). "And thinking makes it so": Cognitive responses to persuasion. In M. E. Roloff & G. R. Miller (Eds.), *Persuasion: New directions in theory and research* (pp. 67–99). Beverly Hills, CA: Sage.

Perloff, R. M., & Pettey, G. (1991). Designing an AIDS information campaign to reach intravenous drug users and sex partners. *Public Health Reports, 106,* 460–463.

Pervin, L. A. (1978). Definitions, measurements and classifications of stimuli, situations and environments. *Human Ecology, 6,* 71–105.

Peterson, P. D., & Koulack, D. (1969). Attitude change as a function of latitudes of acceptance and rejection. *Journal of Personality and Social Psychology, 11,* 309–311.

Petty, R. E., & Brock, T. C. (1981). Thought disruption and persuasion: Assessing the validity of attitude change experiments. In R. E. Petty, T. M. Ostrom, & T. C. Brock (Eds.), *Cognitive responses in persuasion* (pp. 55–79). Hillsdale, NJ: Lawrence Erlbaum Associates.

Petty, R. E., & Cacioppo, J. T. (1977). Forewarning, cognitive responding, and resistance to persuasion. *Journal of Personality and Social Psychology, 35,* 645–655.

Petty, R. E., & Cacioppo, J. T. (1981). *Attitudes and persuasion: Classic and contemporary approaches.* Dubuque, IA: Wm. Brown.

Petty, R. E., & Cacioppo, J. T. (1984). The effects of involvement on responses to argument quantity and quality: Central and peripheral routes to persuasion. *Journal of Personality and Social Psychology, 46,* 69–81.

Petty, R. E., & Cacioppo, J. T. (1986). The elaboration likelihood model of persuasion. In L. Berkowitz (Ed.), *Advances in experimental social psychology* (Vol. 19, pp. 123–205). New York: Academic Press.

Petty, R. E., & Cacioppo, J. T. (1990). Involvement and persuasion: Tradition versus integration. *Psychological Bulletin, 107,* 367–374.

Petty, R. E., Cacioppo, J. T., & Goldman, R. (1981). Personal involvement as a determinant of argument-based persuasion. *Journal of Personality and Social Psychology, 41,* 847–855.

Petty, R. E., Cacioppo, J. T., & Heesacker, M. (1985). *Persistence of persuasion: A test of the Elaboration Likelihood Model.* Unpublished manuscript, University of Missouri, Columbia.

Petty, R. E., Cacioppo, J. T., Kasmer, J. A., & Haugtvedt, C. P. (1987). A reply to Stiff and Boster. *Communication Monographs, 54,* 257–263.

Petty, R. E., Gleicher, F., & Baker, S. M. (1991). Multiple roles for affect in persuasion. In J. Forgas (Ed.), *Emotion and social judgments* (pp. 181–200). Oxford: Pergamon.

Petty, R. E., Ostrom, T. M., & Brock, T. C. (1981). Historical foundations of the cognitive response approach to attitudes and persuasion. In R. E. Petty, T. M. Ostrom, & T. C. Brock (Eds.), *Cognitive responses in persuasion* (pp. 5–29). Hillsdale, NJ: Lawrence Erlbaum Associates.

Petty, R. E., Wells, G. L., & Brock, T. C. (1976). Distraction can enhance or reduce yielding to propaganda: Thought disruption versus effort justification. *Journal of Personality and Social Psychology, 34,* 874–884.

Pfau, M., & Burgoon, M. (1988). Inoculation in political campaign communication. *Human Communication Research, 15,* 91–111.

Pfau, M., & Kenski, H. C. (1990). *Attack politics: Strategy and defense.* New York: Praeger.

Piliavin, J. A., Piliavin, I. M., Loewenton, E. P., McCauley, C., & Hammond, P. (1969). On observers' reproductions of dissonance effects: The right answers for the wrong reasons? *Journal of Personality and Social Psychology, 13,* 98–105.

Pliner, P., Hart, H., Kohl, J., & Saari, D. (1974). Compliance without pressure: Some further data on the foot-in-the-door technique. *Journal of Experimental Social Psychology, 10,* 17–22.

Pollay, R. W. (1989). Campaigns, change and culture: On the polluting potential of persuasion. In C. T. Salmon (Ed.), *Information campaigns: Balancing social values and social change* (pp. 185–196). Newbury Park, CA: Sage.

Pratkanis, A. R. (1989). The cognitive representation of attitudes. In A. R. Pratkanis, S. J. Breckler, & A. G. Greenwald (Eds.), *Attitude structure and function* (pp. 71–98). Hillsdale, NJ: Lawrence Erlbaum Associates.

Pratkanis, A. R., & Aronson E. (1992). *Age of propaganda: The everyday use and abuse of persuasion.* New York: W.H. Freeman.

Pratkanis, A. R., & Greenwald, A. G. (1989). A sociocognitive model of attitude structure and function. In L. Berkowitz (Ed.), *Advances in experimental social psychology* (Vol. 22, pp. 245–285). San Diego: Academic Press.

Prime ribbing. (1974, March 26). *Time, 123,* p. 54.

Pryor, J. B., Gibbons, F. X., Wicklund, R. A., Fazio, R. H., & Hood, R. (1977). Self-focused attention and self-report validity. *Journal of Personality, 45,* 514–527.

Puska, P., Koskela, K., McAlister, A., Pallonen, U., Vartiainen, E., & Homan, K. (1979). A comprehensive television smoking cessation programme in Finland. *International Journal of Health Education, 22* (Suppl.), 1–29.

Putnam, L. L., & Wilson, C. E. (1982). Communicative strategies in organizational conflicts: Reliability and validity of a measurement scale. In M. Burgoon (Ed.), *Communication yearbook 6* (pp. 629–652). Beverly Hills, CA: Sage.

Quigley-Fernandez, B., & Tedeschi, J. T. (1978). The bogus pipeline as lie-detector: Two validity studies. *Journal of Personality and Social Psychology, 36,* 247–256.

Rajecki, D. W. (1990). *Attitudes* (2nd ed.). Sunderland, MA: Sinauer.

Rajecki, D. W., & Wolfson, C. (1973). The ratings of materials found in the mailbox: Effects of frequency of receipt. *Public Opinion Quarterly, 37,* 110–114.

Rakow, L. F. (1989). Information and power: Toward a critical theory of information campaigns. In C. T. Salmon (Ed.), *Information campaigns: Balancing social values and social change* (pp. 164–184). Newbury Park, CA: Sage.

Ray, G. B. (1986). Vocally cued personality prototypes: An implicit personality theory approach. *Communication Monographs, 53,* 266–276.

Ray, M. L. (1973). Marketing communication and the hierarchy of effects. In P. Clarke (Ed.), *New models for mass communication research* (pp. 147–176). Beverly Hills, CA: Sage.

Ray, M. L. (1982). *Advertising and communication management.* Englewood Cliffs, NJ: Prentice-Hall.

Razran, G. H. S. (1940). Conditioned response changes in rating and appraising sociopolitical slogans. *Psychological Bulletin, 37,* 481.

Reardon, K. K. (1981). *Persuasion: Theory and context.* Beverly Hills, CA: Sage.

Reardon, K. K. (1987). *Interpersonal communication: Where minds meet.* Belmont, CA: Wadsworth.

Reardon, K. K. (1989). The potential role of persuasion in adolescent AIDS prevention. In R. E. Rice & C. K. Atkin (Eds.), *Public communication campaigns* (2nd ed., pp. 273–289). Newbury Park, CA: Sage.

Reardon, K. K. (1991). *Persuasion in practice.* Newbury Park, CA: Sage.

Reardon, K. K., Sussman, S., & Flay, B. R. (1989). Are we marketing the right message: Can kids "just say, 'no' " to smoking? *Communication Monographs, 56,* 307–324.

Regan, D. T., & Kilduff, M. (1988). Optimism about elections: Dissonance reduction at the ballot box. *Political Psychology, 9,* 101–107.

Reinard, J. C. (1988). The empirical study of the persuasive effects of evidence: The status after fifty years of research. *Human Communication Research, 15,* 3–59.

Rhodes, N., & Wood, W. (1992). Self-esteem and intelligence affect influenceability: The mediating role of message reception. *Psychological Bulletin, 111,* 156–171.

Riess, M., Kalle, R. J., & Tedeschi, J. T. (1981). Bogus pipeline attitude assessment, impression management, and misattribution in induced compliance settings. *Journal of Social Psychology, 115,* 247–258.

Riggio, R. (1987). *The charisma quotient: What it is, how to get it, how to use it.* New York: Dodd, Mead.

Roberts, W. R. (Trans.). (1954). *Aristotle.* New York: Modern Library.

Robertson, L. S. (1976). The great seat belt campaign flop. *Journal of Communication, 26,* 41–45.

Robertson, L. S., Kelley, A. B., O'Neill, B., Wixom, C. W., Eiswirth, R. S., & Haddon, W., Jr. (1974). A controlled study of the effect of television messages on safety belt use. *American Journal of Public Health, 64,* 1071–1080.

Robertson, N. (1988). *Getting better: Inside Alcoholics Anonymous.* New York: Morrow.

Robinson, J. P., & Meadow, R. (1982). *Polls apart.* Cabin John, MD: Seven Locks Press.

Rogers, E. M. (1983). *Diffusion of innovations* (3rd ed.). New York: Free Press.

Rogers, E. M., & Storey, J. D. (1987). Communication campaigns. In C. R. Berger & S. H. Chaffee (Eds.), *Handbook of communication science* (pp. 817–846). Newbury Park, CA: Sage.

Rogers, R. W. (1975). A protection motivation theory of fear appeals and attitude change. *Journal of Psychology, 91,* 93–114.

Rogers, R. W., & Mewborn, C. R. (1976). Fear appeals and attitude change: Effects of a threat's noxiousness, probability of occurrence, and the efficacy of coping responses. *Journal of Personality and Social Psychology, 34,* 54–61.

Rokeach, M. (1971). Long-range experimental modification of values, attitudes, and behavior. *American Psychologist, 26,* 453–459.

Rokeach, M. (1973). *The nature of human values.* New York: Free Press.

Rokeach, M., & Rothman, G. (1965). The principle of belief congruence and the congruity principle as models of cognitive interaction. *Psychological Review, 72,* 128–142.

Roloff, M. E. (1980). Self-awareness and the persuasion process: Do we really *know* what we're doing? In M. E. Roloff & G. R. Miller (Eds.), *Persuasion: New directions in theory and research* (pp. 29–66). Beverly Hills, CA: Sage.

Roloff, M. E., & Barnicott, E. (1978). The situational use of pro- and anti-social compliance-gaining strategies by high and low Machiavellians. In B. D. Ruben (Ed.), *Communication yearbook 2* (pp. 193–208). New Brunswick, NJ: Transaction Books.

Romano, C. (1987). The grisly truth about bare facts. In R. K. Manoff & M. Schudson (Eds.), *Reading the news* (pp. 38–78). New York: Pantheon.

Room, R. (1977). *The prevention of alcohol problems.* Social Research Group Working Paper F-63, Berkeley, CA.

Rosen, S. (1961). Postdecision affinity for incompatible information. *Journal of Abnormal and Social Psychology, 63,* 188–190.

Rosenbaum, A. S. (1986). *Coercion and autonomy: Philosophical foundations, issues, and practices.* Westport, CT: Greenwood.

Rosenberg, M. J. (1960). An analysis of affective-cognitive consistency. In C. Hovland & M. Rosenberg (Eds.), *Attitude organization and change* (pp. 15–64). New Haven, CT: Yale University Press.

Rosenberg, M. J. (1965). When dissonance fails: On eliminating evaluation apprehension from attitude measurement. *Journal of Personality and Social Psychology, 1,* 28–42.

Rosenberg, M. J., & Hovland, C. I. (1960). Cognitive, affective, and behavioral components of attitude. In M. J. Rosenberg, C. I. Hovland, W. J. McGuire, R. P. Abelson, & J. W. Brehm (Eds.), *Attitude organization and change: An analysis of consistency among attitude components* (pp. 1–14). New Haven, CT: Yale University Press.

Roser, C., Flora, J. A., Chaffee, S. H., & Farquhar, J. W. (1990). Using research to predict learning from a PR campaign. *Public Relations Review, 16,* 61–77.

Rosnow, R. L., & Robinson, E. J. (Eds.). (1967). *Experiments in persuasion.* New York: Academic Press.

Rouner, D., & Perloff, R. M. (1988). Selective perceptions of outcome of first 1984 presidential debate. *Journalism Quarterly, 65,* 141–147.

Rule, B. G., Bisanz, G. L., & Kohn, M. (1985). Anatomy of a persuasion schema: Targets, goals, and strategies. *Journal of Personality and Social Psychology, 48,* 1127–1140.

Saegert, J. (1979). Another look at subliminal perception. *Journal of Advertising Research, 19,* 55–57.

Salancik, G. R. (1982). Attitude–behavior consistencies as social logics. In M. P. Zanna, E. T. Higgins, & C. P. Herman (Eds.), *Consistency in social behavior* (Vol. 2, pp. 51–73). Hillsdale, NJ: Lawrence Erlbaum Associates.

Salmon, C. T. (1989). Campaigns for social "improvement": An overview of values, rationales, and impacts. In C. T. Salmon (Ed.), *Information campaigns: Balancing social values and social change* (pp. 19–53). Newbury Park, CA: Sage.

Salzman, M., & O'Reilly, A. (1991). *War and peace in the Persian Gulf: What teenagers want to know.* Princeton, NJ: Peterson's Guides.

Sawyer, A. G. (1975). Demand artifacts in laboratory experiments in consumer research. *Journal of Consumer Research, 1,* 20–30.

Sawyer, A. G. (1981). Repetition, cognitive responses, and persuasion. In R. E.

Petty, T. M. Ostrom, & T. C. Brock (Eds.), *Cognitive responses in persuasion* (pp. 237–261). Hillsdale, NJ: Lawrence Erlbaum Associates.

Sawyer, A. G. (1988). Can there be effective advertising without explicit conclusions? Decide for yourself. In S. Hecker & D. W. Stewart (Eds.), *Nonverbal communication in advertising* (pp. 159–184). Lexington, MA: D.C. Heath.

Schachter, S., & Singer, J. E. (1962). Cognitive, social and physiological determinants of emotional state. *Psychological Review, 69,* 379–399.

Schacter, D. L. (1982). *Stranger behind the engram: Theories of memory and the psychology of science.* Hillsdale, NJ: Lawrence Erlbaum Associates.

Schank, R. C., & Abelson, R. P. (1977). *Scripts, plans, goals, and understanding: An inquiry into human knowledge structures.* Hillsdale, NJ: Lawrence Erlbaum Associates.

Scheflin, A. W., & Opton, E. M., Jr. (1978). *The mind manipulators: A non-fictional account.* New York: Paddington.

Scheidel, T. M. (1967). *Persuasive speaking.* Glenview, IL: Scott, Foresman.

Scheier, M. F., & Carver, C. S. (1980). Private and public self-attention, resistance to change, and dissonance reduction. *Journal of Personality and Social Psychology, 39,* 390–405.

Schein, E. H. (1961). *Coercive persuasion: A socio-psychological analysis of the "brainwashing" of the American civilian prisoners by the Chinese Communists.* New York: W.W. Norton.

Schenck-Hamlin, W. J., Georgacarakos, G. N., & Wiseman, R. L. (1982). A formal account of interpersonal compliance-gaining. *Communication Quarterly, 30,* 173–180.

Schenck-Hamlin, W. J., Wiseman, R. L., & Georgacarakos, G. N. (1982). A model of properties of compliance-gaining strategies. *Communication Quarterly, 30,* 92–100.

Scher, S. J., & Cooper, J. (1989). Motivational basis of dissonance: The singular role of behavioral consequences. *Journal of Personality and Social Psychology, 56,* 899–906.

Scherer, K. R. (1979). Voice and speech correlates of perceived social influence in simulated juries. In H. Giles & R. St. Clair (Eds.), *Language and social psychology* (pp. 88–120). London: Basil Blackwell.

Schifter, D. B., & Ajzen, I. (1985). Intention, perceived control, and weight loss: An application of the theory of planned behavior. *Journal of Personality and Social Psychology, 49,* 843–851.

Schlegel, R. P., & DiTecco, D. (1982). Attitudinal structures and the attitude-behavior relation. In M. P. Zanna, E. T. Higgins, & C. P. Herman (Eds.), *Consistency in social behavior: The Ontario symposium* (Vol. 2, pp. 17–49). Hillsdale, NJ: Lawrence Erlbaum Associates.

Schlenker, B. R. (1982). Translating actions into attitudes: An identity-analytic approach to the explanation of social conduct. In L. Berkowitz (Ed.), *Advances in experimental social psychology* (Vol. 15, pp. 194–247). New York: Academic Press.

Schopler, J., & Bateson, N. (1962). A dependence interpretation of the effects of a severe initiation. *Journal of Personality, 30,* 633–649.

Schuman, H., & Johnson, M. P. (1976). Attitudes and behavior. *Annual Review of Sociology, 2,* 161–207.

Schuman, H., & Kalton, G. (1985). Survey methods. In G. Lindzey & E. Aronson

(Eds.), *Handbook of social psychology* (3rd ed., Vol. 1, pp. 635–697). New York: Random House.

Schwartz, T. (1973). *The responsive chord*. Garden City, NY: Anchor Press.

Schwarz, N., Bless, H., & Bohner, G. (1991). Mood and persuasion: Affective states influence the processing of persuasive communications. In M. P. Zanna (Ed.), *Advances in experimental social psychology* (Vol. 24, pp. 161–199). San Diego: Academic Press.

Scott, C., Klein, D. M., & Bryant, J. (1990). Consumer response to humor in advertising: A series of field studies using behavioral observation. *Journal of Consumer Research, 16,* 498–501.

Scott, W. A. (1957). Attitude change through reward of verbal behavior. *Journal of Abnormal and Social Psychology, 55,* 72–75.

Scott, W. A. (1969). Attitude measurement. In G. L. Lindzey & E. Aronson (Eds.), *Handbook of social psychology* (2nd ed., Vol. 2, pp. 204–273). Reading, MA: Addison-Wesley.

Sears, D. O., & Chaffee, S. H. (1979). Uses and effects of the 1976 debates: An overview of empirical studies. In S. Kraus (Ed.), *The great debates: Carter vs. Ford, 1976* (pp. 223–261). Bloomington, IN: Indiana University Press.

Sears, D. O., Huddie, L., & Schaffer, L. G. (1986). A schematic variant of symbolic politics theory, as applied to racial and gender equality. In R. R. Lau & D. O. Sears (Eds.), *Political cognition: The 19th annual Carnegie symposium on cognition* (pp. 159–202). Hillsdale, NJ: Lawrence Erlbaum Associates.

Sears, D. O., & Whitney, R. E. (1973). Political persuasion. In I. de Sola Pool, F. W. Frey, W. Schramm, N. Maccoby, & E. B. Parker (Eds.), *Handbook of communication* (pp. 253–289). Chicago: Rand McNally.

Seibold, D. R., Cantrill, J. G., & Meyers, R. A. (1985). Communication and interpersonal influence. In M. L. Knapp & G. R. Miller (Eds.), *Handbook of interpersonal communication* (pp. 551–611). Newbury Park, CA: Sage.

Seligman, C., Bush, M., & Kirsch, K. (1976). Relationship between compliance in the foot-in-the door paradigm and size of first request. *Journal of Personality and Social Psychology, 33,* 517–520.

Sereno, K. K., & Hawkins, G. J. (1967). The effects of variations in speakers' nonfluency upon audience ratings of attitude toward the speech topic and speakers' credibility. *Speech Monographs, 34,* 58–64.

Shavitt, S. (1989). Operationalizing functional theories of attitude. In A. R. Pratkanis, S. J. Breckler, & A. G. Greenwald (Eds.), *Attitude structure and function* (pp. 311–337). Hillsdale, NJ: Lawrence Erlbaum Associates.

Shavitt, S. (1990). The role of attitude objects in attitude functions. *Journal of Experimental Social Psychology, 26,* 124–148.

Shavitt, S., & Brock, T. C. (1986). Self-relevant responses in commercial persuasion: Field and experimental tests. In J. Olson & K. Sentis (Eds.), *Advertising and consumer psychology* (Vol. 3, pp. 149–171). New York: Praeger.

Sherif, C. W., Sherif, M., & Nebergall, R. E. (1965). *Attitude and attitude change: The social judgment-involvement approach*. Philadelphia: W.B. Saunders.

Sherif, M. (1967). Introduction. In C. W. Sherif & M. Sherif (Eds.), *Attitude, ego-involvement, and change* (pp. 1–5). New York: Wiley.

Sherif, M., & Hovland, C. I. (1961). *Social judgment: Assimilation and contrast effects in communication and attitude change*. New Haven, CT: Yale University Press.

Sherif, M., & Sherif, C. W. (1967). Attitude as the individual's own categories: The social judgment-involvement approach to attitude and attitude change. In. C. W. Sherif & M. Sherif (Eds.), *Attitude, ego-involvement, and change* (pp. 105–139). New York: Wiley.

Sherif, M., Taub, D., & Hovland, C. I. (1958). Assimilation and contrast effects of anchoring stimuli on judgments. *Journal of Experimental Psychology, 55,* 150–155.

Sherman, S. J., & Fazio, R. H. (1983). Parallels between attitudes and traits as predictors of behavior. *Journal of Personality, 51,* 308–345.

Sherman, S. J., Presson, C. C., Chassin, L., Bensenberg, M., Corty, E., & Olshavsky, R. W. (1982). Smoking intentions in adolescents: Direct experience and predictability. *Personality and Social Psychology Bulletin, 8,* 376–383.

Shingi, P. M., & Mody, B. (1976). The communication effects gap: A field experiment on television and agricultural ignorance in India. *Communication Research, 3,* 171–190.

Shupe, A. D., Jr., & Bromley, D. G. (1980). *New vigilantes: Deprogrammers, anti-cultists, and the new religions.* Beverly Hills, CA: Sage.

Sigall, H., & Page, R. (1971). Current stereotypes: A little fading, a little faking. *Journal of Personality and Social Psychology, 18,* 247–255.

Silverman, L. H., & Spiro, R. H. (1967). Further investigation of the effects of subliminal aggressive stimulation on the ego functioning of schizophrenics. *Journal of Consulting Psychology, 31,* 225–232.

Simons, H. W. (1971). Persuasion and attitude change. In L. L. Barker & R. J. Kibler (Eds.), *Speech communication behavior: Perspectives and principles* (pp. 227–248). Englewood Cliffs, NJ: Prentice-Hall.

Simons, H. W., Berkowitz, N. N., & Moyer, R. J. (1970). Similarity, credibility, and attitude change: A review and a theory. *Psychological Bulletin, 73,* 1–16.

60 Minutes. (1984, December 23). Vol. 18, No. 15.

Skinner, B. F. (1957). *Verbal behavior.* New York: Appleton-Century-Crofts.

Skolnick, P., & Heslin, R. (1971). Quality versus difficulty: Alternative interpretations of the relationship between self-esteem and persuasibility. *Journal of Personality, 39,* 242–251.

Slamecka, N. J., & Graf, P. (1978). The generation effect: Delineation of a phenomenon. *Journal of Experimental Psychology: Human Learning and Memory, 4,* 592–604.

Smith, G. H., & Engel, R. (1968). Influence of a female model on perceived characteristics of an automobile. *Proceedings of the 76th annual convention of the American Psychological Association, 3,* 681–682.

Smith, L. J. (1991). *Art of advocacy: Summation.* New York: Matthew Bender.

Smith, M. B., Bruner, J. B., & White, R. S. (1956). *Opinions and personality.* New York: Wiley.

Smith, M. J. (1982). *Persuasion and human action: A review and critique of social influence theories.* Belmont, CA: Wadsworth.

Smith, M. J. (1984). Contingency rules theory, context, and compliance behaviors. *Human Communication Research, 10,* 489–512.

Snyder, M. (1974). The self-monitoring of expressive behavior. *Journal of Personality and Social Psychology, 30,* 526–537.

Snyder, M. (1982). When believing means doing: Creating links between attitudes and behavior. In M. P. Zanna, E. T. Higgins, & C. P. Herman (Eds.), *Consistency in social behavior: The Ontario symposium* (Vol. 2, pp. 105–130). Hillsdale, NJ: Lawrence Erlbaum Associates.

Snyder, M. (1987). *Public appearances/Private realities: The psychology of self-monitoring.* New York: W.H. Freeman.

Snyder, M., & DeBono, K. G. (1985). Appeals to images and claims about quality: Understanding the psychology of advertising. *Journal of Personality and Social Psychology, 49,* 586–597.

Snyder, M., & DeBono, K. G. (1989). Understanding the functions of attitudes: Lessons from personality and social behavior. In A. R. Pratkanis, S. J. Breckler, & A. G. Greenwald (Eds.), *Attitude structure and function* (pp. 339–359). Hillsdale, NJ: Lawrence Erlbaum Associates.

Snyder, M., & Ebbesen, E. (1972). Dissonance awareness: A test of dissonance theory versus self-perception theory. *Journal of Experimental Social Psychology, 8,* 502–517.

Snyder, M., & Kendzierski, D. (1982). Acting on one's attitudes: Procedures for linking attitude and behavior. *Journal of Experimental Social Psychology, 18,* 165–183.

Snyder, M., & Rothbart, M. (1971). Communicator attractiveness and opinion change. *Canadian Journal of Behavioral Science, 3,* 377–387.

Snyder, M., & Swann, W. B., Jr. (1976). When actions reflect attitudes: The politics of impression management. *Journal of Personality and Social Psychology, 34,* 1034–1042.

Snyder, M., & Tanke, E. D. (1976). Behavior and attitude: Some people are more consistent than others. *Journal of Personality, 44,* 510–517.

Soames Job, R. F. (1988). Effective and ineffective use of fear in health promotion campaigns. *American Journal of Public Health, 78,* 163–167.

Solomon, D. S. (1989). A social marketing perspective on communication campaigns. In R. E. Rice & C. K. Atkin (Eds.), *Public communication campaigns* (2nd ed., pp. 87–104). Newbury Park, CA: Sage.

Songer-Nocks, E. (1976). Situational factors affecting the weighting of predictor components in the Fishbein model. *Journal of Experimental Social Psychology, 12,* 56–69.

Sperber, B. M., Fishbein, M., & Ajzen, I. (1980). Predicting and understanding women's occupational orientations: Factors underlying choice intentions. In I. Ajzen & M. Fishbein (Eds.), *Understanding attitudes and predicting social behavior* (pp. 113–129). Engelwood Cliffs, NJ: Prentice-Hall.

Staats, A. W., & Staats, C. K. (1958). Attitudes established by classical conditioning. *Journal of Abnormal and Social Psychology, 57,* 37–40.

Staats, A. W., Staats, C. K., & Crawford, H. L. (1962). First-order conditioning of meaning and the parallel conditioning of a GSR. *Journal of General Psychology, 67,* 159–167.

Staats, C. K., & Staats, A. W. (1957). Meaning established by classical conditioning. *Journal of Experimental Psychology, 54,* 74–80.

Star, S. A., & Hughes, H. M. (1950). Report on an educational campaign: The Cincinnati plan for the United Nations. *American Journal of Sociology, 55,* 389–400.

Stang, D. J. (1974). Methodological factors in mere exposure research. *Psychological Bulletin, 81,* 1014–1025.

Steele, C. M. (1988). The psychology of self-affirmation: Sustaining the integrity of the self. In L. Berkowitz (Ed.), *Advances in experimental social psychology* (Vol. 21, pp. 261–302). San Diego: Academic Press.

Steele, C. M., & Liu, T. J. (1981). Making the dissonance act unreflective of the self: Dissonance avoidance and the expectancy of a value-affirming response. *Personality and Social Psychology Bulletin, 7,* 393–397.

Steele, C. M., & Liu, T. J. (1983). Dissonance processes as self-affirmation. *Journal of Personality and Social Psychology, 45,* 5–19.

Sternthal, B., Dholakia, R., & Leavitt, C. (1978). The persuasive effect of source credibility: Tests of cognitive response. *Journal of Consumer Research, 4,* 252–260.

Stevens, S. S. (1950). Mathematics, measurement, and psychophysics. In S. S. Stevens (Ed.), *Handbook of experimental psychology* (pp. 1–49). New York: Wiley.

Stiff, J. B. (1986). Cognitive processing of persuasive message cues: A meta-analytic review of the effects of supporting information on attitudes. *Communication Monographs, 53,* 75–89.

Stiff, J. B., & Boster, F. J. (1987). Cognitive processing: Additional thoughts and a reply to Petty, Kasmer, Haugtvedt, and Cacioppo. *Communication Monographs, 54,* 250–256.

Stoner, C., & Parke, J. A. (1977). *All Gods children: The cult experience—salvation or slavery?* Radnor, PA: Chilton.

Street, R. L., Jr., & Brady, R. M. (1982). Speech rate acceptance ranges as a function of evaluative domain, listener speech rate, and communication context. *Communication Monographs, 49,* 290–308.

Street, R. L., Jr., Brady, R. M., & Lee, R. (1984). Evaluative responses to communicators: The effects of speech rate, sex, and interaction context. *Western Journal of Speech Communication, 48,* 14–27.

Stuart, E. W., Shimp, T. A., & Engle, R. W. (1987). Classical conditioning of consumer attitudes: Four experiments in an advertising context. *Journal of Consumer Research, 14,* 334–349.

Suedfeld, P. (Ed.). (1990). *Psychology and torture.* New York: Hemisphere.

Sutton, S. R. (1982). Fear-arousing communications: A critical examination of theory and research. In J. R. Eiser (Ed.), *Social psychology and behavioral medicine* (pp. 303–337). New York: Wiley.

Sutton, S. R., & Eiser, J. R. (1984). The effect of fear-arousing communications on cigarette smoking: An expectancy-value approach. *Journal of Behavioral Medicine, 7,* 13–33.

Sypher, H. E., & Sypher, B. D. (1987). Affect and message generation. In L. Donohew, H. E. Sypher, & E. T. Higgins (Eds.), *Communication, social cognition, and affect* (pp. 81–92). Hillsdale, NJ: Lawrence Erlbaum Associates.

Taylor, S. E., & Thompson, S. C. (1982). Stalking the elusive "vividness" effect. *Psychological Review, 89,* 155–181.

Tedeschi, J. T., Schlenker, B. R., & Bonoma, T. V. (1971). Cognitive dissonance: Private ratiocination or public spectacle? *American Psychologist, 26,* 685–695.

Tesser, A. (1978). Self-generated attitude change. In L. Berkowitz (Ed.), *Advances in experimental social psychology* (Vol. 11, pp. 181–227). New York: Academic Press.

Tesser, A., & Shaffer, D. R. (1990). Attitudes and attitude change. *Annual Review of Psychology, 41,* 479–523.

Tetlock, P. E., & Manstead, A. S. R. (1985). Impression management versus intrapsychic explanations in social psychology: A useful dichotomy? *Psychological Review, 92,* 59–72.

Thistlethwaite, D. L., de Haan, H., & Kamenetzky, J. (1955). The effects of "directive" and "nondirective" communication procedures on attitudes. *Journal of Abnormal and Social Psychology, 51,* 107–113.

Thompson, W. N. (1975). *The process of persuasion: Principles and readings.* New York: Harper & Row.

Thorson, E. (1989). Television commercials as mass media messages. In J. J. Bradac (Ed.), *Message effects in communication science* (pp. 195–230). Newbury Park, CA: Sage.

Thurstone, L. L. (1928). Attitudes can be measured. *American Journal of Sociology, 33,* 529–544.

Tichenor, P. J., Donohue, G. A., & Olien, C. N. (1970). Mass media flow and differential growth in knowledge. *Public Opinion Quarterly, 34,* 158–170.

Tourangeau, R., Rasinski, K. A., Bradburn, N., & D'Andrade, R. (1989). Carryover effects in attitude surveys. *Public Opinion Quarterly, 53,* 495–524.

Traugott, M. W., & Price, V. E. (1991 November). *Exit polls in the 1989 Virginia gubernatorial race: Where did they go wrong?* Paper presented at the annual meeting of the Midwest Association for Public Opinion Research, Chicago.

Uranowitz, S. W. (1975). Helping and self-attributions: A field experiment. *Journal of Personality and Social Psychology, 31,* 852–854.

Vidmar, N., & Rokeach, M. (1974). Archie Bunker's bigotry: A study of selective perception and exposure. *Journal of Communication, 24,* 36–47.

Vokey, J. R., & Read, D. J. (1985). Subliminal messages: Between the devil and the media. *American Psychologist, 40,* 1231–1239.

Walker, L., Thibaut, J., & Andreoli, V. (1972). Order of presentation at trial. *Yale Law Journal, 82,* 216–226.

Wall, V. D. (1972). Evidential attitudes and attitude change. *Western Speech, 36,* 115–123.

Wallack, L. M. (1981). Mass media campaigns: The odds against finding behavior change. *Health Education Quarterly, 8,* 209–260.

Walster, E. (1964). The temporal sequence of post-decision processes. In L. Festinger (Ed.), *Conflict, decision and dissonance* (pp. 112–127). Stanford, CA: Stanford University Press.

Ward, C. D., & McGinnies, E. (1974). Persuasive effects of early and late mention of credible and noncredible sources. *Journal of Psychology, 86,* 17–23.

Warner, K. E. (1977). The effects of the anti-smoking campaign on cigarette consumption. *American Journal of Public Health, 67,* 645–650.

Warner, L. G., & DeFleur, M. L. (1969). Attitudes as an interactional concept: Social constraint and social distance as intervening variables between attitudes and action. *American Sociological Review, 34,* 153–169.

Wartella, E., & Middlestadt, S. (1991). Mass communication and persuasion: The evolution of direct effects, limited effects, information processing, and affect and arousal models. In L. Donohew, H. E. Sypher, & W. J. Bukoski (Eds.), *Persuasive communication and drug abuse prevention* (pp. 53–69). Hillsdale, NJ: Lawrence Erlbaum Associates.

Wartella, E., & Reeves, B. (1985). Historical trends in research on children and the media: 1900–1960. *Journal of Communication, 35,* 118–133.

Waterman, C. K., & Katkin, E. S. (1967). The energizing (dynamogenic) effect of cognitive dissonance on task performance. *Journal of Personality and Social Psychology, 6,* 126–131.

Watts, W. A., & Holt, L. E. (1979). Persistence of opinion change induced under conditions of forewarning and distraction. *Journal of Personality and Social Psychology, 37*, 778–789.

Weaver, R. M. (1953). *The ethics of rhetoric*. Chicago: H. Regnery.

Webb, E. J., Campbell, D. T., Schwartz, R. D., & Sechrest, L. (1966). *Unobtrusive measures: Nonreactive research in the social sciences*. Chicago: Rand McNally.

Weber, M. (1968). *On charisma and institution building*. Chicago: University of Chicago Press.

Webster's Third New International Dictionary. (1986). Springfield, MA: Merriam-Webster.

Weigel, R. H., & Newman, L. S. (1976). Increasing attitude–behavior correspondence by broadening the scope of the behavioral measure. *Journal of Personality and Social Psychology, 33*, 793–802.

Weinstein, N. D. (1980). Unrealistic optimism for future life events. *Journal of Personality and Social Psychology, 39*, 806–820.

Weitz, B. (1981). Effectiveness in sales interactions: A contingency framework. *Journal of Marketing, 45*, 85–103.

Werner, H. (1957). The concept of development from a comparative and organismic point of view. In D. B. Harris (Ed.), *The concept of development* (pp. 125–148). Minneapolis: University of Minnesota Press.

Westie, F. R., & DeFleur, M. L. (1959). Autonomic responses and their relationship to race attitudes. *Journal of Abnormal and Social Psychology, 58*, 340–347.

Wheatley, J. J., & Oshikawa, S. (1970). The relationship between anxiety and positive and negative advertising appeals. *Journal of Marketing Research, 7*, 85–89.

Wheeless, L. R., Barraclough, R., & Stewart, R. (1983). Compliance-gaining and power in persuasion. In R. Bostrom (Ed.), *Communication yearbook 7* (pp. 105–145). Beverly Hills, CA: Sage.

Whitehead, J. L., Jr. (1968). Factors of source credibility. *Quarterly Journal of Speech, 54*, 59–63.

Whittaker, J. O. (1967). Resolution of the communication discrepancy issue in attitude change. In C. W. Sherif & M. Sherif (Eds.), *Attitude, ego-involvement, and change* (pp. 159–177). New York: Wiley.

Why did many GI captives cave in? Interview with Army expert. (1956, February 24). *U.S. News and World Report, 40*, 56–72.

Wicker, A. W. (1969). Attitudes vs. actions: The relationship of verbal and overt behavioral responses to attitude objects. *Journal of Social Issues, 25*, 41–78.

Wicklund, R. A., & Brehm, J. W. (1976). *Perspectives on cognitive dissonance*. Hillsdale, NJ: Lawrence Erlbaum Associates.

Wiebe, G. D. (1952). Merchandising commodities and citizenship on television. *Public Opinion Quarterly, 15*, 679–691.

Wilson, C. E. (1974). The effect of medium on loss of information. *Journalism Quarterly, 51*, 111–115.

Wilson, T. D., Dunn, D. S., Kraft, D., & Lisle, D. J. (1989). Introspection, attitude change, and attitude–behavior consistency: The disruptive effects of explaining why we feel the way we do. In L. Berkowitz (Ed.), *Advances in experimental social psychology* (Vol. 22, pp. 287–343). San Diego: Academic Press.

Wiseman, R. L., & Schenck-Hamlin, W. J. (1981). A multi-dimensional scaling validation of an inductively-derived set of compliance-gaining strategies. *Communication Monographs, 48*, 251–270.

Wolff, H. G. (1960 February). Every man has his breaking point—The conduct of prisoners of war. *Military Medicine, 125,* 88.

Wood, W., Kallgren, C. A., & Preisler, R. M. (1985). Access to attitude-relevant information in memory as a determinant of persuasion: The role of message attributes. *Journal of Experimental Social Psychology, 21,* 73–85.

Woodall, W. G., & Burgoon, J. K. (1983). Talking fast and changing attitudes: A critique and clarification. *Journal of Nonverbal Behavior, 8,* 126–142.

Worth, L. T., & Mackie, D. M. (1987). Cognitive mediation of positive affect in persuasion. *Social Cognition, 5,* 76–94.

Wright, P. (1966). Attitude change under direct and indirect interpersonal influence. *Human Relations, 19,* 199–211.

Wright, P. L. (1981). Cognitive responses to mass media advocacy. In R. E. Petty, T. M. Ostrom, & T. C. Brock (Eds.), *Cognitive responses in persuasion* (pp. 263–282). Hillsdale, NJ: Lawrence Erlbaum Associates.

Wu, C., & Shaffer, D. R. (1987). Susceptibility to persuasive appeals as a function of source credibility and prior experience with the attitude object. *Journal of Personality and Social Psychology, 52,* 677–688.

Zahn, C. J. (1989 November). *Sex-linked language revisited: A critical review of research on gender and language.* Paper presented at the annual meeting of the Speech Communication Association, San Francisco.

Zajonc, R. B. (1968). Attitudinal effects of mere exposure. *Journal of Personality and Social Psychology Monographs Supplement, 9* (2, Pt. 2), 1–27.

Zajonc, R. B. (1980). Feeling and thinking: Preferences need no inferences. *American Psychologist, 35,* 151–175.

Zanna, M. P., & Cooper, J. (1974). Dissonance and the pill: An attribution approach to studying the arousal properties of dissonance. *Journal of Personality and Social Psychology, 29,* 703–709.

Zanna, M. P., & Fazio, R. H. (1982). The attitude–behavior relation: Moving toward a third generation of research. In M. P. Zanna, E. T. Higgins, & C. P. Herman (Eds.), *Consistency in social behavior: The Ontario symposium* (Vol. 2, pp. 283–301). Hillsdale, NJ: Lawrence Erlbaum Associates.

Zanna, M. P., Kiesler, C. A., & Pilkonis, P. A. (1970). Positive and negative attitudinal affect established by classical conditioning. *Journal of Personality and Social Psychology, 14,* 321–328.

Zanna, M. P., Olson, J. M., & Fazio, R. H. (1980). Attitude–behavior consistency: An individual difference perspective. *Journal of Personality and Social Psychology, 38,* 432–440.

Zanna, M. P., & Rempel, J. K. (1988). Attitudes: A new look at an old concept. In D. Bar-Tal & A. Kruglanski (Eds.), *The social psychology of knowledge* (pp. 315–334). New York: Cambridge University Press.

Zanot, E. J., Pincus, J. D., & Lamp, E. J. (1983). Public perceptions of subliminal advertising. *Journal of Advertising, 12,* 39–45.

Zillmann, D., Williams, B. R., Bryant, J., Boynton, K. R., & Wolf, M. A. (1980). Acquisition of information from educational television programs as a function of differently paced humorous inserts. *Journal of Educational Psychology, 72,* 170–180.

Zimbardo, P. G. (1960). Involvement and communication discrepancy as determinants of opinion conformity. *Journal of Abnormal and Social Psychology, 60,* 86–94.

Zimbardo, P. G. (1972). The tactics and ethics of persuasion. In B. T. King & E.

McGinnies (Eds.), *Attitudes, conflict, and social change* (pp. 84-99). New York: Academic Press.

Zimbardo, P. G., Ebbesen, E. B., & Maslach, C. (1977). *Influencing attitudes and changing behavior* (2nd ed.). Reading, MA: Addison-Wesley.

Zimbardo, P. G., Weisenberg, M., Firestone, I., & Levy, B. (1965). Communicator effectiveness in producing public conformity and private attitude change. *Journal of Personality, 33*, 233-255.

Zuckerman, M., & Reis, H. T. (1978). Comparison of three models for predicting altruistic behavior. *Journal of Personality and Social Psychology, 36*, 498-510.

Author Index

Subject Index